Ruffed Grouse

The Wildlife Series

Ruffed Grouse

Edited by
Sally Atwater and Judith Schnell

STACKPOLE
BOOKS

Copyright © 1989 by Stackpole Books

Published by
STACKPOLE BOOKS
Cameron and Kelker Streets
P.O. Box 1831
Harrisburg, PA 17105

Printed in the United States of America

10 9 8 7 6 5 4 3 2 1

The map on page 49 is reprinted courtesy of
Houghton Mifflin Company from *The Journals of
Lewis and Clark,* edited by Bernard DeVoto, © 1953.

Library of Congress Cataloging-in-Publication Data

Ruffed grouse / edited by Sally Atwater and Judith Schnell.
    p.   cm. – (The Wildlife Series)
    Bibliography: p.
    Includes index.
    ISBN 0-8117-1650-3
    1. Ruffed grouse. I. Atwater, Sally
II. Schnell, Judith. III. Series.
QL696.G285R83 1989
598'.616–dc20   89-4636
                                                           CIP

Contents

The place
of the ruffed grouse

A description

THE PATTERN OF LIFE

POPULATION DYNAMICS

THE KINGDOM
OF THE RUFFED GROUSE

Contributors

HAROLD L. BARBER is a former chief forest wildlife biologist for the Kentucky Department of Fish and Wildlife Resources. The author of numerous articles for both technical journals and lay magazines, he designed and implemented a grouse management program for the state of Kentucky.

FRED J. BRENNER is a certified wildlife biologist, a professor of biology at Grove City College in Pennsylvania, and a certified senior ecologist.

ROBERT CHAMBERS, recipient of the Outstanding Professional Award from the New York chapter of the Wildlife Society, is a professor of wildlife management at S.U.N.Y. College of Environmental Science and Forestry.

SCOTT R. CRAVEN is an extension wildlife specialist and an associate professor of wildlife ecology at the University of Wisconsin–Madison.

WILLIAM R. DAVIDSON is an assistant professor with the Southeastern Cooperative Wildlife Disease Study and School of Forest Resources at the University of Georgia.

STEPHEN DESTEFANO is pursuing a doctorate of wildlife resources at the University of Idaho. He studied grouse and other woodland wildlife for two years with the Wisconsin Cooperative Wildlife Research Unit and the University of Wisconsin–Madison's Extension Service.

GORDON W. GULLION is a leading researcher and writer on ruffed grouse habitat. His findings have been widely published, and as leader of the University of Minnesota Forest Wildlife Project at Cloquet, he continues his research in forest wildlife management. He is active in the Ruffed Grouse Society and other wildlife organizations.

WILLIAM L. HUDSON has done graduate work in wildlife science at West Virginia University. He is employed as a preserve manager by Ohio's De-

partment of Natural Resources, Division of Natural Areas and Preserves.

PAUL A. JOHNSGARD is the foundation professor of biological sciences at the University of Nebraska–Lincoln. A winner of the Wildlife Society's annual award for the outstanding book on terrestrial wildlife biology, he is the author of twenty-five books.

RICHARD O. KIMMEL is the project leader of upland game bird research for the Farmland Wildlife Populations and Research Group. He is a wildlife biologist with the Minnesota Department of Natural Resources.

ROY KIRKPATRICK is a professor of wildlife science at Virginia Polytechnic Institute and State University. He is the author or co-author of more than 90 technical papers, most of which deal with the nutritional ecology of wild birds and mammals.

JOHN KUBISIAK has been the project leader of forest wildlife research for the Wisconsin Department of Natural Resources since 1966. He received the Upland Conservation Award from the central Wisconsin chapter of the Ruffed Grouse Society in 1983 and the Award for Excellence from the Wisconsin DNR Bureau of Research in 1987.

R. SCOTT MCBURNEY holds a master's degree in wildlife biology from Iowa State University. He is a general science teacher at Wheatland Center School in southeastern Wisconsin.

STEPHEN J. MAXSON is a waterfowl research biologist with the Wetland Wildlife Populations and Research Group of the Minnesota Department of Natural Resources. He is also an adjunct assistant professor in the biology department of the University of North Dakota.

RONALD R. RUNKLES has been studying orni-

ix

thology with Dr. Ernest Willoughby of St. Mary's College in Maryland since 1983. He is a member of the Mid-Atlantic Bird Banding Group.

DONALD H. RUSCH has studied populations of ruffed grouse in Alberta, Manitoba, and Wisconsin and is the leader of the Wisconsin Cooperative Wildlife Research Unit at the University of Wisconsin–Madison.

DAVID E. SAMUEL has published more than 100 papers in scientific journals, contributed several chapters to various scientific books, and written more than 300 magazine articles. He is a professor of wildlife biology at West Virginia University.

JOHN G. SCOTT, a biologist for Charles T. Main, Inc., is studying to complete his master's degree in wildlife science.

FREDERICK A. SERVELLO recently completed four years of doctoral research at Virginia Polytechnic Institute and State University on ruffed grouse nutrition and the ecology of the ruffed grouse in the Southeast. He is an assistant professor of wildlife at the University of Maine.

ROBERT J. SMALL is a wildlife ecologist and research associate for the department of wildlife ecology at the University of Wisconsin–Madison.

STEVEN K. STAFFORD, SR., is a regional wildlife biologist for the Florida Game and Freshwater Fish Commission. He holds a master's degree in wildlife ecology from the University of Tennessee at Knoxville.

DEAN F. STAUFFER is an assistant professor of wildlife science at Virginia Polytechnic Institute and State University. His research centers on developing models that relate wildlife species to their habitats.

GERALD L. STORM is a research wildlife biologist and an adjunct associate professor of wildlife management at the Pennsylvania State University. During the last ten years, he has studied the responses of rabbits, woodcock, and ruffed grouse to land use and habitat manipulation.

FRANK R. THOMPSON, III is a research wildlife biologist for the North Central Forest Experiment Station in Missouri. He conducts forest wildlife research for the U.S. Forest Service.

GARY TURBAK is a freelance journalist specializing in wildlife. His work has been published in many major magazines, and he is the author of two books about predators.

BILL VOGT, a freelance writer, has contributed many articles to the major nature magazines.

EMILY JO WENTWORTH is a research technician with the Southeastern Cooperative Wildlife Disease Study at the University of Georgia. She received the Stoddard-Burleigh-Sutton Wildlife Conservation Award in 1987.

Photographers and artists

Hans Aschenbrenner

David Besenger

Sherry Blankenship

Steve Bonney

Cindie Brunner

Hope Sawyer Buyukmihci

Peter Doran

W. Greene

Gary W. Griffen

Gordon W. Gullion

Heiner C. Hertling

William L. Hudson

Paul A. Johnsgard

Richard O. Kimmel

Eric W. Kurzejeski

Herbert J. Lange

Ted Levin

Bob Lollo

Karen Lollo

Tom C. Martinson

Karl H. Maslowski

Steve Maslowski

Stephen J. Maxson

David Mohrhardt

Wendover Neefus

Bob Pratt

Leonard Lee Rue III

Rod Sando

Frederick A. Servello

Richard P. Smith

Steven K. Stafford, Sr.

Mark Sullivan

Frank R. Thompson III

Michael Todoroff

John Trott

Emily Jo Wentworth

Jack Wilburn

Henry F. Zeman

Foreword

Represented in this comprehensive exploration of the ruffed grouse are incredible investments of time and money. Several of the researchers featured here, such as Gordon Gullion, whose famous Minnesota grouse studies span decades, have dedicated much of their careers to the ruffed grouse. And some of the most important results of their efforts have been combined into this tremendous reference book. Considering the scope of that knowledge in the first place, this volume may rank as one of the all-time great bargains.

Many of the wildlife researchers whose works appear here have already made a significant impact on ruffed grouse management. And no doubt others will also have an influence, perhaps through the pages of this volume.

What is most impressive is that although this is certainly a bona fide textbook of superb detail, there are qualities that will bring an individual back to it time and again, just for the pleasure of reading it and savoring the magnificent color photographs.

And that's worth a lot to the Ruffed Grouse Society, for the more people understand and appreciate the ruffed grouse and what this game bird must have to survive, the easier will be the society's job of teaching and helping implement forest habitat improvement techniques.

In these pages Paul Johnsgard aptly points out that the incomparably beautiful ruffed grouse deserves the attention of poets and artists. Even more, the bird is worthy of the attention of all who value healthy and productive woodlands. Because the grouse has such stringent habitat requirements, his very presence tells us his chosen coverts are places not merely where he alone can live but where many, many other wildlife species will also thrive.

The Ruffed Grouse Society is pleased and proud to be associated with Stackpole Books in presenting this first volume of the Wildlife Series.

−Samuel R. Pursglove, Jr.
Executive Director, Ruffed Grouse Society

Publisher's note

In making this book we have tried to evoke the drama, the beauty and nobility, of the ruffed grouse and its life in the wild. We have tried to paint you a living canvas, to make you feel, vividly, what it is like for the grouse to hatch, mature, mate, and die in its natural habitat. This is a scientific work, but we have tried also to capture the color, the power and grace, the rhythm and mystery, that make the ruffed grouse one of North America's most beloved birds.

How might a grouse move about its territory during the first hours of a summer's day? Where does the bird fit into the forest hierarchy? What is it about the grouse's musculature that allows it to explode into flight and streak through densest cover without touching a branch? What do the baby chicks eat? Why does the cock drum? When a bobcat begins her stalk, what defense mechanisms activate in the bird's physiology?

Volumes such as the one you are holding are generally intended to serve a practical end—reference text for the wildlife manager, guide for the hunter, aide for the wildlife artist—and indeed, the pages that follow will provide the wildlife manager with more data on population and behavior than any book has heretofore been able to make available. The hunter will achieve a better understand-

ing of where to find the bird, the artist a better understanding of anatomy and coloration . . . but the central inspiration behind this project is a desire to understand for understanding's sake, a desire to study our ecosystem's processes in order to relish them.

It is quite possible to seek knowledge for its own sake. It is quite possible, and honorable, to analyze the natural world merely to enjoy it. If we would more often take time to study nature's workings with no end in mind beyond enjoyment, perhaps as a race we would find ourselves managing our environment a little more sanely.

We have felt a measure of reverence during the preparation of this book, reverence for the grouse, reverence for the natural world of which the grouse is a part—this fascinating, complicated planet we, and the grouse, inhabit and whose workings we humans may be less able to control than we think.

We hope you will lose yourself in what follows. We hope you will feel the same sense of excitement we did as we put these pages together. We hope you will slip easily, deeply, into the magical life-cycle of this truly magnificent bird.

—M. David Detweiler
President, Stackpole Books

NEEFUS

The place
of the ruffed grouse

The king of game birds

The ruffed grouse is an incomparably beautiful bird. Its plumage is a study in subtle coloring, worthy of the attention of both poets and artists. In the intricate pattern of grays, blacks, buffs, and browns can be found the results of millions of years of evolutionary processes. Through the countless generations of birds, the species' feather pigments have come to match its forest surroundings. To the human eye, however, this eminently functional coloration seems to suggest avian artistry, as if ruffed grouse have been continually refining the aesthetic sensibilities of their ancestors. Anthropomorphism aside, the female ruffed grouse must have an innate ability to recognize and appreciate the male's unique plum-

age pattern as well as his postures, calls, and sounds, for it is she who selects which of all the drummers competing for her attention shall pass on his genes to the next generation of ruffed grouse.

Ensuring that there will be a next generation is the challenge for wildlife managers and the concern of all who love the ruffed grouse, wing shooters and bird-watchers alike. This handsome bird does not clamor for their attention, however, and though important to them, it is only a bit player on the ecological stage. The ruffed grouse is a small animal. It is shy, retiring, wary. It does not dam streams, or trample vegetation, or strip bark from trees. In the scheme of things, it contributes an insignificant part to the total

The ruffed grouse is a characteristic species of young forests. Such woodlands often consist of aspen and, as here, alder, but tall shrubs also can make good grouse coverts.

KUBISIAK

Left: A dirt road cuts through a stand of aspens in Wisconsin. These trees, ranging from saplings to mature 56-year-olds, provide both food and cover in close proximity for the ruffed grouse. Right: The flower buds of the male aspen, which will soon open into catkins, sustain the birds through the winter.

living biomass provided by all the plants and animals of North American forests. Yet its role should not be underestimated, for it is one of the characteristic, "indicator" species of certain forest types.

The ruffed grouse's overall geographic range corresponds to that of certain species of *Populus,* the poplars, primarily the quaking aspen and the balsam poplar. Both trees are part of the boreal coniferous forest of Canada and the northeastern United States, where they are the primary transitional species during the natural succession from grassland to mature forest and, to a more limited extent, a permanent but minor part of the temperate deciduous forest community of eastern North America.

Poplars grow rapidly, especially in sunny and fairly moist areas. Their tiny and numerous seeds, lofted by cottony hairs, are carried far and wide on the wind. Poplars are thus ideally suited for colonizing newly exposed areas following forest fires, logging, landslides, or other major disturbances. Their tiny flowers, those of the two sexes growing on separate trees, are rich in pollen because the species relies on the wind for pollination. The hanging clusters of flowers, or catkins, as well as the sugar-rich leaf buds that gradually develop and enlarge over the winter, provide a prime source of energy and nutrients for animals that can nip them off the branches. Given such a ready-made feast, within easy reach of a bird, it should not be too surprising that the distribution

and ranges of *Bonasa umbellus,* the ruffed grouse, and *Populus* coincide so remarkably.

The ruffed grouse is not wholly dependent upon poplars, however. Indeed, the species is catholic in its diet for much of the year, and any attempt to discuss its foods ends up in a long list of plants. If such a list were to include all the foods eaten in various parts of the birds' range, and if it were complete—at least insofar as our knowledge permits—it might well run more than five hundred plant species and still not prove exhaustive. In an early study by the New York State Conservation Department, during which Bump and his colleagues examined more than a thousand ruffed grouse crops and stomachs, some 330 species of plants were found to have been consumed; the bird was pronounced "omnivorous."

Certain tree and shrub species, however, provide the bulk of the bird's diet. Most of these woody plants are ecological pioneers, transition species in forest succession—the largest number of which are normally present from three to five years after heavy lumbering. In New York, the most commonly taken foods were aspens, which accounted for 12 percent of the total volume, cherries (11 percent), birches (9 percent), raspberries and blackberries (9 percent), and hop hornbeams (6 percent). Animal foods, mainly insects, are eaten primarily by young chicks, but among adults the consumption of insects (mostly ants, beetles, and caterpillars) is largely limited to summer months

KUBISIAK

GULLION

Good grouse habitat depends on the periodic devastation of forests, whether by logging or by wildfire, and the renewal that follows. The Little Sioux fire of northern Minnesota burned in mid-May 1971.

GULLION

Aspens are opportunistic, sun-loving pioneer trees. Six weeks after the Little Sioux fire, these seedlings were standing thick and tall.

GULLION

Thirteen years later, the Little Sioux aspens show the characteristics of excellent habitat for ruffed grouse. The dense vertical cover and the shrubby understory protect the birds from predators and offer sources of food.

and amounts to a mere 1 percent of volume. Most of the year's protein needs must come from plant sources. Besides solid foods, grouse need water, but this is normally readily available in most of the habitats they occupy.

A more recent study than Bump's included a comparison of ruffed grouse foods in Missouri with the results of twenty-four published studies from around the species' range. Aspen and poplars were the principal foods in seventeen of these studies, Korschgen reported, and birch was cited in eleven; all other food sources were mentioned less often. Basically, winter foods consist of tree buds and twigs. Buds and catkins, the primary spring foods, are gradually supplemented by green leaves as they become available. In early summer the grouse begins feeding on berries, and also on some insects, but by late summer berries and fruits of various shrubs have become the more important foods.

The broad array of foods acceptable to the ruffed grouse allows it to survive in the great variety of temperate forest ecosystems whose successional or climax stages include one or more species of aspen, poplar, or birch. These forests typically have the heavy shrub understory and fallen trees that are needed for the males' spring courtship and fall territorial displays. These drumming logs are carefully chosen for their height, length, condition, aspect, and surrounding cover. Males seem to prefer logs that are partially

After a forest fire, the first plants to appear are light-loving grasses and other herbaceous species, as well as seedlings of shrubs and trees. As the seedlings grow and create more shade, the area becomes less hospitable to herbaceous plants.

decayed, for example, apparently so that they can imbed their claws in the wood for a better grip. Drumming sites are usually surrounded by relatively little ground cover but thick shrub and tree cover above—a combination that presumably allows for maximum protection from overhead predators and maximum potential for scanning the ground for rivals, mates, and terrestrial predators. If well-situated logs are not available, the

drummers select rocks or other elevated stages.

Other types of vegetation within the same forests offer food and cover for ruffed grouse in other stages of their life cycle. Small, shrubby clearings seem to be important as brood-raising habitat and sources of fruits and berries in summer and autumn. Both conifers and deciduous tree species may provide the basic forest canopy, and a mixture

6

of these tree types seems to be more favorable to grouse than are hardwoods alone. It is possible that the presence of a few thickly foliaged conifers provides valuable roosting cover during winter, and the predominant hardwoods favor the development of a shrubby undercover with its ground-level food sources.

Despite all that has been learned from all the many studies over so many years, in some respects the ruffed grouse remains an enigma. What, exactly, does the bird need to eat to survive? What triggers the fall dispersal of young grouse? What causes the ten-year cycle of highs and lows in the grouse population? What habitat best ensures the bird's survival? Questions, perhaps, for the next generation of students of the ruffed grouse.

—Paul A. Johnsgard

Softwood species (aspen and birch) mature first, followed by the coniferous trees. Finally, the slow-growing hardwoods (maple and oak) break through the canopy; succession is complete.

A proud pedigree

What makes the ruffed grouse a ruffed grouse is a collection of special characteristics, such as the neck ruff and the distinctive tail bands found in both sexes of adults. These characteristics are specific to the species, and although the ruff is most fully developed in adult males, it is typical of adult females, too.

The ruffed grouse has two close relatives: the Eurasian hazel grouse, *Bonasa bonasia,* and the black-breasted hazel grouse of China, *Bonasa severzowi*. Both the ruffed grouse and the two species of hazel grouse are more like one another than any other kind of grouse: in all these species the upper leg is feathered, the lower leg is bare, and the rounded and banded tail is almost two-thirds the length of the folded wing. These similarities are considered genus-level traits that point to an older order of evolutionary relationships.

The three *Bonasa* birds are part of the larger grouse assemblage, which can be characterized in a fairly simple manner. All the species of grouse–sixteen in Johnsgard's recent revision–have variably feathered lower legs, or tarsi, and nostrils that are hidden by short feathers. Both traits help the birds retain heat in cold climates, and indeed grouse are better adapted to arctic and alpine conditions than any of the other pheasantlike birds. Some taxonomists have therefore placed the sixteen grouse in a family by themselves, called Tetraonidae. Recent au-

The feathered leg is a physical characteristic shared with other members of the grouse family. The most remarkable feature of the ruffed grouse is behavioral: only the ruffed grouse calls his mate by drumming from a fallen tree.

THE PLACE OF THE RUFFED GROUSE

The hazel grouse (left, female; right, male) might be considered a Eurasian version of the ruffed grouse. The legs and nostrils of both species are feathered, permitting them to inhabit cold regions.

thorities, however, generally regard these traits more as climatic adaptations than as indications of some definite evolutionary divergence, and they have designated the grouse as a subfamily, Tetraoninae, of the larger family of pheasants, Phasianidae.

Apart from the grouse, the pheasant family Phasianidae includes the large pheasants typical of the Old World—the tribe Phasianini, whose males have long tails, sharp tarsal spurs, and often iridescent plumage. Closely related to these are the Old World partridges, quails, and francolins of tribe Perdicini, which are variably smaller, usually have short tails, often lack tarsal spurs, and never have iridescent plumage. The New World quails, which include such familiar species as the northern bobwhite, the scaled and California quails, plus some tropical wood partridges, are externally almost identical to the Old World quails and partridges, save for the irregular serrations on the cutting edge of the lower mandible. Because of this trait they are called odontophorine, or "tooth-bearing," partridges, and are usually considered a subfamily (Odontophorinae) or sometimes a family (Odontophoridae).

Also in the pheasant family are two species of turkeys, *Meleagris,* that are native to the woodlands of Mexico and the southern United States; these might almost be thought of as gigantic grouse that have specialized for eating acorns or other large nuts and seeds of the forest. They are usually considered a separate family, Meleagrididae.

Lastly, the African guinea fowl (Numidinae) and various tropical groups, such as the Old World megapodes (Megapodidae) and the New World chachalaca-guan-curassow assemblage (Cracidae), are related, in various degrees, to the grouse.

Together, all these families are the chick-enlike, or gallinaceous, birds that constitute the large order Galliformes. Precisely how, when, and where these birds differentiated themselves from other orders of birds—the songbirds of the order Passeriformes, for example, and the waterfowl of the order Anseriformes—are questions that will probably never have satisfactory answers. For it is an unfortunate fact that evolution works so slowly and leaves so few fossilized traces of its processes that most of what might be said about the evolution of almost any species is as much conjecture as documented fact. This is doubly true with birds: their bones are hollow, thin, and highly fragile, and thus tend to deform or disintegrate before they are ever fossilized. Yet, on the basis of comparative anatomy of the sixteen or so living species of grouse, and from what we know about the climatic and physical changes in the environment in the last thirty million to fifty million years, we can make some fairly solid conclusions about the probable evolutionary pathways that led to the modern species *Bonasa umbellus.*

Let us first establish the space and time for our discussion. We know that the entire assemblage of grouse is confined to the north-

Paleocene	Eocene	Pleistocene	Oligocene	Miocene	Pliocene
60	50	40	30	20	10

Millions of years before the present

ern hemisphere, and is primarily associated with temperate to arctic environments. Thus, we can perhaps safely exclude tropical areas and the southern hemisphere from consideration, especially since no grouse fossils are known from such places. As to time, Sibley and Ahlquist have calculated that the Phasianini—the pheasants, turkeys, jungle fowl, and grouse—separated from the closely related Old World quails, partridges, and francolins of tribe Perdicini about fifty million years ago. This was early in the Cenozoic era, or the Age of Mammals, when climates were mild throughout nearly the entire world. Hardwood forests probably dominated much of the land masses of North America and Eurasia. This Arcto-

Tertiary geoflora completely encircled the north temperate regions with little variation in character or composition. A land bridge between North America and Europe across the North Atlantic might have persisted for a time; certainly there was extensive land contact between western North America and eastern Asia with the result that both plants and terrestrial animal life were similar throughout these areas. To the north, the forest flora included such plants as pines, spruces, willows, birches, poplars, alders, and many other familiar genera of trees; the climate was probably humid with moderate temperatures and summer rainfall.

The earliest known fossil grouse is *Paleoalectoris incertus,* from about twenty-five mil-

The Miocene epoch saw the world's first grouse. Plant life was becoming much like our modern floras. Evidence suggests large browsing animals from the Oligocene and placental mammals from the Paleocene were still populating the earth, but they were overshadowed by the rise of whales, apes, and grazing animals. Warm temperatures prevailed, and much of today's coastline was submerged.

THE PLACE OF THE RUFFED GROUSE

BESENGER

The subgroups of the order Galliformes are distinguished on the basis of physical characteristics and habitat. Only grouse, for example, have pectinated toes and feathered nostrils and ankles. Unlike other Galliformes, they occur throughout the northern hemisphere.

Phasianini (pheasants)

Tetraoninae (grouse)

Odontophorinae (New World quail)

Perdicini (partridges)

Meleagridinae (turkeys)

Numidinae (guineafowl)

Cracidae

lion years ago in North American lower Miocene deposits. It is an old form, from a genus with no surviving examples. Somewhat more recent is another North American fossil, *Tympanuchus stirtoni,* from the middle Miocene. This is the oldest fossil grouse belonging to a modern-day genus, that of the prairie chickens, and appears to suggest that grassland grouse already existed. This is unlikely, however, as grasslands were then just beginning to develop as offshoots of temperate savannas and forest edges. As the Rocky Mountains in western North America began to lift during the Miocene epoch, a progressively drier area to the east was formed by rain-shadow effects, and the once-continuous deciduous forest that had occupied the area began to shrink and was confined to shady slopes and wetter river valleys. Farther north the predominantly coniferous forests began to subdivide into more northerly lowland (boreal) and western mountain-adapted (montane) types, and tundralike communities of plants formed on high mountain peaks and extreme northern portions of the land masses.

During this period of roughly ten million to thirty million years ago, the grouse must have been actively evolving, too. Few fossils are available to document the process, however. Besides an upper Miocene fossil from North America *(Archeophasianus),* there is the first Eurasian fossil grouse *(Tetrao macropus)* from the upper Pliocene epoch, less than ten million years ago. These do not provide good evidence of the evolutionary pattern, but one can make some reasonable guesses based on the sequence and pattern of diversification of the major plant communities, or ecosystems.

First, we might postulate that the earliest grouselike birds were forest-dwelling members of the Old World pheasant assemblage, which by and large is more tropical than the present-day grouse family. To become grouse, these birds needed feathers to cover both their tarsi (lower legs) and the nostrils. These two adaptations, the major ones that identify grouse as grouse, offer better insulation against the cold, protecting the legs (and also the toes in the three ptarmigan species) from freezing and providing a kind of muffler to warm frigid air entering the

Lagopus mutus
Dendragapus falcipennis
Bonasa bonasia
Bonasa severzowi
Tetrao tetrix
Lagopus lagopus
Lagopus leucurus
Tetrao urogallus
Tetrao mlokosiewiczi
Tetrao parvirostris
Dendragapus canadensis
Dendragapus obscurus
Centrocercus urophasianus
Tympanuchus phasianellus
Tympanuchus cupido
Bonasa umbellus

BESENGER

nostrils. The extra feathers enabled these birds to occupy the deciduous forests of the Arcto-Tertiary geoflora: in Eurasia, a bird probably resembling the modern hazel grouse settled into this ecological niche, and in North America it was an ancestor of the ruffed grouse. These birds presumably fed on berries, seeds, and leaves in the summer, and on the buds and flowers of willows, alders, and poplars during the winter and spring.

Farther north, where spruce and pines dominated the Arcto-Tertiary geoflora, other ancestral grouse were adapting to a diet of needles and related foods; these birds were larger, with less surface area per total mass, and thus better able to conserve body heat in their extreme climate. In North America the modern blue grouse (*Dendragapus obscurus*) and spruce grouse (*D. canadensis*) probably closely approximate the ancestral conifer-adapted grouse; in Eurasia the modern capercaillie (*Tetrao urogallus*) and sharp-winged grouse (*Dendragapus falcipennis*), their evolutionary counterparts, descended from the ancestral grouse in the northern reaches of Eurasia.

With the drying and cooling trends of Pliocene times, and the corresponding expansion of grasslands and tundra, it is likely that offshoots from forest-adapted grouse moved out to exploit these newly developing habitats. The modern sage grouse (*Centrocercus urophasianus*) can be seen as a derivative of

The pressures of natural selection encourage animals to exploit available niches. Thus resources help determine the direction in which species evolve. Each of the several species of grouse is adapted to the climate, habitat, and food availability of its particular region.

the ancestral conifer-adapted grouse that re-adapted to the expanding semiarid sagelands of western North America, just below the forests of ponderosa pine. The pinnated grouse (*Tympanuchus cupido*) and the sharp-tailed grouse *(T. phasianellus)* are clearly derived from species of deciduous-woodland grouse that gradually spread from the forest edges into the prairies of central North America. A similar process probably occurred simultaneously in Eurasia, with the expansion of the ancestral black grouse *(Tetrao tetrix)* into forest-edge and moorland habitats. In both continents the developing tundra communities of the Far North were being colonized by ptarmigans (*Lagopus* sp.). These tundra-adapted grouse turn variably white during winter and acquire long, feath-ered snowshoes that support them in soft snow and keep their toes warm—two adaptations for their habitat that distinguish them from other grouse.

Like its ecological counterpart in Eurasia, the hazel grouse, the ancestral grouse saw its range altered and disrupted as mountain ranges rose and a changing climate splintered the deciduous habitats into isolated forests. The bird's cover and food species changed as well. Some deciduous trees, such as the poplars, remained a part of the mostly coniferous boreal forest by becoming transient successional forms, exploiting the stages of forest development and appearing after major disturbances, such as forest fires. The ruffed grouse and hazel grouse became part of such communities, perhaps increasingly adapting their diet to one rich in buds and catkins, whose nutrients got them through the usually severe winters and prepared them for the rigors of spring breeding. In Eurasia the hazel grouse found its range split into two major components, the one in China becoming sufficiently different as to warrant designation of a separate species, the black-breasted hazel grouse. In North America the degree of disruption was less, yet enough to allow the ruffed grouse to evolve into almost a dozen geographic races, or subspecies.

Besides this geographic diversification, the ruffed grouse has also evolved two distinct and genetically controlled color phases. The differences between the gray and the red show up best in the tail feathers. With the exception of the reddish brown Pacific Northwest race *castanea*, all subspecies occur in both phases, but the frequency of the two types varies greatly in different parts of the species' range and correlates with the dominant forest cover. Generally, the gray birds are much more common in northern and typically drier parts of the range, which often have a grayish, lichen-rich ground covering; the red birds are more typical of warmer and more humid areas, which are rich in the broad-leaved understory plants that turn rusty brown in fall. Gullion and Marshall have suggested that gray-phased birds may be better adapted physiologically for tolerating cold and are thus more likely to survive the extremes of northern winters.

—*Paul A. Johnsgard*

Winter snows expose the ruffed grouse to cold and predation, but the species has evolved a variety of physical characteristics and behavioral strategies to survive.

The ecological niche

Ruffed grouse occupy a similar ecological niche wherever they are found, even though their habitat varies considerably in the different portions of their range. A plant that accounts for a major part of the birds' diet in one region, for example, may be absent entirely from some other region. Likewise, the habitat differs from region to region in the species of trees, shrubs, and vines that provide cover. Nevertheless, the habitat remains similar in terms of its structure—the size of the plants and their density. The one constant: dense woody cover.

Ruffed grouse find all their annual habitat needs in brushy mixed-age woodlands. Their seasonal cover requirements include a need for dense woody vegetation, but unlike some other species of grouse and their relatives, such as pheasants and quail, they usually avoid the rank cover provided by tall grasses or herbs.

Since a food supply is of little value without good cover, and cover is not attractive unless it also offers food, the degree of interspersion of different habitat components is important. The farther grouse have to travel to get from cover to food, the fewer the grouse. The kind of habitat ruffed grouse need also varies according to the birds' age and the time of year, and no single cover type can be ideal in satisfying all these needs. There are, in fact, at least four basic types—drumming log cover, nesting cover, brood

The pendulous catkins of black birch are important to the grouse diet in winter, especially when the temperatures dip below freezing and snow covers the ground.

cover, and fall and winter cover—each of which the ruffed grouse finds despite the enormous differences in vegetation throughout its range. To appreciate the species' adaptability, consider the characteristic grouse habitats in each region.

THE NORTH

In Canada and the northern portion of the Lake States of Wisconsin, Minnesota, and Michigan, the range of the ruffed grouse is generally synonymous with the boreal forest formation and its forest ecotone—the aspen parkland and the hemlock-hardwood forests. The climate of the region is characterized by a short growing season (June-August), very cold winters, and moderate but regionally variable precipitation, averaging about 20 inches per year. Deep, powdery snow is typical of the winters and usually allows snow-roosting grouse to find refuge from the extremely cold temperatures. Although the land is typically flat and poorly drained, with numerous lakes and bogs, elevations vary from the Hudson Bay lowlands (near sea level) to the montane regions of western Canada (4,000 to 10,000 feet).

Common climax trees in the boreal forests include white spruce, balsam fir, paper birch, black spruce, and tamarack. Jack pine, white cedar, and aspen are important species in the successional and transitional forests of the region. Sparse populations of ruffed grouse occur in forests of spruce, fir, and birch, but it is the early successional and transitional forests, especially those dominated by aspen, that support the majority of ruffed grouse in the North.

Aspen forests dominate the southern fringe and the parkland ecotone of the boreal forest formation, and successional aspen forests resulting from fires occur sporadically throughout much of the region. In the North, young aspen stands with stems less than 3 to 4 inches in diameter and lacking other tree canopy are not usually occupied by ruffed grouse, except for an occasional brood. Even-aged stands of somewhat larger, more mature aspens constitute good grouse habitat in most of the region—if they contain a well-developed shrub understory of willows, viburnums, hazel, red-osier dogwoods, and other shrubs. The spotty impacts of fire often create mixed-age aspen stands that, perhaps, make the finest ruffed grouse habitat in North America. Such stands often satisfy all the food and cover requirements of ruffed grouse, and it is in these mixed-age aspen forests of southern Canada that the birds typically attain their highest densities.

THE WEST

In the West the ruffed grouse may be found in forests at elevations ranging from sea level to more than 8,000 feet. Over this range, the climate varies greatly: In the coastal areas and western slopes of the Cascade mountains, climate is moderated by the Pacific Ocean, and temperatures are relatively mild—neither excessively cold in the winter nor excessively hot in the summer. Precipitation is relatively high, coming as year-round rain in the lower elevations and as substantial snowfall in the higher elevations during winter. On the east slope of the Cascades and the Rocky Mountain area, however, the climate is harsher. Summers are drier and hotter, and winters may be much colder and more rugged, often with temperatures below 0°F. and more than 10 feet of snow in many areas of the Rockies.

Deciduous forests are preferred by the grouse: selection of hardwoods has been noted in western Washington, Alberta, northern Utah, and southeastern Idaho. Aspen is the favorite, but when available, birch, maples, alders, and cottonwoods may also be chosen. In central and northern Idaho, however, where little deciduous vegetation grows, viable grouse populations have been found thriving in coniferous forests, and Douglas fir, grand fir, western white pine, and lodgepole pine are commonly used by ruffed grouse. In southeastern Idaho, grouse have often been found in areas where Douglas fir and subalpine fir flourish.

Regardless of the type of forest, early successional stages are preferred over more mature forests, with typical high-quality grouse cover consisting of dense, brushy conditions. Such cover may include serviceberry, chokecherry, Rocky Mountain maple, huckleberry, snowberry, ninebark, and Utah honeysuckle. These shrubs provide not only

the cover necessary for the birds' anonymity but also the berries and buds needed for their nourishment.

THE MIDWEST

The midwestern portion of the ruffed grouse's range—Iowa, Missouri, northern Arkansas, and Illinois—is dominated by oak-hickory forest, similar to that in the East but distinctly different from the northern hardwoods. The following are important grouse habitats in this region:

• Upland oak-hickory forests, dominated by white, chinkapin, northern red, and black oaks; shagbark, mockernut, and bitternut hickories; and sugar maple. The understory in mature stands ranges from open to dense and may contain sugar maple, serviceberry, hop hornbeam, flowering dogwood, and blackhaw viburnum. Young stands, eight to twenty years old, provide the best grouse habitat.

• Narrow bands of bottomland hardwoods typically along streams and creeks. They contain oaks and hickories but also black walnut, basswood, sycamore, elm, and sugar maple. Their understories usually comprise sugar maple, elm, American hornbeam, American bladdernut, Ohio buckeye, spicebush, pawpaw, and rough-leaf dogwood. Young stands provide the best cover, but mature stands with dense understories are also used by grouse.

• Old field habitats, where agricultural land was abandoned twenty to fifty years

An old field in the midst of second-growth hardwoods provides a variety of plant foods, including leaves and fruits of vines and shrubs.

A stand of conifers at the edge of an oak woodlot: though very different from the northern aspen forests, this habitat can support huntable populations of ruffed grouse.

ago. They contain a mixture of eastern red cedar, oaks, hickories, American plum, persimmon, black locust, multiflora rose, American bittersweet, and flowering and gray dogwood.

Despite these major differences in forest composition, grouse habitat here has remarkably similar features to those in other parts of the grouse range. Of prime importance is a high density of shrubs, saplings, and pole-size timber.

Climate in the Midwest is typically continental, with cold winters and hot summers. Winter daily low temperatures average in the single digits in the northern part of the Midwest, and summer daily high temperatures are above 90°F. in the southern part. The region receives an average of 25 to 40 inches of rain per year and 10 to 30 inches of snow. Although significant accumulations of snow occur occasionally, snow is rarely persistent and grouse cannot usually snow-roost.

THE SOUTHEAST

In the eastern United States, *the South* designates the region from the Ohio River to the Gulf of Mexico. That definition suffices well enough for political purposes, but it has no relationship to ecology, or to the ruffed grouse. The heart of the ruffed grouse range lies in the forests of southern Canada and the northern United States, and any grouse that live south of that border region might, in one sense, be considered southern. For most students of the ruffed grouse, however,

the South refers to the eastern United States from the edge of the northern hardwood forests to the southern limit of the species' range: Indiana, Ohio, part of Pennsylvania, and south to northern Georgia and western South Carolina.

Grouse are present wherever they can find suitable habitats throughout this region, but in the extreme southern portion of their Appalachian range, they usually live only where the elevation exceeds 2,000 feet.

The ecology of the southern grouse range accounts for a curious feature: the region's most "northern" habitats are on upper elevations in the southern Appalachians. Oak forests dominate most of the southeastern grouse region, but northern forest species, such as white pine, hemlock, yew, and mountain maple, extend into the southern Appalachians at high elevations. The western Appalachian slopes in Kentucky and Tennessee support a great diversity of trees and shrubs, including some more northerly species, like beech and sugar maple.

Ruffed grouse in the Southeast appear to occupy structurally similar habitats and have roughly the same requirements as grouse in northern areas. The differences demonstrate the adaptability of this species. In this region, ruffed grouse are largely restricted to the mountainous parts of Virginia, West Virginia, North Carolina, Georgia, Tennessee, and Kentucky. At these higher elevations the hardwoods characteristic of northern forests still predominate. Some birds live

in lower areas: Seehorn has reported that hunters have shot grouse at elevations of 366 to 1,768 meters in Virginia, North Carolina, and Georgia, and Stafford and Dimmick have reported on grouse collected in the Great Valley of Tennessee, where elevations range from 183 to 640 meters. In general, however, grouse seem to be more common at higher elevations. Hein, for example, observed few grouse below 1,100 meters on a study area in North Carolina that dipped as low as 650 meters. Ruffed grouse have recently been stocked at low elevations in western Tennessee and eastern Virginia, but whether the birds will make these sites their permanent home is unknown.

The regional climate is temperate. Snow rarely covers the ground for more than a few days at a time, and below freezing temperatures rarely continue for more than three or four days. Snowfall may range from 10 to 20 inches a year in the valley to as high as 40 inches in the Blue Ridge—accumulations that pale in comparison with the deep snows in the northern heart of the grouse's range. Generally, grouse here are able to forage for green leafy foods throughout the winter. Late spring and early fall freezes, however, can ruin the fruit production of some desirable food plant species.

Portions of the southern grouse range were extensively farmed. Logging in the early 1900s has created today's second-growth forests, mostly upland hardwoods and pines. The American chestnut was a

Left: *In the southern Appalachians, grazed mountain pastures interspersed with hawthorn and evergreens are preferred grouse feeding sites in fall.* Center: *Southern grouse are largely restricted to the Appalachians, where deciduous trees predominate. The habitat tends toward steep slopes and narrow ridges.* Right: *Rhododendron thickets in mature forest stands provide winter cover, but poor forage at such sites appears to limit their value for grouse.*

dominant timber species in the entire Appalachian region before the chestnut blight.

The rolling foothills and mountains of the Southeast support a diversity of woodland types. At elevations above 5,000 feet, the red spruce and Frasier fir forests resemble those of many areas in the northeastern United States. A curiosity of sorts are the laurel slicks—nearly treeless expanses of mountain laurel and Catawba rhododendron on the high mountain slopes. These broad-leaved evergreens took over after the slopes had been cleared by fire or landslides but are constantly being invaded by hardwoods. Also scattered throughout these upper mountains are large treeless areas known as grass or heath "balds," which support low-growing grasses and ground-hugging shrubs, such as blueberries and other heathlike plants. Balds, the relics of some former climatic period, are maintained by constant exposure to prevailing winds. In some ways balds resemble the alpine meadows of the northern United States.

The more moist sites at midelevation generally include a mixture of oaks, beech, black and yellow birch, and red maple. These same species also occur at lower elevations in the plateau. Fire cherry is a dominant species in many mountainous areas that have been disturbed by fire or cutting. On rich, dry sites at midelevation, several oak species occur. Moist coves and north-facing slopes are characterized by eastern white pine, eastern hemlock, northern red oak, and black walnut. Drier, south-facing slopes support the oaks and hickories interspersed with stands of Virginia pine and pitch pine. At lower elevations, mountain coves display an association of yellow poplar, basswood, maples, hemlock, beech, birches, and northern red oak. The aspens, so important to grouse in the North, are virtually nonexistent here except in isolated stands. The abandoned homesteads, pastures, and old apple orchards scattered throughout the mountains are often overgrown with pioneers, such as black locust, hawthorn, blackberries, honeysuckle, and wild rose.

The dominant understory plants in the region are mountain laurel on the drier mountain slopes and ridges, rhododendron on moist mountain slopes, flowering dogwood and tag alder along streams and in coves, and sourwood, flame azalea, and other heathlike plants on a combination of understory sites. Oak and pines are typical of the woodland ridges. Chestnut oak, scarlet oak, and shortleaf pine are the principal overstory trees. On the poorer rocky sites, thick stands of Virginia pine are common. Where limestone is near the soil surface, dense stands of Eastern red cedar occur. Common understory species in the valley are honeysuckle, dogwood, redbud, and sourwood.

—Harold L. Barber, Roy Kirkpatrick,
John Kubisiak, Donald Rusch,
Frederick A. Servello,
Steven K. Stafford, Dean F. Stauffer,
and Frank R. Thompson III

Forests of aspen trees and conifers most easily come to mind when ruffed grouse habitat is mentioned, but the birds use other settings as well.

MARTINSON

A
description

The subtleties of plumage

*I*t has happened many times. The woods are quiet but for the flutter of yellowing aspen leaves and the crackle of twigs underfoot. Suddenly an explosive roar assaults the ears. The heart leaps. But before the human intruder can turn toward the noise and focus in its direction, its source has disappeared through the branches. Silence returns to the woods almost as quickly as it was shattered.

Or perhaps the ruffed grouse—for this is the explanation for the startling noise—is not close enough to be disturbed by the footsteps. It continues its fall ritual of beating its wings, creating miniature thunderclaps to warn its rivals.

This bird, *Bonasa umbellus,* is indeed more often heard than seen. Nature has equipped it with such superb camouflage that if it is not flushed, it is practically invisible. It is no accident that information on nesting hens is scant. And who knows how many grouse have sat immobile on the forest floor while a hunter passed by, or perched in a hemlock while he walked beneath, only to slip away through the forest behind his back? For grouse can flush without a sound.

The ruffed grouse, a ground-dwelling bird of young deciduous and mixed woodlands, is mottled with various shades of brown, black, and gray, with lighter underparts that have dark bars. Both sexes are similar, but there are two color phases, independent of sex or age: brown and gray. The brown

Soft shadings of chestnut and cream conceal this hen as she incubates her eggs at the base of a tree. As long as she remains quiet and still, she is unlikely to be noticed.

phase is often called the red or reddish brown phase. Whatever the nomenclature, the difference is most noticeable in the tail feathers.

Two field marks of plumage that help distinguish the ruffed grouse from its cousins are the broad black band on the fan-shaped tail and the somewhat triangular patch of dark feathers on each side of the neck that, when erected, form an umbrellalike ruff from which the bird derives its species name, *umbellus*.

The name *Bonasa umbellus* is itself an umbrella for the approximately one dozen recognized subspecies. The subspecies' names provide convenient "handles" for populations of grouse that vary in plumage, range, and habitat. But the brown phase of *Bonasa umbellus umbellus*—the nominate subspecies, the one for which the species is named—will be our starting point. This will give us a basis of comparison for the subtle differences among the color phases, sexes, and subspecies.

PLUMAGE

Because the beautiful coloration of the ruffed grouse is complex and subtle, it is necessary to make fine distinctions in color. The following descriptive material relies on those colors defined in Smithe's *Naturalist's Color Guide*.

The feathers of the crown are long, with distinct blotches of dark brownish gray, or fuscous. Their tips lie along the back of the head, protected from wear as the bird forages under brush, but when erected, they form a conspicuous crest.

The upper parts of the head, back, rump, and wings are basically cinnamon brown and chestnut but include a variety of other colors: fuscous, Sayal brown, pale smoke gray, tawny, and light clay. The upper back feathers have a distinct but variously shaped spot of Sayal brown at the tip; each of the remaining back feathers and rump feathers has a large, distinct arrowhead of light drab, lightly stippled and narrowly edged with fuscous; it is located distally along the shaft.

Left: *His blackish ruff whirring into an umbrella that frames his head, this gray-phase male puts on his display.* Right: *A brown-phase female reveals the bars of her ventral plumage. Like the male, the hen bears a crest.*

MARTINSON

The tail feathers, or rectrices, vary from light cinnamon brown at the base to dark cinnamon brown toward the tip. Seven to nine fuscous bands cross these feathers, together with a broad, fuscous-black band just below the tip. Both proximally and distally to this subterminal band are bands of smoke gray stippled with fuscous.

Between the eye and the bill is the loreal stripe, white with a pale buff wash on the male, a light salmon wash on the female. The auriculars, the feathers covering the "little ears" under and behind the eyes, are stiff feathers. Their shafts are light smoke gray, almost white, with a pale smoke gray streak along each side. The remaining portions of the vanes are cinnamon brown and fuscous.

The ruff feathers are large and blunt. They lie in a triangular patch on each side of the neck until erected. Each has a long fuscous base that darkens distally, a dark subterminal band with a blue or violet sheen, and a fuscous terminal band. The longest of the ruff feathers measure about 70 millimeters on an adult male; those of the female and subadult are generally shorter and duller.

Ventral plumage is generally light gray, but the feathers on the throat, breast, sides, and flanks have bands of cinnamon brown or fuscous that give the underparts of the grouse its barred effect. The bars are indistinct on the abdomen. The chin, throat, breast, and sides have a pale buff wash on the male; there is a pale salmon wash on the throat and breast of a female, but her sides have a pale buff wash.

These ventral and other contour feathers have afterfeathers, which are typical of gallinaceous birds. The afterfeather on the grouse is a small secondary feather whose shaft is attached to the base of the shaft of a contour feather. Being well developed in the ruffed grouse, these afterfeathers make the plumage very thick. They are downy and fully pigmented—usually gray, except at their tips, where they may have some brown coloration. Afterfeathers are not present on

The feathers that cover the nostrils are an adaptation for cold, as are the feathers of the legs. The grouse's toes can grip even smooth branches.

the flight feathers of either the tail or the wings.

The carpal remex is another oddity of the ruffed grouse and some other birds. It is an extra flight feather with a covert, on the upper surface of the wing between the primaries and the secondaries. A stiff feather, like the primaries and secondaries, it is about half the length of a secondary. The function of this feather is questionable; some ornithologists consider it a vestige.

THE BILL

The bill of a ruffed grouse is generally brown, short and thick, and curved downward. The tip of the upper mandible bends down slightly over the tip of the lower mandible. Feathers cover the base of the upper mandible and the nostrils, making the bill look shorter and smaller than it is.

THE TARSI

The tarsi, or "ankles," are half-covered with fine, hairlike feathers, usually pale gray with a light russet vinaceous (almost wine-colored) wash at the base, and very pale gray at the tips. The amount of feathering on the legs tends to decrease with increasing mean temperature; grouse in the southern and warmer portions of their range have almost bare tarsi. The lower, bare portion of the leg is scutellate, covered with scales—*scutella* in Latin, meaning "little shields."

Tails of both the brown phase (top three fans) and the gray phase (bottom three fans) can have black or chocolate subterminal bands. The fan in the middle is a split phase.

THE FEET

A ruffed grouse's feet are generally brown with hues of pink, gray, or blue. The three forward toes are slightly webbed; the hind toe is short and slightly elevated. The nails are short, thick, moderately curved, and sometimes blunt, adapted to scratching in the leaf litter of the forest floor. In winter a grouse has many comblike teeth about 2 millimeters in length along the sides of all the toes. These pectinations (from Latin *pectere,* "to comb") grow in early autumn and are shed irregularly in the spring. They tend to grow longer in the northern part of the grouse's range, where they, together with the slight webbing between the forward toes, may serve to distribute the weight of the grouse over a greater area, thus enabling it to walk on snow as if on snowshoes.

COLOR PHASES

Color-phase differences are most noticeable in the tail feathers. In birds of the gray phase, the basic tail color is light smoke gray

The gray-phase grouse tail (left) stands out on the russet leaves that cover the ground in a mature forest of oaks and maples. In stands of birch and aspen, however, it is the brown-phase grouse (right) that fails to blend into the surroundings.

with a faint brown wash, rather than cinnamon brown. The large spots on the back and rump are also light gray, and these feathers have broader, gray terminal bands than those of brown-phase birds. The shafts of the rectrices differ, too: tawny with fuscous bands on the gray-phase grouse, a reddish cinnamon, or cinnamon rufous, with fuscous bands on the brown-phase bird.

Given that the color phases are not due to sex, season, or developmental stages, why do they exist? Their geographical distribution yields a clue.

The brown phase prevails on both the Atlantic and the Pacific coasts; the gray phase is predominant in the interior and the North, the Rocky Mountains and the Great Plains. The brownest of the brown grouse inhabit the coastal areas of Washington and Oregon and the Appalachian Mountains of the Southeast; the grayest of the gray grouse dwell in northwestern Canada and Alaska.

Predation rates are a second clue. In northern Minnesota, according to studies by Gullion and Marshall, gray grouse tended to be less vulnerable to predation than brown grouse. This was particularly true during winters when there was little snow cover into which grouse could burrow to hide from their enemies. There lies the possible answer. The forest floor in that area of Minnesota has a grayish hue from dead aspen and birch leaves and needle litter. Gray

grouse blend right in. Brown grouse tend to blend better in the southern part of the state, where leaf litter under oaks and maples has a brown hue. If this hypothesis is correct, then the color phases of the grouse are linked with their environments.

The difference in predation and mortality rates between the two phases may be related to another factor, however. The eastern screech owl *(Otus asio)*, like the ruffed grouse, comes in two color phases. Ornithologists have noticed that owls of the gray phase are better able to endure harsh winters. Although ornithologists are not quite sure why, the red-phase owls have a significantly higher energy demand in cold weather, which simply means that they need more food. The increased demand occurs just when extremely cold weather reduces the owls' hunting efficiency, according to Terres. Perhaps the red- or brown-phase ruffed grouse likewise experience an increased demand for food coupled with a reduction in foraging efficiency; certainly this would lead to greater predation among brown-phase grouse.

One day there may be a definitive reason for the color phases of ruffed grouse. With release programs in various states, it will be possible to investigate the environmental selection of color phase because in certain instances populations may be isolated for study. Studies are now under way. In Missouri, Appalachian ruffed grouse of the brown phase have been released, but there have been no observations of gray-phase birds among their progeny.

There is also a correlation between the colors of grouse and the amount of moisture in their environment. Some of the darkest grouse dwell in the rain forests of the Olympic peninsula in western Washington; some of the palest grouse inhabit the dry aspen stands of the Utah mountains. In these cases ruffed grouse conform to Gloger's Rule, which maintains that birds dwelling in humid climates tend to be dark in coloration, and birds inhabiting dry climates tend to be light.

Within the two recognized color phases of brown and gray, infinite color variations exist, known as polychromatism. Like the phases, polychromatism is not related to sex, season, or age.

Occasionally, individuals of either color phase may have reddish ruffs. In these birds the base of the large ruff feathers is closest to robin rufous with a dark subterminal band that has a blue or violet sheen. The fuscous subterminal band on the tail feathers is washed with rufous. The overall appearance of the plumage of such a grouse is often more reddish brown than that of other birds of its subspecies and phase.

Gray phase or brown, the ruffed grouse has evolved plumage that conceals it from its predators. This camouflage, known as cryptic coloration, consists of three factors: protective coloration, disruptive coloration, and countershading. The bird's *protective coloration* lies in the various hues of brown, gray, and black of the feather coat, particularly on the forehead, crown, nape, back, rump, wings, and tail: these colors mimic those of the forest detritus. The *disruptive coloration* breaks up the silhouette of a grouse with the distinct light spots on the back, the streaks of the auriculars, and the bands of the tail: these ensure that the predator will not even discern the outline of a bird. The *countershading* is produced by the generally light colors of the underparts, which offset the effect of a shadow cast by the body of the grouse: thus the three-dimensional mass of the bird dissolves into the flat forest floor.

—*Ronald R. Runkles*

Even bright sunlight cannot expose any flaws in this hen's perfect camouflage. In color, shading, and form, she is all but invisible.

Preening and dusting

Locked feather barbs (left) keep the flight feathers smooth. When the feather barbs become unlocked (right), the bird preens, restoring them to their locked position.

*A*s a ruffed grouse brushes against twigs and leaves, as it rests on the forest floor or roosts in a tree, tiny insects jump in between its feathers: lice, fleas, mites, flies, and ticks. The feathers themselves pick up dirt, and their barbs become unhooked. But a grouse cannot tolerate ectoparasites or feathers in disrepair and still remain competitive. It must preen and dust.

A grouse has an oil gland, also known as a preen gland or uropygial gland, on the rump at the base of the tail. This gland secretes a greasy, waxy substance that repels water and makes the feathers more flexible; it may also secrete substances that inhibit the growth of bacteria and fungi.

Preening is often done in the open on a log, rock, or tree limb, or on the ground near the edge of a body of water—wherever the bird's field of vision permits it to detect approaching predators. The grouse begins by squeezing the area of the oil gland between its mandibles or by rubbing its closed bill against the area until the waxy material is released. Then it usually fluffs its feathers to make them more accessible. The grouse preens a feather by grasping its base and either gently nibbling it as it passes through the bill or pulling the feather through a partly closed bill. The preening serves to remove dirt, oil, and ectoparasites, while relocking the feather barbs. Preening the head presents a bit of a challenge: the bird must rub these feathers against another part of its body.

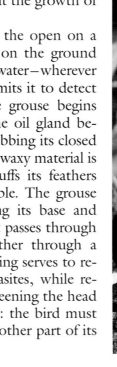

A flea, a tick, or just an itch: the ruffed grouse balances on one leg to scratch its head.

Dusting is characteristic of birds living in dry habitats, where it seems to replace water bathing: birds that dust, like the grouse, tend not to bathe in water except when it rains.

Grouse begin dusting when they are chicks, and there are special places where the entire brood goes; occasionally, two or three adult males gather to dust. They seek areas

with exposed soil—an ant hill, a path, a pile of ashes from burned brush, where a tree was uprooted, or where there is rotted wood. One grouse may have several sites. The birds dust all year. But in the Appalachians at least, the behavior seems most frequent in the summer during the postbreeding molt, when dusting may help remove sheath fragments and loose feathers, and least frequent in winter, when the ground is frozen or covered with snow.

Dusting takes place in three stages. First, the birds loosen the soil by scratching and pecking. They next work dust into their feathers by tossing loose dirt with their feet, throwing it onto their backs with their wings, and working it into the head feathers by rubbing their heads into the dirt. Finally, they ruffle their feathers to spread the dust and then shake it out.

Research done by Healy and Thomas with Japanese quail, *Coturnix japonica,* suggests that dusting helps the bird improve the alignment of feather barbs; reduces dandruff, oil, and moisture; makes the contour feathers dry and fluffy so that the down feathers can occupy the spaces in between, thereby improving the insulating ability of the feather coat; and dislodges ectoparasites. That dusting is of value to feather maintenance was ascertained by Edminster, who observed that the plumages of grouse kept in captivity without places to dust became ragged and worn.

—*Ronald R. Runkles*

Above: *By working dust into its feathers, the ruffed grouse makes its plumage a less desirable habitat for parasites.* Left: *Dust baths are smooth depressions of exposed soil; often a ruffed grouse feather is the only clue that betrays the site.*

Molting

The down of the newly hatched chick has its functions. It insulates and camouflages the young grouse, keeping it safe from cold winds and predators. But as the chick grows and takes to the air, its feather requirements change. It needs flight feathers—remiges and rectrices. Moreover, the old feathers become worn as it scurries through underbrush in search of food. As the bird approaches adulthood, it needs still longer, stronger, and thicker feathers over its entire body. And adults must replace their frayed feathers if they are to keep themselves in top condition.

Given the choice, a bird would rather not shed all its feathers at once, as a snake sheds its skin. That would leave it utterly defense-less against the elements and its enemies. The molt of the ruffed grouse—the word *molt* referring to both the loss of the old feathers and the growth of the new—includes safeguards that minimize the danger of being less than fully feathered.

First, the new feather begins to grow in the follicle before the old one falls out: the growth of the new one actually pushes out the old feather. An incoming feather emerges from the follicle as a *pinfeather,* totally enclosed in a sheath and looking like a thick pin. The sheath breaks open at the tip, and some barbs of the feather emerge. At this stage the feather is referred to as a *brush,* simply because it looks like artists' bristles. As the feather continues to grow, the sheath

The molt of feathers—annual for adults, nearly continual for chicks—proceeds in such a way that the bird is always capable of flight. Nevertheless, adults in the midst of their molt may flee danger on foot.

BESENGER

MARTINSON

continues to break apart toward the base, exposing even more barbs. The feather is now a *sheathed feather*, ready to be released from the remainder of the sheath and replace the old feather. All the tiny sheath fragments in the feather coat may make the grouse feel waxy and slippery in the hand.

Second, as Bump and his colleagues noted in 1947, the first feathers to appear cover and protect the bases of developing feathers.

Third, the body molt progresses in such a way as to maximize the area covered by the new incoming feathers, making the plumage appear complete before it is.

Fourth, a bird's first two molts proceed rather rapidly, the second beginning before the first has concluded. By mid-October the five-month-old grouse is wearing its sub-adult plumage.

Finally, the primaries, the most important flight feathers, are replaced not all at once, which would render the bird flightless, but gradually. A grouse usually lacks only one or two primary flight feathers per wing at any one time.

The ruffed grouse wears several coats during its lifetime. The downy plumage with which it has hatched is shed in the postnatal molt, resulting in juvenal plumage; the post-juvenal molt brings subadult plumage; a postbreeding molt introduces the adult plumage. The postbreeding molt becomes an annual occasion for grouse that live long enough.

*Feather development: first the completely sheathed **pin-feather** emerges. As it develops, some feather barbs break out from the sheath to form the **brush**. Nearing full size, the **sheathed feather** remains partially enclosed. Finally, the feather is released from the sheath.*

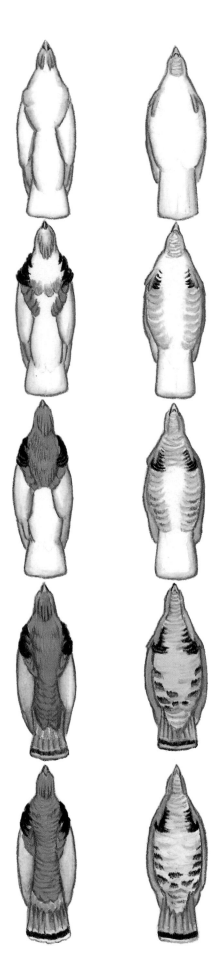

Right: A chick two or three days old wears protective coloration. The dark stripe from eye to nape is characteristic of eastern ruffed grouse chicks.

DOWNY PLUMAGE

When ruffed grouse emerge from their eggs, they are covered with natal down both above and below. A down feather is soft and fluffy: it lacks the long, stiff, central shaft of the contour feather that will later emerge. These down feathers, like the contour feathers to come, grow only on certain areas of the body, called *feather tracts*. Between these tracts are naked *apteria,* unfeathered bare spots, but the feathers grow in such a way as to cover the entire body.

The downy plumage provides not only insulation but also protective coloration for the chicks. A chick of the *Bonasa umbellus umbellus* subspecies has a distinctive dark fuscous stripe from the eye to the nape. The forehead, crown, occiput, and nape are russet, paling toward buff at the sides. The back and rump are slightly variegated with cinnamon brown and russet. This patch of color broadens posteriorly but pales laterally and ventrally. The upper wing surfaces are pale russet. The area on each side of the neck, where the ruffs will be, is a pale cinnamon. The chin, throat, breast, and abdomen are light buff. In general, the chicks are darkest along the dorsal midline and lightest along the ventral midline.

POSTNATAL MOLT

The chick's first molt begins quickly after it has hatched—perhaps within a few hours. By the end of the first week, several of the scapulars are evident, and some of the ten primary feathers have started to emerge, developing from the innermost (number 1) to the outermost (number 10). During the second week, the secondaries begin to emerge and develop, starting with the outermost and continuing to the innermost. (Accordingly,

The postbreeding molt progresses along a definite bilaterally symmetrical pattern. The first new feathers appear on the throat (left, ventral view) and the crown (right, dorsal view). The molt continues along the wings. The rump and abdomen are the last to fill in.

the numbering of the secondaries begins with the outermost, 1, and ends with the innermost, 15.) As these flight feathers develop, their corresponding coverts also grow. More scapulars appear, along with feathers on the center of the forehead and crown, the face, and the upper back. New feathers on the sides and flanks have also started to develop, and pinfeathers begin to appear on the sides of the neck, abdomen, and legs. Next, the central pair of rectrices emerge, followed by the adjoining rectrix on each side. The development of the rectrices progresses from the central pair outward on each side. After the rectrices have started to develop, pinfeathers appear on the chin and throat, and then the breast. One of the last areas to finish molting is the nape.

The general progression of the postnatal molt on top of the head is outward from the midline; on the back it progresses from the scapulars to the upper back and then toward the rump. On the underparts, scattered feathers appear first on the sides and flanks, and next the molt moves inwardly toward the midline of the abdomen and begins on the upper legs. Then the molt begins on the chin and progresses toward the breast.

Once the retrices and the feathers on the nape, rump, and breast are fully developed, the grouse has attained its so-called juvenal plumage, except that the growing inner primaries are those of the subadult plumage. During this time body feathers are easily shed when the grouse is handled because

they are loosely attached in their follicles: the postjuvenal molt is about to begin.

JUVENAL PLUMAGE

This plumage is alike for both sexes, but the color phase to which a juvenile belongs may occasionally be distinguished by the color of its tail. The ruffs are not fully developed and do not have the dark colors or sheen of the adult. The back and rump feathers lack the distinct light-colored spots

An immature male ruffed grouse lacks the iridescent black ruff feathers of the drummer.

of the adult plumage. The rectrices are rounded instead of blunt and have only narrow fuscous bands—the broad subterminal band is missing. The chin and throat are light gray, almost white, but barring similar to that on the adults is present on the underparts.

POSTJUVENAL MOLT

Even before the postnatal molt is complete, the next molt begins. At about the time the number 5 juvenile primary has completed its growth, juvenile primaries 1 and 2 are dropped and replaced with subadult primaries. As juvenile primaries 6 through 10 continue to grow, the inner primaries are likewise replaced by subadult primaries. The subadult primaries continue to grow through number 8; juvenile primaries number 9 and 10 are usually retained through the first breeding season.

The postjuvenal molt on the body proper begins in the areas of the upper back and scapulars and proceeds to the remainder of the back and rump. At the same time, it begins with scattered feathers on the sides and flanks and continues to the abdomen and legs and then to the breast and ruffs. This molt differs from the postnatal and

At one week, tiny flight feathers have appeared. The chicks grow quickly, however, and therefore outgrow their primaries.

postbreeding molts in that the head is often the last area of the body to shed its plumage. The molt here begins on the forehead, chin, and face, and continues posteriorly along the center of the crown, occiput, and nape. The crown and occiput feathers molt from the center laterally toward the eyes.

All the while the primaries continue to molt from the innermost outward, but the secondaries may molt in a scattered fashion. The flight feathers on the wings and the body feathers are well along in their molt when the rectrices are shed–occasionally all at once. The rectrices complete their growth at about the same time that the molt on the head is completed.

Even though the subadult plumage is achieved by mid-October, a young grouse may continue to show evidence of several growing contour feathers into early winter.

Wildlife biologists and game managers have discovered that for stocking programs to succeed, grouse should be at least thirteen weeks old. Age for this purpose may be estimated by the degree of completion of the postjuvenal molt, based on studies conducted in Ohio and New York. On a young grouse thirteen weeks old, primary 8 should have dropped, and primary 7 should at least be a partially grown subadult primary.

SUBADULT PLUMAGE

The young grouse now resembles the adults of its phase, but the subadult rectrices

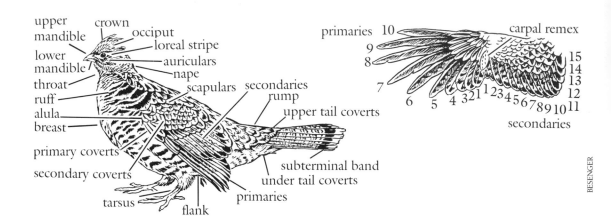

BESENGER

The body plan

*F*ollowing biologists around the body of a bilaterally symmetrical animal, like a bird, is as easy as reading compass directions. The head and front end constitute the *anterior,* and the rear section is the *posterior:* these are the anatomical before and after. *Dorsal,* from Latin *dorsum,* "back," refers to anything on the bird's back; *ventral,* from the stem *ventr-,* "belly," describes the breast and underparts. *Proximal,* meaning "nearest," describes something close to the point of attachment, such as the insertion point of a feather; *distal* is its opposite, the tip of a feather.

are sometimes slightly more rounded than those of the adults, and the ruff feathers are generally shorter, duller, and sometimes without the distinct dark band with its blue or violet sheen. The ninth and tenth juvenile primaries are usually retained in this plumage, and the subterminal band on the inner pair of rectrices is often incomplete on subadult males.

POSTBREEDING MOLT

As the weather warms in the spring, both males and females shed feathers of their thick winter plumage, particularly along the feather tracts, since the extra insulation is no longer needed. However, the first evidence of this molt, which occurs in both subadults and adults, often appears on the ruffed grouse hen: she begins to shed feathers that cover the bare *apterium* of the abdomen to make a brood, or incubation, patch. Without those feathers in the way, she can better transmit her warmth to the eggs.

The problem for both sexes in the summer is worn feathers. Abraded feathers lose their functions of flight, display, and protection from the elements. The light-colored tips of feathers are often worn or broken, feather edges appear scalloped, and feathers look generally ragged. The longer flight feathers of the wings and tail may even be broken.

Wear shows first—and is greatest—on the forehead, upper back, scapulars, and breast on the body proper, and also on the inner secondaries, outer primaries, and inner and outer rectrices of the flight feathers. As the breeding season progresses, wear intensifies and affects feathers on the rest of the body.

Females generally suffer greater wear than males in the late spring and early summer, while they are rearing their broods. Habitat is one explanation for the difference: the hens select brush and slashings for their chicks, habitats that naturally result in more abrasion to the feathers than open woodlands. Moreover, males generally show signs that new feathers are replacing worn ones sooner than females, whose biological priority remains the care of the chicks.

As early as April, the postbreeding molt begins about the head on a few individuals, with a noticeable shedding of feathers on the chin and throat and on the feather tracts

An incubating hen molts her abdomen feathers to provide more direct heat to her eggs.

near the bare spaces. A few growing feathers may even be found on the chin, throat, or occiput. However, this feather growth may be interrupted during breeding, or at least progress very slowly. Most individuals do not exhibit growing feathers until at least mid-June.

The molt occurs in stages. Initially it affects the chin, throat, and occiput, although occasionally, females with incubation patches exhibit growing feathers on the abdomen before growing feathers appear on these areas about the head. Next, the flight feathers on the wings begin to be replaced. In examining specimens taken throughout the breeding range, Runkles has found that the primaries begin to drop as early as the first week of June and continue growing until mid-September. The first secondaries are lost about as early as July 1. The replacement of the primaries progresses from the inside out; that of the secondaries seems to be scattered. As the remiges begin to molt, the postbreeding molt spreads to the forehead, center of the crown, face, and upper back. The chin and throat continue to molt, while growing feathers appear scattered on the sides and flanks. On the underparts the molt progresses from the sides and flanks to the abdomen and legs and then the breast. On top of the head, the molt spreads laterally, while it progresses posteriorly on the back. As the molt continues down the back, it also spreads to the sides of the neck and to the area of the ruffs. During this stage the

This bird, photographed in the rain in mid-September, molted all its tail feathers at once. Until the new rectrices are well along, it will conceal itself in thick cover.

molt is the heaviest. When the molt of the remiges and body proper is well along, the rectrices and their corresponding upper and under tail coverts are shed, beginning with the innermost rectrices. Nevertheless, in late summer one often finds a tailless grouse, whose rectrices all dropped simultaneously. The rectrices finish growing at about the time the postbreeding molt is complete on the body proper (about mid-September), and they are replaced very rapidly. The feathers of the nape are often the last to molt.

Even though the postbreeding molt, which is a complete molt like the postnatal and postjuvenal molts, may begin with a few individuals exhibiting growing feathers as early as April, it is heaviest during July, August, and early September. During this time grouse may be extremely hard to find as they seek thick cover. Observing Appalachian ruffed grouse, Runkles has occasionally found that, when discovered, they also have a tendency to run on the ground like mice, taking refuge under a bush or beside a log. Such birds as can be found show signs that feathers are growing over the entire body, in somewhat scattered patches. The birds appear ragged and ratty, especially in the earlier stages of this molt, since the degree of feather wear also peaks just prior to the peak of the molt. This molt is largely completed by early October, but there may be growing feathers scattered over the body for another month or more.

PREBREEDING MOLT

Since the beginning of this century, there has been a question as to whether ruffed grouse have a partial prebreeding molt. Dwight discovered two grouse of the subspecies *Bonasa umbellus sabini*, collected in British Columbia, that had growing feathers about the head and throat in May. In 1942, Trainer reexamined these two grouse and likewise found growing feathers, but he believed that they were an exception and that ruffed grouse do not generally molt in the spring. He based his claim, at least in part, on his examination of thirty birds in the Cornell University collection that could have exhibited this molt but did not.

An examination by Runkles of 111 specimens at the National Museum of Natural History in Washington, D.C., revealed the following: none of the grouse collected in March had growing feathers (0 of 9), but 11 percent of the birds collected in April (4 of 37), 21 percent of those collected in May (5 of 24), 58 percent of those collected in June (14 of 24), and 94 percent of those collected in July (16 of 17) exhibited feathers in some stage of growth.

Even though grouse were found growing new feathers as early as April, these findings do not indicate a prebreeding molt, separate and distinct from the postbreeding molt, but rather the early beginning of the postbreeding molt. There are several reasons for this conclusion: First, the number of birds with growing feathers in April and May did not favor either sex. Therefore, a renewal of feathers for the males for courtship was not likely. Second, the growing feathers appeared in the same areas—chin, throat, or occiput—where they are initially found on birds molting later in June and July. Finally, there were only a few feathers growing on both sides of the midline on any one bird, an indication that it was not merely incidental feather replacement and yet not a full-scale feather replacement either.

—*Ronald R. Runkles*

Studying the molt

_____

Over the years information has been acquired by basically three methods. Foremost has been the study of birds raised in captivity. This method has yielded data on the timing of the molt for various populations of grouse, especially on the molt of the flight feathers, which is used to age young birds. It has also yielded general information on the progression of the molt over the body. The major disadvantage, however, is that birds raised under artificial and controlled conditions do not necessarily reflect the experience of wild birds.

Study skins, found in the collections of museums and universities, have also been evaluated for molt and wear. This method provides data on the topographical progression and the timing of the molt, as well as on the general progression and timing of wear. One drawback to this method is that feathers are often lost, especially growing feathers, as the skins are prepared and examined. Another problem is that the information applies only to a single point in time for each bird—the moment the bird was "collected."

Another way to obtain information on the molt is to use simple field observation, such as gathering primary flight feathers shed at or near drumming sites. This method has yielded information that pertains not only to the timing of the postbreeding molt but also to the sequence of the primary flight feather molt.

In examining the molt of a captive grouse or a specimen, the ornithologist looks for evidence of the molt in the loss of feathers and the degree of development of new feathers. He scrutinizes the feathers that distinguish, say, subadult from adult plumage. And he studies the degree of wear, which may help differentiate the old and new adult plumages. To accomplish all this, he must carefully consider four things when examining a specimen: the color patterns of the feathers on different parts of the grouse, the contour of the feathers, their texture, and their degree of development.

The dark colors and sheen of an adult's ruff are not present on the juvenile grouse. In fact, the juvenile ruffs are not even as dark as those of a subadult, and the back and rump feathers lack the distinct light-colored, arrow-shaped spots of the subadult and adult plumages.

The general contour of certain feathers varies from one plumage to the next. But generally, the rectrices of juveniles are more rounded than those of adults, and the tips of the outer primaries are more pointed on juveniles than on adults. To determine the progression of wear, the ornithologist examines the contour of feathers on different areas of the body and compares their degree of wear. Heavily worn feathers may be deeply notched or even truncated, the tips broken off. Moderate wear is characterized by ragged or scalloped outer edges. In contrast, the outer edges of new or unworn feathers form clean, distinct lines.

The contour feathers of the juvenile are more loosely textured than those of the subadult, and this difference is particularly noticeable on the nape and the back.

Besides color, contour, and texture, the most important factor in determining the progression of the molt is the degree of feather development. Ornithologists look for pin feathers, brushes, sheathed feathers, new or worn feathers, or small patches of bare skin with red spots, indicating active feather follicles.

—_Ronald R. Runkles_

The subspecies

Since the differences in plumage coloration between the subspecies are often very subtle, an unknown specimen should be compared with the various subspecies in a collection of study skins with a good representation of each form. To someone unfamiliar with the different subspecies, grouse all look the same, except some have gray tails and some, brown. The material in this section provides a starting point for sorting out the differences between the various subspecies.

EASTERN RUFFED GROUSE
(Bonasa umbellus umbellus)

This, the nominate subspecies, inhabits subclimax and climax deciduous woodlands from southern Massachusetts and central New York south through western Connecticut, Rhode Island, eastern Long Island, New Jersey, and eastern Pennsylvania.

At one time the range of the eastern ruffed grouse extended through coastal Maryland as far south as Amelia County, Virginia. Grouse are still reported from Amelia County and to the east and north along the Piedmont Plateau. Could it be that an isolated, remnant population of this subspecies still exists in Virginia?

In the spring of 1986, two ruffed grouse were seen in northeastern Maryland, Cecil County, in part of their former range, but their subspecies is questionable. They could have been eastern ruffed grouse occupying

The tail fan, being brighter and more distinctive than the contour feathers of the body, is the best determinant of a bird's color phase, which in turn helps identify its subspecies.

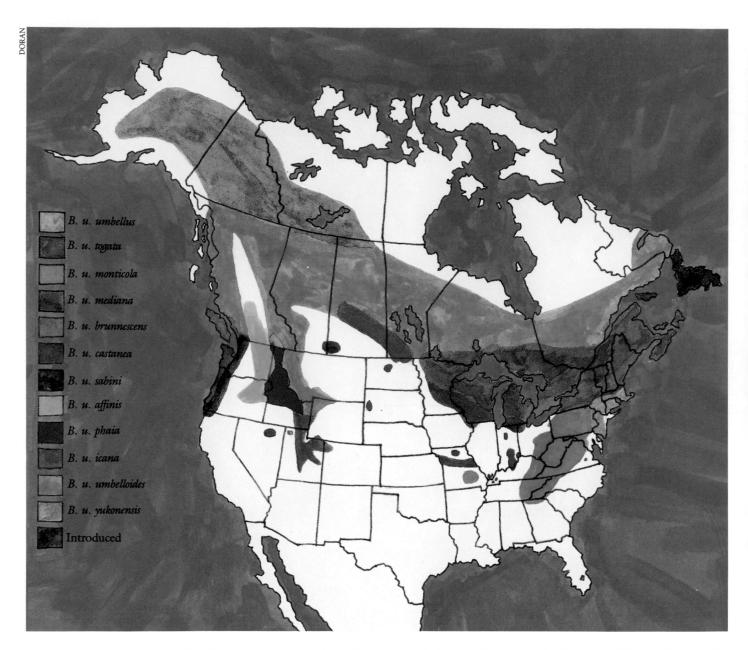

B. u. umbellus

B. u. togata

B. u. monticola

B. u. mediana

B. u. brunnescens

B. u. castanea

B. u. sabini

B. u. affinis

B. u. phaia

B. u. icana

B. u. umbelloides

B. u. yukonensis

Introduced

The twelve subspecies are fractional populations of Bonasa umbellus. Geographical distribution is a major criterion in subspecies designation.

their former range or Appalachian ruffed grouse from private release attempts.

In the population of *umbellus umbellus* as a whole, the brown phase occurs more frequently than the gray phase. Robert Erikson has reported that of the 170 ruffed grouse live-trapped in New Jersey in 1984 and 1985, at least 90 percent were brown.

MIDWESTERN RUFFED GROUSE
(Bonasa umbellus mediana)

So named because their range lies in the middle, these grouse live in the subclimax and climax oak-hickory forests in east-central Minnesota, southern Wisconsin, and southwestern Michigan, along with isolated areas in Iowa, extreme northwestern Illinois,

south-central Indiana, and in northern Missouri.

This subspecies has been extirpated from extreme western Tennessee, and those grouse now in the western part of Kentucky have been released and may not be of the midwestern form.

Most of the present grouse population in Illinois, especially the southern part, is the result of stocking programs between 1953 and 1986. Some of these birds may be Appalachian ruffed grouse.

Since 1978 the state of Missouri has had a rather extensive release program to reestablish the ruffed grouse in three areas: along the north side of the Missouri River across the state, in the north-central part of the state, and in the southeastern section of the state. The grouse released in the northern part of the state have been mostly the midwestern subspecies; those released in the southern sections have generally been Appalachian birds.

Because the midwestern race is so similar in color to the eastern ruffed grouse, it was not recognized as a distinct subspecies in the 1957 *Checklist of North American Birds;* however, it is geographically separated from the nominate subspecies.

St. Lawrence or Canada ### ruffed grouse *(Bonasa umbellus togata)*

This subspecies lives in subclimax deciduous woodlands in the transitional area between the northern coniferous and eastern deciduous forests: from northeastern Minnesota through southern Ontario and Quebec to New Brunswick, Nova Scotia, and Prince Edward Island, south through Maine, New Hampshire, and Vermont into northern Massachusetts, and west through central New York, central Michigan, and northern Wisconsin.

The gray phase is more predominant than the brown—not surprisingly, since these birds dwell in birch and aspen stands. This subspecies is slightly larger and scarcely heavier than the nominate subspecies.

Appalachian ruffed grouse *(Bonasa umbellus monticola)*

This mountain-dwelling grouse lives in the eastern deciduous forests and the ecotone between them and the northern coniferous forests of the Appalachians, from southeastern Michigan, extreme southern Ontario, and the western half of Pennsylvania south through eastern Ohio, West Virginia, the mountains of Maryland, eastern Kentucky, the mountains and piedmont of Virginia, eastern Tennessee, western North Carolina, western South Carolina, and northern Georgia. It has also been introduced in southern Missouri. The brown phase predominates.

Gray ruffed grouse *(Bonasa umbellus umbelloides)*

Despite the common name, a brown phase does exist in this subspecies. This subspecies

dwells in the subclimax deciduous woodlands (aspen, poplar, and willow stands) of the northern coniferous forests from extreme southeastern Alaska, northern and eastern British Columbia, central and southern Alberta through northern Saskatchewan, central Manitoba, Ontario, central Quebec, and southeastern Labrador south of the forty-eighth parallel in western Montana, northwestern Wyoming, and southeastern Idaho.

Hoary ruffed grouse *(Bonasa umbellus incana)*

This grouse, which appears white and gray with age as its subspecific name implies (*incana* is the Latin for "hoary"), lives in subclimax deciduous woodlands and thickets (cottonwood, willow, and aspen stands) of the northern coniferous forests and the grasslands in extreme southeastern Idaho, west-central Wyoming, northwestern Colorado, and as far south as northeastern and central Utah, with isolated populations in North Dakota and western South Dakota. In Canada the hoary ruffed grouse breeds across central and southeastern Saskatchewan and southwestern Manitoba.

This subspecies is native to the Turtle Mountains and Pembina Hills of North Dakota. Release programs using grouse from the Turtle Mountains have been successful in the Salyer National Wildlife Refuge and the Killdeer Mountains, and similar programs are planned for other counties.

This New York hen, leaving her nest to feed, demonstrates the reason gray-phase birds tend to be more numerous in the gray-hued northern regions.

IDAHO RUFFED GROUSE
(Bonasa umbellus phaia)

This predominantly gray grouse (*phaios* is the Greek word for "gray"), aside from being found in northern Idaho and along the western slopes of the Rocky Mountains into south-central Idaho, inhabits subclimax deciduous woodlands in extreme northeastern Washington, extreme northeastern Oregon and southeastern British Columbia. The extent of its range in Canada is uncertain.

YUKON RUFFED GROUSE
(Bonasa umbellus yukonensis)

This, the largest and grayest grouse, has the most extensive tarsal feathering of any of the subspecies.

As its name implies, the population is concentrated along the upper Yukon River. It inhabits subclimax deciduous woodlands between the northern coniferous forests and the tundra from western Alaska, along the Yukon and Kuskokwim rivers, east across

By any other name

*B*esides its generally accepted English name—and some colloquial ones, such as "partridge"—the ruffed grouse goes by a Latin name, *Bonasa umbellus*, which enables ornithologists around the world to recognize it regardless of their native language. This "scientific" name starts with a general or generic name, *Bonasa*, which in Latin means "like a *bonasum*," or bison, perhaps because the male's drumming is like the sound of a thundering herd. Or perhaps the word derives from *bonus* and *assum*, meaning "a good roast." There follows a specific or species name, *umbellus*, meaning "umbrella" and referring to the ruff of blackish neck feathers that the bird erects into an umbrellalike shape during its display.

The numerous local populations of ruffed grouse, which on close inspection appear slightly larger or smaller, darker or lighter than ruffed grouse from other regions, also have Latinized names. A total of twelve such races, or subspecies, were identified by Aldrich and Friedmann in 1943.

• *Bonasa umbellus umbellus*, with a repetition of the "umbrella," is the subspecies for which the species is named—the nominate subspecies. The term applies to the grouse of eastern North America.

• *B. u. monticola*, the "mountain-dwelling" grouse, refers to Appalachian birds.

• *B. u. mediana* is the midwestern, or "middle," grouse.

• *B. u. sabini*, the Pacific ruffed grouse, is named for Joseph Sabine.

• Grouse of the Olympic Peninsula and Puget Sound are called *B. u. castanea*, "chestnut," for their rich brown color.

• *B. u. brunnescens*, referring to the birds of Vancouver Island and the adjacent mainland, is the race "tending toward brown."

• The grouse of Canada and the northern United States are *B. u. togata*, the "toga" referring to the male's cape.

• The Columbia ruffed grouse of British Columbia and environs is *B. u. affinis*, "related to *Bonasa umbellus*."

• *B. u. phaia*, meaning "dusky" or "dark," describes the Idaho ruffed grouse.

• Another subspecies of the West is *B. u. incana*, the hoary ruffed grouse, so called because of its frosted appearance.

• Grouse of the Yukon river drainage system are identified by a simple place name, *B. u. yukonensis*, "of the Yukon."

• *B. u. umbelloides*, "similar to *Bonasa umbellus*," is the gray ruffed grouse of Canada.

—*Paul A. Johnsgard*

the central part of the Yukon Territory in Canada to the Great Slave Lake and south into northern Alberta and northwestern Saskatchewan.

COLUMBIAN RUFFED GROUSE
(Bonasa umbellus affinis)

The Columbian ruffed grouse, of which the gray phase predominates, breeds in the subclimax deciduous woodlands (aspen, poplar, and willow stands) of the coniferous forest biome from south-central Oregon, east of the Cascade Mountains, along a strip north through interior Washington and north into central British Columbia along the west slopes of the Rocky Mountains and the east slopes of the Coast Mountains. The northern extension of its range in British Columbia is uncertain.

In color the Columbian grouse is closely related (*affinis* is Latin for "related") to the gray ruffed grouse (*B.u. umbelloides*). For this reason, it was not recognized as a distinct subspecies in the 1957 *Checklist of North American Birds* but was simply considered a darker form of *B. u. umbelloides*.

PACIFIC RUFFED GROUSE
(Bonasa umbellus sabini)

The breeding range of this grouse (named in honor of Joseph Sabine) includes the subclimax deciduous woodlands in the moist coniferous forests from southwestern British Columbia (excluding the territory of the Vancouver ruffed grouse: Vancouver Island and the adjoining mainland coastal area) on the west side of the Cascade Range through central Washington and eastern Oregon into northwestern California. The Pacific ruffed grouse inhabits a drier range than the Vancouver and Olympic ruffed grouse within the Pacific rain forests.

The brown phase of this subspecies is closest in appearance to the brown phase of the Appalachian ruffed grouse.

VANCOUVER RUFFED GROUSE
(Bonasa umbellus brunnescens)

This predominantly brown subspecies dwells in the subclimax, moist coniferous forests on Vancouver Island and the adjacent mainland from Vancouver north to Lund, British Columbia.

A red-phase male's tail is surrounded by tails from four females. Except for the red tail (upper right), they are split-phase, with the central feathers redder than the laterals. Upper left: *The hen lost half her tail, and the replacement feathers are smaller and grayer. Three tails have only one central rectrix, the other having been plucked.*

The color of these red tails from two widely separated populations (above, Minnesota; below, Tennessee) of two different races is nearly identical. Chocolate or bronze bands are on the left, black bands on the right. The Tennessee tails are about 10 to 15 millimeters longer.

The five Minnesota tails all have black bands. Center: A split-phase female. Clockwise from upper right: Red-phase male, intermediate gray male, silver-gray male, brown-phase male.

OLYMPIC RUFFED GROUSE
(Bonasa umbellus castanea)

The subspecific name appropriately refers to its chestnut coloration. No gray phase is known. This ruffed grouse inhabits the subclimax woodlands of the moist forests along the Pacific Coast from the Olympic Peninsula and the shores of Puget Sound south through extreme western Washington and Oregon.

—Ronald R. Runkles

A history of the subspecies

As all students of the subject know, there are a dozen subspecies, more or less, of ruffed grouse. Two hundred-plus years ago, however, there were two distinct *species*—at least in an early version of scientific classification of living organisms.

In the 1750s Carolus Linnaeus, a professor of botany and medicine at the University of Uppsala in Sweden, invented a taxonomic system that, with modifications, is still in use today. The most important legacy of his system is binomial nomenclature, the two italicized, Latinized names that taxonomists attach to plants and animals. Predating Charles Darwin by a century, Linnaeus probably had no concept of evolution and considered each species an unchanging entity. He simply grouped organisms according to similar morphological characteristics, such as (in the case of birds) bill, feet, and plumage.

Linnaeus had received two descriptions of ruffed grouse: one from eastern Pennsylvania, and one from Quebec. Recognizing the birds' affinity to other fowl, and to other grouse in particular, Linnaeus in 1766 put these New World grouse into order Gallinae (*gallus* is the Latin word for "cock") and genus *Tetrao* (a Greek word meaning "grouse"). The Pennsylvania bird he called *Tetrao umbellus,* and the Quebec bird, *Tetrao togata.*

Today we recognize only one genus of ruffed grouse—called *Bonasa* instead of *Tetrao*—and Linnaeus's two distinct species are really just two of the subspecies. What has

happened since 1766 is that species are now defined in a much broader way.

A species is first a population of mutually fertile individuals. These individuals are reproductively isolated from individuals of other populations, and they possess common characters that distinguish them from other, similar populations. Because any species shows variation among its individuals, and because the variations tend to be grouped in local populations, or races, the category of subspecies is often used. A subspecies is, therefore, a local population with a combination of characters making it sufficiently distinct from other populations. These characters must be morphological, such as size, shape, and color, but may also extend to ecological requirements and reproductive traits, such as song, type of nest, and general behavior patterns.

Note that Linnaeus's basis for distinguishing species, because it was based on morphological characters, more closely approximates the modern concept of subspecies than that of species. His *Tetrao umbellus* and *T. togata* are today considered subspecies (*Bonasa umbellus umbellus* and *B. u. togata,* respectively) because neither population is reproductively isolated, as required by the modern definition of *species.* Along the boundaries of their populations, there are many intermediate forms of plumage coloration. Therefore, they cannot be separate species, as Linnaeus had classified them.

According to the modern form of Linnaean classification, these two grouse are assigned as follows:

kingdom	Animalia (animals)
phylum	Chordata (animals with notochords and hollow nerve cords)
subphylum	Vertebrata (animals with backbones)
class	Aves (birds)
order	Galliformes (chickenlike birds)
family	Phasianidae (the pheasants)
subfamily	Tetraoninae (the grouse)
genus	*Bonasa* (drumming sounds like a herd of bison)
species	*umbellus* (the ruff is like an umbrella)
subspecies	*umbellus* and *togata*

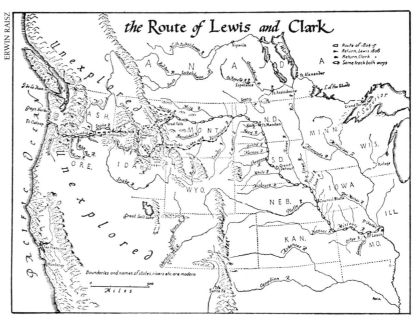

Carolus Linnaeus, the father of binomial nomenclature, first classified the ruffed grouse.

During the westward expansion in America, other distinctive populations of grouse were recognized and named. Lewis and Clark described a variation they saw on their 1805 to 1806 expedition, but this bird was not officially named until 1829. Then, David Douglas, a Scottish-born botanist and traveler to the Far West, named it *Tetrao sabini* (now designated *B. u. sabini*) in honor of Joseph Sabine, the elder brother of Sir Edward Sabine, an eminent British astronomer and physicist. (Both Sabine brothers had accompanied Sir John Ross and Sir William Parry on their Arctic expeditions of 1818 to 1820.) In 1829 Douglas, remembered for the Douglas fir named in his honor, also described *Tetrao umbelloides* (now *B. u. umbelloides*).

Those four grouse were the sole representatives of the genus for the next eighty years. But during this time, the name was changed from *Tetrao* to *Bonasa* as the definition of *species* expanded and the Linnaean system of classification became more complex. A zoologist named Stephens had first proposed the genus name *Bonasa* in Shaw's *General Zoology* in 1819. Thus, the four species of ruffed grouse became recognized as subspecies.

In 1916 Dr. Joseph Grinnell, director of vertebrate zoology at the University of California and editor of *The Condor,* the publication of the Cooper Ornithological Society, introduced the subspecies *B. u. yukonensis.*

Since 1931, the number of subspecies has

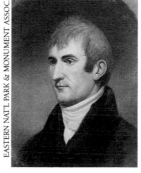

In 1803 Thomas Jefferson charged Meriwether Lewis (left) and William Clark (right) with surveying the West, including its plant and animal life. This expedition yielded, among other things, the description of a new subspecies of ruffed grouse.

ebbed and flowed. Outram Bangs, an amateur ornithologist, described the subspecies *B. u. thayeri* in honor of John Eliot Thayer (1862–1933), of Lancaster, Massachusetts. Thayer, an ornithologist and a patron of science, had established the Thayer Museum, which contained one of the largest private collections of birds in the United States at the time. *B. u. thayeri*, the Nova Scotia ruffed grouse, differs from *B. u. togata* in that both color phases have darker gray upperparts and more distinct banding on the underparts.

Note that the gray and brown color phases of grouse have not given rise to designations of different subspecies, since these color phases occur together in differing frequencies in most all populations. Both color phases sometimes occur in a single brood.

In 1935 H.B. Conover added *B. u. brunnescens*, and in 1940, W.E.C. Todd described subspecies *monticola*, *mediana*, and *canescens*. The first two are the Appalachian and midwestern ruffed grouse; *canescens*, the northern ruffed grouse, is similar to *umbelloides* but is lighter overall. It is also grayer, with less brown on the upperparts than *togata*, and generally lighter underparts. Its range extends from Labrador west to James Bay and into central Ontario.

Another subspecies, *helmei*, was added to the list in 1941 by H.H. Bailey. Known as the Long Island ruffed grouse, this bird is similar in coloration to *umbellus* but is smaller, and its range is now limited to northeastern Long Island.

A taxonomic revision was proposed in 1943 by Aldrich and Friedmann, who based their classification not just on the size and plumage of the birds but also on their habitats. Three subspecies were dropped: *thayeri* was considered to be the same as *togata*, *canescens* was subsumed under *umbelloides*, and *helmei* was absorbed into *umbellus*. Four new subspecies were proposed: *castanea*, *affinis*, *phaia*, and *incana*. That made twelve subspecies.

The 1957 *Checklist of North American Birds* reduced the number to ten by incorporating *affinis* into *umbelloides*, and *mediana* into *umbellus*. That left *umbellus*, *togata*, *umbelloides*, *sabini*, *yukonensis*, *brunnescens*, *monticola*, *castanea*, *phaia*, and *incana*.

The following description of the subspecies follows the 1943 delineation by Aldrich and Friedmann because of its ecological foundation—an important consideration in release programs. *Ecological* here means the interaction of grouse with their environment, which includes such things as light, temperature, rainfall, humidity, and vegetative habitat. In restoring grouse to their former range in Missouri, for example, success has been attributed to a decision to release birds of the original subspecies from similar habitat and approximately the same latitude. However, in private stocking attempts, Appalachian grouse have not survived in areas of the Atlantic coastal plain, once inhabited by the eastern ruffed grouse.

Evidently, natural selection has acted upon the different populations of ruffed grouse such that each has adapted to its special ecological conditions. Natural selection proposes that the ancestral populations of grouse throughout its range had numerous variations in plumage coloration. Gray-phase grouse and grouse with lighter and grayer plumages that live in the drier and more open forest habitats survived longer and left more offspring than the others. One reason may have been that their lighter and grayer plumage helped hide them from predators. In the humid and closed forest habitats, however, brown-phase grouse and grouse of the redder and darker plumages gradually predominated. Thus the hoary ruffed grouse, lightest and grayest of the subspecies, dwells in the dry and open stands of cottonwood, willow, and aspen on the east side of the Rocky Mountains, but the Olympic ruffed grouse, darkest and reddest of the species, with no known gray phase, lives in the moist and closed forests of the Pacific Northwest.

This tendency for the plumage coloration to be darker in humid climates and lighter in dry climates has been noted in other avian species and is known as Gloger's Rule. Another general principle operates in the different populations of ruffed grouse: Bergman's Rule, which holds that body size tends to be larger in cooler climates, smaller in warmer ones. The Yukon ruffed grouse is the largest of the grouse.

—*Ronald R. Runkles*

Plumage of the subspecies

Subspecies	Brown phase	Gray phase
Bonasa umbellus umbellus	Underparts: lighter and less extensive barring and buff wash than on other subspecies	Underparts: lighter and less extensive barring and buff wash than on other subspecies
B. u. mediana	Same as umbellus	Same as umbellus
B. u. togata	Upperparts: slightly darker brown and less rufous than on umbellus Rectrices: basic color varies between tawny olive and Sayal brown	Upperparts: slightly darker browns and grays, with more extensive black markings than on umbellus
B. u. monticola	Upperparts: slightly darker brown; more dark fuscous and black markings Rectrices: basic color tends toward raw sienna	Upperparts: darker grays and browns Rectrices: trace of Sayal brown wash in the basic color
B. u. umbelloides	Upperparts: similar to the gray phase of umbellus but darker Rectrices: basic color tends toward cinnamon	Upperparts: less brown, except on upper back; lower back and rump grayer than those areas on the gray phase of umbellus Underparts: much darker and grayer, with a much heavier buff wash
B. u. incana	Upperparts: similar to gray phase of umbellus but paler and with less brown; paler than phaia, with less brown on upper back and upper wing surfaces Underparts: lighter barring than phaia, but heavier than umbellus Rectrices: basic color is clay	Upperparts: similar to gray phase of umbellus Rectrices: much grayer tail than on gray phase of umbellus–dark bands are even-washed with gray
B. u. phaia	Upperparts: much darker; less rufous; and grayer Underparts: generally much darker	Upperparts: darker gray and less brown Underparts: generally much darker
B. u. yukonensis	Upperparts: much more gray on back, rump, and upper tail coverts Rectrices: lighter brown in both the basic color and the bands	Upperparts: much grayer and paler on the back, rump, and upper tail coverts
B. u. affinis	Upperparts: darker, especially the crest feathers Rectrices: basic color tends toward cinnamon, occasionally with a pale tawny wash	Upperparts: generally darker Rectrices: darker gray with a Sayal brown wash; similar to gray phase of umbelloides, but tarsal feathering of umbelloides is greater than that of affinis; brown wash on the rectrices is heavier than on umbelloides
B. u. sabini	Upperparts: darker–black spots rather than fuscous; brown colors tend toward chestnut; more rufous above than on affinis	Upperparts: dark spots on upper back, black; darker smoke gray Rectrices: basic color dark smoke gray with a brown wash Ruffs: black
B. u. brunnescens	Upperparts: darker and more brown; less reddish and darker than sabini Rectrices: basic color tends toward raw umber	Upperparts: generally darker smoke gray Rectrices: basic color is dark smoke gray with a brown wash
B. u. castanea	Upperparts: dark chestnut; less gray; darker and browner than sabini; redder than brunnescens	No gray phase known

Southern and Appalachian grouse

---

*T*he Appalachian ruffed grouse, formally known as subspecies *monticola,* is the only racial variety left in the southern grouse range, according to the 1963 classification by Aldrich. The midwestern subspecies, *mediana,* was once present in Arkansas, Missouri, Illinois, and northern Indiana, but extensive forest removal eventually dislodged these midwestern grouse from the southern portion of their range.

The classification of ruffed grouse into twelve subspecies mainly on the basis of coloration appears, however, to be of questionable validity and usefulness. About thirty color variations are currently recognized among Minnesota grouse alone, Gullion has reported, which suggests that predicting color in a brood of grouse may be about as reliable as predicting color in a litter of kittens. If coloration does have a taxonomic significance, the classification of all southern grouse as members of the Appalachian race, *monticola,* is puzzling, for they come in three distinct color phases and various intermediate shades.

One color phase, the relatively dark "gray" grouse common in northern forests, is present only in the upper elevations of the southern Appalachians, where vegetation and climate approach the conditions of southern Canada. There is a lack of agreement among grouse students as to the proper terminology for the other two color phases. Brown and red grouse have often been lumped together as one color but are very different. The reddish bird, regarded by many as the most beautiful of all the grouse, appears most often near the southern and western fringes of the inhabited southeastern grouse range. The brown phase nevertheless predominates, accounting for 85 percent of the hunter-killed grouse examined in Kentucky. Both colors provide ideal camouflage against the dead-leaf background of the southern forest floor, and birds of either color are practically invisible as long as they stay motionless.

The grouse of southern Indiana are distinctive, being paler in color than any I have seen elsewhere, except for one partial albino from eastern Kentucky, and are exceptionally handsome birds. The population is an interesting case, being completely isolated from other grouse populations, and its range may represent the most southern ecological conditions anywhere in the eastern region where native grouse survive.

Southern grouse are approximately the same size as their northern counterparts. In southeastern Ohio, adult male grouse have been found to average about 698 grams (25 ounces), and adult females, 605 grams (21 ounces). Those weights are probably representative for grouse throughout much of the southern and Appalachian region. In Stoll and McClain's four-year survey involving nearly 1,400 grouse, the heaviest male bird weighed 794 grams (28 ounces), and the heaviest female, 737 grams (26 ounces).

—Harold L. Barber

Birds of all sizes

---

*T*he farther south you go, the bigger the grouse. Davis found significant differences between grouse in northeastern Ohio and birds in east-central and southeastern Ohio. And the birds became increasingly larger in West Virginia, Virginia, and Georgia. It appears that the grouse were larger in all dimensions—long tails, longer wings, larger feathers, and, according to Uhlig, heavier weights as well.

All one really needs to judge bird size, though, is tail length, since this measurement has a significant positive correlation with weight. But despite the ease of this calculation, the subject becomes complicated once we get beyond the generalization that southerners are bigger.

Across the continent there are some differences in bird sizes. Unfortunately, data have been recorded in only a few places. Most of the information available has come from the Great Lakes states, all of it on the St. Lawrence ruffed grouse, *Bonasa umbellus togata*. Comparable measurements from Michigan, Minnesota, and Wisconsin show little difference in bird size. Even among the birds from North Dakota—evidently a different subspecies, *B. u. incana*—sizes are very similar.

Examination of 11,147 ruffed grouse taken in Minnesota from 1961 to 1977 showed no regional variation. The state was divided into eight regions and tail lengths were compared by region, but no consistent or significant differences were evident.

Birds studied by Brewer in Washington's Puget Sound area showed more variation than those from the interior of the continent. Working with the subspecies *B. u. sabini,* the Pacific ruffed grouse, he found much greater overlap between sex and age classes than is common farther east. Nevertheless, the overall sizes of these ruffed grouse differed little from those of the Great Lakes.

The data from museum specimens published in 1946 by Ridgway and Friedmann did suggest regional differences, but problems compromise their conclusions. The number of specimens was too small, for one thing. Thus the 11.3-millimeter difference in average tail-feather length between three adult hens of subspecies *mediana* and twenty-one hens of subspecies *togata* would vanish completely in a sample size of several thousand specimens.

Moreover, Ridgway and Friedmann made no distinction between first-year and adult plumage. Consequently, the data mix feathers from both young and adult grouse. And adult males often have slightly longer rectrices.

What are we to make of all this conflicting and inconclusive evidence? Perhaps only that bird size may differ more from year to year, due to environmental conditions, than between supposed races. And that the hunter who wants to bag the big ones should go south.

—Gordon W. Gullion

Determining sex

So far, no one has ever seen a male ruffed grouse incubating eggs, and no one has ever witnessed a hen drumming—or at least no one has ever reported such a sight. It is therefore safe to say that the bird on the nest is a hen, and the one drumming on the log is a cock. But unless you come upon ruffed grouse engaged in such sex-determined activities, you would be hard pressed to tell the males from the females. And once a bird has lost its baby fluff and acquired its postjuvenile plumage, you would have equal difficulty telling its age.

Ruffed grouse are monomorphic: that is, all the birds look alike, whatever their sex or age. For decades, researchers have been probing and poking and plucking these birds in their efforts to identify sex and age criteria reliable enough to satisfy wildlife managers yet simple enough to please hunters and bird-watchers. Along the way they have discovered as many caveats as criteria.

The population samples used in research studies, for one. Older grouse, which get to be older because they are smarter, are less vulnerable to hunters' shots, so data based on harvested birds are skewed to the younger set. Hunters using dogs find birds that elude hunters without dogs, and similarly, hunters who take their birds along trails and roads sample different populations than those who beat the bush. For the same reasons, trapped grouse provide less-than-ideal population

Glimpsed through the branches of alder, the ruffed grouse keeps its sex a secret. Observation of behavior and analysis of particular feathers are the keys.

samples. Even samples based on mirror trapping, which captures virtually every drumming male in a particular area, carry a caveat: since there may be a number of nondrumming males—mostly young birds—such samples cannot presume to reflect the total male population. Nevertheless, there are consistent, if subtle, differences that can be used to sex and age grouse.

Field identification. The careful observer can be fairly certain of the sex of a grouse in the bush, even without having it in the hand, provided he gets a good look at it. Although a young male and the occasional adult male may be smaller than a large hen, male ruffed grouse are usually larger and more robust than females. The barring on the flanks tends to be blacker and more pronounced on hens than on males, whose bars are usually less distinct and often brownish. The ruff feathers, though, are more prominent on the male than on the female.

Most reliable is the relative length of the bird's back and tail. The tail of a hen usually looks about the same length as its back, but the tail of a cock always appears somewhat longer than the back.

Sexing internally. It is a simple matter to field dress a bird and find the sex organs, or gonads. Open the bird's abdominal cavity and remove the intestines and gizzard, as is normally done in preparing the bird for table. Then lay the bird on its back. A pair of flesh-colored organs roughly 2 inches long—

Field guides

Abbreviated guides to sex and age determination of ruffed grouse have been published by various groups. The classic is certainly the Wisconsin Conservation Department guide, by Hale et al. Published in 1954, it is now out of print. Two other guides are currently available:

A Grouse in the Hand: Tips for Examining, Aging and Sexing Ruffed Grouse, by S. DeStefano, R.L. Ruff, and S.R. Craven (Madison: University of Wisconsin Extension, 1983). This twelve-page very useful guide was published by the university's extension service in conjunction with the Ruffed Grouse Society.

Sequence of Materials Handling for Sex and Age Discrimination of Ruffed Grouse and Comments Concerning Tail Patterns and Colors, by G.W. Gullion (University of Minnesota, Forest Wildlife Project, SOP No. 5, 1972). This detailed guide of sixteen pages has been in use in Minnesota for a number of years.

the kidneys—will be seen lying on either side of the backbone. The gonads are at the anterior, or forward, end of the kidneys, in a position that in the living bird would have been immediately dorsal to, or above, the gizzard.

A male has two small black or dark gray testes about the size and color of a piece of lead pencil. They are spaced about half an inch apart on each side of the backbone. In a young male the testes can be inconspicuous, no more than one-quarter inch long, and you may have to look closely to see them. After the breeding season, the testes of an adult male will be somewhat larger, nearly one-half inch, and a lighter gray.

A hen has a single more-or-less heart-shaped ovary about the size of your little fingernail, lying at the head of the left kidney. In an adult female the ovary resembles a clump of tiny white grapes. This granular appearance is less pronounced in young females.

A note of caution: as the bird lies on its back, the gonads usually rest on top of some yellow material, the adrenal glands. Since the testes are inconspicuous, you might mistake a male's adrenal gland for an ovary and incorrectly sex your bird. In a hen the two organs—ovary and adrenal gland—are about the same size.

Feather length. In the absence of internal examination, the lengths of tail and wing feathers, alone or in combination, provide the most reliable criteria for sexing ruffed grouse.

The tail feathers are called rectrices (singular *rectrix,* a feminine form of the Latin *rector,* meaning "director") because they control the direction of flight. A ruffed grouse may have sixteen to eighteen rectrices, but the two central rectrices—and these are the significant ones—usually look slightly different. First, they are inserted in the bird's body a little above and forward of the plane of insertion of the remaining rectrices. Second, they exhibit some difference in pattern, even if it's nothing more than a fuzzier transition from the subterminal band into the bordering colors.

The wing has several sets of feathers: a series of coverts, the alula (Latin for "little

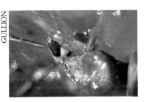

Top: *The testes of the male ruffed grouse are small and dark gray. The yellowish adrenal glands, immediately beneath the testes, are sometimes mistaken for ovaries.* Bottom: *The ovaries are whiter and may have a granular appearance.*

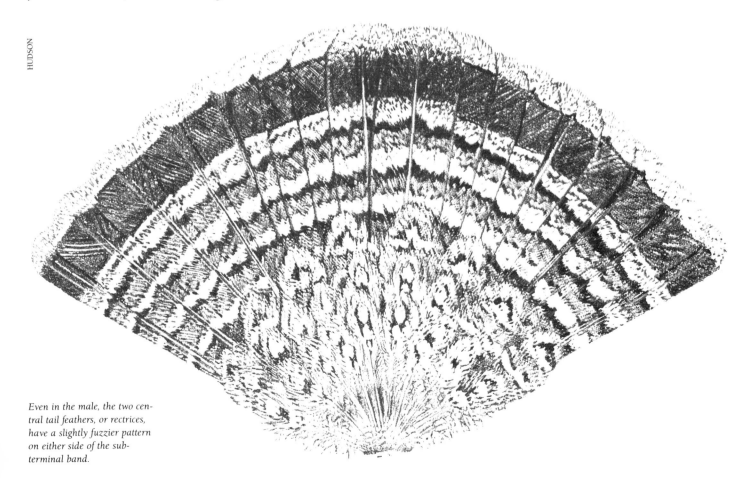

Even in the male, the two central tail feathers, or rectrices, have a slightly fuzzier pattern on either side of the subterminal band.

wing") at the wingtip, and the primary, secondary, and tertiary flight feathers. The primaries, also called remiges (singular *remex*, Latin for "oarsman"), are numbered from the inside out, 1 to 10. It is the outermost remiges, numbers 8, 9, and 10, that yield information on age.

For determining sex and age, the appropriate feathers are normally plucked before being measured. To be comparable to the Minnesota data presented in this chapter, your measurement should follow the natural curve of the feather, and the outer edge should not extend more than 15 millimeters from the cord.

Among a Minnesota sample of 299 grouse whose age and sex were known, there was a highly significant, close correlation between tail length and the bird's sex and age. In statisticians' terms, 81 percent of the variation in tail-feather length was due to age and sex. In laymen's terms, the longer the length of the central rectrices, the more likely the bird is an adult male.

The length of the flight feathers, however, tends to be related to the bird's overall size and age, rather than its sex. But if the rectrices fail to make a definitive sexing, the length of the remiges becomes important because there are fairly constant relationships between remex-rectrix pairs of feathers. That is, a small male may have shorter tail feathers than a large hen, but the length of his tail feathers in relation to the length of his flight feathers will remain constant, and

that ratio will identify him as a male. To see how this works, first consider the way tail feathers are used to sex grouse.

In a sample of 2,030 grouse from Minnesota, 98.5 percent of the males had rectrices longer than 150 millimeters. On the other hand, 88.2 percent of the females had tails shorter than 144 millimeters. No males had rectrices shorter than 144 millimeters, and no females had rectrices longer than 150 millimeters. There is, then, a gray area—from 144 to 150 millimeters—where male and female tail lengths overlap and consequently cannot be definite indicators of sex.

Now let's throw in another factor: age. Among the females in the area of overlap, 70.5 percent were adult hens, but all the males in this category were young. If you had a bird whose rectrices fell into the gray area, and you knew it was a young bird, you might be willing to bet it was a male; if you knew it to be old, you might put your money on a hen.

But what if you didn't know its age? Here is where the remex-rectrix ratio comes into play.

In the overlap group the central rectrices of the young males were always 5 millimeters or more *longer* than the ninth primaries. In females the central rectrices were always the same as or *shorter* than the ninth primaries.

The rule holds for the eighth primaries—at least for females. Their central rectrices are nearly always shorter than the eighth primaries—99.7 percent of the time, in fact.

The primary flight feathers of the wing, called remiges, are numbered from innermost to outermost. These feathers reveal the bird's age but can also be used in conjunction with tail feathers to determine sex.

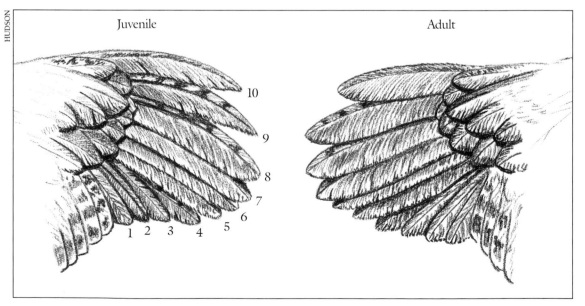

But only a very few males (2.7 percent in this study) had an eighth primary *longer* than the central rectrix. In each case, however, the male's rectrix was at least 6 millimeters longer than the ninth primary and the tail exceeded 149 millimeters in length. Thus the bird would already have been sexed male on the basis of these two criteria.

Comparisons of remex-rectrix length to determine sex have a confidence rating of 94 percent. Of 681 males, only 5 (a mere 0.7 percent) had rectrices that were 5 to 10 millimeters shorter than the ninth primaries; and of 104 females, only 12 (11.5 percent) had rectrices 5 to 10 millimeters longer than their ninth primaries.

But when all is said and done, these remex-rectrix intricacies may not even be necessary. As long ago as 1948 Ammann concluded that although a few birds might be misclassified on the basis of rectrix measurement alone, in a large sample the erroneous males and the erroneous females would cancel each other out. And in 1954 Hale found that for Wisconsin grouse, the 150-millimeter yardstick for tail feathers would place 99.2 percent of the males and 98.8 percent of the females in their proper categories.

Rump spots. Although Bump and his colleagues noted sexual differences in rump feather coloration, it was not until 1975 that rump spots were recognized as useful for identifying sex. In a sample of 366 Quebec grouse, whose sex was determined internally, Roussel and Ouellet found that only one hen of 164 had more than a single white spot on its rump feathers, and all of 202 males had two or three white spots. Servello and Kirkpatrick have also found this procedure reliable among a sample of 62 birds sexed internally in Virginia.

In Minnesota we recently reexamined 397 grouse taken in the Grand Rapids National Grouse Hunt from 1982 to 1986 and found quite a bit of overlap in rump spots. Although 16 percent of the females had no white spots on the rump feathers, and 51 percent of the males had two or more white spots, the rest of the birds could not be distinguished on this basis. Indeed, 49 percent of the males had one white spot or one white and one brown spot. In other words, the technique fails to sex half the males and

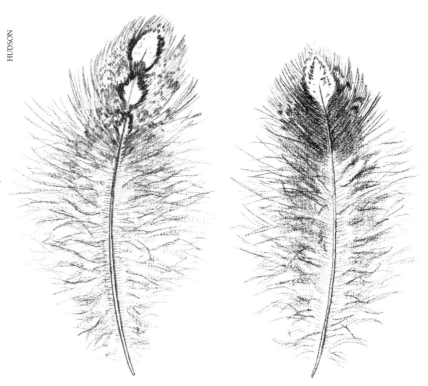

one-sixth of the females. Furthermore, feathers collected from the center of the rump are most likely to have the "correct" number of spots. Toward the sides the number of spots is often fewer, or none at all. In Minnesota, then, this technique should be used only when more reliable criteria are not available.

Midtoe. A measurement that has some validity for sex determination is the length of the midtoe, from the joint to the end of the skin at the base of the claw (the length of the claw itself is not included, since it can vary from season to season, depending on wear).

There is a significant correlation between midtoe length and the bird's sex: males have longer toes. The longest midtoe of any of 44 females was 41 millimeters; 26 percent of the 576 males had toes longer than that. The shortest midtoe on any male was 37 millimeters; 18 percent of females had shorter toes. When we used 40 millimeters as a cutoff, we found that only 10 percent of females didn't fit the short-is-female guideline.

Admittedly, there is a great deal of overlap in midtoe length, but it can provide a basis for sexing a bird when other evidence is lacking. And occasionally, all that remains of a grouse at the site of a goshawk kill is the pelvic girdle with the legs.

A central rump feather with two spots is most likely to be from a male (left). The feather of a female (right) can have just one spot. The accuracy of this method has been high in some studies, mixed in others.

Field conditions often make sex identification difficult. Measuring the length of the midtoe is sometimes a practical method.

In both pattern and length, the central rectrix indicates the sex of the bird. Left: The male's subterminal band is clear, and the feather is longer. Right: This hen's subterminal band is blotched. Also compare the number of tail bars; hens tend to have fewer.

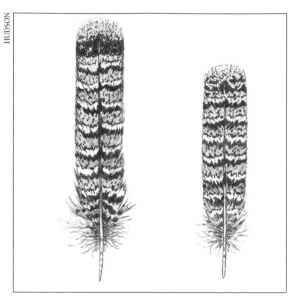

The Minnesota study

*T*he analysis presented in this section and in "Determining Age" is more detailed than anything published to date. It is based on material from 2,433 samples of grouse whose sex was determined by internal examination or by observation of nesting or drumming, plus 1,121 samples of grouse whose age was known as a result of being trapped and leg-banded, then recaptured at a later date. For 945 samples, both age and sex were certain.

The grouse came from three Minnesota research projects and the National Ruffed Grouse Hunt near Grand Rapids, Minnesota. Criteria developed and refined in the study were used to determine the sex and age of another 27,700 grouse from various Minnesota sources.

Research procedures allowed nearly total accuracy. If all the necessary feathers were available and normal, according to Gordon Gullion, the error was probably less than one bird in a thousand.

Tail band. The traditional basis for sexing grouse—clear tail band for males, mottled tail band for females— is not even as reliable as the midtoe measurement. To complicate matters, among Minnesota ruffed grouse, five tail-band patterns are recognized.

Among 1,441 males, 79 percent had the clear or nearly clear band that indicates maleness. Various degrees of tail-band obscurity marked 18 percent of the males, and 9, or 0.6 percent, lacked evidence of any subterminal tail band. An occasional female (4.2 percent among 188 females) may have a clear band, but most have varying degrees of obscurity.

Then there is the "blotched" or "pooled" band pattern. This distinctive pattern evidently reflects a melding of the band with the most distal tail bar—that is, the bar farthest from the body of the bird. Among females, 68.6 percent exhibited this pattern, but it also occurred on 2.4 percent of the males. Some 13 percent of the females had no distinct band across the central rectrices.

Regional differences should be noted. In Michigan, Ammann found that only 44 of 91 males had complete bands. And although 86 of 87 females had interrupted bands, so did 47 of the males. In Wisconsin, Hale found that 73 percent of 365 males had complete bands; the rest shared the interrupted pattern with 97 percent of 403 females. A few females had the clear bands typical of males.

Tail bars. If a fox has sheared the tail near its base, or if rectrices have been carelessly snipped, a count of the transverse bars on the central rectrix can be useful. These bars are the dark stripes across the tail. They may be dark in red-phased grouse but alternate dark and lighter hues in the gray and brown phases. Start at the proximal or insertion end of the feather and begin counting with the first complete bar. If the bar pattern is asymmetrical—and it often is—base the count on the vane with the most bars.

In our study of 1,552 Minnesota males, 51.2 percent had nine or more bars, and none had fewer than six. Among 217 hens, 82 percent had seven or fewer bars, and only 4.6 percent had nine or more. To make the roughest sort of generalization: more bars means male.

Part of this sexual dimorphism results from the melding of the most distal bar into the tail band on many hens, producing the pattern called blotched or pooled. In the Cloquet population, 27 percent of the grouse had eight bars, whatever their sex.

Tail barb. The length of the central tail feather barbs provides a way to sex grouse whose tails are not fully grown. Dorney took his measurements on the central rectrix, at a point 50 millimeters from the tip.

Males tend to have longer tail barbs. Among 1,207 males in Minnesota, barbs ranged from 31 to 45 millimeters long for young birds, and 35 to 49 for yearlings and adults. Among 61 females, barbs measured 31 to 37 millimeters in young birds and 33 to 39 in adults.

A separation point of 38 millimeters would misclassify 7 percent of the males and 22 percent of the females. But all birds with barbs 40 millimeters or longer were males.

Tail color. It is not always necessary to pluck feathers and make painstaking measurements. When more than one color phase exists—and this means most of the range for the species—differences in tail colors may reliably classify females. At least in Minnesota, among the hens that are not red phased, the two central tail feathers are often markedly redder than the bordering rectrices. This characteristic, termed the split phase, was recorded for 88.5 percent of 261 nonred females. None of the 2,179 males in the sample showed this female characteristic.

Although this difference has been noted in tails from grouse in other regions, there are no data concerning its frequency outside Minnesota. But this pattern of tail coloration is characteristic of the closely related Eurasian hazel grouse, *Bonasa bonasia.*

The eye patch is simply the unfeathered rim above the eye. The male's may range from bright red during mating to orange in the off-season. The female's eye patch is more subdued.

Eyebrow color. If the bird's eye patch is glowing like a fiery coal, with surrounding feathers drawn back to reveal its brilliance, odds are it's a male. This characteristic, part of the cock's displaying behavior, is most reliable if the bird knows a hen is nearby, and if it's April. At other times of the year, the color of the eye patch is more subdued—but still useful for sexing a grouse in hand.

Palmer found this method helpful for sexing Michigan juveniles too young to be sexed by plumage. Checking it against internal examination, he reported a 95 percent accuracy among juvenile grouse, compared with 85 percent among adults.

In a Minnesota sample, we found that among 901 males 32.5 percent had light to bright red eye patches, 62 percent had orange, and 2.5 percent were without coloration. Among 56 females, 9 percent were red, 14 percent orange, and the rest showed no coloration.

Using the rump spot count with the eye patch color test should permit nearly complete confidence in determining the sex of young grouse older than about ten weeks.

—*Gordon W. Gullion*

The barb of the central rectrix is measured as shown, 50 millimeters from the tip. Males usually have longer tail barbs.

In the field

No one acquainted with the ruffed grouse should be surprised that it can be a difficult creature to sex: a bird as cryptically colored and elusive as the ruffed grouse does not easily reveal its secrets. But live birds can be reliably sexed in the field, sometimes from a good distance.

Behavior is a useful tool. Besides nesting, only a female grouse will feign a broken wing to lure predators away from her nest or brood. And besides drumming, males engage in characteristic shows of machismo. From February through April, and also for a short period in the fall, you may catch grouse crossing a country road. One bird may be strutting back and forth, its tail spread and its head held high; it is probably

Male or female? Style of flight is not a reliable determinant of the sex of the bird, but other behaviors are. Only males ascend logs to drum, and only females incubate eggs and brood their young.

a male. A closer look at the neck area of the strutting grouse will reveal a conspicuous ruff. These feathers, after which the bird is named, are jet black with iridescent green and purple highlights. Although present in both sexes, the ruff is much more prominent in the cock, especially when he is displaying to an eligible hen.

Cocks are even alleged to flush in a stereotypically masculine way, "hurtling upward . . . toward the treetops," while hens, true to the feminine stereotype, "are more likely to rise in a much more gradual arc," Bump wrote. Hunters have argued over this one for years, and since, often as not, the flushed birds get away, its veracity cannot be easily proved.

A bird in the hand can be more reliably identified. What may turn out to be the most accurate method throughout the ruffed grouse's range is the relatively new technique discovered by Quebec researchers Roussel and Ouellet. It requires only a simple examination of the rump feathers, and it works with nearly 100 percent accuracy for birds collected during and after September, when all grouse are more than thirteen weeks old.

A female grouse has only one white dot along the center of each rump feather; a male nearly always has two or even three. There are only a few cautions: do not confuse the rump feathers with the upper tail coverts, which lie immediately over the tail feathers; check several rump feathers from

Male attire and female finery

each bird; count only distinct white dots.

The most publicized technique for sexing ruffed grouse costs its practitioner no more than a dollar. The length of a U.S. Treasury note is very slightly less than 15 centimeters, and that's the measurement that distinguishes male from female when it comes to the two central tail feathers, or rectrices. If the plucked feathers are longer than 15 centimeters, the bird is judged a male; if shorter, a female.

As ruffed grouse specialist Gordon Gullion has noted, however, tail feather lengths vary by region. In Minnesota a shorter yardstick must be used: tail feathers shorter than 14.2 centimeters represent females, longer than 14.7 identify males. In the southern part of the ruffed grouse's range, not only are overall tail feather lengths greater, but so is the span between the sexes, above which the bird is definitely male and below which it is assuredly female. In Virginia, for example, Servello and Kirkpatrick found the average length of central tail feathers to be 14.4 centimeters in females but 17.8 centimeters in males.

Because atypical birds can easily be assigned the wrong sex, the best bet is to test an initial identification against several other criteria. And remember that if the ruffed grouse brazenly advertised its identity, it would lose the very mystique that attracts its many admirers.

—David E. Samuel and William L. Hudson

*T*he soft flecks and gentle shading of the body, the iridescent violets and purples of the ruff, the bold black subterminal band of the tail: the inimitable coloration of the ruffed grouse is one of the foremost features of this beautiful bird. With practice, the eye may discern ever-so-subtle differences between the sexes.

The base of the ruff feathers, for example, tends to be darker on the male than on the female in both gray- and brown-phase grouse. Across the ventral portion of the neck, the dark ruff is continuous on the male but fades on the female. Usually uninterrupted in males, the subterminal band on the tail may be partially complete only on the central pair of tail feathers of the females.

Upon close inspection of grouse of the nominate subspecies *(B. u. umbellus)* and in particular the brown-phase birds, hens appear to have light beige washes on the spots of the upper back; these spots are Sayal brown on males. Even the arrow-shaped spots on the back and rump of hens have a light beige wash, but they are light drab in males. On hens the loreal stripe, throat, and breast have a pale salmon wash; on cocks these areas are more buff.

Among gray-phase grouse, the smoke-gray edging of the feathers on the forehead and crown seems to be broader, more pronounced, on males than on females. The spots on the back of the male tend to have more smoke-gray coloration and less brown.

—Ronald R. Runkles

Determining age

Once the first full, postnuptial molt is completed at fourteen to fifteen months, age cannot easily be determined unless the grouse has been banded or marked in some other manner. Size and weight alone, for example, are not reliable indicators. Occasionally, two-year-old adult males are smaller and lighter than ten-month-old hens. And hens at seventeen weeks are often as large as they will ever be. Similarly, by the time young males complete their wing molts at seventeen weeks, they are usually within 5 percent of their ultimate weight. But there are ways to tell a bird's age.

Molt sequence. The easiest aging technique is based on the molt sequence of growing grouse. Obviously, the wing feathers that support the flight of a five-day-old, 15-gram grouse will not generate enough lift to get a sixteen-week-old weighing 600 grams off the ground.

So as young grouse grow, they undergo a molt that replaces juvenile wing feathers with adult feathers. An eleven-week-old grouse has a complete first generation of ten primary flight feathers. Replacements progress from number 1, the innermost, toward number 10 at the wingtip. By the time the bird is sixteen weeks old, the first molt has progressed as far as the eighth primary. The ninth and tenth primaries are not replaced until the bird is about fourteen months old.

To determine a bird's age, compare the condition of the most recently replaced pri-

Two immature ruffed grouse are roosting in a conifer. They could pass for adults undergoing a summer molt of tail feathers, but close inspection of plumage reveals age.

Top: *At ten weeks of age this bird's wing was dyed red. When it was killed in October, it had not yet molted the ninth and tenth primaries. The eighth is a replacement feather of post-juvenile plumage. Only the tip of the seventh was exposed when the bird was dyed.* Bottom: *On the left is the wing of a seven-week-old bird; primaries 1 to 4 are the first generation of adult flight feathers. The wing on the right is from a twelve-week-old grouse; replacement of primaries 7 and 8 is under way.*

Top to bottom: *Primaries 10, 9, and 8. Calamus measurements are taken just below the first barbs. Note the sheathing remnant on the eighth primary.*

mary, the eighth, with that of the adjacent, older ninth primary. Look at the remnant of the blood quill, which nurtured the developing primary. On a young bird this tissue-paper-like sheathing will usually be much more pronounced on the base of the eighth primary than on the ninth, which is six weeks older.

Adult grouse follow the same molt pattern, but replace all the primary feathers each summer. For adult males this molt begins in early June with primary number 1 and ends in late August or early September with the loss and replacement of the ninth and tenth primaries. On an adult grouse, therefore, the sheathing on the ninth primary is at least as heavy as on the eighth. In this case the ninth primary is the newer feather, and you have an adult bird.

However, grouse examined in September or early October (especially hens that raised broods) may not have completed the molt, and then aging is quite certain. Follow these guidelines:

If the seventh or eighth primaries, or both, are still quilled and growing, and the ninth and tenth primaries are fully grown, the bird is less than sixteen weeks old.

If the ninth or the tenth primaries, or both, are still quilled and growing on both wings, the grouse is at least fourteen months old.

After handling a considerable number of ruffed grouse during all seasons in Minnesota, we see no reason to question the validity of the wing molt progression as a basis for separating age groups. The problem arises when telltale indicators are missing. Sheathing, for example, is frequently absent from grouse examined in late winter and during the drumming season. Then it becomes necessary to turn to the more tedious process of measuring feather diameters.

Feather diameter. The most useful criteria take advantage of the differences between the slender shafts of the juvenile outer primaries and first postjuvenile rectrices and the larger feathers that replace them in a grouse's first postnuptial molt.

Before measuring, let the feathers dry for at least a month, since a certain amount of shrinkage occurs in the diameter of a feather shaft (this shrinkage does not affect feather length). Once dried, feathers remain stable.

The dimension usually measured is the diameter of the calamus (Latin for "reed"), or the bare part of the shaft just below the feather vane. If you use a screw micrometer, take the measurement at the setting that just holds the feather in place; don't let the instrument squeeze the calamus.

Most apparent is the increased diameter of the calamus of the ninth primary, which on the average increases 0.199 millimeter as a male's first adult ninth primary replaces the juvenile feather. The increase averages 0.173 millimeter among females. Dorney and Holzer demonstrated the usefulness of this technique and found that a diameter of 0.117 inch (2.97 millimeters) could separate young from adult grouse, even though 14 percent of the young birds were larger and 18 percent of the adults smaller than the 0.116-inch (2.93-millimeter) size.

This method contains a large margin for error. But Rodgers refined the technique by comparing the diameter of the ninth primary with the diameter of the eighth. His reasoning was as follows. By the time it is fully grown on the seventeen-week-old grouse, the eighth primary is an adult feather that will not increase in size during subsequent molts. But the juvenile ninth primary will be replaced a year later by a feather with a larger diameter. So there is a greater difference in diameters of the shafts of the eighth and ninth primaries of young grouse than on birds more than a year old.

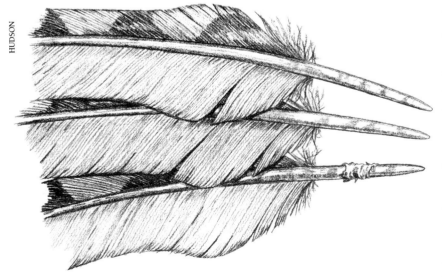

Calamus diameters of the eighth primary are nearly the same for both males and females and, surprisingly, average slightly larger among young grouse than among adults of either sex. But the variations are great enough that this criterion alone is undependable as a means of separating age groups.

Rodgers found in Wisconsin that the calamus diameters of juvenile ninth primaries were never larger than 88 percent of the eighth, but that among adult grouse the ratio of primary 9 to primary 8 most often exceeded 0.90.

Among 433 adult male grouse handled in Minnesota, in only 3 percent was the ratio of the ninth to the eighth primary calamus diameter less than 0.885. Among 883 males regarded as young based on molt status, the ratio in 99 percent was less than 0.885. Of 1,316 male Minnesota grouse of known or quite certain age, there was 1.7 percent overlap between age classes. In other words, fewer than 2 birds of 100 would be misclassified by this criterion alone, and the error is negligible when birds already aged by other means are considered.

Among females, a ratio of 0.885 or even 0.880 separates young and old. Of 24 known adult females the ninth:eighth primary calamus diameter ratio was less than expected in very few birds: in only one was it 0.879, and in four it was less than 0.90. Of 256 females believed to be young on the basis of wing molt, only one had a ratio larger than 0.880, and only eight had ratios greater than 0.870.

Diameter of the central rectrix. Another useful criterion for determining age, first identified by Dorney and Holzer, is the diameter of the central rectrix. The overlap here between age groups is somewhat larger than for the ninth primary calamus, but among Wisconsin males only 11 percent of the adults had rectrix diameters of less than 2.22 millimeters, and only 6 percent of the young birds had diameters larger than 2.3 millimeters. Tail diameter, then, is useful for aging some ruffed grouse that cannot be aged by other criteria, but this is at the bottom of the list of useful methods.

Among the Minnesota sample, 318 known yearling males had rectrix calamus diameters ranging from 2.00 to 2.66 millimeters, and those of 413 known adults ranged from 1.98 to 2.69 millimeters. Among 413 males classed as young on the basis of primary molt, the range was 1.77 to 2.48 millimeters.

Using a 2.25-millimeter separation point for this sample of 1,256 Minnesota ruffed grouse, 22.9 percent of the young male grouse would have been erroneously classi-

Young and old

*B*y the time a chick is three weeks old, its juvenile plumage begins to be replaced by adult feathers, which change little regardless of how long the bird lives. Technically, this is the *first basic* or *postjuvenile* plumage.

At seventeen weeks the bird has only four juvenile feathers left: the two outermost primaries (numbers 9 and 10) on each wing. These are usually not replaced until the bird is fourteen or fifteen months old and completing its first postnuptial molt.

The juvenile primaries permit researchers to assign the bird to a specific cohort of grouse—*young*, or *immatures*. But the latter term may mislead, since some young males are sufficiently mature to engage in adult activities, such as drumming, at twenty weeks and to breed at ten to eleven months.

In this chapter, grouse termed *young* had clearly identifiable juvenile plumage in addition to the ninth and tenth primaries.

The term *yearling* here refers to twelve- to twenty-three-month-old birds that were first handled and banded when young. A yearling can sometimes be identified among grouse trapped or taken by hunters in September or early October. These birds have the seventh, eighth, and ninth primaries still quilled and a worn, faded, and usually pointed tenth primary not yet molted.

The term *adult* is restricted to grouse at least twenty-four months old.

—*Gordon W. Gullion*

fied as adults, and 19 percent of the adult males would be misclassified as young. In a sample of 1,386 known sex males, 47.8 percent had central rectrix diameters larger than the 2.28-millimeter maximum diameter recorded for a known female.

Among Minnesota females, the rectrix diameters ranged from 1.62 to 2.18 millimeters for 141 known and assumed young grouse, and 1.85 to 2.28 millimeters for 30 known yearlings and adults. If a separation point of 2.01 millimeters is used for females, 31.9 percent of the young and 43.3 percent of the adults would be misclassified.

Tips of the ninth and tenth primaries. This aging technique has been popular for many years, but it is much less reliable than stage of wing molt. Supposedly, if the tips of the ninth and tenth primaries are pointed, the bird is young, and if the feathers are rounded, it's an adult. This is only approximately so. Nevertheless, the technique is sometimes useful when age cannot be determined on the basis of other features.

The tenth primary, grown when the bird is only eleven weeks old, usually has the shape of a paring knife. But the ninth primary is seldom, if ever, so pointed. Among 41 young grouse of both sexes handled in Minnesota, 88 percent had the pointed tenth-primary tip, 10 percent exhibited a more triangular shape, and in 2 percent the tip was as rounded as the other primaries.

Among 946 males believed to be young on the basis of other characteristics, the tenth primaries were pointed in 76 percent, triangular in 5 percent, and rounded like adults' in 19 percent. The frequency of pointed tenth primaries was somewhat different among 518 females believed to be young birds: the tips were pointed in 80 percent, triangular in 10 percent, and rounded in only 10 percent.

On adult grouse the tip of the tenth primary tends to be as rounded as the tips of the eighth and ninth. Among 296 yearlings of both sexes, 7 percent had pointed tenth primaries, and 1 percent had the triangular shape. Among 369 adults, pointed tips were recorded on 9 percent and triangular on 2 percent.

Condition of the ninth primary. Young Minnesota grouse often exhibit pronounced

damage, or "foxing," of the outer portion of this feather. This was noted by Ammann in 1948 and has recently been recorded for 72 percent of 573 young Minnesota grouse.

Evidently, damage to this feather occurs as the eighth is being replaced, leaving the ninth as the longest feather on the bird's wingtip. In the postnuptial molt sequence the damaged ninth is replaced by a new feather that is shorter and hence protected by the fully grown eighth primary, so foxing was found on only 36 percent of 628 adult wings.

Bursa of Fabricius. This is a blind, dead-end, pocket that opens into a bird's vent, or cloaca. Although its function has not been determined, it is deepest in young birds and atrophies as the bird grows older. This feature has been much used to separate age classes of a wide range of birds, including waterfowl, pheasants, rails, and grouse.

During the period when bursal measurements are most useful, however, it is much easier and just as reliable to age ruffed grouse on the basis of wing feather molt. Also, the carcass must not have been field dressed—something most hunters do right away.

SIGNS OF AGING

Ruffed grouse that manage to survive into their second or even third year undergo certain changes in feathers and other characteristics. The data, based on the records of 822 ruffed grouse handled again a year or more after initial banding, indicate that these signs of aging vary with the sex of the bird.

Weight changes. Adult female grouse tend to be somewhat heavier than young birds, but this seems to be more the result of better survival among heavier young hens than an increase in weights as they grow older. The weights of 41 fall-trapped young females that lived at least a year were significantly greater than the weights of the 291 that were not known to have survived, 512.4 versus 529.8 grams.

The same is true among young males. The fall weights of 128 young males known to have survived to the next spring averaged 19.7 grams heavier than 142 young males from the same cohorts that were not known to have survived.

Two generations: on the young grouse (left) the eighth primary is fully grown but still heavily sheathed at its base, and the tenth is pointed. The ninth and tenth primaries of the adult bird (right) are still growing and have more rounded tips.

Unlike females, the surviving young males do become heavier during their first two years. The mean weight gains for 282 males handled as young birds and later as yearlings was 31.8 grams, significantly greater than the mean 8.1-gram weight gain for 138 birds growing from yearlings to adults. The young males showed an average gain of 5.5 percent over their 574-gram mean weight a season earlier.

Once males have attained full growth, weight changes are more related to wintering conditions. One long-lived drummer, for example, weighed 533 grams as a young male in 1964; he grew and shrank to 587, 621, 576, 569, 550, 593, and 568 grams when captured on his drumming log at about the same date in seven successive seasons.

Primary growth. The ninth primary tends to lengthen as a young grouse's juvenile feathers are replaced by adult feathers, with a mean increase of 4.6 millimeters among 181 young males and 3.21 millimeters among 19 young hens. But once adult length has been achieved, subsequent feathers are as likely to be shorter as longer.

Tail growth. Young males grow signifi-cantly longer tails when they become year-lings. The mean growth was 9.7 millimeters among 326 males first handled as young and later as yearlings. Growth was much less—only 1.69 millimeters—among 42 young hens and not significant.

Once tail length has been attained among yearling males, it tends to remain static. Among grouse older than twenty-four months, tail lengths are as likely to be slightly shorter as slightly longer following subsequent molts.

Along with the increased length of the central rectrix as the bird replaces its first tail, there is an increase in barb length. This aver-ages 4.16 millimeters as young males become yearlings but tends not to change as the grouse becomes older. For 102 yearling males the mean increase in barb length was only 0.471 millimeter, very significantly less than the young-to-yearling growth.

Among 32 females, the barb increased only 1.37 millimeters as they grew from young to yearling birds—significantly less than among young males.

An increase in size occurs in calamus diam-eters as feather lengths increase. Among 272

Clues for feather sleuths

When a grouse is in the hand, the identi-fication of feathers for use in aging and sex-ing is relatively easy. Spread the wing. The outermost primary is number 10, the next in is number 9, then 8, and so forth. But occa-sionally a feather is missing—through acci-dent, abnormality, or normal molt.

In early fall, for example, a young bird may have lost its eighth primary and not yet grown its replacement. Or there may be only a scattering of feathers left where a grouse was plucked by a predator. If the remains are to be sexed and aged, the proper feathers must be identified. And the sixth, seventh, and eighth primaries, being all about the same length, are easily confused with one another. But there are two clues to their identity.

First is the number and placement of light spots on the leading edge of each feather. Although there are the same number of spots on each feather, their positioning dif-fers and is consistent among all the grouse we have examined. Usually, a reference col-lection for comparison provides the most reliable method for establishing feather iden-tity.

Second is the distance from the inner tip, or umbilicus, to the beginning of the vane. This distance is always greater on the sixth and seventh primaries than on the eighth.

—Gordon W. Gullion

The configuration of bars and flecks of the tail feathers (right, detail) is unique to each bird. The pattern persists through successive molts.

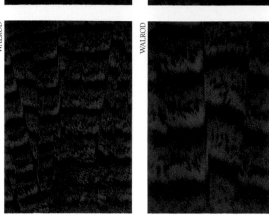

Another bird, another pattern. These markings form the cryptic coloration that conceals the grouse from its enemies.

young males, the calamus diameter of the central rectrix increased by 0.151 millimeter; the increase was only 0.063 for 31 young females. Among 173 adult males, the tail calamus diameters showed no significant changes as they grew older.

Tail color and pattern are generally stable as ruffed grouse grow older. The tail bar count, terminal band pattern, and general coloration of the rectrices remain much the same. Sometimes, however, the adult rectrices will be a little darker and richer in color than the first generation of feathers, especially among gray- and brown-phased grouse.

Most tail bands remain constant from one feather generation to another, except for the female's blotched and pooled patterns. Sometimes a blotched tail is replaced by a pooled pattern, or vice versa.

The general pattern of each ruffed grouse's tail is as distinctive for that bird as a fingerprint. On several occasions in Minnesota it has been possible to identify specific birds on the basis of one or two rectrices shed during an encounter with a predator, molted beside a drumming log, or lost for some other reason.

–Gordon W. Gullion

A feather card shows how consistent the individual patterns are. Two tail feathers were plucked when the bird was first trapped in 1974; another two were plucked in 1975. The following year the grouse was picked off by a raptor.

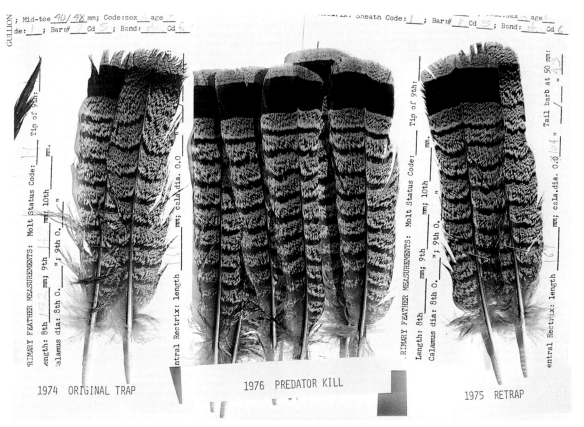

1974 ORIGINAL TRAP

1976 PREDATOR KILL

1975 RETRAP

Complications, cautions, and close calls

The most common source of material for sex and age determination is grouse bagged by hunters. Frequently, local or state officials ask hunters to put feathers in bags or envelopes and deposit them in boxes or send them by mail to a central collection point. Requests most commonly specify the tail and one wing, but recently rump feathers have been added to some samplings.

The value of these collections is considerable, because of their magnitude. In 1963 Dorney reported on his examination of feathers from 22,942 grouse taken by Wisconsin hunters from 1953 to 1957. And from 1958 to 1980 Minnesota hunters submitted material from nearly 28,000 grouse.

But the cooperating hunter who sends only wings or only tails can complicate life for grouse students. And if he mixes the feathers from several birds in the same envelope, the material may almost be useless.

Other sources include road and accidental kills and the remains from predators' kills. Identifying these birds taxes researchers' techniques most severely, for often few of the critical feathers are available or intact.

Trapped grouse provide a good source of material for researchers. In Minnesota studies, a central and lateral rectrix and an eighth and ninth primary are collected and saved from every grouse handled. If a bird is taken again after it has gone through a molt, the collection is repeated. All collected feathers are saved on the bird's personal feather card.

Because plucking primaries often damages the tissues that produce new feathers, replacement feathers may be deformed. Sometimes this deformation is pronounced and obvious; at other times it is very subtle but still enough to compromise the measurements. In Minnesota research, therefore, feathers are taken from right wings in even-numbered years and left wings in odd-numbered years, to avoid collecting the same feathers from the same wing in successive years. After the second collection there is not much point in plucking primary feathers from the same bird, since feathers taken from a wing plucked two years earlier are likely to be abnormal.

A second precaution involves measuring rectrix lengths to determine sex. Ruffed grouse shed rectrices easily under stress, and a close call with a predator often results in the loss of some or all of the grouse's tail feathers. Although these grow back rapidly and are fully replaced in a few weeks, feathers regrown during periods of winter stress are seldom as long or wide as the bird's normal tail. Such replacement feathers on males, even adult males, may be short enough to fall in the range that is exclusively female for normal feathers.

Yet the incidence of near misses yields valuable information on ruffed grouse survival. It provides another measure of winter predation pressure—assuming the same percentage of grouse that are attacked escape from predators each year.

—*Gordon W. Gullion*

The signs of age

In the dorsal wall of the cloaca of a ruffed grouse is an opening leading to a blind, dead-end pouch known as the bursa of Fabricius. This pouch reaches its maximum size in juvenile grouse, becomes smaller as the bird enters its first autumn, and is resorbed during the first winter. Its depth can therefore be used as a criterion for separating juveniles from adults: any bird with a bursa deeper than 5 millimeters is considered a juvenile. Since researchers don't enjoy taking such measurements any more than grouse like being measured, this technique is not widely used.

The best method for determining whether a grouse is a juvenile depends on the fact that, unlike adults, juveniles do not replace all of their wing primaries during the first year of life. Grouse, like many other game birds, have ten major flight feathers. They are numbered 1 through 10, from the innermost feather to the outermost. Molting of these feathers begins with the innermost feather, number 1, in the summer months and proceeds to the outermost primaries later in the fall. The molt pattern of chicks is regular and can therefore be used to determine age.

Birds collected in the fall can be reliably aged by comparing the outer two primaries (9 and 10) with the new feathers on the rest of the wing. Juvenile grouse still have their old ninth and tenth primaries, and the contour and shape of these feathers differ greatly from those of new adult feathers. Over time,

the action of flight wears primary feathers to a pointed shape. Since molting proceeds from the innermost primaries out, primaries 9 and 10 are the newest and least worn of the flight feathers on an adult bird, and the oldest and most worn in a juvenile. So if, compared with number 8, the trailing edges of numbers 9 and 10 seem worn, and their overall shape appears more sharply pointed, the bird is classed as a juvenile. If the trailing edges of these outer primaries are not worn and the feathers are rounded, the bird is classed as an adult.

Don't expect this difference to jump out at you, however. The classification is reliable but subjective, and it takes some practice to discern the difference.

On occasion, while examining wingtips in the fall, you may find a bird whose ninth and tenth primaries are not fully grown. If there are incompletely developed feathers on both wings, the bird is definitely an adult. The gradual molting of flight feathers in the ruffed grouse assures that this bird does not experience a flightless period, as do waterfowl and some other birds.

How can a full-sized grouse be aged in the spring when the outer primaries of both one- and two-year-old birds are worn? Researchers faced with this problem developed a technique of using the diameter of the calamus, or feather quill, measured where the first barbs come out of the shaft of primaries 8, 9, and 10.

In an Ohio study, the diameter of the calamus of primary 9 was found to be 0.1195 inch in an adult male grouse, and 0.1113 inch in a juvenile male. Similar differences between adult and juvenile females were also detected. The method may seem obscure, but it has been found to work about 85 percent of the time. If the technique is taken a step further, however, and a ratio of the calamus diameters of primaries 8 and 9 is computed, it is possible to separate almost all juveniles from adults, as well as males from females.

To the average person this information is of little value as well as difficult to obtain, since measurements must be taken with a micrometer or calipers. To the grouse biologist working in the early springtime, however, this criterion can be crucial.

For the sake of completeness, one additional method for aging ruffed grouse should be mentioned. This technique is also based on primary feather characteristics but can be a bit trickier than the methods already mentioned. New feathers grow inside a sheath made of a clear, flaky material resembling cellophane. Some sheathing remains on the shaft of a plucked feather. On an adult grouse, primaries 9 and 10 are new in the fall; not much difference should be evident in the amount of sheathing present on these outer primaries and the sheathing present on the eighth primary. On a juvenile, however, you should see less sheathing, if any, on primaries 9 and 10 than on the other newly replaced feathers.

BESENGER

Above: *Primaries 8, 9, and 10 are blunt on an adult bird.* Below: *Primary 8 is blunt, as on the adult, but 9 and 10 are sharply pointed and worn, indicating that these feathers have not yet molted: the bird is a juvenile.*

Aging the ruffed grouse can be difficult. To improve their chances of accuracy, most researchers combine various methods when trying to determine the birds' ages. Note that no method other than banding has been developed to distinguish between two- and three-year-olds. Such an effort would hardly pay off, given that so few grouse ever see their third summer.

*—David E. Samuel and
William L. Hudson*

Sexing and aging by plumage

Many plumage characteristics may be used to determine the age and sex of a grouse. Because none of these methods are totally reliable, as many characteristics as possible should be considered. Also, because plumage characteristics may vary considerably from one population to another, each population should be studied separately.

SEXING

Plumage characteristics can also establish a grouse's sex. The length of the tail feathers is one such factor. In populations of ruffed grouse in the state of Washington, a tail length of 15.2 centimeters or more indicated a male; less than 15.2 centimeters, a female. The tail length was measured from the skin at the base of the central pair of rectrices to the tip of the longest rectrix. However, in populations of grouse in Wisconsin, if one of the two middle tail feathers, plucked, was longer than 14.9 centimeters, the bird was a male; if less than 14.0 centimeters, a female. Birds with intermediate measurements could have been of either sex.

Another means of sexing by the rectrices is the completeness of the dark subterminal band on the central pair, which is bordered by smoke gray bands on both sides. This band is generally complete on an adult male, but on a female it is missing or indistinct. The difficulty with this method is that this band may be partial—that is, its proximal and distal borders are broken by the smoke gray of the surrounding bands—on both subadult males and some females. (A male grouse in the northern part of the birds' range may have a lighter subterminal band of fuscous that appears partial, but look closely: the incomplete appearance is due to lighter cinnamon brown spots that are actually part of the band.) Therefore, if the subterminal band on the central pair of rectrices is complete, the bird is a male; if missing or only a trace, a female; and if partial, the sex cannot be determined by this method alone.

Grouse usually have eighteen tail feathers. Count them anyway, for the atypical tail often reveals its owner's sex. Edminster checked many tail tallies against other criteria and in 1947 reported that a bird with twenty rectrices was most likely a male. And a bird with only sixteen—assuming that no feathers were missing because of the molt—was generally a hen.

In populations of grouse in western Washington, Quebec, and Wisconsin, the number of light-colored spots on a plucked feather taken from the rump, near the upper tail coverts, was used to determine the sex. If there were two or three spots, the grouse was a male, but if there was only one spot or an indistinct one, it was a female.

As a further aid to determining the sex of a grouse, remember that the female often has a pinkish or salmon wash on the throat and breast and, during the breeding season, has an incubation patch.

The sex of a chick eight to fourteen weeks old may be determined from the color of the

The eye patch of the drummer in full display glows bright red.

bare spot over its eye. If it is subdued orange to a bright red-orange, it is a male, but if there is little or no color, it is a female. During the breeding season, the bare spot over the eye of an adult male is also bright red.

AGING

Since a ruffed grouse does not usually shed the outer two primaries, numbers 9 and 10, of its juvenile plumage until its first postbreeding molt, when it is about one year old, the outer primaries may be used to estimate age. In the fall, check the bases of primaries 8 through 10. If there are remnants of a sheath at the base of primary number 8, but not at the bases of number 9 and 10, the bird is probably no more than a year old—a subadult. If remnants of sheath exist at the bases of all three, the grouse is at least one year old—an adult.

The contour of the tenth primary may also indicate age. If it is a juvenile primary retained by a first-year bird, this feather may be pointed at the tip or have a straight edge along the inner web at the tip. If the grouse is an adult, the tip will be rounded. Nevertheless, priority should be given to the presence of sheathing, as it takes some practice to use the contour method to estimate age. Also, during late winter and spring, the tip of the tenth primary may be worn, making a determination by contour impossible.

Since the wear of the outer primaries may complicate matters, the diameter of the calamus, or quill, of the ninth primary may be used to determine age. For population studies by Brewer in western Washington, the ninth primary was plucked and oven-dried for forty-eight hours. When the diameter of the quill of a male grouse was larger than 2.6 millimeters, the grouse was an adult; if smaller, the grouse was a subadult, or it had not yet gone through its first postbreeding molt. If the diameter of this particular quill from a female grouse was larger than 2.7 millimeters, the bird was an adult; if less, a subadult. The catch is that you have to determine the bird's sex first.

To study populations in Wisconsin, ornithologists also used the diameter of the ninth primary to determine the age of live birds because the shaft of this primary is sufficiently exposed. If the diameter, measured where the larger proximal barbs begin, was more than 3 millimeters, the bird was an adult; if less than 3 millimeters, a subadult.

Two other methods have been used to age Wisconsin populations in the spring and early summer. In one, the shaft diameter of a dried, central rectrix was measured. If the diameter was greater than 2.3 millimeters, the bird was an adult; if less than 2.2 millimeters, a subadult; and if between 2.2 and 2.3 millimeters, unknown. Second, the length of a plucked, central rectrix was measured. If it was 170 millimeters or more, the bird was an adult; if 159 millimeters or less, a subadult; and if between 160 and 169 millimeters, unknown.

—Ronald R. Runkles

Key for identifying ruffed grouse

This guide, based on the external characteristics of 2,723 Minnesota grouse of known age and sex, appears to be valid through the north-central part of the continent. Racial variation may require different points of separation in other regions.

Sex separation

	Male	Female	Unclassified
Central rectrix (CR)	Longer than 150 mm	Shorter than 144 mm Between 144 and 150 mm and is an adult	
Central rectrix compared with ninth primary (P9)	Length of CR more than 5 mm longer than P9	Length of CR less than 5 mm longer than P9	
Central rectrix compared with eighth primary (P8)	CR longer than P8	P8 longer than CR	
Ratio of P9 to CR	Less than 0.910	Greater than 0.960	
Ratio of P8 to CR	Less than 1.02	Greater than 1.04	
Midtoe	Longer than 41 mm	Shorter than 37 mm	
Tail bar count	More than 9	Less than 6	
Tail feathers		Two central rectrices markedly redder than laterals	All tail feathers same color
Terminal tail band	Clear or fuzzy	Obscured or blotched	Not as described for male and female
Eyebrow	Bright red or orange	Without pigmentation	
Length of tail barb	Over 40 mm	50 mm from distal end of CR less than 34 mm	
Rump spots	Three or more white spots	No white spots	
Ruff feathers	Conspicuous		Not conspicuously longer than other neck plumage

Age separation

	Males		Females		
	Young	*Adult*	*Young*	*Adult*	*Unclassified*
Condition of ninth and tenth primaries	Fully grown; tips probably foxed; eighth primary absent, growing, or more heavily sheathed at base than the ninth primary	One or both missing, growing, or more heavily sheathed at base than the eighth primary	Fully grown but probably showing foxed tips; eighth primary absent, growing, or with more evident sheathing at its base than the ninth	One or both absent, growing, or more heavily sheathed at base than the eighth	
Central rectrix	Shorter than 151 mm	Longer than 175 mm	Shorter than 132 mm	Longer than 146 mm	
Ninth primary	Shorter than 132 mm	Longer than 151 mm	Shorter than 132 mm	Longer than 143 mm	
Diameter of ninth primary calamus	Less than 2.82 mm	Greater than 3.04 mm	Less than 2.82 mm	Greater than 2.96 mm	
Ratio of ninth to eighth primary calamus diameters	Less than 0.885	Greater than 0.885	Less than 0.885	Greater than 0.885	
Diameter of central rectrix calamus	Less than 2.04 mm	Greater than 2.44 mm	Less than 1.86 mm	Greater than 2.16 mm	
Rectrix barb at 50 mm	Less than 37 mm	Greater than 45 mm	Less than 32 mm		No difference at upper limit
Tip of tenth primary	Sharply pointed or triangular	As rounded as tips of eighth and ninth	Sharply pointed or triangular	As rounded as tips of eighth and ninth	
Tip of ninth primary	Pronounced foxing		Pronounced foxing		Intact, undamaged

Racial variations

Two dimensions important for determining the age and sex of a ruffed grouse – the length of a central tail feather and the length of the midtoe – vary among the subspecies. This table presents the racial variations found by Ridgway and Fried-mann in 1946; it includes some subspecies not recognized in the 1957 checklist of the American Ornithological Union.

No distinction was made between postjuvenal replacement tail feathers and post-nuptial replacements. That is, both young and adult birds are included. The tails were measured with the feathers intact; a plucked rectrix would be about 10 millimeters longer. The midtoe was measured without the claw.

Data were based on samples of different sizes, from three Appalachian females to forty-three gray males.

	Females		Males	
	Range (mm)	Mean (mm)	Range (mm)	Mean (mm)
Gray (B. u. umbelloides)				
Tail	125–134	130.4	144–174	157.7
Midtoe	33.8–36.3	34.9	35.0–40.6	37.5
St. Lawrence (B. u. togata)				
Tail	119–144	130.6	142–174	156.9
Midtoe	31.3–36.7	34.6	33.0–39.9	35.9
Eastern (B. u. umbellus)				
Tail	123–141	132.6	144–174	159.0
Midtoe	32.7–36.9	34.2	32.4–39.0	36.7
Appalachian (B. u. monticola)				
Tail	121–156	134.8	139–181	160.0
Midtoe	32.2–39.6	35.1	32.8–40.0	36.5
Midwestern (B. u. mediana)				
Tail	127–159	141.3	140–163	150.6
Midtoe	34.3–37.4	35.4	34.5–39.5	36.8
Hoary (B. u. incana)				
Tail	120–147	133.2	138–164	151.8
Midtoe	33.2–38.8	35.0	35.0–39.9	37.4
Idaho (B. u. phaia)				
Tail	124–134	130.2	141–171	157.7
Midtoe	34.4–37.5	36.2	34.8–39.7	37.6
Columbian (B. u. affinis)				
Tail	123–157	132.4	130–170	152.4
Midtoe	32.5–39.3	35.2	34.2–41.0	37.6
Pacific (B. u. sabini)				
Tail	124–137	130.2	142–159	151.7
Midtoe	33.0–39.0	36.5	39.0–41.9	40.1
Olympic (B. u. castanea)				
Tail	130–139	131.8	145–168	153.9
Midtoe	37.0–39.7	38.6	38.9–42.2	40.7
Vancouver Island (B. u. brunnescens)				
Tail	124–134	128.4	144–157	148.6
Midtoe	37.0–39.9	38.4	40.0–41.0	40.3
Yukon (B. u. yukonensis)				
Tail	127–137	130.8	129–168	148.5
Midtoe	33.0–37.0	34.9	34.0–38.5	36.7

Chicks

The age of a juvenile grouse can be determined by the condition of its primaries *(P)*. The data below are from Bump et al. (1947).

Age	
1 week	P1, P2, P3 half-grown; P5 emerging
2	P1, P2, P3 grown; P8 emerging
3	P1 and P2 shed; P3, P4, P5 grown; P9 and P10 emerging
4	P3 shed; P4, P5, P6, P7 grown; P1 and P2 emerging
5	P4 shed; P5, P6, P7 grown; P3 emerging
6	P5 shed; P1, P2, P6, P7, P8 grown; P4 emerging
7	P1, P2, P6, P7, P8 full-grown; P5 growing
8	P1, P2, P3, P7, P8 full-grown; P5 and P6 growing
9	P1, P2, P3, P4, P8 full-grown; P7 shed
10	P1, P2, P3, P4, P5, P8 full-grown; P7 emerging
11	P1, P2, P3, P4, P5, P6, P9, P10 full-grown; P8 shed
12	P1, P2, P3, P4, P5, P6, P9, P10 full-grown; P8 emerging
13	P8 half the length of P9
14	P8 10 mm shorter than P9
15	P8 equal in length to P9
16	P8 5 mm or longer than P9
17	P8 full-grown but umbilicus not sealed

Inside the bird

For the upland bird hunter—or for anyone walking through the woods on an autumn day—the thunderous sound and fleeting sight of a flushing ruffed grouse are a common event. What is going on inside that ruffed grouse, however, is an astoundingly complex series of physiological events: the bird's eyes pick up the forest intruder, its brain registers the threat, adrenalin flows, muscles contract, and in the briefest of instants, the grouse is airborne, hurtling through tree branches at alarming speed.

Or perhaps the visitor does not come so close as to flush the bird, which continues its territorial defense, outdrumming its rivals. Or the grouse is a juvenile, undergoing the molt that will usher in its richly patterned adult plumage. Anatomically, just how does it all work?

SIGHT

Anyone who has ever hunted the ruffed grouse has marveled at the bird's ability to place a tree between itself and its pursuer in an all-too-brief moment of time. The grouse's response to potential danger is mediated through the central nervous system, primarily through the well-developed cerebellum, which coordinates the activities of the muscular and nervous systems. This structure receives stimuli from the body via fibers in the spinal cord and from the inner ear, all of which are assembled and coordi-

Takeoff: the ruffed grouse is considered the king of game birds precisely because it thunders into flight with such great speed. Adaptations special to the ruffed grouse, with an assist from features common to all birds, account for this characteristic.

Unlike migratory waterfowl, which may fly thousands of miles, the ruffed grouse is built for short bursts of speed.

nated to initiate movement and maintain body balance.

Survival of the ruffed grouse depends on the ability of the bird to receive and respond to stimuli from the environment. Receptors in the skin note heat, cold, and touch, for example. A bird's sense of smell is less than acute, as suggested by the small size of the olfactory lobes. Because the avian cochlea, site of the sense of hearing, is only a tenth the length of the mammalian cochlea, birds may be less sensitive to the wide range of sound frequencies that mammals perceive; but with ten times the number of hair receptor cells, birds may be more sensitive to different intensities of sound, according to Pumphrey.

It is a grouse's sight, however, that is most important. Birds probably obtain more information through their eyes than from all the other senses combined. The dorsal region of the midbrain, called the tectum, has evolved into a major correlation center, especially for sight. The optic lobes in the brain are large, as are the orbits of the skull and the eyes themselves, all suggesting that avian vision has evolved to a perfection not found in other vertebrates. And indeed, grouse can detect the direction, distance, size, shape, brightness, color, depth, and motion of an object with special acuity. They are also capable of binocular vision in dim light. In its structure, the avian eye is similar to that of lizards, and little variation exists among members of the entire class of Aves.

A keen sense of sight is important for the behavior of the species as well as for its ability to find food and escape predators. Visual displays, not vocalizations, are the basis for both courtship and brooding behavior.

Courtship, for example, consists of a strutting and feather-ruffle display. The male raises his tail and fans the feathers while lowering his wings to the ground. He holds his head back and erects the ruff until it forms an almost complete circle of iridescent black or brown feathers. True, the female is attracted to the male in the first place by the sound of his drumming, but even that may not be as important to her as the availability of good nesting habitat nearby.

When danger approaches, the female gives

Grouse have a highly evolved sense of sight. The eyes are large, as are the optic lobes, the parts of the brain that receive visual stimuli.

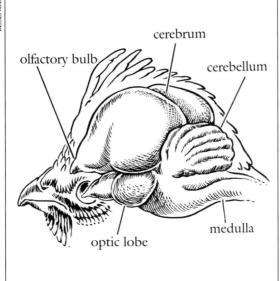

cerebrum

olfactory bulb

cerebellum

medulla

optic lobe

RUFFED GROUSE

a warning call, but her defense of the chicks —now virtually invisible in cover—depends on a visual display. She feigns a broken wing to lure the predator away.

FLIGHT

The ruffed grouse might never get off the ground were it not for the numerous air spaces within its delicate bones. These pockets of air, common to all birds, reduce the grouse's weight. Such delicacy is all well and good, but it cannot be at the expense of strength. The wings and large flight muscles must be firmly attached if they are to launch a bird into flight and keep it aloft. The trunk portion of the skeleton is therefore rigid, its vertebrae fused together and the ribs fused with the sternum, allowing a firm point of attachment for the wings. Only the vertebrae at the opposite ends—neck and tail—are free to move independently. For additional rigidity, the bones that form a girdle at the shoulders (scapula, clavicle, and coracoids) are more or less united and joined to the sternum. The pronounced keel is an adaptation for the insertion of the two large flight muscles: the pectoralis, which depresses the wing, and the supracoracoideus, which raises the wing.

The bones of the wing—comparable to the forelimbs of other vertebrates—are highly modified for flight. Each wing consists of a humerus, an ulna, a radius, two carpals, and digits 2, 3, and 4. The remaining three carpals are fused to the metacarpals, forming the carpometacarpus. The fusion and the reduction in the number of bones in the wing result in reduced mobility. Only three fingers remain. The stubby thumb supports three or four small feathers of the alula. The second finger is the largest, consisting of two broad segments for the attachment of the primary flight feathers. The third finger is reduced to a single small bone.

The flight muscles (pectoralis, supracoracoideus) that depress the wing are more ventrally located than the muscles in the forelimbs of ground-dwellers, enabling the bird to lift rapidly off the ground and improving its aerodynamic balance. A comparison of the amount and location of white and red muscles—light and dark meat—reveals what

The avian backbone is rigid, a necessity for both flight and standing posture. Highly porous bones reduce body weight, another adaptation for flight.

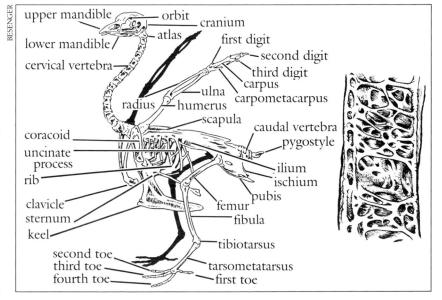

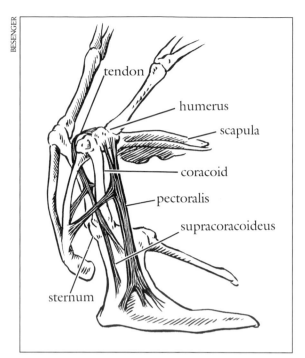

BESENGER

tendon

humerus

scapula

coracoid

pectoralis

supracoracoideus

sternum

kind of flier a bird is. The flight muscles of waterfowl, for example, are primarily red (recall the dark breast meat of a duck), with finer fibers than white muscles, and with nuclei located at the edges of the fibers, rather than scattered throughout. The red color is due to the presence of the oxygen-carrying compounds, myoglobin and cytochrome, which are absent or rare in white muscles. Furthermore, red muscles have more of the respiratory structures called mitochondria, which supply the high energy demands of sustained flight. Migratory birds, after all, must fly the avian equivalent of a marathon twice a year. The ruffed grouse, however, has white flight muscles, which cannot sustain long flights. White muscle contracts more

rapidly, however, and these fast contractions help it burst into flight in a way that ducks and geese cannot.

Since grouse escape their predators by flying away, their leg muscles and bone articulations do not need to permit the complicated lateral motions characteristic of certain mammals, such as rabbits or, for that matter, tennis pros. Birds need only walk, run a bit, leap to the air, land with some cushioning, and grasp branches with their toes. The major leg muscles provide for the necessary forward and backward motion with little, if any, lateral movement or rotation. Thirty-eight leg muscles have been identified in birds. There are some muscles in the shank (tibiotarsus), and six small, thin muscles are located just above the toes, in the tarsometatarsus. But most are in the thigh region over the femur. This concentration of muscles in the upper leg keeps the weight near the bird's center of gravity; the lighter weight of the extremities of the leg, moreover, permits the bird to move it quickly without expending a lot of energy. Still, grouse are relatively slow runners, at least compared with other

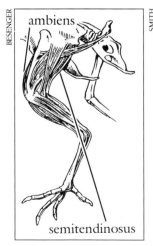

BESENGER

ambiens

semitendinosus

SMITH

The hexagonal pattern of the contour feathers provides the grouse with its remarkable coloring.

gallinaceous birds, such as pheasants and turkeys, because their legs are short.

SKIN AND FEATHERS

Feathers, which grow from the dermis of the skin, perform a variety of functions, primarily heat conservation and flight. They are effective in insulating the birds against heat loss, and for this reason, grouse have more feathers in winter than in summer. The flat, rounded contour feather is primarily an adaptation for flight, but it also sheds rain and has other protective functions. A unique characteristic of the feathers of the grouse is the aftershaft, a second shaft that bears most of the typical feather parts and is attached near the base of the main shaft. This is best observed in the contour feathers.

The contour feathers of the ruffed grouse are arranged in crossing rows such that any given feather is at the center of a hexagon consisting of its six nearest neighbors. The reason for this arrangement is not clear, but it accounts for the distinctive color patterns of this species.

In response to cold, the ruffed grouse often fluffs itself up in such a way that the feathers trap insulating air. It accomplishes this by extending the contour feather follicles, which are attached to muscles in the skin. These dermal muscles—smooth, involuntary muscles controlled by the sympathetic nervous system—can move the follicles, and thus the contour feathers, up or down or sideways. The extension of the follicles is also an involuntary response to danger. This is a stereotypical behavior pattern that is part of the defensive-aggressive behavior pattern of the species.

Other smooth and skeletal muscles move entire patches of feathers, such as those

Muscles just beneath the skin extend the contour feathers, creating an insulating blanket of trapped air. These dermal muscles act involuntarily, much like the human mechanisms that account for goosebumps and shivering.

This ruffed grouse hen, photographed on a day of below-zero temperatures, has fluffed up the feathers of her neck and breast. If, come spring, she is disturbed on her nest, the dermal muscles will again move the feathers up, making her appear more formidable to the intruder.

Muscles of the rump move the pygostyle, which supports the tail feathers. The full fan is part of the male's courtship display, but when threatened, hens also fan their tails.

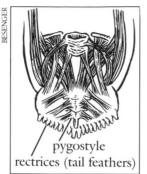

pygostyle
rectrices (tail feathers)

involved in courtship displays. The male's characteristic fanning behavior, intended to impress a potential mate or discourage a rival, involves a complex set of muscles in the rump and tail. These muscles move the pygostyle, which supports the tail feathers, and the ruffed grouse's tail expands into an impressive fan.

The process by which a bird replaces its plumage is molting, an event controlled, apparently, by thyroid hormone in conjunction with reproductive hormones. Molting begins when feathers become worn out and loose in their follicles. Next they fall out and the germ layer at the base of each follicle promptly begins to grow a new feather. Occasionally, it is the growing of a new feather that pushes out the old one. In a typical molt, however, a bird loses a few feathers at a time, usually corresponding feathers on opposite sides of the body. Tail feathers usually molt from the center outward, so the outer feathers begin molting only after the center ones have been replaced. If for some reason other than molting a feather is lost, a new one begins growing almost immediately.

As an aid in the care of feathers, the grouse has a uropygial or preen gland, located at the base of the tail. This gland secretes an oil that the bird squeezes out with its mandibles and then places on the feather to waterproof and condition it.

Scales on the bird's legs are also produced from the dermis of the skin and are remnants of its reptilian ancestors.

The scales of the leg and foot betray a bird's reptilian ancestry. Modern evolutionary theory holds that elsewhere on the avian body, scales developed into feathers. Note the pectinations, commonly called snowshoes, along the toes of the ruffed grouse.

RUFFED GROUSE

DRUMMING

The male ruffed grouse marks his territory and calls his mates in a fashion unique to the species, by drumming. The bird rotates his wings forward, creating rapid air movements. The main muscles responsible for this action are the numerous smaller muscles of the wing and shoulder girdle, which pull the wing forward or backward, rotating the humerus so as to raise or depress the leading edge of the wing.

That accounts for the mechanics of drumming. But this drumming behavior, like the ruffed grouse's courtship and brooding, has as its ultimate source the animal's tendency toward stereotyped behavior patterns. These instinctive behaviors have a genetic basis, and control over them is located in the nervous and endocrine (hormonal) systems of the species.

The nervous system of the grouse, like that of other birds and all vertebrates, consists of two parts: the central nervous system (brain and spinal cord) and the autonomic nervous system, which controls reflex actions of the heart, lungs, and other organs. The difference between birds and other vertebrates is in the relative development of different areas of the brain.

The cerebral cortex of birds is thin, not fissured, and not as well developed as in mammals: it lacks direct motor pathways to the spinal cord. As a result, it is likely that direct, conscious control of body motions is greatly reduced in birds, compared with mammals. Within the cortex is a major nerve relay center, the corpus striatum, which controls many of the innate behaviors of the ruffed grouse, such as sensory perception, locomotion, feeding, courtship, brooding, and, of course, drumming. If the cerebral cortex is removed but the corpus striatum left intact, researchers have found, pigeons can complete complex behavior patterns. But removing the corpus striatum has a quite different effect: the birds can pick up grain but cannot complete the sequence of motions necessary to feed themselves.

The behavior of birds is thus more mechanical and stereotyped than that of, say, mammals, whose behavior is coordinated in the upper regions of the cortex, not in the corpus striatum.

Drumming, peculiar to the ruffed grouse, is a stereotyped behavior, controlled by hormones and the nervous system. It is accomplished not by the up-and-down motion of flight, but by a rotation of the wings.

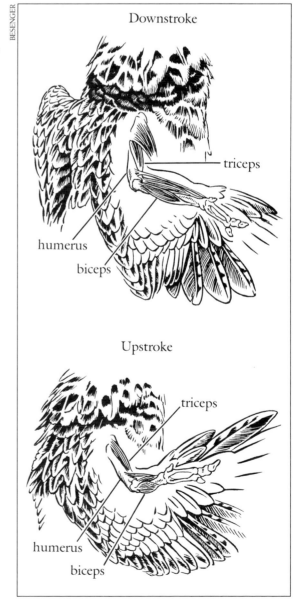

Downstroke

triceps

humerus

biceps

Upstroke

triceps

humerus

biceps

FEEDING

However powerful and acrobatic the wings of the ruffed grouse, they are still just wings: they cannot help the bird preen itself or build a nest or pick aspen buds for the evening meal. The bird must rely instead on its skull and jaws, which have become modified to perform such tasks.

The beak, an elongation of the anterior bones of the skull, consists of the heavy sheath—the bill—and the jaws. The beak of the ruffed grouse is specially adapted to pick up the bird's diet of seeds, fruits, buds, and other plant material. Muscles in the neck compensate for the lack of teeth by allowing the beak a wide range of movements. These muscles are complex, being interwoven and subdivided and attached to each other in such a way that the contraction of one depends on the contractions of its neighbors.

It is doubtful, by the way, that a ruffed grouse enjoys its diet of buds and twigs, or even relishes the succulent fruits of late summer and autumn. The sense of taste appears to be poorly developed in birds, which rely primarily on sight to locate their preferred foods.

Once food has been taken up, further adaptations for the vegetarian diet help the bird obtain the most from its food. As in mammals, the mouth is roofed with a hard palate. Small mucous glands in the soft portions of the mouth lubricate the food to prepare it for swallowing. The small, pointed tongue, used to manipulate food, is covered by cornified epithelium with nipple-shaped papillae at the rear. Salivary glands in the pharynx secrete enzymes that aid in the digestion of the grouse's starchy food.

In gallinaceous birds and many other species as well, the esophagus, designed to carry food from the throat to the stomach, has enlarged into a storage chamber. The crop, as this chamber is called, allows foragers like the ruffed grouse to eat quickly, thereby minimizing the time they are away from the safety of their roosts; the food stored in the crop can be digested at leisure. The crop has another function as well: although no digestive glands have been identified in its walls, seeds and other hard bits of food are softened with mucus before they pass, with the aid of certain neck muscles, into the stomach.

Actually, birds have two stomachs: an anterior glandular stomach, and a posterior muscular stomach better known as a gizzard. The glandular stomach is lined by columnar epithelium cells, and the mucous membrane contains tubular mucous glands that lubricate the digestive tract. The thickest tract of the stomach is the submucosa, which contains digestive glands. In the gizzard these glands secrete a keratinous fluid, which hardens into horny plates or ridges that act like a millstone and grind food. The grinding action is enhanced by small stones, sand, and other grit, which the bird knows to eat for just this purpose.

As in mammals, the small intestine is

Left: A complex arrangement of muscles enables the ruffed grouse to nip aspen buds and other foods. Right: The birds often visit road shoulders to pick up grit, which helps grind food in the gizzard and compensates for the lack of teeth.

where food is chemically digested and absorbed into the body. A bird's small intestine is a coiled tube, consisting of alternating longitudinal and circular bands of smooth muscle between the gizzard and the cloaca, the "sewer" for waste products. The small intestine is not differentiated into regions (duodenum, ileum, and jejunum), as in mammals. Microscopic fingerlike projections, called villi, increase the surface area available for absorption, which takes place through the mucous epithelium layer of the intestinal wall and villi. Bile, which helps break down fats, is secreted into the small intestine via the bile duct from the liver; lipase, carbohydrase, and proteinase enzymes from the pancreas arrive via the pancreatic ducts. There also appears to be a narrow zone of tubular digestive glands in the anterior portion of the small intestine, which probably correspond to Brunner's glands in mammals.

Dissolving in this bath of enzymes, all the ground-up food arrives at the ceca, two dead-end sacs at the junction of the small and large intestines. These ceca are unique to birds. Here, apparently, water is absorbed, proteins are digested, and complex carbohydrates decompose under the action of bacteria. What little digestible material is left is discharged into the large intestine.

Through the walls of the large intestine more water is reabsorbed. Undigested, unabsorbed material passes into the anterior of cloaca, a region called the coprodaeum (liter-

From the crop these seeds and leaves would have entered the forward glandular stomach. Note the expandable capacity of the ruffed grouse crop.

ally, the "highway for dung"). In the middle region the undigested material is joined by nitrogenous wastes from the kidney and reproductive cells through the vas deferens or oviduct. Now excrement, all this matter enters the terminal proctodaeum, which is equipped with massive muscles to eject the waste through the cloaca and out of the body.

On the dorsal wall at the end of the cloaca is a lymphatic pocket called the bursa Fabricii. Prominent in young grouse, it is usually atrophied in adults. The size of the bursa Fabricii can therefore be used to distinguish juvenile from adult grouse, but for the living bird it functions like the thymus gland, by producing white blood cells. It also appears to be involved in some way in sexual development.

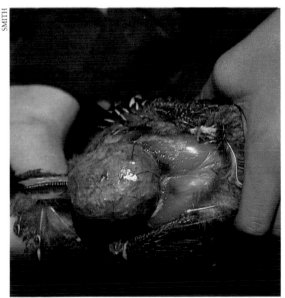

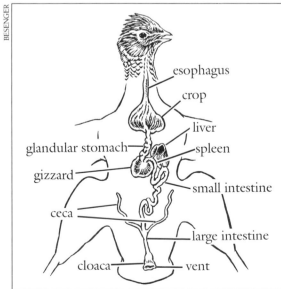

esophagus
crop
liver
glandular stomach
spleen
gizzard
small intestine
ceca
large intestine
cloaca
vent

Left: *The crop, an enlargement of the esophagus, expands into a storage chamber. Its contents are digested after the bird has finished foraging.* Right: *A grouse's liver is larger than that of a mammal of equal size. In addition to bile production, the liver has storage and excretion functions.*

Nearly 180 degrees: because a cross-vessel connects the two jugular veins, the grouse can twist its head, thereby shutting off one vein in its neck, without interrupting the flow of blood.

The heart and kidneys of a grouse are much larger than those of the similarly sized squirrel because of the high oxygen demand and rapid metabolism required for flight.

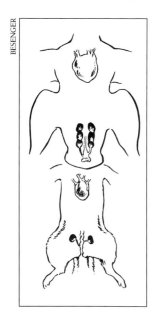

CIRCULATION

The circulatory system of the ruffed grouse, like that of other birds, has evolved for an aerial mode of life. Its general pattern, however, resembles that of reptiles and mammals: it transports oxygen, digested food material, and hormones throughout the body; there are separate pathways for arterial and venous blood; the four-chambered heart has two atria and two ventricles; the right side of the heart pumps blood to the lungs, and the left side handles blood flow to the rest of the body. There the similarities end.

Probably as an adaptation for flight, the bird heart is larger and more powerful than that of mammals of comparable size. To pump blood throughout the body, the muscular walls of the left ventricle have more than three times the mass of the right ventricle. The brachial and pectoral arteries supplying the wing and breast muscles are relatively large. The two jugular veins, which drain blood from the head, are joined by a cross-vessel so that if by turning its head, the bird cramps one vein, blood is shunted to the other and so returned to the heart. This allows for a greater rotation of the head.

To ward off bacterial infections, reptiles and mammals have well developed lym-phatic systems. Birds rely instead on a higher body temperature—40° to 42°C. (104° to 108°F.)—to combat bacterial infections. What remains of such a system are small, dead-end vessels that run parallel to larger blood vessels, draining into the thoracic duct, and small lymph hearts that appear in the embryo near the sacral vertebrae and then disappear in almost all adult birds.

The spleen of birds is also of less importance to birds than to mammals. Although it functions in the formation of white blood cells and the destruction of old red blood cells, it is apparently of little importance in the storage of blood. The size of this weak-muscled organ for some reason varies by season: larger in summer, smaller in winter.

The cargo that the blood transports—salts, nutrients, proteins, wastes, hormones—varies according to several factors. The number of red blood cells, for example, varies by time of day and season of year but is generally higher in males than in females, which suggests that sex hormones may have a role in their formation and destruction. This has been demonstrated by the experimental injection of androgens, the male hormone, into castrated males and females, whose red blood cell count then increased. The thyroid hormone has also been shown to function in the regulation of red blood cells: if the thyroid is removed, the red blood cell count drops approximately 25 percent in males but remains unaffected in females. The reason for this is unknown.

Red blood cells get their color from hemoglobin, a pigment that has the ability to take up and release oxygen. Although birds possess less hemoglobin than mammals, avian hemoglobin is more efficient in handling the muscles' great demands for oxygen during flight. The job of transporting gases and keeping the muscles well supplied apparently wears hemoglobin out: the life expectancy of a red blood cell in a bird is only 30 days, compared with 120 days in a human being. Birds also possess a higher ratio of red to white cells than mammals. In birds there are 100 to 200 red blood cells for every white cell, compared with 700 to 1 in humans, demonstrating the birds' need for more red cells because of their reduced hemoglobin content.

As in other vertebrates, the kidneys are responsible for removing the waste products of metabolism from the blood. Because a bird's metabolism is so rapid, however, its kidneys are twice as large as those of mammals of comparable size. The kidney has three lobes, each divided into small lobules containing a vein from which radiate the renal bodies, or nephrons, that do the work of the kidney. Here water, salts, and glucose are filtered from the blood into the renal tubule, which then allows them to be selectively reabsorbed into the blood via surrounding capillaries. An antidiuretic hormone secreted by the pituitary directs the reabsorption of water from the urine. The now-concentrated waste products enter the ureter, which dumps them into the cloaca. Given the bird's need to handle the wastes quickly and efficiently, a typical avian kidney contains between 90 and 500 renal corpuscles per milliliter of tissue, compared with 4 to 15 in mammals. More than 200,000 renal corpuscles have been reported for the domestic chicken, a close relative of the grouse.

Note that the bird lacks a urinary bladder—an evolutionary adaptation that saves weight. There are other avian adaptations in the treatment of waste as well. Like the reptiles from which they arose, birds excrete uric acid instead of urea. The physiological advantage of uric acid is that it is relatively insoluble in water; water may be reabsorbed until the uric acid is nearly dry, and thus the body can eliminate the waste without losing precious fluid. The evolutionary advantage, however, is not weight reduction. Rather, it allows the concentration and harmless storage of wastes until the bird hatches.

The embryos of birds, like those of reptiles, develop not in an aqueous medium (like the water of a lake or the amniotic fluid in the uterus) but in a gaseous medium. And nitrogenous wastes cannot be eliminated in the exchange of gases that occurs through the egg shell. Were it to accumulate inside the shell, urea would soon poison the developing bird, but uric acid, being insoluble, can be stored in a structure known as the allantois. Once the chick has hatched, the uric acid crystals are eliminated via the intestines.

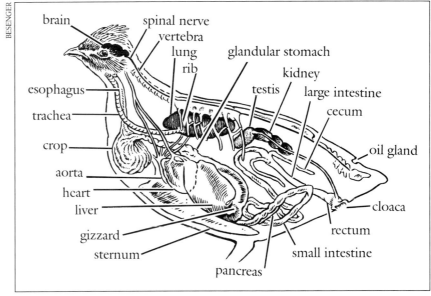

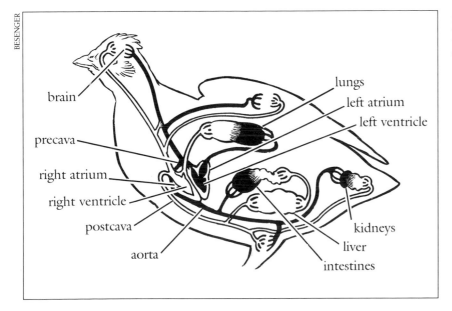

Above: *The low, stable center of gravity provided by a compact body cavity helps the grouse achieve balance in flight.* Left: *Only warm-blooded animals—mammals and birds—have separate arterial and venous pathways for blood.*

GAS EXCHANGE

Birds have a gas exchange system that is the most efficient among the vertebrates. Its primary function is the same—to obtain oxygen and eliminate carbon dioxide—but without special avian adaptations, the ruffed grouse could not burst into flight and reach top speed so quickly. The metabolic rate, the rate at which chemical and energy reactions take place within a bird, is higher than in other animals of comparable size, and this rapid expenditure of energy demands that oxygen be taken up instantaneously. A bird's complex system of air sacs and interconnecting tubes permits this by allowing for a more complete exchange of air. (A mammal's lungs, in contrast, retain a good amount of stale air even during exhalation.)

When the bird breathes, air passes from the nasal region through the mouth and pharynx, via the glottis through the larynx, and into the trachea. The trachea branches into two tubes—bronchi—which connect to the lungs. (In young birds, the trachea is reinforced by rings of cartilage, which turn into bone in adults. Although it may be possible to use the rings to distinguish between juvenile and adult birds, other methods of aging are easier.)

Each bronchus enters the ventral side of the lung, where it is termed a mesobronchus. From it develop four to six secondary tubes, the ventrobronchi, which in turn subdivide into parabronchi—the ultimate units for gas exchange.

This complex system of sacs and interconnecting tubes assures that the grouse will have sufficient oxygen to maintain its high metabolic rate.

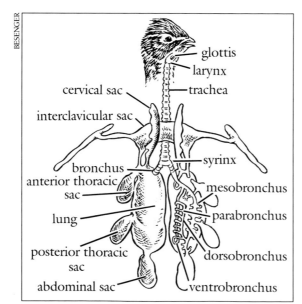

No one has counted the number of parabronchi in the lungs of the ruffed grouse, but a related bird, the domestic chicken, has about one thousand. Each parabronchus is a small tube—several millimeters long, half a millimeter in diameter—whose walls have openings, or air capillaries, that project into a network of blood capillaries. It is at this interface that oxygen diffuses into and carbon dioxide diffuses out of the blood capillaries.

The parabronchi are not a bird's only specialization. There are air sacs as well, nine of them, which act like reservoirs to ensure a continuous flow of air across the respiratory surfaces. These air sacs reach into different parts of the bird's body, but they are generally dorsal, a location that keeps the bird from becoming top-heavy and thus helps stabilize the animal in flight by lowering its center of gravity. They are thin-walled, with little musculature for expansion and contraction, and they have but a poor blood supply: hence they cannot be considered important in gas exchange. But they aerate the lungs and probably also help maintain body temperature by providing a site for internal evaporative cooling.

Each of the nine air sacs—four pairs plus one single—is connected to the lungs by the mesobronchi. The unpaired air sac, the interclavicular, sends its branches into the larger air-filled bones, such as the sternum, pectoral girdle, and humerus. The paired cervical air sacs are associated with the vertebrae of the neck. The prethoracic sacs are associated with the forward section of the chest. The posterior thoracic abdominal sacs supply the pneumatic bones of the legs, sacrum, and pelvic regions. In addition to the breathing tubes previously mentioned, each air sac (with the exception of the cervical air sacs) has recurrent bronchi or sacrobronchi that branch out into the lungs and the parabronchi for the exchange of air between the lungs and the air sacs.

The lungs are the center of the breathing system, where the exchange of oxygen and carbon dioxide between air and blood occurs. The lungs are small, highly vascularized, and relatively inelastic. They are attached to the ribs and the thorax. Birds, in contrast to mammals, possess two diaphragms, the pulmonary and the abdominal. The pulmonary diaphragm originates on the ventral surface of the vertebral column and inserts on the posterior region of the abdomen. Since the diaphragms of birds are not well developed, breathing depends on the movement of the body wall, especially the thoracic region.

A bird's breathing rate is regulated by the breathing center in the medulla region of the brain. The rate varies, depending on age, sex, body size, activity, temperature, time of day, and other factors. But birds do not breathe as rapidly as mammals of comparable size, probably because the large air sacs give birds a larger amount of fresh air per breath.

No voice to sing

*T*he ruffed grouse does not have the voice of a nightingale. In fact, it has hardly any voice at all. Its voice box—the syrinx, a structure found above the sternum at the junction of the trachea and bronchi—is a primitive instrument of the bronchial-tracheo type. In this type of syrinx, the last three to six rings at the base of the trachea enlarge to form the tympanum; to these are added two chambers consisting of the last two rings of each bronchi. The syrinx is supplied with muscles and vibrating membranes. The perfection of song is closely related to the number of syrinx muscles that act on these membranes and rings. Poor rings, such as those in the ruffed grouse, may have two or three pairs of syringeal muscles, while songbirds may have seven to nine.

Although its vocal organs are of a primitive type, the ruffed grouse, is capable of producing a wide variety of sounds, according to Bump and associates. When alarmed, a hen grouse emits a drawn-out nasal squeal or a hissing sound. Brooding hens produce a scolding call to quiet the chicks, or coo a low humming call to call them in. Other calls include a *cherp* call that resembles the common vocalization of a red squirrel, and a *pete-*

MARTINSON

pete-peta-peta that may be emitted prior to flushing. The *peta* call is not frequently heard by the hunter, probably because it is drowned out by the sound of the bird's wings when it takes flight.

The principal calls of grouse chicks include alarm, inquiry, and distress calls, all of which are variations of a basic *peep*. For the first two or three weeks after hatching, chicks emit an inquiry call that consists of two or three *peeps* in descending scale, each having a downward inflection. Older chicks emit a definite warning call, which consists of several notes in a descending pattern. The first two notes are rather sharp, while the others diminish progressively in intensity and length.

—Fred J. Brenner

Left: *Using soft clucks, the hen keeps her brood safely together.* Below: *The grouse's repertoire of sounds includes hissing, cooing, peeping, and scolding—all produced in the syrinx.*

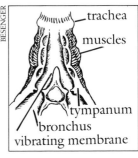

BESENGER

trachea
muscles
tympanum
bronchus
vibrating membrane

GROWTH, BREEDING, AND REPRODUCTION

The maturation, behaviors, and activities of breeding ruffed grouse begin with the pituitary, the "master gland" whose chemical secretions prompt other glands to produce their chemicals. These secretions, called hormones, are transported by the blood to target tissues. They can cause rapid growth of particular tissues, or stimulate or inhibit chemical processes. The pituitary can even instruct another gland to increase or decrease its production—which generally results in feedback to the pituitary, which in turn alters its instructions.

Located at the base of the midbrain behind the optic nerves, the pituitary, with help from the thyroid and adrenal glands and the pancreas, regulates metabolism. But it is especially important in the development and growth of the young bird and in reproduction.

During spring, the male ruffed grouse enters into the breeding season. The male's reproductive system consists of paired testes, each shaped like a lima bean, with the left testis commonly larger than the right. Certain cells in the testes, called Leydig cells, increase their production of male hormones, or androgens. It is these hormones that prompt the ruffed grouse to stake out his territory by drumming and begin courting the local hens.

The testes enlarge considerably, often to 200 or 300 times their off-season size. Each

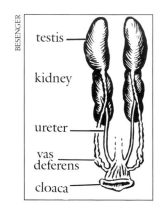

Above: *The testes are enlarged for the breeding season.*
Below: *The trip from ovary to nest takes twenty-four hours. On the way the ovum will acquire albumen and a shell.*

testis contains numerous tubules where sperm develop and, by vibrating their taillike flagella, move into the vas deferens, where they are stored until the bird finds a mate. The vas deferens enlarges for this purpose, especially at the caudal end next to the cloaca, and acts as a storage sac. At each copulation as many as four billion sperm cells may pass from male to female in the domestic chicken; the numbers for ruffed grouse are probably similar.

In the domestic chicken, sperm travel the length of the oviduct in as little as twenty-six minutes. The domestic hen, whose reproductive cycle is regulated by secretions of the ovary, usually lays her first egg seventy-two hours later.

Females can store sperm in the oviduct, but with seasonal breeders like the ruffed grouse, which lay only one clutch, one copulation suffices for the season. If the hen loses her clutch, a second mating may be necessary, depending on the length of time between breeding and the loss of her clutch. The longer she incubates or broods her young, the longer the interval until she can renest, if she renests at all.

The eggs begin as ova, released from the ovary in the middle of the hen's abdominal cavity. Only the left ovary develops; if it has been removed, the vestigial right ovary develops into a testis. The ovary also releases estrogen and progesterone, the hormones responsible for the development of secondary sex characteristics, such as the male's longer

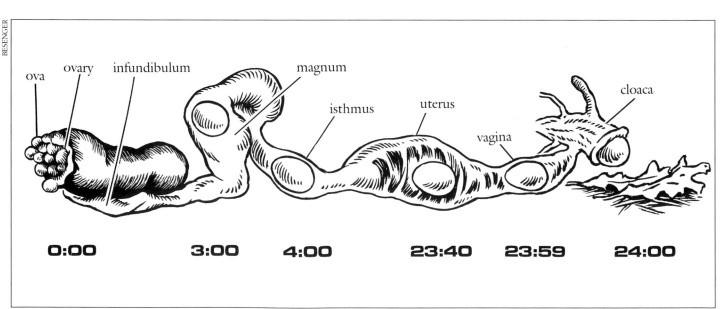

By constricting selected blood vessels, hormones from the adrenal gland increase blood pressure, ensuring a ready supply of oxygen and fuel to the flight muscles as the bird flushes.

hackles and darker ruff, as well as reproductive and parental behaviors. The ovary, like the testis, enlarges during the grouse's breeding season. At maturity, the ovarian follicles resemble a bunch of grapes, each of which is an ovum, ready to grow into the yolk of a mature egg under the direction of the follicle-stimulating hormone.

Once it reaches maturity, the ovum is released into the oviduct, usually within fifteen to seventy-five minutes after the laying of the preceding egg. As it moves down the oviduct, the ovum begins to look more and more like an egg: in the largest section of the oviduct, the magnum, it spends approximately three hours acquiring layers of albumen, or egg white; in the narrow isthmus it is encased in a shell membrane; in the muscular uterus the whole is surrounded by the limey shell, colored buff by the pigment glands. And finally the egg enters the vagina, whose muscular walls and mucous glands aid in its laying. Total time for an ovum to become an egg and land in the nest: approximately twenty-four hours.

Throughout breeding and brooding, hormones are involved. Thyroid hormone, which generally stimulates metabolism and is associated with normal growth and development of the young bird, increases egg production. Increased testicular activity by the drummer, on the other hand, appears to suppress the release of the thyroid stimulating hormone, which then slows down the thyroid. The changes apparently induce de-

Hormones released from the anterior pituitary and their functions

Gonadotropins

Follicle stimulating hormone (FSH)
Stimulates ovarian follicle and spermatogenesis

Lutenizing hormone (LH)
Stimulates interstitial cells of testis

Interstitial cell stimulating hormone
May be present; isolated in chickens and demonstrated in the pheasant

Thyroid stimulating hormone (TSH)
Stimulates the thyroid

Adrenocorticotropic hormone (ACTH)
Stimulates adrenal interrenal tissue

Prolactin
Stimulates maternal behavior

creases in the level of hormones, the size of the gonads, and the production of sperm or ova; this gonadal regression occurs despite artificial increases in daylight.

In the hen, a secretion of the pituitary, called oxytocin, induces the contraction of the oviduct to expel the egg. The thymus gland, whose primary function is the formation of white blood cells, enlarges during the breeding season in sexually mature birds, suggesting the existence of some as-yet-unknown hormonal function. The adrenal glands, too, have sexual functions: their gonadoid secretions can cause male characteristics to develop in female chickens; their removal results in a shrinking of the testes and atrophy of the cock's comb; and adrenal steroids, or cortisone, cause testicular enlargement and stimulate the production of androgens.

The hormones for which the adrenal glands are most noted, however, have nothing to do with sex and are not controlled by the pituitary. They are adrenalin and noradrenalin, both regulated by the sympathetic nervous tissue. In an emergency—say, at the first sighting of an English setter—a ruffed grouse needs to concentrate all its faculties and forces on its survival. Adrenalin constricts blood vessels primarily in the skeletal and heart muscles, while noradrenalin constricts blood vessels in all parts of the body: the two thus act together to increase blood pressure. Blood sugar level goes up as glycogen in the liver is converted to glucose and released into the bloodstream. Action in the digestive system decreases. The heart rate increases. As the bird explodes into flight, the rush of adrenalin continues, enabling the bloodstream to carry the glucose and oxygen needed by the flight muscles as their contractions accelerate and the bird wings to safety.

—*Fred J. Brenner*

MARTINSON

Breakout

MARTINSON

A point on top of the beak enables the tiny chick to peck and hammer a way out of its shell prison.

An eggshell is such a fragile thing that commercial producers package each egg in its own Styrofoam nest, and supermarket checkout clerks tenderly lay the carton of a dozen on top of all a shopper's other groceries. For the ruffed grouse chick, however, an eggshell is a secure prison, and breaking out requires two special adaptations.

The first is an egg tooth, a short, pointed, horny projection on the upper mandible; the second is a pair of hatching muscles, located on the upper neck and back. The muscles reach their maximum size the day before hatching, when they enable the chick to propel its head and egg tooth upward against the inside of the shell. Thus the puncturing, or pipping, of the shell begins. Both the egg tooth and the muscles disappear after they have served their functions.

—Fred J. Brenner

Facts and figures

The skeleton of the ruffed grouse, with its hollow ilium, humerus, coracoid, scapula, and femur, is the lightest of all the grouse.

Unique to the ruffed grouse are the cutaneous muscles under the ruff feather tracts, which erect these feathers into the characteristic ruff.

The heart weighs between 1.3 and 3.7 grams. If the grouse is at rest, it beats 342 times per minute.

Respiration rate is 63 breaths per minute.

The esophagus is highly elastic and can pass foods as large as 1.5 centimeters in diameter: acorns, for example, and hawthorn fruits. The crop, too, is elastic. It commonly contains 30 to 45 grams of food—about 5 to 7 percent of body weight—but in 1947 Bump reported that one grouse's crop contained no less than 153 cubic centimeters of food, which was probably at least twice the normal amount.

After being stored in the crop, food is ground in the bird's gizzard, typically 3 to 4 centimeters long. This organ usually weighs 15 to 16 grams, but weights may vary from 10 to 26 grams. Like all muscles, the gizzard increases in size with increases in activity. Although not studied specifically in grouse, the gizzard in related species undergoes changes in weight when the bird eats more food and especially more fiber.

The small intestine is highly coiled, varying in length from 81 to 106 centimeters. At the junction of the small and large intestines are the openings to the ceca, two long, cylindrical pockets typically 0.5 to 1 centimeter in diameter and 37 to 57 centimeters long. Cecal length changes seasonally, appar-ently in response to changes in the quality of the bird's forage. Six to eight folds inside each cecum increase the area available for absorption of nutrients. The ceca typically appear green or gray because the contents are visible through the thin cecal walls.

The cecum evacuates whatever is not digestible into the large intestine two or three times per day. The large intestine, which measures about 11 centimeters in length, widens into the cloaca, which also receives material from the ureters and, in hens, the oviduct. In related species, and presumably in the ruffed grouse, the lengths of both large and small intestines change with seasonal variations in diet.

Recessed in the dorsal wall along the vertebrae are the kidneys, which may weigh 2.1 to 5.5 grams. The liver may range from 6.1 to 9.7 grams.

The testes, which weigh a half-gram most of the year, increase to 1 to 1.7 grams during the breeding season. The female reproductive organs undergo a much more dramatic transformation, from 0.2 gram in the off-season to twenty or thirty times that—about 19 grams—in the breeding season. During egg laying, the ovaries contain twenty or more easily visible follicles in various stages of development. The largest are typically 5 to 12 millimeters in diameter. When a follicle ovulates to begin the final stages of egg development, a visible follicle sheath, or sac, is left behind on the ovary, making the ovulated follicle easy to identify. The sheath eventually degenerates.

—Frederick A. Servello and
Roy Kirkpatrick

Diseases and parasites: Enemies within

Ruffed grouse are susceptible to infection by a variety of diseases and parasites, and although occurrence is well documented, the influence of these diseases and parasites on wild ruffed grouse populations is uncertain. The actual amount of mortality due to these agents is virtually impossible to determine, simply because most wild birds that die as a result are not discovered by people. Nevertheless, as factors that impinge on the health and the survival of ruffed grouse, diseases and parasites are important to researchers studying the population dynamics of the species, to wildlife managers attempting to restore this grouse to portions of its historic range, and to sportsmen, naturalists, and bird-watchers concerned with the numbers and vitality of this handsome bird.

NUTRITIONAL DISEASES

Wild birds typically receive adequate nutrients from natural foods. Although ruffed grouse diet quality may vary among regions (Servello 1985), nutritional deficiencies or excesses typically do not result in disease. Grouse may actually select more nutritious foods and prefer feeding on male aspen buds with higher protein and potassium contents (Doerr et al. 1974), or they may select foods so as to avoid protective plant chemicals (Bryant and Kuropat 1980). Still, visceral gout, which may result from nutritional factors as well as from other causes, has been

Ruffed grouse are beset by diseases and parasites, some relatively minor, others fatal.

reported. In a wild ruffed grouse from Vancouver, British Columbia, the cloaca and the ureters were filled with a white, pasty mass, and the heart and the liver were covered with white deposits of uric acid salts (Cowan and Fowle 1944). The primary lesions were associated with the kidney, which was pale, slightly enlarged, and covered with many fine white spots. Visceral gout is caused by kidney failure, which may result from excess dietary protein, toxic levels of calcium, vitamin A deficiency, toxins, or infectious diseases.

TOXICOLOGIC DISEASES

The devastating effects of environmental toxicants and contaminants on wild birds, particularly birds of prey, are well recognized. Ruffed grouse may also be exposed to these compounds. In addition, because ruffed grouse are neither migratory nor wide-ranging, they may be valuable in the comparison of contaminant levels of specific areas or regions.

Blevins (1979) tested muscle tissue of ruffed grouse from eastern Tennessee for concentrations of organochlorine (OC) pesticides. Organochlorine pesticides, such as DDT, dieldrin, endrin, and lindane, were widely used beginning in the late 1940s. Because of their persistence in the environment and their detrimental effects on both people and wildlife, most have since been banned or restricted in the United States. Blevins detected several OC compounds in grouse muscle and noted that the levels of dieldrin and endrin were elevated. Elevated levels of OC compounds are often associated with long-term disease, especially reproductive problems in heavily contaminated species. Such problems have not been found in ruffed grouse.

Neave and Wright (1969) reported that DDT, which had been aerially applied to control spruce budworm in New Brunswick, was associated with significantly smaller ruffed grouse broods in June. Grouse chicks appeared to be most vulnerable during their first few weeks because they fed heavily on contaminated insects. Age ratios in the fall disclosed fewer immature birds in areas sprayed with DDT than in unsprayed areas. The authors attributed these differences to the loss of entire broods on sprayed areas.

Ruffed grouse exposed to copper, nickel, and iron emissions from smelters in Ontario, Canada, exhibited higher concentrations of metallic elements in feathers (Rose and Parker 1982) and body tissues, food items consumed, and feces (Rose and Parker 1983) than in ruffed grouse from uncontaminated environments (Scanlon et al. 1980; Kendall et al. 1984; Parker 1985). The effects of these elevated levels were uncertain.

TUMORS

Tumors, or neoplasms, are reported infrequently in free-flying birds and probably are an insignificant source of mortality in most wild avian populations. Only a few tumors have been reported in ruffed grouse. An adult female grouse with a large fibrous mass that involved the bone and the skin of one foot was diagnosed as having a chondrosarcoma, or malignant tumor of the bone and cartilage (Siegfried 1983). Howerth et al. (1986) reported tumors in three hunter-killed ruffed grouse. A soft, yellow-white mass that was diagnosed as a lipoma, or fatty tumor, was found on one leg of a female grouse from Rabun County, Georgia. An adult female from Botetourt County, Virginia, had a subcutaneous nodule at the corner of the right eye; the firm, white mass, which did not involve the skin or the underlying muscle, was diagnosed as a fibroma durum, or hard, fibrous tumor. An adult female ruffed grouse from Greenbrier County, West Virginia, with tumorous masses in the liver and the kidney, was diagnosed as having a renal carcinoma, or malignant tumor of the kidney.

VIRAL DISEASES

The only viral disease known to strike ruffed grouse is avian pox, and this condition has been reported very rarely. Avian pox viruses occur in a wide variety of birds from virtually all orders. Avian pox was diagnosed in a single hunter-harvested ruffed grouse from Wayne County, West Virginia; the bird was submitted to the Southeastern Cooperative Wildlife Disease Study in January 1983. Blood-feeding insects, especially mosquitoes, are important mechanical vectors of avian pox viruses in other birds, but inhalation or ingestion of virus-contaminated scabs shed from lesions can also spread this disease. Avian pox infection is characterized by discrete, cream-colored nodules that are usually restricted to the oral cavity, unfeathered areas of the head and the legs, or the respiratory tract. Birds often have lesions only on the skin of the head, feet, or legs, or only in the oral cavity; however, occasionally both skin and oral or respiratory lesions occur in a single bird. Depending on their severity and location, pox lesions may cause vision impairment, respiratory distress, emaciation, and weakness. Lesions in the bird from West Virginia were proliferative masses around one eye.

Wild ruffed grouse populations are almost certainly subject to infection by many other avian viruses. The entire field of viral diseases has been inadequately investigated during studies of disease in ruffed grouse, and these viral diseases should receive more attention in future work on this species.

BACTERIAL DISEASES

Several bacterial diseases, including avian tuberculosis, ulcerative enteritis, fowl cholera, and tularemia, have been reported in ruffed grouse. Such reports are rare, however, and these diseases are not known to be important causes of death in wild grouse populations. Under confinement conditions associated with captive propagation, bacterial diseases can result in heavy mortality, but such large-scale effects have not been noted in wild ruffed grouse populations.

Avian tuberculosis is a chronic, contagious disease caused by organisms in the genus *Mycobacterium* and is spread by infective feces. The tubercle bacilli shed from ulcerated lesions in the intestines and the liver and from infections in the respiratory tract are responsible for transmission of the disease. In the soil, these bacilli can persist several years (Schalk et al. 1935). Avian tuberculosis has been reported in ruffed grouse from New England and the Lake States (Gross 1925; Snoeyenbos 1966). Diagnosed as having tuberculosis, a hunter-killed ruffed grouse from Massachusetts was emaciated, and the liver and the spleen were enlarged with numerous small, yellowish gray nodules

A hard, fibrous tumor obstructs the vision of this ruffed grouse hen. Such tumors are rare.

Avian pox, a viral disease, can cause lesions in the skin and in the respiratory tract.

(Snoeyenbos 1966). Similar nodules were also found in the lungs and the peritoneum, and *Mycobacterium* bacilli were evident in smears from the nodules. Infection may have been attained from poultry, for the grouse was killed in a woodlot near several residences that may have maintained flocks of free-ranging chickens. This disease is probably uncommon in wild birds not exposed to farms.

Ulcerative enteritis, also known as quail disease, is an acute, bacterial disease that is infectious to a wide variety of galliform birds but has been reported only in pen-reared ruffed grouse (Levine 1932). This disease is transmitted when birds ingest food or water contaminated by feces containing the bacterium *Clostridium colini*. Birds dying acutely may not exhibit obvious signs of disease and may have normal muscle tone and fat deposits. The intestines and ceca may become inflamed and ulcerated. Ulcers, which appear as small, yellow foci with hemorrhagic borders, may penetrate the intestinal wall, resulting in peritonitis. Liver lesions may include irregular areas of dead tissue, and the spleen may be enlarged and reddened with hemorrhage. Ulcerative enteritis appears to be primarily a disease of confinement that occurs occasionally in captive galliform birds and apparently is very rare among wild, free-ranging birds.

Fowl cholera is an infectious disease caused by the bacterium *Pasteurella multocida*. Fowl cholera occurs rarely in wild ruffed grouse, and *P. multocida* has been isolated from only one wild bird (Green and Shillinger 1936). Cholera is transmitted through bacteria-laden excretions of the mouth, rectum, or nares. Lesions associated with the disease in most species of birds typically include small hemorrhages of the heart and the gizzard, and a liver studded with focal spots of necrosis. Occasionally, the lungs may become firm as the air spaces fill with exudate and fluid.

Tularemia, caused by the bacterium *Francisella tularensis,* is often spread by biting arthropods. Tularemia vectors include the rabbit tick *(Haemaphysalis leporispalustris)* and the common bird tick *(H. chordeilis),* both of which have been found on ruffed grouse. Lesions typical of tularemia were described in a ruffed grouse from St. Louis County,

Minnesota, and cultures from the bird yielded *F. tularensis* (Green and Shillinger 1932). Tularemia is more commonly associated with mammals, particularly rabbits. Although this disease has been reported to occur among many wild game birds, including bobwhite quail, sage grouse, sharp-tailed grouse, and ruffed grouse, it has not been verified as a cause of significant losses (Shillinger and Morley 1937). Birds with tularemia reportedly exhibit gradual weakening prior to death. Characteristic lesions of tularemia are white or yellowish white spots on the liver and the spleen, both on the surface and the interior of the organs. Lesions may include darker coloration of lungs, liver, and spleen, and the spleen may be enlarged.

FUNGAL DISEASES

Only one fungal disease, aspergillosis, has been reported in ruffed grouse. Although more commonly observed in waterfowl, aspergillosis has been observed in a variety of wild birds, including ruffed grouse (Gross 1925; SCWDS unpublished data). The disease is transmitted when a bird inhales spores of the fungus *Aspergillus fumigatus* from moldy food or surroundings. Infection may be acute, but observations suggest that in wild birds the disease more often is chronic, with gradual weakening and death. Obvious signs of the disease include gasping, droopiness, emaciation, and possibly diarrhea. The disease typically affects the respiratory tract and may also involve the air sacs and the abdominal organs. Fungal plaques, which may resemble bread mold, form on air sacs and in the lungs as well as on the surface of the liver and other organs. Aspergillosis typically is a sporadic disease of individual birds and is not important at the population level.

PROTOZOAN PARASITES

Ruffed grouse are susceptible to infection by several species of minute, one-celled animals. Most of these protozoans are not considered harmful, but some may cause diseases such as histomoniasis or coccidiosis. The importance of these diseases in wild populations is largely unknown, although they can cause substantial mortality in captive grouse as well as other species of gallinaceous birds.

Histomoniasis, a disease caused by the protozoan *Histomonas meleagridis,* has not been reported from wild grouse but was a major disease problem during early captive propagation efforts (Bump et al. 1947). The disease, which is also known as blackhead disease, is severe in captive ruffed grouse with morbidity and mortality rates often more than 75 percent. Characteristic lesions are found in the ceca and the liver. Cecal walls become ulcerated, hemorrhagic, and swollen, and large plugs of yellowish debris, called cecal cores, fill the ceca. The liver often has numerous discrete, circular lesions with depressed gray centers. These lesions often become larger and white to yellow as damaged liver tissue becomes fibrous.

Histomonas meleagridis has a complex life cycle and utilizes a worm parasite as a vector. The histomonads infect the ovary of the cecal worm, *Heterakis gallinarum,* and become incorporated within the worm eggs. Cecal worm eggs are passed in the droppings, and birds become infected by ingesting worm eggs containing the cecal worm larvae and histomonads. Earthworms also contribute to transmission by storing cecal worm larvae and histomonads in their bodies when they feed on soil containing droppings from infected birds. Birds may become infected by ingesting these earthworms. Avian species that are tolerant of infection, such as pheasants and chickens, are inapparent carriers and serve as a source of infection for other birds.

Coccidiosis is a disease of the digestive tract caused by any of a group of protozoans called coccidia. These parasites, particularly those of the common genus *Eimeria,* are very host specific, and most occur in only one host species. Three such parasites have been found in ruffed grouse: *Eimeria angusta* and *E. bonasae* infect the ceca, and *E. dispersa* occurs in the small intestine (Boughton and Volk 1938; Hardcastle 1943; Todd and Hammond 1971). Crowded conditions, like those of captive propagation programs, favor the spread and buildup of high levels of coccidia, but such conditions are not likely to be encountered by wild birds.

Birds become infected when they ingest the infective coccidian stage, called oocysts. The coccidia undergo a period of growth

A fungus, Aspergillus fumigatus, causes the formation of a fungal plaque resembling bread mold.

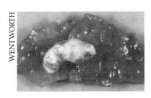

Histomoniasis is a serious and often fatal disease. Yellowish debris may fill the ceca.

Necrotic lesions damage the liver of a ruffed grouse afflicted by histomoniasis.

and multiplication within the epithelial cells lining the intestinal tract, and as the parasites multiply, they damage these cells. The coccidia produce oocysts that are passed with the birds' droppings. Under appropriate environmental conditions, which include sufficient moisture, temperature, and oxygen, the oocysts develop into the infective stage. They do not survive dessication caused by direct sunlight but are persistent in moist soil. Oocysts can also tolerate freezing during moderate winters and, when thawed, can infect new hosts.

Although coccidia may be readily detected by microscopic examination of the feces, clinical signs and lesions have not been identified in infected wild ruffed grouse, and coccidiosis probably is not an important source of mortality in the wild. Barker et al. (1984) experimentally infected immature ruffed grouse with *Eimeria angusta* obtained from a naturally infected ruffed grouse. Attempts to infect mature grouse were unsuccessful. The young experimental birds developed diarrhea, occasional blood-tinged cecal droppings, depression, and loss of appetite. Lesions were restricted to the cecal epithelium and included small hemorrhages, fibrinous exudate adhering to the mucosa, thickening of the mucosa, and erosion of the surface epithelium. Although the captive ruffed grouse that was the source of *E. angusta* died of coccidiosis, none of the experimentally infected birds died as a result of the coccidian parasites.

Four genera of protozoan parasites have been found in the blood of ruffed grouse. *Leucocytozoon, Haemoproteus,* and *Plasmodium* occur within the circulating blood cells, and *Trypanosoma* organisms are found in the fluid portion of the blood. All are transmitted by one or more blood-feeding arthropods, such as blackflies, biting midges, mosquitoes, and possibly louse flies. The protozoans are ingested and reproduce within the arthropod vector. After a period of development, the parasites move to the arthropod's mouthparts and are transferred to an avian host when the insect feeds. Within the bird, the protozoans continue to develop in such internal organs as the liver, the spleen, and the lungs (*Leucocytozoon*), in the cells lining the vessels of these organs (*Haemoproteus*), or

within both the internal organs and the blood (*Plasmodium* and *Trypanosoma*). The protozoans then enter the circulating blood. Although blood protozoans are commonly found in ruffed grouse and their prevalence, particularly of *Leucocytozoon* and *Haemoproteus,* can be high in some populations of ruffed grouse (Erickson 1953; Bennett and Fallis 1960; Dorney and Todd 1960; Eve and Davidson 1976), they have yet to be associated with any significant diseases.

HELMINTH PARASITES

Numerous flukes, tapeworms, and roundworms live within ruffed grouse, but with the exception of the stomach worm, *Dispharynx nasuta,* and the tracheal worm, *Syngamus trachea,* most are not considered pathogenic. Nevertheless, several are obvious because of their size or location.

The eye worm, *Oxyspirura petrowi,* is a conspicuous slender, white or cream roundworm up to 12 millimeters long, found beneath the nictitating membrane of the eye. Occasionally, eyeworm infections may produce inflammation and watering of the eye, and the nictitating membrane may become swollen. The eyelids may stick together with a pasty matter collecting beneath the lids, and in severe cases, damage to the eye may result. Preoccupation with the worms or vision impairment may increase susceptibility of infected ruffed grouse to predation.

Transmission occurs when a bird ingests an intermediate host, such as a cockroach, containing infective larvae. The larvae are released in the bird's crop and travel up the esophagus to the mouth and through the nasolacrimal duct to the eye. A mature female lays eggs in the eye; the eggs are then washed down the tear ducts, swallowed, and passed out with the droppings. The eggs are ingested by an invertebrate intermediate host and develop into infective larvae within the invertebrate's body (Sanders 1927).

The tracheal worm or gapeworm, *Syngamus trachea,* is a large red worm found attached to the mucous membrane of the trachea. This helminth is sometimes called the Y or forked worm because the small, 6-millimeter-long male is permanently attached to the 20-millimeter-long female in a Y configuration. The female gapeworm deposits eggs in the bird's trachea; the eggs are coughed up, swallowed, and passed out with the droppings. In moist, shaded soil, eggs develop to contain infective larvae, or in some cases the larvae hatch. Such invertebrates as earthworms or snails may ingest and store some of these eggs and larvae within their bodies. Birds are infected when they ingest eggs or larvae directly, or when they eat infected invertebrates. Once in the bird, the larvae quickly migrate to the lungs and continue their development. Adult males and females pair and attach to each other in the lungs before moving up the bronchi to the trachea.

Gapeworms can mechanically block the trachea, causing death by suffocation. Infections are most detrimental in young birds, which become emaciated and often stand with their eyes closed and mouths open, gasping for air. This gasping is sometimes referred to as the "gapes," hence the name *gapeworm*. Lesions attributed to the tracheal worm are mild to severe tracheitis with nodules in tracheal tissues. This parasite is widely distributed and may cause disease and mortality in free-ranging poultry and pen-raised game birds. Intensity of infection in wild ruffed grouse is typically low, and gapeworms are probably not an important cause of mortality.

The stomach worm, *Dispharynx nasuta,* is probably the most pathogenic parasite harbored by ruffed grouse (Goble and Kutz 1945; Bump et al. 1947). This short (7 to 10 millimeters), thick, frequently coiled roundworm occurs in the proventriculus or glandular stomach of many species of birds, particularly the terrestrial galliforms and the perching songbirds, or passeriforms.

Within the proventriculus, a mature female lays her eggs, which are passed out with the droppings. After ingestion by a pill bug or sow bug intermediate host, the eggs hatch and develop into infective larvae. Ruffed grouse and other hosts are infected by ingesting the infected intermediate host, and the larvae are released in the bird's proventriculus, where they develop into adults.

Lesions associated with *D. nasuta* vary with intensity of infection; larger numbers of worms generally cause more severe damage to the proventriculus. Only a few

Eimeria dispersa
coccidia

BESENGER

Brachylecithum orfi
fluke

Raillietina tetragona
tapeworm

Ascaridia bonasae
roundworm

A large white roundworm is commonly found in the small intestine. Its name reflects its incidence in Bonasa umbellus, the ruffed grouse: Ascaridia bonasae.

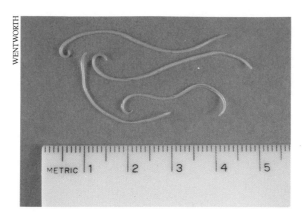

worms, however, may cause problems (Bump et al. 1947; Davidson et al. 1977; Marquenski 1986). Lesions often include hemorrhages and ulcers in the stomach wall where the parasite attaches, necrosis and sloughing of the mucosa, thickening of the stomach wall, and damage to surrounding glandular and muscular tissue. Damaged, sloughing tissues may partially or completely occlude passage of food through the stomach, and infected birds may become emaciated and weak. Stomach worms may cause death of grouse directly or may increase susceptibility to other mortality factors, such as predation.

The gizzard worm, *Cheilospirura spinosa*, is found beneath the lining of the gizzard. This roundworm, which may measure 20 to 40 millimeters long, is easily seen when the hard gizzard lining is removed. The parasite's eggs are shed in the feces of infected birds and ingested by grasshoppers that serve as intermediate hosts. Larvae hatch and encyst in the muscles of the legs and body cavities of the grasshoppers. Grouse then eat the grasshoppers and the cycle continues.

Light gizzard worm infections produce relatively minor lesions, but pathways made by the parasite's movements may be evident between the gizzard lining and muscle. Heavy infestations can cause hemorrhage and necrosis of the gizzard lining as well as damage to the musculature (Stafseth and Kotlan 1925; Bump 1947; Ruff 1984). The low levels found in wild grouse, however, have not been associated with mortality.

The large white roundworm, *Ascaridia bonasae*, is commonly found in the small intestine of ruffed grouse. Adult male worms may reach 35 millimeters in length, and females, 50 millimeters. In the small intestine,

mature females lay eggs that are passed in the feces. The eggs develop to the infective stage under warm, moist environmental conditions, but the eggs do not tolerate extreme temperatures or dessication. Grouse become infected with ascarid roundworms when they ingest eggs that they pick up during feeding. The eggs hatch in the proventriculus or the intestine, and the larvae develop in the mucosa and interior of the intestine.

Although one of the most common and easily found internal parasites of ruffed grouse, *A. bonasae* is not considered pathogenic. Even large numbers of these roundworms do not produce apparent lesions.

The cecal worm, *Heterakis isolonche* (synonymous with *Heterakis bonasae*) is a short, white roundworm found in the ceca of ruffed grouse mainly from the southern portions of the grouse range. Mature female worms deposit their eggs in the ceca, and the eggs are shed with the droppings. Although the eggs can survive freezing temperatures and prolonged periods in the soil, development of the larvae to the infective stage occurs with average temperatures and moisture. Earthworms may ingest cecal worm eggs and store the larvae within their bodies. The larvae do not develop further while in the earthworm; therefore, the earthworms serve as transport hosts for the parasite. Transmission of cecal worms occurs when infective eggs or larvae-containing earthworms are ingested by grouse. The larvae are released in the upper part of the intestine and quickly move to the ceca, where they mature.

Although infections in grouse may involve hundreds of worms, they typically cause no remarkable lesions or significant damage in the ceca. Primary importance of this parasite to ruffed grouse is as a potential vector for the transmission of the histomonad protozoan *Histomonas meleagridis* that causes histomoniasis, or blackhead disease. *Heterakis isolonche*, which typically infects ruffed grouse, has not been proven to transmit this histomonad. Grouse are, however, susceptible to infection by *H. gallinarum*, the common cecal worm of domestic poultry and pen-raised game birds, which is known to transmit the protozoan. Pen-raised grouse and wild grouse in contact with domestic poultry or game birds or poultry litter may acquire histomoniasis from these sources.

Brachylecithum orfi is a small (5 to 11 millimeters) slender, fluke found in the bile ducts of the liver. The life cycle of *B. orfi* probably requires two intermediate hosts (Kingston 1965). Eggs deposited by mature flukes are carried in the bile to the intestine and are shed in the feces. The eggs are initially ingested by snails, and the larvae hatch in the digestive tract of the snail. The larvae develop within the snail before exiting through the respiratory pore and being deposited in slimeballs on the ground or vegetation. A second intermediate host, probably an arthropod, then ingests the larvae, and a ruffed grouse becomes infected with flukes when it eats this arthropod. The flukes burrow into the bird's intestinal wall and make their way to the liver, where they develop into adults.

These flukes can cause the bile ducts to become enlarged and fibrous. Infection in the liver is not readily apparent, but on close examination the large bile ducts surrounded by yellow, bile-stained rings may be noticeable. Although these parasites produce some tissue damage in the liver, they are not considered detrimental to the health of wild grouse.

EXTERNAL PARASITES

A variety of fleas, ticks, mites, lice, and louse flies are found on the skin and the feathers of ruffed grouse. One of the more common ectoparasites, the louse fly *(Lynchia americana)* has a flattened, brownish-gray body and rather long wings. These winged parasitic flies move rapidly through the feathers and have been called flying ticks. While on their avian host, adult louse flies mate, and the eggs develop within the female to contain larvae. The female probably leaves the host to deposit the larvae on nearby vegetation or leaf litter. The pupae develop, metamorphose into winged flies, and seek out suitable avian hosts.

Louse flies are found on a variety of birds from several orders. No pathologic effects have been ascribed to this parasite. Although louse flies often fly quickly from the carcasses of dead grouse, hunters handling the dead birds may see these flies, which may alight on people.

Ceratophyllus diffinis
flea

BESENGER

Lynchia americana
louse fly

Liponyssus sylvarium
mite

Haemaphysalis chordeilis
tick

SUMMARY

A great variety and number of diseases and parasites have been found in ruffed grouse. Although several infectious diseases have caused substantial mortality of grouse during captive propagation efforts, they have not been associated with significant disease losses among wild ruffed grouse populations. Most parasitic infections are considered non-pathogenic or mildly pathogenic and, with the exceptions of the stomach worm and the gapeworm, probably do not cause mortality directly. Although disease and parasitism have often been suggested as potential factors causing periodic fluctuations of ruffed grouse populations, scientific evidence is insufficient to confirm or refute these theories. Future research should focus on the impact of pathogens on populations rather than simply cataloging what occurs. An especially fruitful area should be better delineation of infectious diseases.

—Emily Jo Wentworth and
William R. Davidson

Parasites of the ruffed grouse

The presence of parasites on grouse can be noted but their impact hard to determine. The information below is based largely on Bump et al. (1947), Braun and Willers (1967), and Davidson et al. (1977).

	Location in host	Distribution	Pathogenicity	Intermediate hosts
Protozoans				
Eimeria angusta	cecum	Alaska, Minnesota, Labrador	★ ★ ★	none
Eimeria bonasae	cecum	Alaska, Maine, Minnesota, Labrador, Quebec	★	none
Eimeria dispersa	intestine	Minnesota	★	none
Haemoproteus canachites	blood	Kentucky, Michigan, West Virginia	★	culicoid midge
Haemoproteus sp.	blood	Wisconsin, Ontario	★	culicoid midge
Histomonas meleagrides	cecum, liver	New York	★ ★ ★ ★	cecal worm, earthworm
Leucocytozoon bonasae	blood	Kentucky, Michigan, Minnesota, West Virginia	★ ★	blackfly
Leucocytozoon sp	blood	Wisconsin, Alberta, Ontario	★	blackfly
Plasmodium circumflexum	blood	Maine	★	mosquito
Plasmodium sp.	blood	Wisconsin, Ontario	★	mosquito
Trichomonas bonasae	crop, esophagus	New England	★ ★ ★ ★	none
Trypanosoma gallinarum	blood	Michigan, Ontario	★	mosquito, blackfly
Trypanosoma sp.	blood	Minnesota, Wisconsin, Ontario	★	mosquito, blackfly
Flukes				
Agamodistomum sp.	muscle cysts	Minnesota	unknown	snail
Athesmia heterolecithodes	liver	West Virginia	★ ★	snail
Brachylaima virginiana	cecum	Kentucky, Michigan, New York, West Virginia	★	snail
Brachylaima fuscata	cecum	Alaska, Michigan, Minnesota, New Hampshire, New York, Ontario	★	snail
Brachylecithum orfi	liver	Michigan, Minnesota, Alberta, Ontario	★ ★	snail
Echinoparyphium aconiatum	intestine	Minnesota	★ ★	snail
Echinoparyphium recurvatum	intestine	Michigan	★ ★	snail, tadpole
Echinoparyphium sp.	intestine	Maine	★ ★	snail
Echinostoma revolutum	intestine	Michigan	★ ★	snail, tadpole
Glaphyrostomum sp.	intestine	Labrador	unknown	snail, insect
Leuchochloridium pricei	cloaca, rectum	Maine, New Hampshire	★	snail
Lyperosomum monenteron	liver	Minnesota	★	snail
Prosthogonimus macrorchis	cloaca	New Hampshire, Lake States	★	snail, dragonfly
Prosthogonimus sp.	cloaca	Michigan	unknown	snail, dragonfly
Strigea sp.	intestine	Michigan, Minnesota	unknown	snail
Tanasia zarudnyi	kidney	Michigan, Ontario	★	snail
Tetracotyle bonasae	muscle cysts	Minnesota	unknown	snail

	Location in host	Distribution	Pathogenicity	Intermediate hosts
Tapeworms				
Choanotaenia infundibulum	intestine	Minnesota	★	fly
Davainea proglottina	intestine	Minnesota, New Hampshire, Labrador	★ ★	snail
Davainea tetraoensis	intestine	New York, Michigan, West Virginia, Alberta, Ontario	★ ★	snail
Hymenolepis carioca	intestine	New Hampshire	★	beetle
Hymenolepis microps	intestine	New York, Ontario	★	beetle
Hymenolepis sp.	intestine	Michigan, Minnesota, New York, West Virginia	unknown	beetle
Raillietina tetragona	intestine	Minnesota, New York, New Hampshire, Alberta, Ontario	★ ★ ★	fly, ant
Raillietina sp.	intestine	West Virginia	unknown	fly, ant
Rhabdometra nullicolis	intestine	Alberta	★	unknown
Roundworms				
Ascaridia bonasae	intestine	Georgia, Kentucky, Maine, Michigan, Minnesota, Missouri, New York, Washington, West Virginia	★ ★ ★	earthworm, grasshopper
Aproctella stoddardi	body cavity	New England, Michigan		unknown
Capillaria annulata	crop	New England, Michigan	★ ★	earthworm
Capillaria caudinflata	crop	Georgia, Maine, Michigan, New York, West Virginia	★ ★	earthworm
Cheilospirura spinosa	gizzard	New England, Michigan, Minnesota, Washington, West Virginia	★ ★ ★	grasshopper
Contracaecum sp.	intestine	unknown	unknown	none
Dispharynx nasuta	stomach	New England, Michigan, Wisconsin, West Virginia, Nova Scotia	★ ★ ★	pillbug, sow bug
Diplotriaenoides sp.	air sacs	Michigan	★	grasshopper
Gongylonema sp.	crop	West Virginia	★	insect
Heterakis bonasae	cecum	Georgia, Kentucky, Michigan, Minnesota, New York, Pennsylvania, West Virginia	★	earthworm, sow bug
Oxyspirura petrowi	eye	Michigan, Minnesota, West Virginia	★ ★	cockroach
Oxyspirura mansoni	eye	unreported	★ ★	cockroach
Physaloptera sp.	muscle cysts	Minnesota	★	none
Strongyloides sp.	intestine	New York, West Virginia	unknown	none
Subulura strongylina	cecum	Minnesota, New York	★	beetle
Syngamus trachea	trachea	New York, West Virginia	★ ★	earthworm
Fleas				
Ceratophyllus diffinis	feathers	Alaska, New Hampshire, Alberta, British Columbia, Labrador, Ontario	★	none
Ceratophyllus garei	feathers	Alaska, New Hampshire, Alberta, British Columbia, Labrador, Ontario	★	none
Lice and louse flies				
Goniodes corpulentis	feathers	Ontario	★	none
Goniodes bonasus	feathers	Colorado, Montana, New York	★	none
Goniocotes sp.	feathers	Massachusetts, New Hampshire	★	none
Gallipeurus cameratus	feathers	Ontario	★	none
Lagopoecus perplexus	feathers	Idaho, New York, Pennsylvania, Ontario	★	none
Lagopoecus umbellus	feathers	Idaho, New York, Ontario	★	none
Lipeurus perplexus	feathers	New York, Pennsylvania	★	none
Lynchia americana	feathers	New England, Ontario	★	none
Ornithoica vicina	feathers	New York	★	none
Mites				
Cnemidocoptes mutans	feathers, skin	British Columbia	★ ★	none
Laelaptinae	feathers, skin	New Hampshire	★	none
Liponyssus sylvarium	feathers, skin	Maine, Quebec	★	none
Megninia sp.	feathers, skin	New Hampshire, Ontario	★	none
Trombicula microti	feathers, skin	Ontario	★ ★	none
Ticks				
Haemaphysalis leporispalustris	skin	Michigan, Minnesota, New England, Labrador, Ontario, Quebec	★ ★	none
Haemaphysalis chordeilis	skin	Michigan, New Hampshire, New York, Ontario	★ ★	none
Haemaphysalis punctatus	skin	Michigan	★ ★	none

★ no noticeable effect; ★ ★ localized lesions, subclinical disease; ★ ★ ★ mildly to moderately severe clinical disease, possible mortality; ★ ★ ★ ★ moderately to highly pathogenic, with morbidity and mortality common.

MARTINSON

The pattern
of life

Courtship and mating

*T*he reproductive fires burn long and fiercely in male ruffed grouse. The snows have not yet disappeared from the forest floor when the distant sounds of drumming are heard from the woodlands in early morning and late afternoon. Long before the spring peepers have tuned their voices, even before optimistic hepaticas have opened their petals under the blanket of last year's dead leaves, these muffled drum rolls proclaim the presence of the male ruffed grouse.

It is a sound both eerie and hypnotic. It seemingly comes from no single direction but pervades the leafless woods. Even if you cup your ears with your hands, rarely can you locate the drumming bird. But when you are very near, the drumming becomes so strong that it almost seems to pulse and throb within your own head. Then, if you are quiet and attentive, you might locate the drumming log and, if you are very lucky, glimpse the drummer himself before he descends from his log and disappears into the undergrowth.

The drumming is part of the ruffed grouse's unique version of a mating pattern typical among members of *Bonasa,* the grouse genus. With this noise he defends his territory against rival claims and advertises to attract females willing to pass on his genes. The only real social contact between the adult sexes occurs with fertilization; thereafter the female departs to lay her eggs and

His wings poised, the drummer prepares to send his signal through the woods, fending off rivals and calling for a mate.

tend her young, without any further participation on the part of the male.

This pattern is perhaps nearest the ancestral grouse's reproductive behavior. Some grouse species have evolved variations. Ptarmigans have a monogamous or near-monogamous mating system and occupy very large territories—adaptive advantages for the rigors of arctic and alpine breeding. Species that dwell in prairies, sagebrush, or the forest edge have developed "lek" mating systems, in which varying numbers of males establish small territories within sight of one another; Johnsgard has found that they compete directly to fertilize the females that are attracted from afar by the group's collective displays.

The male ruffed grouse operates alone. His home range, the territory in which he seeks his food, is relatively small. His core area, the place of concentrated activity, averages about 5 acres, and the bird rarely moves more than about a quarter-mile after becoming sexually mature and establishing his territory. By comparison, the female ruffed grouse may have a winter home range of up to 26 acres, and during spring her home range may overlap the territories of several drumming males. Probably she is attracted to a particular male within her home range by the effectiveness of his display behavior.

The male grouse must signal his presence and desirability if he is to attract and mate with females. In a forest habitat, however, bright colors are essentially useless; indeed, they would increase the danger of predation, sending signals indiscriminately to both friend and foe. However, sound travels well in the woods—especially low-pitched sound. Thus the ruffed grouse, like most forest-dwelling grouse, tends to be concealingly colored and exposes bright colors—the fiery red eye patches—only briefly for short-range courtship; he relies instead on sound.

The sound produced by the male ruffed grouse has appropriately been described as drumming. It consists of a repetitive and stereotyped wing-beating sequence done as the male stands on a drumming log. He drums most often at dawn and again at dusk, when hawks and owls are inactive yet just enough light is present for the bird to see reasonably well. Typically, drumming begins well before daybreak and may continue well past sunrise; it usually begins again about an hour before twilight and continues until dark. Several minutes usually elapse between individual drumming sequences, but during the peak display periods the bird may rest only a few seconds before resuming.

The drumming sounds are caused not by the wings striking one another but by the sudden compression and release of air pressure as the wings are quickly brought forward and upwards, stopping suddenly in front of the breast. The speed of the wing beats gradually increases, like a quickening drumroll, until the throbbing sounds continuous. At any distance the sound is something like that made by a distant two-cycle

RUFFED GROUSE

NEEFUS

Above: *The male ruffed grouse communicates his presence not through gaudy plumage or attention-getting visual displays, but through low-frequency thunderclaps.* Left: *The performance begins with a few measured drumbeats, then climaxes with a sustained drumroll of some forty-eight wingbeats. The spread tail helps the drummer maintain his balance.*

THE PATTERN OF LIFE

Having attracted a mate, the male puts on a full display for the hen: fanned tail, erect ruffs, dropped wings, a strutting posture.

balance the effects of wing beating, which would otherwise push him backward off the log. For additional stability he digs his claws deeply into the log. During each drumming sequence, Hjorth has reported, the wings are beaten about fifty times; a single sequence is likely to last about eight to eleven seconds.

Males typically have a preferred, "primary" log from which they regularly display each morning and evening, but Gullion found that they may also have one or more secondary display logs scattered throughout their territories. Females may be attracted to the male at any of these sites.

Should another grouse appear, the resident male responds by "strutting," spreading his blackish neck ruffs, erecting and spreading his tail like a turkey, and dropping his wings. Hissing and violent rotary shakes of the head, which cause the ruff to become a circular blur, usually accompany the strutting. In this imposing and highly aggressive manner the male approaches the other birds. If that bird is an intruding male, it is likely to respond just as aggressively, and a fight is almost certain to ensue. A receptive female, however, will respond submissively, and by her mincing steps, slimmed plumage, and lowered tail she clearly identifies her sex. Copulation attempts are likely to follow directly, especially if the female squats and assumes her receptive pose of slightly spread wings. Mating lasts only a few seconds, and the female leaves the area within a short

motor starting up, but as one gets within 15 to 20 yards of a displaying bird, the air-pressure changes on the eardrum are palpable.

While drumming, the male uses his partially spread tail as a support to counter-

116

time. She probably remains sexually receptive for only a few days: according to Brander, the receptive period ends abruptly about a day before the laying of the first egg.

It is highly likely that all females attempt to breed their first year of life. Although the male ruffed grouse, too, is sexually mature in his first year, it is more difficult for him to breed, for he must compete with other, often older males for territory before he can become an established drummer. Gullion has estimated that as much as 30 percent of the population may be nondrumming males that have not been able to claim territories and are waiting for the deaths of resident drummers. Indeed, sometimes three years elapse before a male becomes established in a breeding territory, and it is probable that a few adult males never do acquire property and breed. Nevertheless, these nondrummers seem to survive just as well as drummers—and perhaps better, since they do not expose themselves so clearly to predators by drumming. Gullion believes that such males, waiting in the wings, can provide a kind of momentum to the growth rate during an upswing in the population cycle.

It is not known how many years a male is able to defend a territory and continue to father chicks; the mortality rate is sufficiently high that few males live through more than a few breeding seasons. Certainly, some very favored drumming logs are used for far longer, but in such cases successive generations of birds are using the same territories

and finding the same logs to their liking.

So far as is known, the female needs to mate only once to receive enough sperm to fertilize her entire clutch of eggs. Unless she should lose her first clutch to predators or other ill fortune, it is unlikely that a second meeting of the sexes will occur in the breeding season. Nevertheless, the male remains on his log, guarding his territory throughout the entire nesting period. Although the intensity of his display slowly diminishes, he probably manages to fertilize several females. As spring progresses, fewer females visit his drumming log, and the sex hormones begin to subside in his bloodstream. Gradually his aggressiveness fades into the more pacific pursuits of searching out succulent berries and fruits, always close to his display site.

As the long days of summer pass into fall, a resurgence of drumming activity begins. Although the fall drumming has nothing to do with fertilizing females, it allows older males to reclaim their territories in preparation for courtship and mating the following spring. It also permits young males and nondrummers to challenge resident birds. This fall drumming can be thought of as warfare in miniature, full of sound and fury, but producing little if any bloodshed, and determining the degree of redistribution of shared habitat among the resident birds. Thus, as the year ebbs and flows into the next, a new generation begins to assume its place in the woods.

—*Paul A. Johnsgard*

Copulation does not usually take place on the drumming log, but the circumstances in this case were unusual. In full display (note the red eye patch), the male approaches the stuffed grouse on his log. A rival bold enough to ascend his log would at least assume a fighting posture, but this strange bird does nothing. Is it a hen? The drummer mounts the decoy.

Patterns of activity

A wary bird that inhabits dense forests, the ruffed grouse easily eludes those who would seek to discover how it lives its life. Not surprisingly, few data on the bird's daily activities were available until the advent of radio-tracking techniques. Researchers have now begun to document the activity patterns of this bird. The grouse is trapped and fitted with a harness, to which is attached a radio transmitter. The radio signal varies in pitch as the bird, now released into the woods, moves about, but the signal remains steady when the bird is at rest.

The most detailed information on activity patterns to date has been for breeding ruffed grouse.

Left: The first ruffed grouse carrying a radio transmitter was released by researcher William H. Marshall in 1960. Right: Hens have been favorite subjects for radiotelemetry studies, and as a result, their movements during the breeding season have been well documented.

Two hens serve as examples of nine birds monitored during preincubation to see how often they attended the nest site.

Preincubation: daily activity

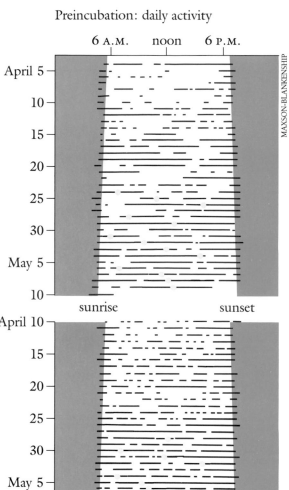

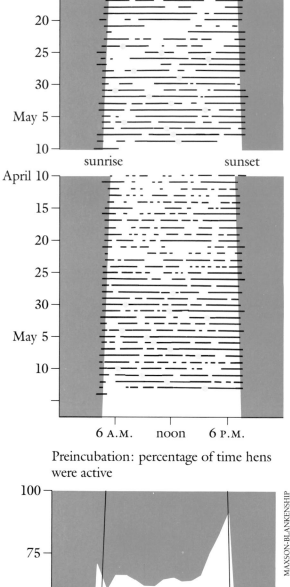

■ Inactive

■ Active

■ At or near nest

　Probable egg laying

During preincubation, hens begin their daily activity at sunrise and remain active most of the day; the cessation of activity coincides with sunset. The chart shows the average percentage of time nine hens were active for each fifteen-minute period.

Note how dramatically the hens' activity levels drop when they begin incubating. Even at sunrise and sunset, these eleven incubating hens were not likely to be off their nests.

Preincubation: percentage of time hens were active

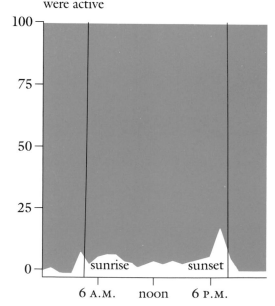

Incubation: percentage of time hens were active

HENS

Maxson found that hens are active 37 percent to 55 percent of the day, with an average of 47 percent, before they begin incubating their eggs.

The birds are seldom active at night. Peaks of activity occur during sunrise and sunset, probably as the grouse feed. Hens are more likely to be active at sunset than at sunrise, a pattern that was consistent for all hens monitored.

Once their activity begins in the morning, the birds typically remain active most of the time during daylight hours. During preincubation, activity usually began thirty to sixty minutes before sunrise and ended fifteen to forty-five minutes after sunset. The precise moment that activity began or ceased varied slightly from day to day, probably according to the weather.

During incubation, from mid-May to early June in northerly portions of the birds' range, activity levels drop to an average of only 4 percent because the hens normally leave their nests only to feed. Activity peaks are still associated with sunrise and sunset, but hens are less likely to be active even at these times than they were during preincubation. A hen may leave her nest from one to five times per day, but usually she is off the nest just two or three times; Maxson reports that some individuals usually made two feeding trips, others three, a finding that agrees with a 1966 study by Kupa. The average length of a feeding period may vary: fifteen to forty minutes among the twelve hens monitored by Maxson, fifteen to thirty minutes among the four studied by Kupa. On average, hens in these studies spent a total of forty-one to ninety minutes off their nests per day. A sudden rain shower can cause feeding hens to return to their nests almost immediately. Yearling hens, Maxson has found, average sixty-six minutes off the nest daily, compared with only forty-six minutes for adult hens, which suggests that experienced birds are more efficient incubators.

The daily pattern of activity is not unchanging, and Maxson has in fact recorded a curious shift that begins four to nineteen days into incubation. Early in incubation, the hens are up and about *before* the sun rises; later, they stay on their nests as long as four to five hours *after* sunrise. Although adverse weather—rain, snow—can cause a hen to delay or even omit a feeding period, this shift does not appear to be related to the weather. The phenomenon remains unexplained, but Maxson has postulated that as the forest canopy leafs out and herbaceous vegetation grows thick, light levels at the nest site remain low until midmorning.

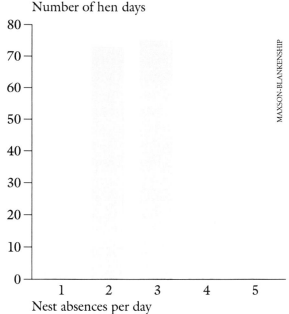

Incubating hens do not leave their nests more than five times a day; the norm for the twelve hens monitored was two or three times a day.

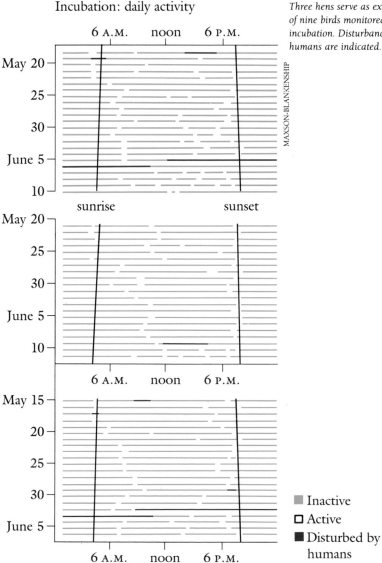

Three hens serve as examples of nine birds monitored during incubation. Disturbances by humans are indicated.

■ Inactive
□ Active
■ Disturbed by humans

When incubation ends—either the eggs hatch, or they are despoiled by predators—activity patterns change once again. The hens are active a high proportion of the time during daylight hours. Some hens in Maxson's study tended to be more active during the evening peak than during the morning, but the pattern was less consistent than during preincubation.

Both hens with broods and hens without are more active than they were during preincubation: 54 percent of the time for brooding hens in June, 60 percent for broodless hens. But the timing of the two groups' activity differs. Brood hens in Maxson's study did not reach their morning peak until one hour to two and three-quarters hours after sunrise; broodless hens reached their peak in only fifteen to thirty minutes. The timing of the evening peak differs similarly: for brood hens, two hours to fifteen minutes before sunset, versus fifteen minutes before to

fifteen minutes after sunset for broodless hens.

Both the brood hens' late morning start and the early end to their evening activity are no doubt related to their care of chicks, which need to be brooded during the cooler portions of the day. As the chicks gain independence, the hens' activity patterns increasingly resemble those of broodless hens.

DRUMMERS

Activity patterns of male ruffed grouse in mid-March to early April, before drumming begins in earnest, are similar in several respects to those of hens during preincuba-

Far right, top: Hens with broods forgo the early morning and evening feedings and instead concentrate their activities during the warmer times of the day, thus protecting their chicks from exposure. The data are based on five hens. Bottom: Hens without broods, meanwhile, take up a pattern of activity resembling that of preincubation: peaks at sunrise and sunset, activity during the daylight hours, and a very high level of activity throughout. The data represent four hens whose nests were destroyed.

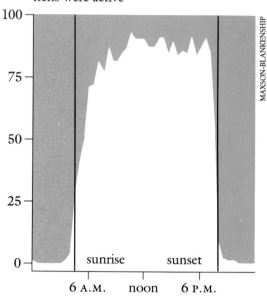

Hens with broods: percentage of time hens were active

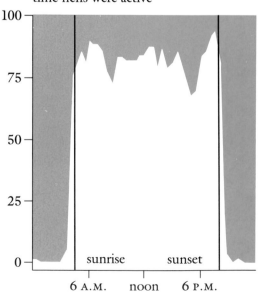

Hens without broods: percentage of time hens were active

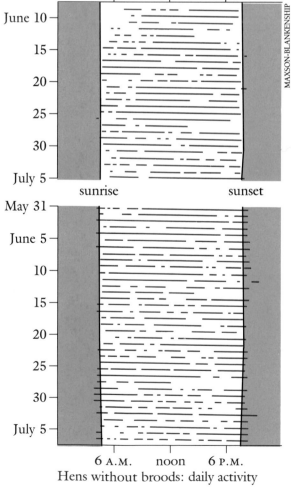

Hens with broods: daily activity

The difference in activity between hens with broods and hens without: for the first few days after her chicks hatched, the hen with a brood did not begin her morning activity until two to three hours after sunrise. Gradually, the onset of activity became earlier until, when the chicks were two weeks old, it approached sunrise. The hen without a brood was nearly always up just before the sun.

☐ Inactive
■ Active

Hens without broods: daily activity

tion, Archibald found: the birds do very little during the hours of darkness, they reach peaks of activity associated with sunrise and sunset; they are more active around sunset than at sunrise. Activity levels during daylight hours, however, typically fluctuate below forty percent, compared with 60 percent for hens during preincubation. Over the twenty-four-hour period as a whole, Archibald reported, male grouse are active only 10 percent to 23 percent of the time.

When springtime drumming becomes regular, drummers' schedules become complicated. The researcher's work is more complicated, too: since the drummer spends most of his time not actually drumming but standing on his log in a more or less stationary position between drums, standard telemetry techniques would mistakenly classify drumming as inactivity. Archibald consequently treated drumming and nondrumming activity separately.

Patterns of nondrumming activity remain generally similar to those recorded the month before: the drummers are not active at night; they become active at sunrise; they are very active (92.5 percent of the time) at sunset, when feeding. As the breeding season approaches, their daytime activity begins to increase but remains lower than for hens during preincubation. Overall, drummers are active 24 to 35 percent of the time.

As for drumming activity, monitored at weekly intervals from early April to early June, Archibald found that males consistently drum at night the first two and a half weeks. Exceptions occurred during windy days and inclement weather. Moonlight, Archibald concluded, was the major external

factor stimulating nocturnal drumming. Thereafter, and for the remainder of the spring season, the birds drum mostly during the day. Drumming usually begins an hour or two before sunrise, and over the entire drumming period, grouse drum most consistently just before sunrise. Drumming at other times of the day varies from week to week, but the birds are usually silent during the sunset feeding period. The proportion of time spent drumming varies from 21 percent to 60 percent over the season. Drumming activity peaks in late April (week 7) and late May (weeks 10 and 11), during which time, taking nondrumming activity into account as well, the birds are active 77 percent to 90 percent of the time.

—Stephen J. Maxson

Ten weeks in spring
Percentage of time drummers were active

□ Drumming
■ Other activity

ARCHIBALD-BLANKENSHIP

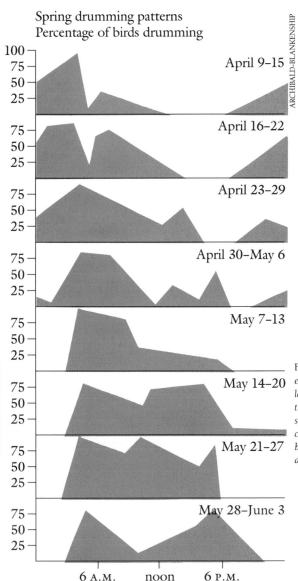

Spring drumming patterns
Percentage of birds drumming

ARCHIBALD-BLANKENSHIP

Early in the season, male ruffed grouse drum mostly before sunrise and after sunset. As the weeks progress, they spend more and more of the daylight hours drumming until week 8, when their drumming tapers off in midday.

Far left: In late winter and early spring, drummers are less active than the hens. Once they begin drumming, they spend more time on this characteristic ruffed grouse behavior than on other activities.

Home range of hens

W here ruffed grouse go in the forest, how much space they need, how much land they cover in a day, a week, a season—these subjects were rather poorly understood until the 1960s, when radio-telemetry techniques were applied to this species. Since that time, a number of telemetry studies in Minnesota have greatly improved our knowledge of the range and movements of ruffed grouse, particularly of hens during the breeding season.

As the term is used by naturalists, *home range* is the area within which an animal lives for extended periods. The area must meet all the animal's day-to-day needs for food and shelter. *Territory,* on the other hand, is an area within the home range that is defended from use by other animals, usually animals of the same species.

Home ranges of different individuals may overlap extensively; territories, by definition, do not.

The boundaries of a home range may shift with changes in the animal's needs, such as those associated with reproduction, and with seasonal changes in the habitat itself. To the extent that an animal depends on certain kinds of habitat, the size and shape of its home range may reflect the distribution and shape of the preferred habitats. It is important for wildlife managers to know how large an area individual ruffed grouse use and how this use of space varies in each stage of each season.

The range of the ruffed grouse hen changes over the course of the breeding season, as the bird seeks habitats suited to nesting and then brooding.

While she is incubating her eggs, the hen's home range is at a minimum. She will not venture far for her food.

AT EACH STAGE

The breeding season for a grouse hen consists of several stages: prelaying, egg laying, incubation, the first four weeks of brooding, and later brood periods. As the needs of the bird change with these reproductive phases, the habitat is also undergoing dramatic changes, from the stark snow cover of late winter to the warmth and lush greenery of summer. Home range use, one might predict, should change too.

In March and early April, before males begin drumming, Archibald reported that weekly home ranges for two hens varied from 5 acres to 11 acres. He suggested that

temperature influenced these movements, with colder temperatures resulting in a smaller home range. Two other hens, tracked by Brander, had March–April home ranges of 7 acres and 26 acres.

Once drumming begins in early April, the hens become more mobile. Archibald noted a steady increase in their average weekly range over a four-week period, from 6 acres to 15 acres. The highest average range size, 30 acres, occurred before laying began for nine ruffed grouse hens, Maxson has reported. This increased movement reflects the hen's response to the drumming she hears from males; a hen may approach the drumming logs of several male birds before selecting her mate.

After copulation, egg laying usually begins within three to seven days. During this interval, the hen must locate a suitable nest site as well as find food. The nest itself is a simple structure that requires little time or energy to build, leaving the hen free to concentrate on building up nutrient reserves adequate for producing eggs.

During the egg-laying period, the hen spends little time near the nest except when she is about to lay an egg. Her visits to the nest may last from one to several hours. Three laying hens monitored by Archibald maintained average weekly home ranges of 15 acres to 16 acres; Maxson's nine hens decreased their average range size from 30 acres to 21 acres. Schladweiler reported home ranges during the laying period that varied from 10 acres to 35 acres and noted that his three subjects ranged as far as 1,300 feet from their nests.

When incubation begins, the hen's home range contracts dramatically. For all practical purposes, the home range becomes the nest site plus one or more nearby feeding sites—usually clumps of aspen in the birds' northern range. The hen spends about 96 percent of her time on the nest, and unless disturbed by a predator, she leaves only to feed during several brief sessions per day. The weekly ranges of Archibald's three incubating hens varied from 2.2 to 7.4 acres; a single hen studied by Schladweiler stayed within 3.5 to 4 acres; the average range of ten incubating hens monitored by Maxson was only 2.2 acres.

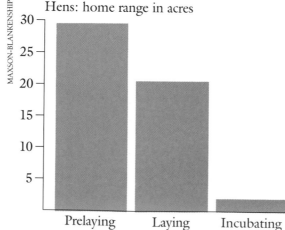

Hens: home range in acres

During the prelaying period, the hen may visit the activity centers of several drummers. Her range then contracts somewhat as laying begins.

By the end of spring, there are two classes of hens: those with broods, and those whose nests have been destroyed by predators. The home ranges and habitat needs of these two groups differ for at least the next several weeks. A broodless hen need consider only her own requirements for food and shelter; a brood hen must behave in ways that benefit the chicks, especially during the first few weeks, when they require a different diet and protection from predators and the elements.

In comparing weekly home ranges of hens with broods and hens without, Maxson noted little difference during the first week: 11 to 12 acres. During the second week, however, all brood hens increased their home ranges to an average of 18 acres, while all broodless hens decreased their ranges to an average of 6 acres. The hens without broods typically moved into dense alder thickets, where they presumably had abundant plant food as well as cover from predators. By contrast, brood hens were using mixed hardwood and birch habitats, which were easier for chicks to traverse and may have contained more insects.

Hens whose nests have been destroyed tend to become secretive and less active than hens with chicks. They often seek particularly dense cover.

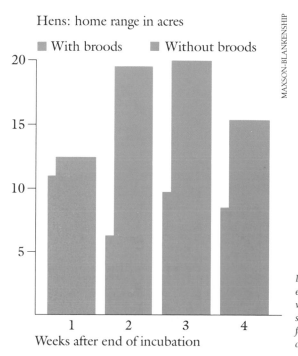

Hens: home range in acres
■ With broods   ■ Without broods

Weeks after end of incubation

In the first four weeks after the eggs have hatched, most hens with broods are very mobile; soon they settle into their preferred habitats for the rest of the summer.

OVER A SEASON

So far we have seen only how the hens use space over each stage of the breeding season. Where they go over the course of the entire breeding season involves the concept of *cumulative home range*. This is the area used during one time period plus any new area used during the subsequent time period. Say a brood hen has a home range of 10 acres during the first week after her eggs hatch, and 10 acres during the second week. If the two areas coincide exactly, the cumulative home range would be 10 acres. If the areas are completely separate, the cumulative range would total 20 acres. To the extent the areas overlap, the cumulative range would fall somewhere in between 10 and 20 acres.

Because cumulative ranges tend to increase over time, comparisons of data from birds monitored for different lengths of time should be made with caution. Of the six broods studied by Godfrey during July and August, for example, two were tracked for nine and eleven days and had home ranges averaging 13 acres; the two broods tracked for eighteen days had ranges averaging 22 acres; the remaining two, tracked for forty-five and forty-eight days, covered an average of 42 acres. The first two broods were not necessarily more sedentary than the last two: there was just less time during which their movements were recorded.

Data from studies of cumulative home range bear out the observation that hens increase their range as they search out mates and, after mating, food and nesting sites. Maxson found that the average cumulative home range for nine hens increased from 30 acres during prelaying to 35 acres during laying, but increased not at all during incubation. The hens' ranges as they laid and incubated their eggs, then, were mostly within the area occupied before laying began.

During the first four weeks after incubation, hens with broods covered more area

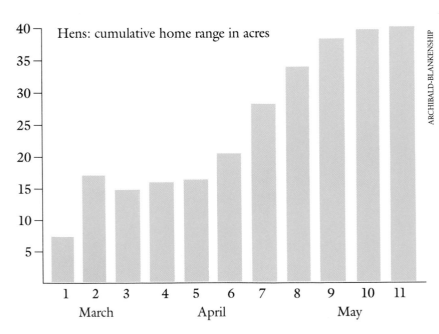

The nest site is likely to be within the range occupied by the hen as she sought her mate.

Below: *Cumulative home range includes the ranges of preceding weeks and thus can only stay the same or increase over time. The lack of a synchronized start for the three hens accounts for the slight decrease in this study.*

Hens: cumulative home range in acres

March April May

than hens without broods, Maxson has found. The brooding hens' average cumulative range—that is, the area used in week 1 plus the areas used in weeks 2, 3, and 4—increased much more rapidly. Not only were broods using a larger weekly home range than broodless hens during weeks 2 through 4, they also continued to move into new areas. Broodless hens, then, tend to be more sedentary.

To what extent the home ranges of breeding hens overlap has not been well documented. Maxson found that the home ranges of twelve egg-laying hens overlapped that of an adjacent hen from 0 percent to 73 percent, with an average of 16 percent. Even in cases of substantial overlap, however, the hens were seldom in close proximity; there was evidence that hens become aggressive toward one another in spring.

Godfrey found that brood home ranges sometimes overlapped but that simultaneous occupancy was avoided. Bump, on the other hand, found no tendency for one brood to object to the presence of another, and Chambers and Sharp presented evidence that two broods were actually traveling together. This aspect of ruffed grouse hen behavior requires further study.

—*Stephen J. Maxson*

The hen must shepherd her chicks into habitats that offer an abundance of insect foods.

Hens with broods use larger home ranges than hens without, and they continue to move into new areas.

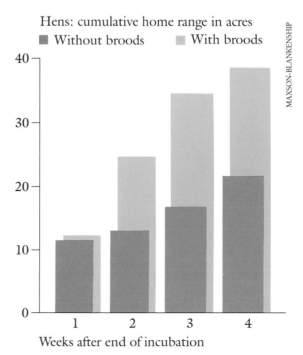

Hens: cumulative home range in acres
■ Without broods   ■ With broods

Weeks after end of incubation

MAXSON-BLANKENSHIP

Nesting

*F*ollowing copulation, the mated hen departs from the male's drumming site. She recognizes no bond with the drummer, and her next priority is to find a nest site, which she does without regard for the boundaries of her mate's territory. She is independent, resourceful, and able to take care of both herself and her chicks without his help.

That is not to say that she has an easy time of it. The female ruffed grouse is entering the most important—and perhaps the most dangerous—period of her life. During this time her nest will be exposed to the dangers of predation. The eggs may be crushed or frozen. She may even be forced to desert them should there be too much disturbance.

All the while she will be expending considerable energy on their behalf.

Ruffed grouse hens begin nesting as yearlings and are capable of producing clutches until they are at least six years old, but few wild birds attain this relatively advanced age. Although Bump and his colleagues suggested that up to 25 percent of hens failed to nest during some years, they were not working with marked birds, and the figure seems excessive. More recent studies using radio-marked hens have found that all hens attempt to nest, and this is probably the norm unless a hen is unhealthy.

Nest building apparently begins after mating occurs, perhaps shortly before the laying of the first egg. The qualifications are neces-

Her back to a boulder, the hen sits warily on her nest. A typical nest site enables her to keep watch for enemies and, if necessary, flush quickly to safety as the forest floor slopes downhill.

At the base of a pine tree, forest litter offers dry needles from which the hen can fashion a nest. It is not built with mud or materials carried from afar, merely scooped out of the debris in situ.

All told, the eggs in a clutch are equivalent to half the hen's weight. To produce them, she must eat heavily during the laying period.

A few twigs and oak leaves nestle this clutch of sixteen eggs. Average clutch size is eleven or twelve.

sary because no data are available for ruffed grouse in the wild. Maxson has noted that hens are seldom in the vicinity of their nests before egg laying begins. The nest does not take long to build, in any case, being little more than a bowl-like depression in the dead leaves and vegetation on the forest floor. Observations of captive ruffed grouse by Allen in 1934 indicated that the hen excavates a bowl, which she then lines with vegetation that is within reach as she sits in it. The bird picks up leaves and other bits of material and tosses them over her shoulder or onto her back—a pattern common among ground-nesting birds. Gradually these materials are incorporated into the nest. There is no evidence that hens transport nesting material any distance to their nests.

The nest is most commonly situated at the base of a solid object, such as a tree or stump. Other sites frequently chosen include deadfalls, brush piles, and boulders, but occasionally the nest is by itself, without any solid object in close proximity. Hardwood stands that are fairly open at ground level, when hens have a good view of their immediate surroundings and a ready escape route from predators, make choice nesting sites. Here, the hens rely on their cryptic plumage to blend into their surroundings and avoid detection.

Bump also found nests in rather dense vegetation but noted that the birds usually had a potential avenue of escape. Although ruffed grouse are generally considered upland nesters, Maxson found seven of twenty-two nests in wet areas despite vacancies in numerous upland sites nearby. Such nests may be more common than is generally realized simply because, difficult as it is to find the well-camouflaged hens on their nests in open areas, it is even more difficult to find them in wet and brushy habitats.

Captive ruffed grouse in Bump's study began laying eggs three to seven days after mating. Maxson has presented limited evidence that adults begin laying about two days earlier than yearlings. This suggests that adult hens come into reproductive condition slightly ahead of yearlings.

A hen spends very little time at or near the nest site except when she is about to lay an egg. At this time, she may be inactive on the nest for one to several hours. As the clutch nears completion, the bird tends to spend an increasing amount of time to lay each egg. Maxson reported two examples of hens spending six to seven hours on the nest by the time they were laying the final egg.

Eggs are laid in a sequence of one to five days, at intervals of twenty-five to thirty hours. Consequently, eggs are laid slightly later each day until at some point the next egg would be due sometime after sunset. In this case the egg is not laid until the following morning. Then a new laying sequence begins, with the typical twenty-five to thirty hours between eggs. Skipping a day between laying sequences is apparently due to a delay in ovulation of the first egg of the next sequence rather than a delay in delivery of a fully developed egg.

The number of days in a laying sequence varies among hens and for individual hens as well. Typical examples include 1–2–2–3–4, 2–3–3–3, and 1–3–5–4; figures indicate the number of consecutive days in a laying sequence, and each dash indicates the skipped day between. Bump reported average laying rates of two eggs every three days. Thus, a typical clutch of eleven eggs would take seventeen days to produce. Maxson's more detailed records indicate a somewhat faster rate of clutch completion: ten to eleven eggs in fourteen days, twelve to thirteen eggs in seventeen days.

The individual female's physical condition probably influences the number of eggs that she is able to lay, and consequently there is some variation around the species' norm. Studies in New York State indicate a highly consistent year-to-year and locality-to-locality average clutch size, although the numbers of eggs laid by individual birds may vary considerably. First clutches typically range from nine to fourteen eggs, with an average of eleven or twelve.

Eggs are smooth surfaced, slightly glossy, milky white to cinnamon buff in color, sometimes with reddish or drab spots. They vary slightly in size and shape within and among clutches, but an average egg is 1.54 inches long and 1.14 inches across.

Each egg weighs about 20 grams at the time of laying, or nearly 4 percent of the adult female's weight. Thus an average clutch of eleven or twelve eggs is equivalent to half of the female's adult weight. During the egg-laying period, she eats heavily, visiting the nest only long enough to lay the next egg; thus she seeks to maintain most of her body weight despite the great energy drain that she undergoes. Indeed, it is important that the hen enter the incubation period at the highest possible weight, since her weight will soon decline sharply, apparently because of reduced feeding opportunities. In New York, for example, an adult female gradually drops from an average weight of nearly 600 grams in late fall to about 520 grams in mid-March, before mating. By mid-April she will have regained some of this weight, but the energy demands of egg laying, which usually begins in late April, and incubation cause a decline to about 500 grams by mid-June. Just when she reaches this lowest point she must begin protecting and rearing her brood, with few, if any, energy reserves but with many more feeding opportunities.

Spacing of nests

When choosing a nest site, hens apparently respect the home range boundaries of adjacent females: Maxson has found little overlap of ranges. Bump and his colleagues likewise found nests most often to be more than 500 feet apart. However, they also found some nests as close as 50 feet. And they cited evidence that two hens may occasionally collaborate in their egg-laying efforts. This may occur when both hens have mated with the same male. Or, according to Storm, perhaps female grouse may lay eggs in the same nest early in the egg-laying phase, if some disturbance has forced one hen from her original site. Another possibility is that the two females are related and both are attracted to a specific site.

— Gerald L. Storm and
John G. Scott

The female's attachment to her nest site increases as the clutch becomes larger, and by the time it nears completion, hormonal changes have physiologically shifted her into a broody state. When she begins intense incubation, usually with the laying of her last egg, she becomes extremely quiet and elusive. She is all but invisible as she crouches down on the nest, her head held low and her entire body immobile.

Lest she betray her position to enemies, the ruffed grouse hen must sit very still for the long hours of incubation. Bump and his researchers likewise sat still in blinds at two nests for three days to observe the hens' behavior; more recently Maxson used a television camera to observe one nest for sixteen days. Both noted that hens remained completely motionless except occasionally to shuffle around on the eggs for a few seconds.

Infrequently, the birds were observed turning an egg or two or picking at insects crawling next to the nest.

Hens leave their nests for only one to five short periods each day, often during the warm hours of the afternoon. They feed quickly on energy-rich aspen leaves and catkins near their nests—usually within 300 feet—and then return. Maxson reported that when his subject left her nest to feed, she stood up, walked one to four feet, usually in the same direction each time, then flew to a feeding site. Return trips were more variable. On five occasions she landed two to five feet from the nest, but more often, she landed at a greater distance and walked home. Her landing sites varied: the hen was observed walking toward the nest from several directions. Once she reached the nest, she was usually settled on the eggs and motionless

Left: *In May this ruffed grouse hen was incubating her eggs.* Right: *Weeks later, the fern fronds had unfurled and the oak seedling had leafed out, but the hen was still in position, even as rain sluiced down. Her chicks had just hatched, and she was awaiting dry weather to lead her brood from the nest.*

NEEFUS

again within thirty seconds. Similar observations were made by Bump and Schladweiler.

Occasionally, the female leaves the nest to defecate, if she has not done so during a foraging break. Droppings produced by incubating females are particularly large, probably because of the recent egg laying. These distinctive droppings, called clockers, are defecated some distance from the nest while flying to a feeding site or while feeding.

Unlike a duck, the ruffed grouse has never been observed covering her eggs with materials that will hide them from view while she is absent from the nest. Their coloration may be similar enough to that of dead vegetation, and the nest site sufficiently well hidden, to make this superfluous. Or perhaps she is not gone long enough to make it worthwhile: hens generally spend 95 percent to 97 percent of the day on their nests, and

While the hen forages, the eggs may resemble mushrooms well enough to fool predators; once she has returned, the nest site is all but invisible.

heavy rain or other inclement weather may cause them to omit one or more of even those short feeding breaks.

Disturbance is another matter. Early in incubation a hen may leave her nest with little protest, but toward the end of incubation she often becomes extremely protective, and she maintains that attitude through the first two weeks or so after hatching, while the chicks are too small to escape readily.

DISTRACTIONS

If a predator approaches the nest, especially in the latter stages of incubation, the incubating hen may try to distract it from her eggs. Hens have two forms of distraction display. First she flies a few feet from the nest and flutters to the ground as if her wing is broken. She then hobbles and flutters along the ground with head and tail held low, all the while making whining or mewing noises. As the predator follows the apparently stricken hen, she keeps slightly ahead of it until the intruder has been lured some distance from the nest, whereupon she flies away. If the predator does not immediately follow her, she may rush at it in a display very similar to that of courting males. The tail is raised and fanned, the short ruffs are extended, and the wings are dropped at the sides. She accompanies this display with a loud hissing. Once the predator takes notice, she resumes feigning the broken wing and again attempts to lure it away. This sequence, alternating vulnerability and scare

tactics, may be repeated several times if the predator is not easily deceived. Such distraction displays are identical to those given by hens defending small chicks.

The intensity of hens' defense of their nests varies. Maxson once observed a hen run from the nest with no display at all, leaving her newly hatched chicks to his mercy. But in general, the fearlessness of incubating ruffed grouse is remarkable. Stories of hens that remained on their nests, enduring commotion and terrifying noises as loggers wielded chainsaws and tall trees toppled about them, are common enough; there is one case of a female who continued to incubate during a forest fire, even as a spray of water was being played over her. While attempting to nest-trap a hen three days before her eggs hatched, Maxson was unable to flush the bird. He poked her gently with a pole. Still on the nest, the hen fanned her tail, raised her ruffs, and bit the pole.

NESTING FAILURES

Despite the hens' tenacity, it is losses from predation and disturbances that force hens to abandon their nests, that account for most nesting failures among ruffed grouse. In a study of more than 1,400 nests in New York, some 38.6 percent were broken up before the eggs hatched, and 89 percent of those failures were attributed to predation. In some cases, a single egg is removed, but more often the entire clutch is destroyed or at least deserted. In New York, foxes were

Sometimes the hen may refuse to budge, even if gently prodded. This hen fluffed up her feathers, erected her ruff, and fanned her tail to intimidate the researcher, then bit the pole.

the major culprits, followed by weasels, skunks, raccoons, dogs, crows, hawks and owls, and woodchucks.

Predation rates may depend on the quality of the habitat. For example, Maxson reported that only two of eight nests were successful in an oak stand that remained fairly open at ground level, whereas eight of nine clutches hatched where a dense fern understory emerged during incubation.

Prolonged chilling is likely to kill developing embryos, but such losses are rare because of the strong incubation instincts and tenacity of the hen. Egg infertility, like nest desertion, is a minor factor in wild ruffed grouse, and on average only 2 percent to 4 percent of the eggs laid are infertile. Dead embryos may account for the loss of, at most, another 4 percent of the eggs. Overall, nest success as reported in the literature ranges from 59 percent to 68 percent.

SECOND CLUTCHES

Should her first clutch be lost, the ruffed grouse hen is likely to attempt a second nesting promptly. Because of the additional energy expenditure this represents, it is not surprising that second clutches average considerably smaller than initial ones—about seven and a half eggs. It is not known whether females that lose both their first and their second clutches attempt to nest a third time. In fact, renesting by ruffed grouse has been proven in only one instance: in 1970 Barrett reported that a second clutch was laid by a radio-marked hen whose first clutch had been destroyed before incubation. Other evidence is circumstantial, based on activity patterns of radioed birds, or on the assumption, probably correct, that late-hatching nests containing only seven or eight eggs are second attempts.

The point during the nesting cycle that a nest is destroyed may determine whether the hen will attempt to renest. If nests are destroyed during laying or very early during incubation, she is likely to try again. But once incubation gets under way, the additional ova that have formed in the bird's ovary begin to be resorbed, and it becomes biologically difficult for her to lay again. In one study, none of the six radio-marked hens that lost their clutches during incubation attempted to renest.

Most ruffed grouse nests hatch during late May and early June, but hatching of late nests may continue into early July. There is, naturally enough, a tendency for hatch dates to occur later in the more northern portions of the birds' range, earlier in the south. However, the peaks may vary by several days from one year to the next even in the same location, probably because of differences in spring weather or plant phenology.

All variables aside, incubation under Bump's game farm conditions lasted twenty-three to twenty-four days; in the wild it typically takes twenty-four to twenty-six days.

—Paul A. Johnsgard and Stephen J. Maxson

THE PATTERN OF LIFE

Food for the hen

In May and early June, deciduous trees are leafing out, seeds and catkins are forming, and herbaceous plants are emerging. The incubating hens would seemingly find themselves surrounded by an abundance of plant foods. But because the female alone incubates the eggs, she cannot enjoy the luxury of a prolonged or casual foraging period: she must rapidly obtain a nutritious meal and return to the nest before the eggs chill. Consequently, each of her feeding trips usually lasts less than thirty minutes, and she leaves the nest only to feed, perhaps making one to five feeding trips per day. Normally, hens fly from the nest site directly to a feeding site, where they remain until returning directly to the nest.

There is little detailed information on the foods selected by incubating ruffed grouse except for two studies of radio-marked hens in Minnesota. In 1968 Schladweiler made eighteen observations of two hens. Both fed in aspen trees on every occasion except one, when a hen chose to feed in a paper birch instead.

Maxson had similar findings in 1978: of fourteen observations of ten hens, all were of birds feeding in trembling aspens except one – a bird feeding in an American elm just when its seeds were ripe. Both researchers saw hens eating aspen leaves, but Maxson also observed female catkins being taken. Schladweiler found hens feeding in only male aspens. Maxson, however, noted that the hens showed no preference. At the time of Maxson's observations, most male catkins had dropped from the trees, female catkins were maturing, and new aspen leaves were emerging. Although male aspens are the preferred food source during fall and winter because of their large flower buds, there may be little advantage for an incubating hen to select only male trees as feeding sites in spring, when leaves are the staple.

There is another difference between winter and spring feeding sites. In winter, ruffed grouse feed primarily in large aspens, twenty-five or more years old, but in spring the hens feed in young aspens as well, with trunk diameters ranging from 1.9 to 8.9 inches.

Schladweiler located his birds feeding 22 to

The aspen seedlings at the edge of a clearcut provide fresh leafy food for the incubating hen.

SMITH

100 yards from the nest and noted that individual trees were used up to four times. Maxson found that hens seldom fed in the aspens closest to the nest. Rather, they flew 28 to 185 yards—an average of 88 yards—even though the nearest aspen was an average of only 32 yards away. Maxson's telemetry record of 590 feeding trips indicated that each hen repeatedly used several feeding sites during her incubation period.

QUALITY FOOD

From these observations it is clear that female ruffed grouse are highly dependent on aspen as a food source during incubation, at least in Minnesota where aspens are relatively abundant. It is likely that incubating hens feed on aspen in other portions of their range where these trees are available. That the hens do not simply fly to the nearest aspen to feed suggests that the birds may be actively selecting certain clones (a group of genetically identical trees arising from a single root system) or individual trees as foraging sites. This selection might be based on the stage of leaf or catkin development of a particular tree, or it could be based on nutrient content, as has been documented during the winter months by Huff. If the latter is the case, the mechanism whereby the bird can distinguish a tree of high nutrient quality from one of low quality remains unexplained.

—*Stephen J. Maxson*

During incubation the hen cannot be away from the nest for long. Her feeding trips are short and infrequent. She walks a few feet from the nest before flying off. On returning, she lands a few feet away and walks back to her eggs.

The young grouse

T he incredible egg: ever since the grouse hen laid it in her nest, it has protected the embryo and permitted the grouse chick to develop in safety and security. Now it presents the chick with life's first challenge. Breaking the eggshell takes considerable amounts of both time and energy, and two days may pass from the appearance of the first small crack in the shell until the chick finally emerges. Making barely audible pip-pip-pip sounds, the chick pecks a circular opening around the large end of the egg and, after a brief rest, forcibly squeezes its body through the opening. To chip its way out of its egg prison, the chick uses a short, pointed, hornlike structure at the tip of the upper beak. This egg tooth will be shed within a day or so after hatching.

But not all chicks get that far in life: a weak chick may be unable to break free from the shell and die trapped in the egg. Of the average eleven or twelve eggs in a nest, perhaps several will not hatch. Just how successful the chicks are depends largely on how well nourished the hen was prior to the onset of laying. Working with ruffed grouse hens in captivity, Beckerton and Middleton found that the amount of protein in the diet of a hen influences such factors as the weight of her eggs, the chicks' ability to break free, and their ultimate survival.

Although the eggs are laid over a period of two weeks or so, they hatch synchronously,

Surprisingly capable at a young age, ruffed grouse chicks can feed themselves, navigate across the forest floor, disappear into brush, and – by the time they are a week old – even fly.

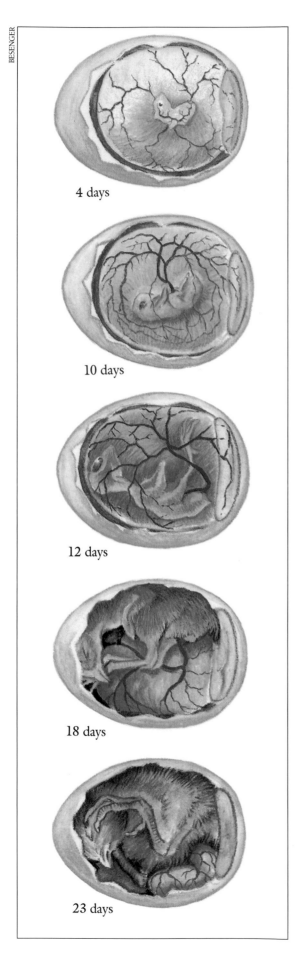

4 days

10 days

12 days

18 days

23 days

The developing embryo receives nourishment from the yellow yolk sac. Shortly before hatching, the chick will absorb the remains of the yolk sac, which continues to sustain it during its first days of life.

usually within a few hours of each other. Certainly, species that produce precocial chicks—that is, chicks that hatch with well-developed locomotor abilities—cannot afford to let hatching go on for as long as the hen took to lay the eggs, for no hen could tend and protect her mobile chicks while waiting two weeks for the last egg to hatch. The ruffed grouse's synchronized hatching behavior may be brought on by the sounds of the other eggs hatching, a trait that has been found among certain species of quails. Or, the onset of hatching may be signaled through vocal communication between hen and unhatched chicks a few days before the chicks emerge. Working with ducks, Hess found that a clutch in an incubator would hatch over two or three days; when the clutch heard hen vocalizations, all ducklings hatched within twenty-four hours. Apparently, the mother's vocalizations synchronized the hatching of the eggs. These vocalizations serve another purpose as well, establishing the beginnings of the mother-to-young bond, for even before hatching, a chick becomes familiar with its mother's voice.

FIRST WEEK

It is astonishing to watch as the wet, almost shapeless creatures struggle out of their shells and are transformed into fluffy and alert chicks in only a few hours. For the first half-day of their lives, the chicks remain under the hen, sharing her warmth and resting to regain the strength lost in their battle with the eggshells. The chicks already recognize their mother's voice, having heard her calls while yet unhatched. During this period the chicks learn more of her characteristics—through sight, the warmth she radiates, the tactile stimulations of her feath-

This chick never hatched: the fifteen-day-old egg was found in an abandoned nest.

The chicks are wet when they emerge from the eggs. Getting dry—and staying dry—is their first priority. The hen will brood them, sharing her warmth, until they are ready to leave the nest.

ers, and the sounds with which she comforts them. These stimuli initiate a complex type of learning called imprinting.

Imprinting is the process through which the chicks learn the characteristics of not only their mother but also their species. Ruffed grouse chicks that were hatched in an incubator and exposed—and thus imprinted—to a human "mother" ultimately responded to humans in such adult social situations as mating and territorial defense, according to a 1987 paper by Kimmel and Healy. It is important that the chicks learn to recognize their mother quickly: she will walk off the nest within twenty-four to forty-eight hours after the first chicks were hatched. They must know to follow.

A combination of good weather and restlessness of the chicks is thought to determine when the hen leaves the nest. By the time the oldest chicks are twelve to twenty-four hours old, they are pushing out from under her. If the weather is warm and dry, she will lead them away. The hen, in suddenly standing up and walking from the nest, signals the end of nesting. She will not return, even for brooding.

Newly hatched chicks are unsteady on their legs, but within an hour or two they can walk about and can travel short distances from the nest site. Early mobility is critical: the chicks must obtain all their own food and be able to run and hide if a predator appears, and a chick unable to keep up with the hen is left behind.

Ruffed grouse chicks become mobile very quickly and are capable of covering substantial distances when necessary. Bump found one brood half a mile from the nest twenty-four hours after hatching. A brood tracked by Barrett had moved 1,300 feet in just four and a half hours the day after hatching. Fol-

Too young and weak to escape into the brush, the newly hatched chicks must rely on their protective coloration for safety.

A half-day-old chick in the hand: about one-eighth of its weight is yolk sac, now absorbed into the body. The chick can survive for three days without food if weather prevents the brood from foraging.

Barely visible when first approached, the hen displays as the photographer draws near. The chicks begin to appear from underneath.

As the chicks change position—popping up now here, now there, to take their first look at the world—the hen spreads her wings, enclosing them in her warmth.

RUFFED GROUSE

She now leaves the nest and calls them to follow. Several of the chicks teeter and stumble; they are still too weak. The hen waits, then turns around, herds them all back to the nest, and resumes brooding.

Once rested, they all follow, leaving behind the broken eggs and the hen's large droppings. She leads the chicks to a fallen log, which will be a smoother road for their first steps, and then takes them into the brush.

At two days of age, the grouse is steady on its feet. Nevertheless, the hen selects fairly open habitat for her brood; dense brush and debris would impede the chicks' movement.

lowing two broods for about their first two weeks, Schladweiler reported that one used an area of 35 acres to 40 acres, but the other moved much more extensively and ended up 4,000 feet from the nest site, having ranged over approximately 400 acres. Why this brood was so peripatetic is unclear. Schladweiler reported flushing the brood on seven occasions, and this repeated disturbance might have influenced the brood's movements. Nevertheless, these data indicate that young broods are able to move large distances—and thus nesting cover need not be adjacent to good brood habitats.

At hatching, the chick weighs 11 to 13 grams, 1.6 grams of which is still yolk sac. Absorbed into the body of the chick as it pulled itself from the shell, the yolk sac constitutes about 12 percent of the chick's weight and is a main source of nourishment during the first day or two; if food is scarce, this food reservoir can supply enough nutrients for the chick to survive three days. Although the chicks eat little food during the first day, they peck at insects or inanimate objects that contrast with the background, such as pebbles, spots on leaves, even another chick's eye. At first their pecking movements are poorly coordinated, and sometimes chicks have to peck several times before hitting their targets. With practice, however, the chicks soon become adept at capturing moving insects. By the second day chicks are active, eager feeders. By the third day, chicks can jump out of a box 6.5 inches high. This jumping ability enables chicks to capture insects clinging to overhead leaves and branches.

On their high-protein diet, new chicks grow rapidly and approximately double their weight during their first week. Males are slightly heavier than females, a difference that will be maintained throughout the growth period.

When hatched, the chick is covered with fluffy down. Already seven of the ten primary and nine of the fifteen secondary flight feathers are visible on the tiny wings. These grow quickly, with the largest feathers reaching a length of 2.3 inches at the end of the chick's first week. Now the chick can fly a few feet off the ground for several yards, awkwardly at first, then with surprising competence. The observer may be reminded of the flight of a large bumblebee. Given the importance of daily feather maintenance to survival, it is not surprising that chicks have been observed preening as early as the day after hatching.

Down, however, is not adequate to keep the chicks warm in the chilly wet days of spring. They rest in the sun during pleasant weather but return to the hen to brood when chilled. All twelve tiny chicks can fit easily under her body and wings.

Down and rudimentary flight feathers are also inadequate to enable the chicks to escape danger. When the brood is threatened by a predator, the chicks respond by crouch-

THOMPSON

ing and freezing, relying on their camouflage coloration to avoid detection. Sometimes the chicks scatter in different directions and run short distances before freezing. They frequently hide under leaves, sticks, exposed tree roots, or other shelters and will remain motionless for ten to fifteen minutes. In this way an entire brood can disappear in a few seconds; the hen, meanwhile, attempts to draw the predator's attention and lure it away from her chicks' hiding places. Because the hen is so important to survival, the brood sticks close to her, and their movements and activity are largely determined by her. By the end of their first week, the chicks are easily capable of traveling a quarter-mile, always in the company of the hen.

A one-week-old chick can stay warm as long as the weather is dry and sunny. Should a cold rain begin, the young bird will need the hen's protection from the elements.

The two-week-old chick loses some of its natal down as the contour feathers of the body begin to grow in.

The yolk sac provides nutrition for the chicks' first day or two, so they don't feed right away. They practice pecking, however, and by their second or third day they are capturing and eating ants, flies, aphids, and other insects. During these first weeks they are growing rapidly and learning important survival skills.

SECOND WEEK

The hen continues to brood her offspring, especially during the cooler hours after sunrise and before sundown, while their flight skills remain rudimentary. It is during these early weeks that her role as a guardian against predators is pronounced. Her continual soft clucks that let the chicks know her location despite dense vegetation, her distress calls (which sound like a cross between a mewing cat and a whining dog), her running and flying charges against intruders, and her broken-wing act to deceive predators all play important roles in the survival of young grouse.

Rapid growth continues. The young chicks have seemingly insatiable appetites and consume large quantities of insects: flies, mosquitoes, grasshoppers, crickets, leafhoppers, dragonflies, damselflies, ants, aphids, caterpillars, butterflies, and moths. Some insects, however, are apparently unpalatable, and the chicks soon learn to avoid them. Stink bugs, small ground beetles, and small scarab beetles are eaten only when the chicks are very hungry. Although Maxson included ants among the unappetizing insects, both Bump in 1947 and Kimmel and Samuel in 1978 have reported that ants are readily taken. This apparent discrepancy can be explained by the chemical defense mechanisms some ant species employ to make themselves undesirable to predators.

Male chicks are now 8 percent heavier than the females. Contour feathers, the short plumage that covers most of the body of the bird, have replaced down on the sides of the neck and upper breast; the rest of the neck and the lower breast, like the belly and head, remain downy. Flight feathers continue to grow, and flight skills with them; if threatened, the brood can now flush in all directions before taking cover and freezing. Dust bathing, which removes excess oil and discourages parasites, has been observed in ten-day-old chicks. Hereafter, dust bathing and sunning become common daytime activities.

By the time the chicks are ten to fourteen days old, they are able to fly proficiently. The hen and her brood settle into their brood range, the best habitat she can find—

usually within 4 miles of the nest. In fact, Godfrey's study in Minnesota revealed that within this period, chicks have covered the majority of the range they will use for the rest of the summer. The average size of a brood's range is about 32 acres, and the grouse move an average 375 yards per day.

THIRD WEEK

The chicks are now capable of making short flights from the ground to low branches of nearby trees. Anyone who encounters them scattering in all directions may be amused by these seemingly inept escape attempts. But those who have tried to capture young grouse by hand soon learn to appreciate their flight capabilities. The hen, too, begins to fly when the brood is disturbed, rather than standing her ground or feigning injury to lure predators away.

Ruffed grouse are ground dwellers, however, and spend most of their time on the forest floor. Although adults tend to feed only twice a day, once at daybreak and again at dusk, the chicks need food more regularly, according to some researchers, and they may seek it at any time, spending perhaps four to nine hours foraging per day. They are able to negotiate their way through dense young forests as long as the ground is relatively clear of tangled vines and dense woody debris.

Ferns, berry bushes or other shrubs, the seedlings and low saplings of deciduous trees provide protective overhead shelter and in-

sects for the chicks, as well as berries for the hen. Young stands of aspen and mixed hardwood stands with ferns are heavily used by broods in the northern parts of ruffed grouse range. In Minnesota, broods have been observed traveling with ease under a continuous canopy of ferns, where they find both food and cover. Old fields are popular brood sites in more southerly regions.

Invertebrates, primarily insects, continue to predominate in the chicks' diet. Males have grown faster than the females and are now 13 percent to 17 percent heavier; they will maintain this differential through sixteen weeks of age. Contour feathers cover most of the back, breast, and belly of both sexes. A few crest feathers are emerging, and

The young chick takes easily to the air and may seek insect foods in the lower branches of trees.

The ruffed grouse chicks begin to range farther from the hen but continue to roost and travel together. The brood moves into habitat that resembles that of adult birds without chicks.

MARTINSON

the tail feathers measure about an inch. Several of the juvenile primary feathers are starting to molt and will be replaced by adult feathers.

The young birds are now better able to regulate their own body temperature, and brooding, which was frequent during the first week, becomes unnecessary except in cold, wet weather. Although considerably larger than they were at hatching, they still all fit under the hen, for mortality has eliminated several chicks. If the brood is too large, the strongest chicks push their way to the warmest places under their mother, forcing weaker chicks to the edges. Those that fail to keep warm and dry during chilly rains may succumb.

By the fourth week, chicks have their juvenile plumage and can fly almost as well as an adult. Insects are still their primary diet, but they are beginning to experiment with plant parts. Six-week-old chicks are quite strong; they can walk long distances and even forage on their own.

The body of the chick is well feathered in its juvenile plumage. Juvenile feathers have replaced down on the head and neck, and the tail has grown to about 2.3 inches. The chick looks like a miniature version of the adult and can fly almost as well.

The chicks begin to show an interest in feeding on plant parts. At first these attempts to vary their diet are unsuccessful: Kimmel has observed chicks having trouble removing the small flower buds from chickweed, plucking leaves from birdsfoot trefoil and sheep sorrell, and taking seeds from panic grass. But during their fourth week they may feed on the leaves of succulent plants, such as jewelweed.

Immature courtship displays are exhibited by young males. Maxson observed a month-old male chick slowly strutting about with its tail raised and fanned, its wings lowered almost to the ground, and its neck feathers erect. At intervals this precocious bird gave a series of side-to-side head shakes, slow at first but increasingly rapid as the sequence progressed. The bird expelled an audible "huff" of air with each shake of its head. At the end of the head shaking sequence, the bird rushed toward another chick, hissing loudly. The tail remained fanned, and the bird held its wings in their dropped position. These displays continued for some thirty minutes.

Similar behavior by another male chick was observed a few days later. Allen noted

similar displays by chicks only seven to eight days old, chicks so young they had no tails to fan. All these displays are fundamentally identical to those of male ruffed grouse during the breeding season.

FIFTH WEEK

As the chicks grow older, they gradually become more independent and range farther from the hen during the daytime, especially when feeding. Most of their travel is on foot. They usually feed alone or in small groups. Dining as a family unit is not the rule for ruffed grouse chicks unless the brood is concentrating on a preferred food item.

Nevertheless, the chicks are rarely more than 10 to 15 yards from the hen. Even if they are not within sight of her, they are aware of her exact location through the soft clucks that she continually gives to assure her brood of her presence. If a chick is disoriented, it gives a lost call, and the mother responds. As long as the chick is strong enough to emit the distress peeps, the hen will remain nearby. It is possible, however, that she recognizes only the brood as a whole and has little idea where the members of her family are or even how many chicks she has. When a chick is too weak to follow, it is simply left behind.

The chicks are fast becoming vegetarian, and their feathers are adequate for both warmth and flight. Now that their physical abilities and needs are similar to those of adults, they require similar cover, and their use of habitat begins to resemble that of adults without broods. Monitoring four broods for eighteen to forty-eight days during July and August, Godfrey found an average home range size of 32 acres. The average daily movement within the home range was 412 yards. The broods spent 64 percent of their time in habitats dominated by alder and only 13 percent in upland habitats.

At night the birds typically roost in the lower branches of trees or shrubs within a few yards of each other. The brood will remain together in this way—feeding on their own or in small groups during the day, roosting as a group at night—until early fall, when the brood breaks up.

Just one month old, this male chick experiments with a courtship display. The tail fan is less than impressive, given the bird's rudimentary feathers.

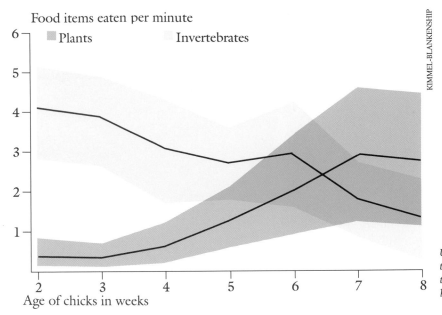

Food items eaten per minute

■ Plants ⬜ Invertebrates

Age of chicks in weeks

Until they are six weeks old, the chicks eat more insects than plants. After that, plants become the preferred diet.

As summer progresses, the chicks' diet becomes gradually more vegetarian; ripe fruits are especially attractive to the young grouse. Between their sixth and ninth weeks subadult plumage begins to come in, and they are nearing their adult size.

SIXTH AND SEVENTH WEEKS

The chicks are eating equal amounts of plant and animal foods. Plants in the diet include seeds of sedges, grasses, and violets; leaf parts from various plants; and fruits, such as raspberries, blackberries, strawberries, and blueberries.

This change in diet is perhaps responsible for the typical shift in habitat within the local range. Stewart reported that broods in Virginia used moist forest edges along streams until July, when they moved to drier, forested mountain slopes where blueberries had ripened. The best brood habitat seems to be in areas that offer a variety of plant species within young forest stands. Lush vegetation is preferred as long as it is not so dense as to restrict the chicks' movement. Indeed, use of an area declines if ground vegetation is too thick or if the canopy closes over, reducing the number of herbaceous plants in the understory.

Data collected by Scott indicate that on an experimental grouse habitat management area in central Pennsylvania, hens with broods liked the ten- to fifteen-year-old plant communities that developed after mixed oak stands had been clear-cut; stands of mature aspen and mixed hardwoods were used less often.

Broods prefer to follow ridges rather than climb them and frequently travel along the interface between upland and lowland habitats, according to a 1975 report by Godfrey,

who tracked grouse with radiotelemetry. He speculated that these border areas allowed for rapid, easy travel on open, dry ground yet also offered easy access to the lowland alder swamps that are used intensively by young broods. Conifers were chosen for nighttime roosting cover.

EIGHTH AND NINTH WEEKS

The chicks are more independent now, and their distance from the hen increases. They often become bold enough to leave the sound of the hen's clucks for short periods. Subadult plumage continues to replace their juvenile feathers.

Plant foods now predominate in the diet, and the chicks concentrate on grazing on various plant parts. Leaves, seeds, and particularly ripe fruits, such as blackberries, are preferred.

The ruffed grouse chicks' metamorphosis from carnivore to omnivore to herbivore is the subject of competing theories. The most common hypothesis, advanced in 1961, is based on Stiven's work with the blue grouse: that insects provide the young chick with a higher source of protein than plants, thus enabling it to grow faster and survive better. Research with domestic fowl and bobwhite quail has demonstrated that hatchlings do indeed have higher protein requirements.

A second theory involves the tough, indigestible character of plant cellulose. During digestion in gallinaceous birds, like the ruffed grouse, cellulose is decomposed by

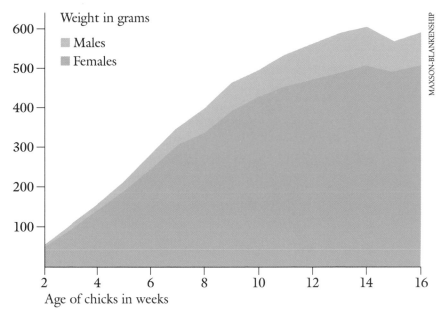

bacteria in the digestive tract. Leopold, in 1953, suggested that the digestive tracts of young birds do not contain the bacteria necessary to break down plant materials.

Both theories are plausible, but another factor may be at work. Kimmel has noted that young ruffed grouse may simply be physically unable to remove plant parts; they therefore concentrate on invertebrates. A soft and juicy aphid, after all, is easily snapped up. Indeed, Bump and his colleagues called ruffed grouse chicks "opportunistic feeders" that eat any food item they are physically able to gather.

The brood continues to move about its habitat in search of desired foods and appropriate cover.

The adult male grouse is larger than the female. Since they mature at the same time, the male's rate of growth is faster.

Tenth and eleventh weeks

Despite the chicks' precocial nature—their ability to escape from predators at an early age, their willingness to eat whatever is available and move if food and cover are inadequate—losses are heavy. Even if weather conditions are good, and predation and accident rates low, the mortality of chicks is substantial. Monitoring broods in Georgia, Harris noted that nearly half of the chicks had died before their tenth week. The younger the chicks, the more vulnerable they are to exposure and predators. Although there is little good information on the sources of chick predation, hawks, owls, and foxes have been implicated in New York.

During the tenth week, all the juvenile tail feathers are molted. Adult tail feathers begin to grow almost immediately but will take several weeks to reach full size. The birds' ability to fly appears unaffected.

Twelfth through fifteenth weeks: breakup

During this period the rate of growth begins to taper off. Ready now for the de-

Two late-summer immatures forage together. The severing of ties among brood members seems to take place gradually.

mands of living alone in the wild, the young spend more and more time traveling independently of their siblings and their mother. Thus begins the first phase in the splitting of family ties: brood breakup. As described by Godfrey in 1975, the young grouse move about the forest as individuals but confine their travels to their original brood range and its adjacent areas. The second phase will take them well beyond.

Brood breakup is not a sudden event. Studying two broods, Godfrey and Marshall noted that the breakup lasted for two and a half weeks, during which the home ranges of four radio-marked juvenile hens averaged 7.7 acres.

To what extent the adult hen influences the breakup is not known. Some biologists believe the process is controlled primarily by changes in day length as the northern hemisphere lapses into winter. These changes in photoperiod, the theory goes, trigger hormonal activity, which in turn promotes aggressive tendencies and increased intolerance among brood members. The breakup may proceed gradually, suggesting a progressive

deterioration of social bonds among siblings. As dispersal gets under way, congregations are likely to consist of unrelated grouse, from different broods.

SIXTEENTH WEEK INTO ADULTHOOD: DISPERSAL

At sixteen or seventeen weeks of age the young grouse is fully feathered in its adult plumage. A notable exception is the two sharply pointed outer primary flight feathers, which will not be replaced by the rounded adult feathers until the bird is in its second year.

It is now early fall, and the young birds embark on the second phase in the splitting of their family ties: they disperse from the brood area to establish home ranges of their own. Dispersal serves to spread out the members of a family, thus enlarging the grouse gene pool, preventing inbreeding, and ensuring the genetic variation that, according to theories of evolution, will allow at least some members of the species to survive in an ever-changing world. Dispersal sometimes distributes members of the spe-

cies into newly created habitats, such as the young growth emerging from forests recently logged or burned by wildfires.

Young male birds are usually first to disperse, according to some researchers, and begin to move out about two weeks after brood breakup. Thus, dispersal usually begins in mid-September in the upper Midwest and New England, later in the more southerly portions of the ruffed grouse's range, but some young birds wait until October or even early November. Females are said to leave home a few days later than the males. But Small's data, compiled while studying 100 grouse marked with transmitters, do not support those findings. He has found no consistent pattern between the time of breakup and dispersal, and no difference between male and female in the timing.

Such disparities aside, researchers do agree on the range of dispersal. Females tend to travel farther—2.5 to 3 miles for females, 1.2 to 1.9 for males. Chambers and Sharp reported in 1958 that 59 percent of the juveniles moved more than 1 mile during fall

As the young birds venture forth on their own, they may colonize new habitats and take the place of adults that failed to survive the summer.

MARTINSON

Fall dispersal: in mid-September the young male grouse leaves its brood habitat in search of an unoccupied activity center. It may encounter a variety of disorienting situations before it discovers an available drumming log.

dispersal. But distances of 5 to 10 miles are not uncommon, and one grouse is known to have traveled 71 miles.

The longer distances traveled by females, Storm theorizes, may be related to predation and to the social organization of ruffed grouse. Males stop when they reach the first suitable habitat from which other males are absent. If this shorter dispersal period results in reduced mortality for males, it is an evolutionary advantage, for it compensates for the likely greater vulnerability of males during the breeding season, when the drummers are advertising their locations. Females, on the other hand, must travel farther during two important periods of their life cycle: while searching for mates, and when rearing their broods. During dispersal, females move twice as far as males, covering roughly 500 yards per day compared with the male's 250 yards. The birds travel alone, mainly by walking, passing through a variety of forest communities and avoiding open areas. Two

or three weeks may pass before the young grouse finally settle into their wintering area, and only a few birds are still moving in November.

But these are averages. Some young birds, perhaps the majority, seem keen on traveling a straight line, and often these birds move quickly, sometimes more than 1 mile per day. Such birds complete their dispersal within a matter of days, a week at most. Godfrey and Marshall have suggested that in some areas ruffed grouse tend to go in one direction more than others, but because the number of grouse studied was small, their results were inconclusive.

Other grouse appear to meander, moving in one direction for several days, then changing course and continuing in a different direction. Some young grouse stop for several days, or a week or more, before continuing their search for a home range. And some birds even return to their brood range, then make a second attempt.

PRATT

What are they looking for? Both sexes need a good wintering area; the male grouse wants an unoccupied breeding site–a drumming log of his own–in addition. Although the species has shown its preference for particular types of vegetative communities, data indicate that young grouse are less selective during the fall dispersal. At other times of the year, drumming males are likely to occupy one sort of area, nesting females another, and broods yet a different habitat, but dispersing juveniles may appear in all types of habitat. Several explanations are possible: these young grouse may be unable to enter the territories of established adults, or inexperienced in identifying ideal habitats, or simply passing through.

As they disperse, the young grouse travel through unfamiliar areas, encountering such strange obstacles as buildings, fences, power lines, and roads. It is at this time that reports of grouse flying into dining room windows and smashing into the sides of barns become common. Such displays of suicidal aviation seem out of character for a bird that, when it encounters a human being with a shotgun, can navigate trees at high speed. But enough young grouse survive this period of stress to reproduce in new areas the following spring, thereby spreading their genetic attributes throughout the population.

WINTER

After the fall dispersal, the young grouse settle into their wintering areas and remain relatively sedentary. During autumn nights they roost on the ground, near such cover as deadfalls or brush piles. During the day they follow the adult ruffed grouse pattern of laying low to conserve energy and reduce their exposure to both predators and cold, now that winter has come and summer's leafy cover lies on the ground.

But the birds must eat. Tester reported that in December, ruffed grouse are up and about just before sunrise 80 percent of the time, and they are active at sunset approximately 98 percent of the time. These activity periods were associated with feeding. Huempfner has reported that the morning feeding averages twelve minutes, the evening feeding, eighteen minutes. Apparently, a ruffed grouse needs to go to its evening roost with a full crop. Feeding at dawn is less critical, perhaps because the bird will have other opportunities to forage during the day.

Indeed, in midmorning and early afternoon, the grouse may emerge from its snow-roost or other cover to feed. Approximately 35 percent to 47 percent of the time, Tester reported, grouse were active at these periods, and Huempfner clocked the feeding durations at twelve to sixty-one minutes, with an average of half an hour. Grouse pause often to roost during these midday feeding periods and seldom feed as rapidly as at sunrise or sunset.

Few birds seem to deviate from this pattern: Tester found that activity levels fluctuated between 0 percent and 20 percent during the rest of the day, when grouse typically rest in snow bowls or snow-burrows. No activity has been recorded during winter nights.

When the grouse does leave its snow-roost or other winter perch, it typically takes to the air and flies only a short distance to feed. These short flights may be intended to lessen the grouse's exposure to cold and predators, and perhaps the bird flies instead of walks to avoid sinking through soft powder. In a

WILBURN/ANIMALS ANIMALS

study in Alberta, 36 percent of the grouse observed leaving their snow-roosts flew less than 90 feet to a feeding site. Males stay especially close to their drumming logs, which they continue to defend throughout the winter. Females, on the other hand, may travel through the activity centers of several males in search of choice food and cover.

The birds' ability to move freely in and around icy branches is particularly important during the winter and early spring, when grouse depend on buds and catkins. Although gallinaceous birds are not so adept at perching as the passerines—the songbirds whose leg tendons are specially designed for hopping along branches and twigs—the ruffed grouse manages a credible job with the help of its "snowshoes," or pectinations, the scaly appendages that grow on the toes in late fall. These are commonly thought to support the birds in deep snow, but Gullion believes they actually provide little extra support; he theorizes that they may be more important in improving the grouse's grip on ice- and snow-covered tree limbs.

When a ruffed grouse arrives at its feeding site, Huempfner reports, it enters at the lower or middle part of the tree. After about a minute, perhaps a time to check for danger, the grouse walks to the outer edges of the canopy to feed. Gullion has reported that the upper part of the tree canopy is the preferred site when the bird is feeding on buds. During a typical fifteen-minute sunrise or sunset feed, the grouse spends only about 10 percent to 15 percent of the time walking along branches, flying from tree to tree, or simply looking around; for the majority of each feeding period, Doerr and his associates reported, the grouse is all business.

Young female ruffed grouse may be more

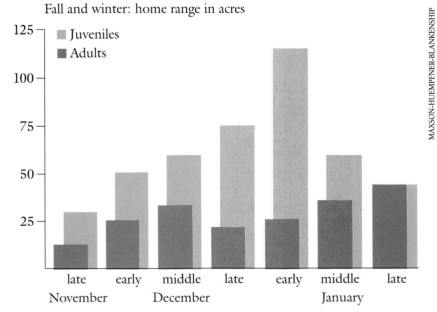

Fall and winter: home range in acres

MAXSON-HUEMPFNER-BLANKENSHIP

mobile than adult hens during the winter. Tracking two adults and one juvenile intermittently from November through January, Huempfner found that the juvenile's home range was 1.6 to 4.6 times larger than the average range of the adults. All three birds used their largest home ranges of the study during January, the month when snow conditions first become suitable for snow-roosting that year. Huempfner believes there may be a relationship between snowfall and home range. When grouse can snow-burrow and thereby protect themselves from predators, he reasons, they need not remain in the sort of dense woody cover that offers secure roosting and feeding sites. The same deep, fluffy snow that is suitable for snow-burrowing also discourages grouse from traveling on foot. Traveling by air to exploit new feeding sites, primarily clones of male aspen, the birds naturally expand their ranges.

As the breeding season approaches, the young grouse reach sexual maturity. The males that were aggressive enough to occupy drumming sites the previous fall—and the males lucky enough to find sites left vacant by birds killed over the winter—now begin spending more and more time at their drumming logs and usually restrict their movements to a 600-foot radius around their activity centers. Some males may use more than one drumming log, periodically moving from one to another. But in an Ontario study, 96 percent of actively drumming males were found within 164 feet of their primary logs.

The young hens, meanwhile, continue to cover the ranges of several males as they seek their first mates and identify good nesting sites. The juvenile hen tracked by Huempfner had home ranges that varied from 24 acres to 41 acres in February, and from 6 acres to 56 acres in March. In general, the range of females is largest during this period; the hens will travel less widely while they lay their eggs and move hardly at all once they start incubating.

Having survived the winter, these ruffed grouse now prepare to ensure the survival of their species: the cycle of life begins anew.

— *Paul A. Johnsgard, Richard O. Kimmel,*
Stephen J. Maxson, John G. Scott,
Robert Small, and Gerald L. Storm

The ruffed grouse places one foot directly in front of the other. Tracks in the snow may lead to a roosting or feeding site.

Avoiding the open field, the grouse keeps out of sight. In winter the bird may delay its feeding excursions until the relative warmth of mid-morning.

Good roosting sites have sufficiently dense cover that the grouse are secure from attack. Nevertheless, the birds remain alert.

Roosting

*I*f a grouse is not feeding, breeding, brooding, or preening, it is probably roosting. In fact, during certain times of the year, such as winter, a grouse may spend as long as twenty-two hours a day on a roost. Roosting makes the bird less susceptible to predation than if it were out and about, attracting the attention of carnivores: the more time a grouse can spend roosting in secure cover, the longer it will probably live.

Grouse normally leave their nighttime roosts an hour or half-hour before sunrise and are active in the early morning. They may roost on and off during the day but have another peak of activity just before they retire for the night. When roosting, they pass the time not sleeping but in a semialert state, usually with their eyes open.

Although a good site may be frequented more than once, a grouse does not have a single roost, the way some animals always return to the same den. Rather, the bird simply roosts wherever cover is suitable. In the spring, the male grouse makes an exception and may roost night after night at his log.

Hens also make an exception when incubating their eggs and remain on their nests almost twenty-four hours a day. After the eggs hatch, hens roost on the ground with their chicks, brooding them to protect them from the cool night air. When they can fly, the family has the option of roosting in trees. A hen and her chicks often roost together in loose groups until fall dispersal.

—Frank R. Thompson III

About to leave the security of its snow-roost, the grouse takes a look around.

Snow-roosting

The coast is clear. With no enemies in sight, the grouse emerges, ready to fly away.

When the leaves have fallen and snow covers the ground, the ruffed grouse—the same bird whose delicately mottled plumage was perfect camouflage in the debris of the forest floor—suddenly becomes vulnerable to predators. And it is cold.

To stay warm and out of danger, grouse take refuge in roosts, which they leave only for short feeding excursions at sunrise, sunset, and possibly midday. The two requirements for a winter roost—security and protection from the cold—are related. The more energy a grouse uses to keep its body temperature up, the more time it must spend feeding to replenish its supply of fuel. And the more it forages for food, the more susceptible it is to predation.

The ruffed grouse's ingenious solution to both problems is snow-roosting. When the snow is at least 10 inches deep, grouse burrow or, more dramatically, plunge into snow cover from flight. A foot or more from the entrance, the bird hollows out a small space, just slightly larger than its body and a few inches below the surface. Depending on the snow, the tunnel may collapse behind the bird as it wiggles in and settles down. Occasionally the grouse may poke its head out to take a look around, particularly if it hears some disturbing noise, just before bursting into flight. The danger gone, or its feeding excursion over, the bird will return to the snow but make a new burrow.

If the snow is not deep enough, the grouse may still burrow into it as far as possible,

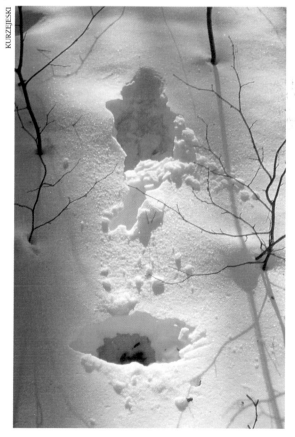

An empty snow-roost: the entrance is at the top, and the imprint of flight feathers marks the exit at the bottom.

The grouse dives headlong into deep snow and hollows out a small roost, where the inside temperature rarely falls below −7°C. When hunger calls or danger threatens, the grouse exits as dramatically as it entered.

leaving its upper body and head exposed. Gullion has referred to these partial burrows as snow-bowl roosts.

Snow-roosts are the most effective form of thermal cover available to grouse. All animals give off thermal radiation as body heat dissipates into colder surrounding air, despite the insulation of fur or feathers. And all receive thermal radiation from their surroundings as a function of the surrounding objects' surface temperatures. An animal in

an enclosed space loses less heat than one in the open because wind chill and radiant heat loss are lower.

Snow both breaks the wind and reduces radiant heat loss. Inside a snow-burrow, a grouse can heat up the surrounding air to just above freezing. At these temperatures the grouse needs to spend little or no additional energy for thermoregulation because of the insulation its plumage provides. In a snow-burrow, it reduces its energy expenditure by 30 percent or more, compared with a grouse in the open.

A snow-roost is not without its own dangers, however. If a few inches of soft powder cover a hard surface, the unwitting grouse that dives in may break its neck. Such fatalities usually involve an underlying crust of ice rather than a hidden rock or log, perhaps because the grouse is familiar with the features of its cover.

A grouse that approaches its snow-roost on foot invariably leaves behind cylindrical droppings about 2.5 centimeters long, consisting mostly of plant fibers. The bird's footprints are about 5 centimeters long, with the toes spread wide. Taking short steps, the bird places one foot directly in front of the other. Because of the comblike appendages that form on each side of the toes in autumn, the toes appear especially broad for a bird with such a short stride.

The ruffed grouse is not the only bird to have discovered the advantages of snow-roosting. All northern grouse, and even pheasants and quail, roost in snow. The black grouse, a Eurasian species, spends as much as 95 percent of its time in snow-burrows during severe weather. Snow-roosting is instinctive, not learned, and young birds that have never before seen snow dive in with the same confidence as their elders.

Roosting in conifers is not so efficient as in snow, but it is better than being out in the open. A dense stand of evergreens may cut wind speeds 75 percent, which enables grouse to realize a 20 percent energy savings. When snow cover is inadequate or unsuitable, then grouse roost in conifers.

In northern states, Bump and Gullion found grouse roosting in spruces, firs, and hemlocks. In the southern part of the birds' range, where winter temperatures are warmer, roosting in conifers reduces heat loss as much as snow-roosts. In Missouri, where snow is rarely deep enough for snow-roosting, grouse prefer eastern red cedar and choose roosts 2 or 3 meters off the ground, close to the trunk on stout limbs. Here there are few branches to impede movement, yet the dense canopy above and to the sides screens them from hungry raptors.
—*Ronald R. Runkles and Frank R. Thompson III*

MARTINSON

Despite the adult ruffed grouse's reputation for solitary life, these five birds fit in the photographer's frame. By late winter they will once again be feeding and roosting alone.

Gregarious grouse

*F*or most of the year ruffed grouse are solitary animals. In the winter some adults continue as loners, but others may cluster in groups of, on average, four or five when feeding or roosting. These groups, of mixed sexes, may form to protect themselves from predators when foraging, since many pairs of eyes are more likely to detect a predator.

The size of the group tends to increase from late fall until January, when the group begins to disband. By March or April the birds are again solitary. This breakup is most probably a result of increasing social pressure as the breeding season approaches.

In early autumn one may still find broods of nearly full-grown young. These broods slowly disband but by midfall may still be going about the forest in loose aggregations of three to seven birds within an area of an acre or two.

Although the range of the ruffed grouse in the West coincides with that of the blue grouse *(Dendragapus obscurus)* and the spruce grouse *(D. canadensis),* it is doubtful that the ruffed grouse competes for food or cover with either of its cousins. In southeastern Idaho, where blue and ruffed grouse inhabit the same mountain range, the birds mostly keep to themselves: the blue grouse winter in conifers at high elevations and breed in the shrublands in the foothills; the ruffed grouse stick to the aspen forests between the blue grouse's wintering and breeding ranges. On several occasions blue grouse, presumably migrating from one range to the other, have been observed near ruffed grouse in aspen stands, but no interaction occurred.

If the western ruffed grouse declines to mingle with its kin, it at least is friendly—in relative terms—with human beings. Compared with eastern birds, grouse in the West are quite tame. It is not uncommon to be able to walk within a few feet of a ruffed grouse, which is just as likely to stroll away as it is to flush. In all likelihood this tameness results from the infrequency of encounters between grouse and man in the West.

—Dean F. Stauffer

A second dispersal

*T*he fall dispersal of ruffed grouse may be a misnomer. A bird's one-way movement from the site of its birth to the place where it will perpetuate the species only begins in fall. This journey may often continue during the drumming and nesting periods of spring. To encompass both the fall dispersal, when the young grouse leaves its brood areas, and the spring movement, when breeding activities are at a peak, we can refer to the whole journey as the natal dispersal.

After the first part of the dispersal, in the fall, the juveniles settle into their wintering areas and remain relatively sedentary during the winter months. In late February or early

March, both adults and juveniles increase the size of their activity area. Adults, however, rarely leave their established sites; juveniles may continue moving into new areas through April and May. If the movement is part of the young grouse's efforts to establish a drumming or nesting site away from the wintering area, it qualifies as part of the natal movement.

This spring dispersal may be more common in males—apparently young males that failed to establish themselves in secure drumming cover during the fall. Although females travel away from their wintering areas for several days in the spring, they often return to nest; their movement in spring may best be described as a search for potential mates.

An understanding of ruffed grouse dispersal is far from complete, and at present we can only speculate on how and why this characteristic behavior, different for each sex, evolved. Asking what the young birds are searching for may give us a clue. Males seek drumming stages and territories; females look for mates and nesting cover. The different patterns of dispersal may reflect these different goals. Or perhaps they serve to separate males and females of the same brood, preventing the risks of inbreeding. Until the solution to the puzzle is found, however, admirers of the ruffed grouse may proceed to cherish a behavior that only adds to ruffed grouse mystique.

—*Robert J. Small*

In early spring the young adult males seek vacant logs. Movement connected with their search may be considered the last leg of the journey begun in the autumn dispersal.

MARTINSON

*The young females, too, may
be on the move, usually
in search of their first mates.*

Tʜᴇ ᴘᴀᴛᴛᴇʀɴ ᴏғ ʟɪғᴇ

In defense of a territory

To assure himself the opportunity to pass his genes on to future generations, a male ruffed grouse must find a mate and minimize interference from rival males. He has evolved a marvelous system of territorial defense and behavioral displays to accomplish just that.

Territorial behavior in ruffed grouse is confined to the males. Both sexes may wander up to several miles from their natal area during their first fall of life in search of a suitable covert. However, once suitable habitat is found, they tend to settle in. From then on the life-styles of male and female grouse are very different. Whereas the female must locate suitable habitat for herself, her nest, and her brood of rapidly growing chicks during the summer, the male need concern himself only with his own survival and ability to mate in the spring. The area over which he wanders regularly during the year to find adequate food, water, and shelter is called the home range. That part of the home range that is defended against intruders of the species is the ruffed grouse's territory.

The male's territory is often referred to as his "core area," "activity center," or "drumming site." Whatever its name, this area must meet several requirements. Of primary importance, Gullion and Marshall found, is a display stage, usually a log, and adequate cover in the form of dense vertical woody plant stems. Selection of a territory is also

With deliberate steps the drummer shifts position on his log. He may aim his next drum in a different direction to signal potential rivals that this territory, this log, is his.

The prairie chicken claps its wings together in flight; the ruffed grouse's drumming may be an earthbound version of its cousin's territorial and courtship display.

affected by the presence of nearby mature aspen trees as a food source and the site's tradition of occupancy as a territory. Its size is determined by the proximity of neighboring males and the quality of the habitat; a territory in prime habitat may be 10 acres or even less, but in poor habitat the bird may require much more room.

During the fall, adult male ruffed grouse already occupy their territories. Young males are dispersing from the area in which they were hatched in search of their own territories. If one finds a suitable site, he may establish a territory in the first fall of his life. But if all suitable sites are occupied by adult birds, it may take him a year or more to find and establish a territory. If an adult landholder dies, a young bird will rapidly move in.

A territory is vital to the male bird. Without it his genetic potential dies unused, and he must remain on the move, a dangerous state of affairs for a prey species. The established drummer is much more secure. He is, in Gullion's words, a very sedentary bird, usually spending the remainder of his life within a radius of 600 to 800 feet of his

When drumming does not dispatch a rival, the ruffed grouse prepares to fight. Bowing movements, head twisting, and a panted hissing are all in the repertoire.

RUFFED GROUSE

drumming log. Once established, the male seeks to maintain his advantageous position. How does he defend his choice area against young males searching for a territory or other adults displaced from their own territories?

THE ROLE OF DRUMMING

The answer lies in an elaborate system of auditory and visual display, backed up by actual fighting. The cornerstone of the behavior of a male grouse is the drumming display, unique among grouse. Drumming may be a ritualized version of the flight display found in other species, Johnsgard has speculated. Among some members of the galliform family, the male takes to the air and claps its wings to deal with rivals and attract females. The ruffed grouse's drumming, in which the male beats its wings without leaving the ground, has the same functions: to proclaim territory, establish dominance over other males, and advertise for a mate.

Drumming can be heard during all months of the year at all times of day, with a peak during the breeding season from March through May. But the flurry of drumming activity during the fall is strictly for territorial defense. Much like Indian drums, a male's drumming conveys two messages: "I'm here, this is my territory, stay away if you know what's good for you," and "I'm here, ready and willing and able, come on over." The interpretation depends on the sex of the auditor.

Besides drumming, the male grouse employs a strutting display when it sees another grouse or something else it finds threatening, confusing, or even just interesting. The bird may fan its tail, erect the ruffs on its neck, droop its wings, and shake its head while parading back and forth or making short rushes at the visitor. Grouse are rarely vocal, but the male may produce a hissing sound in conjunction with head shaking and strutting. As with drumming, the message conveyed by strutting may be a warning to an intruding male or an enticement to a visiting female. In fact, a territorial male apparently determines the sex of another grouse by its response to his strutting: the rival male responds in kind, the female assumes a submissive posture. Strutting represents the final preliminary threat display

MAXSON

The threat display is the fighting posture when two grouse go head to head. The beak is the primary weapon. Birds confined in captivity without barriers may peck each other to death.

SMITH

In the wild, drumming and strutting displays usually suffice to establish one bird's dominance over another. Here, however, two males face off to fight.

prior to an actual confrontation. Grouse can and certainly do fight.

Much of what is known about fighting among ruffed grouse comes from studies of grouse in captivity, reported by Bump and his associates in 1947. Early captive breeding attempts were stymied by intense fighting and territorial behavior. Even with modern propagation techniques, captive grouse remain very difficult to raise.

In captivity, fights were frequent, accompanied by much strutting and bluffing, until a definite social order was established, much the same as in a flock of farmyard chickens. Fighting was noted in birds of all ages beginning at the tender age of only one week. Age, sex, and size were not the sole determi-

nants of a bird's position in social hierarchy, but being larger, adult, or male was an advantage. Overall vigor and aggression could move a presumably subordinate bird up in social rank. An unusually weak bird might be cornered in a pen by a dominant bird and pecked until its skull was laid bare. More often a fight would conclude when the attacked bird ran or flew from its attacker. If the birds were evenly matched, both would eventually give up. Only when boards 10 inches high were placed in the pens at four-foot intervals to establish territorial boundaries and keep the grouse out of each other's sight could the birds live in peace.

During a fight the grouse assumes a low "fighting posture" with the head held low,

RUFFED GROUSE

neck outstretched, feathers flattened, and the tail folded and lowered. The bird's primary weapon is its beak, but wings and occasionally feet are also used.

Fighting in confined situations is well described, but Bump referred to circumstances leading to fighting in the wild as "obscure." Since the grouse is not a social bird, the kinds of aggregations seen in pens are not likely to occur in the wild except when grouse converge at an especially attractive food source or roost site. The drumming and strutting displays, in fact, have evolved as a magnificent behavioral mechanism precisely to avoid the sort of fighting that could harm both combatants. Brood dispersal in the fall is apparently another mechanism by which grouse avoid fighting over dominance. As Bump observed, fighting is most common during the breeding season and the fall "shuffle" of young birds dispersing.

In the wild, the most likely stimulus for an actual fight would be the invasion of a male's territory by a rival male despite the resident bird's drumming and strutting. In most such cases the resident male has the upper hand—he knows his turf, and he is usually stronger precisely because he is established—and wins the dispute. There are accounts of such battles between grouse; one observed by Bradford led to the death of one of the birds. Bump once saw two grouse fighting together against a third bird.

Female grouse also display aggression, but they fight in defense of their nests or broods

rather than territory. Since the selection of the hen's nest site bears no relation to the male's territory, she enjoys no benefit from his defense of the area: she is on her own. Before hatch, the female uses a distraction display, such as a feigned broken wing, to lead a potential threat away from her nest. After the chicks have hatched, she is more likely to stand her ground, spread her tail, and hiss. She may also rush at the intruder in an attempt to drive it off. Grouse biologists relate numerous accounts of "attacks" by protective females during the brood-rearing period. Once the chicks can fly, the hen and her brood are more likely to flee from danger than confront it.

—Scott R. Craven

The resident bird has the advantage of knowing the territory, and the rival is intimidated into retreat.

Fighting

A belligerent male prepares to fight the gloved hand of a researcher. Overt aggressiveness toward people is rare, but physical encounters between male ruffed grouse may occur frequently.

This male, says Gordon Gullion, was defending his territory against the researcher. "I could lift him up but not hold on to him, nor would he allow me even to put a hand over him. When I lay on the ground, he literally danced around me."

While fighting between grouse is of biological interest, there are several fascinating accounts of grouse displaying aggression toward humans. These have often been described as examples of "tame" grouse. However, Gullion in 1981 concluded that these are not tame grouse at all, but rather male birds whose aggression during the breeding season reaches such a pitch that they ignore or "forget" their normal fear of humans.

Bradford told of an encounter with a belligerent grouse along a trail during a spring trout fishing trip in northern Wisconsin. Gullion described several individual male grouse that attacked people. One grouse, banded as part of a research study, attacked a researcher on eight occasions as he passed through the bird's territory. The same bird also attacked parked cars along a nearby road. Gullion also related the story of "Nutsy," an adult male grouse that defended his territory adjacent to a rural Wisconsin tavern and attracted considerable local media attention. Schneiders described a well-known grouse that would appear by a certain tree along the road to shadowbox with all challengers. He also mentioned a farmer's account of a grouse that "boxed" at his children and followed them into the house.

Nevertheless, fighting grouse are more a curiosity than a threat to humans. Their displays, in fact, serve them well in their struggle to survive and reproduce without actually engaging in combat.

—*Scott R. Craven*

A captive grouse takes to the air in mid-attack. This hand-reared grouse treated human beings as though they were rival birds.

MAXSON

Drumming

My reaction to the sound is the same now as it was years ago. Sometimes I seem to feel the preliminary wingbeats, rather than hear them. I still freeze in my tracks and cock an attentive ear, as if that would really help. Somewhere ahead in the woods comes the drumming of a ruffed grouse. Or perhaps it is to the side, or from behind. Four or five minutes later comes another muffled drum. Possibly the bird will be easier to locate this time. But no matter: long ago I learned that a drumming cock grouse is among the wariest of nature's creatures. When approached, more often than not, a drummer silently steals away from his log, leaving the hunter to wonder if he really heard a grouse at all.

Drumming advertises the presence and location of the male ruffed grouse in the forest. The female, attracted by this drumming, seeks out the male at his drumming log; other males are warned that the drummer has claimed this area of the forest as his own. Although active defense of a clearly defined territorial boundary has not been demonstrated in ruffed grouse, evidence gathered by Gullion in Minnesota, and by others, strongly indicates that drumming is a mechanism to ensure the proper spacing of male grouse in the woods.

Drumming may have a third function, less easily demonstrable than attracting hens and establishing territories. It may serve simply as an outlet for the release of excess energy in

As a territorial display, drumming apparently keeps male ruffed grouse a safe distance from one another; as a courtship display, it summons hens.

a bird. Lee Gladfelter of the Iowa Conservation Commission and I once watched a bird that drummed seemingly incessantly after having mated with a female. We both had the distinct, albeit somewhat unscientific, impression that if male 603 had not drummed so furiously and exultingly, he would have exploded.

If he has not already been in position throughout the night, the male grouse usually approaches his drumming log well before sunrise. Upon mounting the log, the bird selects one particular place to drum. This location, called the *drumming stage* by Gullion, is repeatedly used by the bird. The grouse first cautiously surveys his surroundings. When he is ready to drum, his body is at a right angle to the axis of the log. His tail is spread moderately and braced against the log for support; his feet are positioned to obtain a firm clawhold.

A few single wingbeats begin the performance. The number varies among birds and among successive drums of the same bird. These preliminary wingbeats are audible to human ears only if the listener is quite close, perhaps within 100 feet if the wind is still. After a brief pause, four clearly audible beats are given. Another brief pause. The wings beat slowly at first, then rapidly increase in speed until they are a blur of motion.

The performance varies in length. An analysis of the drums from birds in Ontario and West Virginia shows that the length of the drum, beginning with the four clearly audi-

ble wingbeats, ranges from 9.06 to 10.62 seconds. The length of the drum can vary from day to day for the same bird.

The total number of wingbeats per drum also is variable, both among birds and among drums of the same bird. The study in Ontario and West Virginia reported that the average number of wingbeats per drum for most birds was between 45.5 and 49.

At the end of the final stroke, the backward pressure the wingbeats have created ceases and the bird tips forward. The tail rises off the log, then is slowly lowered as the bird regains his balance.

Many descriptions of the drumming performance detail how the male grouse struts and displays on his log. When I watched a drumming grouse for the first time, I was surprised that all the bird did was drum, then remain motionless at his drumming stage until he drummed again. Watching other drumming grouse taught me that this is normal procedure. The cautious male turns only his head as he watches for intruders. A cock grouse generally displays and struts only when he knows he has an audience. Otherwise he does not move until he is ready to drum again—in about two to three minutes, sometimes less, sometimes more.

Might it be possible to identify individual male birds in the field by the patterns of their drums? The West Virginia study by Samuel and his colleagues reported that often there were no significant differences in length of drum or number of wingbeats per

drum between adjacent drumming grouse. Complex computer analysis of tape recordings revealed some minute differences among the drums of various birds, but the authors concluded that this was not a practical technique for identifying individuals.

High-speed photographic techniques have laid to rest the old controversy about exactly what produces the sound made by the drummer. The wings strike neither each other nor the log on which the bird stands. Instead, the sound is a sonic boom in miniature, produced by air rushing to fill a momentary vacuum. But what produces the vacuum remains unclear. It might be the thrusting wingstroke, whose motion is simultaneously forward, upward, and inward.

Or, as postulated by Hjorth, it might actually be the return wingstroke that is responsible.

Such speculations on the physics of drumming matter little to the grouse, but technique is a concern: the drumming sound cannot automatically be produced on a bird's first attempt. Young grouse must learn by practicing. Gullion in 1984 told of one male grouse that made the proper wing motions but for one entire spring season never produced a single drumming sound.

Grouse may be heard drumming during any month of the year. Although they drum only occasionally during the heat of midsummer, male grouse spend a great deal of time at or near their drumming logs. In the

Young males may need some practice before they can send a clear signal. Once they have mastered the technique, variations in individuals' drumming are insignificant.

The characteristic sound of the drumming grouse is not caused by the wings striking each other or the log. The wings' rapid rotation creates a vacuum, and air rushing in produces miniature thunder-claps that announce the grouse's presence.

depth of winter, wing marks on a snow-covered log are evidence of a drummer.

But it is the arrival of spring that most people consider synonymous with the drumming of ruffed grouse. Observers generally agree that drumming activity begins in earnest with the melting of the snow cover on and around drumming logs. On the Cedar Creek Natural History Area in Minnesota, Archibald found that a great deal of early-season drumming was nocturnal. He associated such activity with the amount of moonlight that reached the forest floor.

Drumming in autumn occasionally seems to rival that in spring. Beginning in October, established territorial male grouse are frequently heard drumming. It is not coinci-

dence that this is the same time that young male grouse are searching for suitable areas in which to stake territorial claims of their own. Drumming by young, newly established males occurs later in the fall than the drumming heard from older, previously established males, according to Gullion.

The main factor that prompts male ruffed grouse territorial and mating behavior, especially drumming, is probably the photoperiod, the amount of daylight versus darkness at a particular time of year. This changing of day length as spring approaches, and again as summer fades into fall, apparently stimulates gonadal activity, which in turn tells the male grouse to step up and claim his territory.

BESENGER

THE PATTERN OF LIFE

Having surveyed his territory, the drummer steps into position, at a right angle to his log, and makes a few preparatory wingbeats. After a pause, the real drumming begins.

The cessation of drumming disturbs the bird's equilibrium. He tips forward, then lifts his tail to regain his balance. A look around satisfies him that no predators are watching . . . but no hens, either.

He walks slowly to another stage on the log. After an interval of perhaps several minutes, he begins again: the preparatory wingbeats, the pause, then the drumming with blurred wings.

The drum may include 50 wingbeats. Once again he stops and recovers his balance, then looks around and waits. If he hears a rival, he will most likely respond with another drum.

The moss-covered log is the classic stage for a drummer. The bird prefers a level platform.

A guard object, like the root-mass of the tree, keeps the drummer secure from predators on one side.

Droppings on this pine log attest to its use as a drumming stage. They also provide clues to the grouse's diet.

THE DRUMMING LOG

The log selected by a male grouse serves as an elevated platform for his drumming display. Other forest objects, such as boulders, exposed tree roots, dirt mounds, woodpiles, and rock walls, have all served the purpose. Usually, however, fallen logs are the most plentiful platforms in the forest and the most frequently used by grouse.

The male has two primary requirements for a log, according to Gullion. Its location should provide him with the best opportunity to advertise his presence within the forest, and it should afford maximum protection from predators. Boag and Sumanik found that male grouse in Alberta were particular about two factors: level stages upon which to drum, and sufficient heights above the forest floor to allow them to see at least 20 yards. As long as a log met such needs, a grouse was not choosy about its condition. Therefore, traditional moss-covered logs devoid of bark, as well as newly fallen trees and objects that are not logs, can meet the criteria.

Although logs used for drumming occur in a variety of habitats, there is general agreement among studies about what types of vegetation characterize the best drumming site, the forest habitat immediately surrounding the drumming log. Gullion has listed the following as necessary requirements, at least for grouse in Minnesota: a raised drumming stage; a "guard object," or screen; fairly dense stem growth of small

trees or shrubs on all sides of the log to a radius of 10 to 12 feet; and as a source of food, several mature male aspen trees within sight of the log.

The height of the drumming stage varies. What is important to the drummer is not any particular measurement but adequate vision: he must be able to survey his immediate surroundings and see whether an approaching intruder is friend or foe.

The guard object Gullion refers to is often the rootmass of a downed tree. The drumming stage on such a log is usually about 3 to 5 feet from the rootmass, which screens the grouse for as much as one quarter of his horizon. The guard object may also be a tree trunk, stump, or clump of shrubs growing close to the drumming stage.

Despite regional differences in vegetation, most researchers have found that the quality of the surrounding shrub layer determines whether a log will be selected as a drumming site. In southwestern Alberta, Boag and Sumanik found that logs used for drumming were in forest areas where woody stems were dense. Apparently, an overhead cover of certain species in the shrub layer (especially young white spruce, *Picea glauca*) was desirable; the canopy provided by the tree layer above this was not important. In a follow-up study, they found that the removal of shrubs around the drumming stages made these logs unacceptable to the grouse.

Other studies have produced similar results. In central Wisconsin, drumming sites were characterized by particular densities and structures of certain woody species, especially alder, winterberry, and hazelnut taller than 5 feet. Most drumming grouse selected sites where older aspens, a source of food, were nearby, and most birds settled along upland-lowland edges. In southeastern Ohio, the density of the woody shrub layer was more critical than the mix of species. In northern Georgia, all vegetation layers were factors, but a shrub understory that provided overhead concealment around the stage and good visibility just above ground level appeared most important.

Differences occur, however, among individual grouse, among regions and habitats, and among the findings of grouse researchers. Palmer, reporting on drumming sites in northern Michigan, stated that vegetation over 8 feet in height was significantly denser near drumming logs than in the surrounding general cover. In a study near Rochester, Alberta, Rusch and Keith found a significantly lower density of saplings and a greater density of trees at drumming logs than elsewhere in the aspen woods. These drumming sites were evenly distributed throughout the aspen woods, not concentrated along upland-lowland edges.

Despite such differences, all researchers agree that grouse want drumming sites with high densities of woody stems for protection from avian predators, and sparse growth of very low shrubs to allow clear views of approaching ground predators.

Features other than fallen trees can serve as platforms for drumming. Left: A Michigan drummer has selected a mound in the midst of evergreens. Deciduous woody stems and saplings are more usual drumming cover. Right: A rock was this bird's choice.

Different stages for drumming

*T*he site is chosen with such care, and the stage has such definable characteristics. Why would a grouse need more than one? But the male ruffed grouse often counts more than one drumming log in his activity center. Use of these alternate logs might be a tactic to avoid predation: perhaps by moving around, the bird keeps his enemies guessing about his location at any one time.

Another explanation takes into account the angles at which trees fall in the forest—usually randomly. Grouse, it seems, often choose as alternate drumming sites logs that lie in directions different from those of their primary logs. Archibald, noting this, recorded the drumming sounds of a grouse from various positions and determined that the sound level was greatest when the microphone was directly in front of the bird. The grouse's potential mates and rivals, like the researcher, can hear his drumming best if they are directly facing him. Archibald reasoned that a grouse might use various logs so that he can face different neighboring birds and intensify the effects of his drumming in the desired directions. Moreover, these logs might help him attract females from afar.

Alternate logs are common. Of thirteen occupied activity centers on the Little Paint Creek study area in Iowa, eleven contained more than one drumming log. The variety of angles at which they lay enabled these males both to avoid predation and to advertise their presence to other grouse.

—R. Scott McBurney

TOPOGRAPHY

Over much of the range of the ruffed grouse, the terrain is reasonably level and does not affect the birds' choice of sites for drumming. Parts of the more southerly range of grouse, however, have a quite rugged topography. Unglaciated regions, characterized by steep, wooded slopes, make up the primary grouse habitat in northeastern Iowa, southwestern Wisconsin, and southeastern Ohio. In Iowa, such slopes are the only places grouse can live, agriculture having appropriated the gently sloping uplands and level bottomlands that were once inhabited by grouse. Drumming sites on steep slopes are relatively rare because trees usually fall downhill and thus cannot provide level drumming stages.

In Ohio, male grouse prefer upper slopes or ridgetops for drumming sites, according to Stoll and his colleagues. In Iowa, I found that drumming males occupied only the narrow band of forest between the cultivated uplands and the steeply wooded slopes. Although the number of logs suitable for drumming was greatest here, grouse may have preferred these sites over downslope ones for another reason: the range over which drumming sounds would carry was greater from the higher elevations, which provided male grouse with better opportunities to advertise their presence.

THE ACTIVITY CENTER

The drumming of the male ruffed grouse is believed to be an act of territorial defense, but it bears repeating that no conclusive evidence exists that grouse actively defend territorial boundaries. Certainly a male will defend his drumming log against other male grouse, but the log is only a display object, and it is well known that many grouse use two or more logs for drumming. These logs are the focal points of larger areas, 10 to 30 or more acres in size, where individual males concentrate their activities. Gullion has called these general areas *activity centers*.

Spending as much time at their activity centers as they do, male ruffed grouse unwittingly leave careful records of their presence and behavior. Properly read, their signs indicate the chronology of use of particular logs and the longevity of individual birds. When these signs no longer can be found, the resident male has probably died.

Fecal droppings, one such sign, accumulate at the drumming stages primarily during the spring season and, to a lesser extent, in the fall. Differences between accumulations at various logs may be surprisingly great. During my study in Iowa, for example, males 603 and 605 were active and consistent drummers in the spring of 1969. However, there were 403 droppings in 603's activity center and only 32 droppings in 605's center. Dropping accumulations, then, do not reveal how much time a bird has spent drumming. Based on other observations, male 603 spent considerable time at his drumming logs and often roosted by them at night. But droppings at least enable a researcher to determine whether an activity center is occupied and the degree of attendance at the drumming stage.

Molted wing feathers (primaries) and tail feathers (rectrices) at or near logs are another sign. Male grouse in Iowa begin molting wing primaries at drumming logs as early as mid-May. At Cloquet, Minnesota, the wing primary molt begins in early June. Molted primaries may be found at drumming logs throughout the summer, for the molt is sequential, beginning with the first (innermost) and ending with the tenth (outermost) primary, and the last primaries are not molted until late August or very early September. Molted rectrices may be found at logs beginning in August. The two central rectrices identify the individual bird as well as a fingerprint identifies a human, Gullion and Marshall have noted, and thus molted

feathers can reveal not only whether a site is occupied but also who occupies it.

While molting, grouse seem to be even more secretive in their habits than usual. Porath noted that birds on the Little Paint Creek study area in Iowa were reluctant to flush and tended to freeze or run when approached. However, ruffed grouse are capable of flight throughout their wing molt.

Trapping, marking, and observing signs left by male grouse at drumming logs have enabled Gullion and other researchers at Cloquet, Minnesota, to record the history of use of activity centers. They have found that drumming logs and activity centers may be considered *transient,* that is, used by one grouse for his lifetime, then perhaps not used again, or *perennial,* used year after year by one grouse after another. It is not always easy to determine whether a drumming log is perennial or transient. Data covering a succession of grouse within that activity center are necessary. As Gullion states, the crucial test for the perennial status of a log comes when an activity center has been vacant for two drumming seasons (one spring plus one fall season) or longer. If a new occupant uses the same drumming stage on the same log, the log is considered perennial.

A drumming log may also be classified according to the intensity of use it receives from an individual grouse. A *primary log* is used most often by a grouse during one season. An *alternate log* is an additional log used by the same bird during one season; one grouse may have several alternate logs. If traps are placed on his primary and alternate logs, a bird might use a *secondary log.* The status of logs defined in this manner can change when one male grouse succeeds another in an activity center. For instance, the primary log of one grouse could have been his predecessor's alternate or secondary log.

Gullion has used two other important terms concerning male territories. During times of intense drumming activity, some male grouse temporarily leave their usual logs to drum at logs not normally used. At these so-called *challenge sites* they engage in drumming duels with neighboring males. When there is a low density of drumming male grouse, some birds expand their usual areas of activity to include nearby activity

The number of droppings can indicate whether a log is the primary drumming stage or a less secure, infrequently used alternate log.

centers. These *expanded occupancies* seem to occur when grouse, not within hearing range of neighboring birds, move closer to other active drummers.

Gullion has also recognized three general categories of drumming male grouse. A *dominant bird* is the normal occupant of a primary log and the bird most frequently heard drumming at that site. A second male grouse may sometimes be present in an activity center. This *alternate drummer* is seldom heard drumming unless the dominant bird is confined in a trap; if the dominant bird dies, the alternate will likely succeed him. Alternates are usually immature birds.

Two males that occupy the same activity center and drum on nearby logs—usually together, as rivals—are *satellite drummers*. Neither bird is clearly dominant. Satellite drummers are more common in years of intense drumming activity.

At the Little Paint Creek study area in Iowa, most of my contact was with dominant birds. There was evidence of at least one exception. On May 5, 1969, male 605 was captured in a mirror trap. During his confinement, an audio tape recorder unit was recording at the drumming log. Playback of the tape revealed the sounds made by the bird in the trap. He had been roost-

Clusters of drummers

*T*hough the spacing of drumming birds may change somewhat as habitat is altered by logging, windstorms, natural forest succession, or other events, certain habitats attract drummers year after year. These birds are selecting the best available habitat, of course: drumming males tend to settle where they find good cover and easy access to mature aspens or other food resources. But other factors may be at work, and the density of drummers may sometimes have little to do with either cover or food.

An example: in central Wisconsin, suitable habitats that had been occupied remained vacant for one or more years. This might be expected in years of low grouse populations, but these perfectly good habitats went unoccupied even as grouse numbers were increasing in the surrounding areas. The absence of drummers was largely due to high hunting mortality, Kubisiak determined. Gullion observed a similar phenomenon at the Mille Lacs Wildlife Area in Minnesota, where populations had been depressed to about a third the capacity by hunting.

The spacing of males has varied considerably in central Wisconsin, where the birds generally seek upland-lowland edges with tall shrubs. In some years most birds were at least 200 meters apart, even in the best habitats. And some birds, those that occupied small islands of less than 1 hectare surrounded by water or marsh, were more than 800 meters from the nearest drummer. In high grouse years the drummers were only about 30 meters apart in the best habitats. That figure is roughly comparable to the closest spacing found by Theberge and Gauthier in Ontario—23 meters.

Most tantalizing is Gullion's 1967 speculation that certain dominant males stimulate other males to occupy drumming sites nearby. It would appear that some aggressive young males are positioning themselves to challenge older, established birds, provided cover is suitable. Thus it may be a dominant male, in addition to the irresistible lure of fine habitat, that prompts drummers to cluster together.

—John Kubisiak

ing regularly in this unset trap for several days and did not sound especially upset about being confined in it. Approximately a half-hour after sunrise, there was a faint but distinct drum from outside the trap. Exactly two minutes later, male 605 began nervously pacing in the trap. He was pacing even more frantically two minutes later, when a second drum could be heard. Unfortunately, the tape then ended. I am fairly certain that the trapped bird could see his challenger on a nearby log. This challenge did not occur until more than one hour after the initial confinement of male 605. I assumed, then, that the silence of the dominant bird in-

duced this second male, presumably an alternate drummer, to approach closely and drum. Male 605 was completely unharmed and had lost very few feathers by the time I released him that day. There was no evidence of fighting or anything unusual.

Observations of intruding males at the drumming logs of confined birds have not been lacking in other research studies. In 1978 Rusch and Keith reported eleven such occurrences during their Alberta studies. All the intruders were young males. In 1981 Rodgers reported five similar incidents in southwestern Wisconsin, two of which involved nonterritorial subadult males.

The spacing of drummers depends on the quality of the habitat and the number of birds. When the population reaches a high point, drummers may coexist only 25 or 30 meters apart.

Nondrumming males

Some male ruffed grouse cannot be identified as occupants of any activity centers. They may be unable to find suitable territories of their own for one or more drumming seasons. These nondrummers, immature or adult, are extremely difficult for researchers to enumerate. Their presence often goes undetected until an established drumming male is killed and replaced by a previously unidentified male within the same drumming season. On the Little Paint Creek study area in Iowa, in 1969, three drumming males were killed at or near their logs by predators. This was during April, at the height of the drumming season. All three were replaced by previously unidentified males before the end of the season.

Nondrumming grouse, then, may become drummers in time. At the Cloquet Forestry Center, Gullion has speculated, some nondrummers prefer to wait their turns to occupy prime activity centers—secure stands of aspen saplings—rather than take up residence in older, less secure habitats, even though these previously used sites are vacant. In the secure aspen habitats, survival of nondrumming males equals or exceeds that of established drummers.

The number of nondrumming males in a given year varies, but Gullion has found that it is greater in years of peak grouse abundance. The size of the nondrumming segment is important to any census of a total grouse population. Several researchers have reported that males (drumming plus nondrumming) are represented by an equal number of females in the breeding population.

Young males appear slowly as established drummers on logs in activity centers. At Cloquet, Minnesota, a few young grouse become established on logs in their first autumn and others the following spring, but these birds account for 50 percent or less of the established drummer population. Yet according to other indices of age composition at Cloquet, young, ten- to twelve-month-old males constitute at least 60 percent of the total male population. Most established drummers, then, must be adults twenty-two months or older. The group of unestablished young males each year is the major component of the population of nondrumming grouse.

Certain perennial activity centers, Gullion has noted, attract adult male grouse when former occupants die. Most of these replacement birds, he believed, came from the populations of adult nondrumming males, rather than young birds.

Gullion has also observed that certain perennial activity centers at Cloquet have remained the exclusive domains of grouse of a particular color phase. Eleven perennial centers were occupied strictly by gray males, Gullion reported, and two centers strictly by red birds.

Similar observations have been made elsewhere. Three neighboring activity centers on the Little Paint Creek study area in Iowa were occupied exclusively by gray-phase birds over a three-year period. Although this was not a long span of time, it nevertheless was unusual that consecutive males in three neighboring activity centers were gray-phased when only about 30 percent of Iowan grouse are gray birds.

What qualities might certain forest areas or drumming logs have that would consistently lure a bird of a particular coloration? There is no known explanation.

PREDATION

Male ruffed grouse are never more conspicuous than during the drumming season. On the Little Paint Creek study area in Iowa, three of twelve known, established drummers were killed at or near their logs during April 1969. Yet if the cover surrounding the log is adequate, the grouse is never more secure than when he is at his drumming log, Gullion believes. The problem arises with perennial logs, the ones in good cover that act as "ecological magnets," attracting grouse year after year. Male grouse that select these logs do not survive as long as grouse that select transient logs. According to Gullion and Marshall, perennial activity centers offer better quality habitats; that's why they are perennial rather than transient. Avian predators, however, apparently know the locations of perennial logs and learn how to ambush the birds using them. Male grouse are not usually killed at these logs—which have been selected precisely because they are relatively predator-proof—but are very vulnerable during their daily movements to and from them. Birds that switch to transient logs within perennial activity centers become more difficult for raptors to ambush.

The general habitat of an activity center is as important as the cover immediately adjacent to the drumming log, Gullion and Marshall have reported. Male grouse survive best in hardwood forest areas devoid of evergreen conifers. Pine trees older than fifteen to twenty-five years have high crowns that can conceal avian predators, and they lack lower branches that can protect grouse from surprise attacks. Spruces and firs, which normally possess these dense lower branches, do not provide raptors with the advantage of surprise, and their presence in activity centers does not adversely affect male grouse survival.

Male grouse that have chosen secure drumming logs and activity centers continue to use them as long as they live. Those birds that initially select poorer sites, however, often move to better ones before the next drumming season. Apparently, some grouse recognize the hazards that exist in certain forest areas: they abandon their activity centers and search for different ones.

When the pine tree behind the drummer grows tall and its lower branches die from lack of light, it will permit raptors to launch sneak attacks. The log will then lose its value as a drumming site.

Twigs and branches help protect this drummer. A grouse in less secure surroundings may abandon his log and risk a search for something better.

SPACING OF ACTIVITY CENTERS

The activity centers of male ruffed grouse are not usually circular, with the drumming log in the middle. Instead, Gullion and Marshall have found, they often are elliptical or triangular, with the drumming log well off center. Two factors seem to determine the size and shape of activity centers: the forest habitat in which these centers are located, and the proximity of neighboring male grouse.

In unbroken, good ruffed grouse habitat, drumming males are often evenly spaced, about 148 to 159 yards apart, so that each bird's activity center encompasses some 8 to 10 acres.

Grouse, however, cannot always occupy ideal habitat. In Iowa, for instance, activity centers were elongated by topographic necessity, bordered by cultivated uplands on one side and precipitous slopes on the other. Nonetheless, within this relatively narrow belt of suitable habitat, activity centers were fairly evenly spaced.

An exception to this general rule is activity clustering, a type of spacing reported by Gullion in 1967. Certain areas of the forest, although apparently similar to areas where grouse are evenly spaced, may contain aggregations of activity centers. Gullion believes that such a cluster reflects an attraction exerted by one dominant male grouse that induces younger males to establish new activity centers in his vicinity. Gullion further suggests that these activity clusters might

be expanded leks, or communal display grounds similar to those of the prairie grouse species.

Aubin reported in 1972 that the distribution of drumming logs in the Bow River Forest Reserve in southwestern Alberta showed similar clustering, but he was uncertain what factors were involved.

Radiotelemetry studies of grouse on the Cedar Creek Natural History Area in Minnesota provided some interesting insights into the spatial relationships of neighboring drummers. Using data from birds fitted with radio transmitters, Archibald reported that the ranges of male grouse became more fixed with the onset of the drumming season. The drumming males' centrally located "core areas" were used intensively and consistently; these areas averaged 2.26 hectares (about 5.6 acres) in size. But the ranges of adult males (twenty-two months or older) were significantly greater than those of juvenile males (ten to twelve months old), which suggested that adult males were capable of defending larger territories.

Territories were not exclusive: the boundaries between the ranges of two neighboring males overlapped. Within this area of overlap, however, a boundary line could be drawn that each male grouse usually declined to cross. If one male died and no newcomer took his place, the neighboring male crossed the line into the late bird's territory more frequently. Perhaps, then, real territorial boundaries exist.

A challenge to drum

*E*arly in the dawn of May 18, 1969, Lee Gladfelter and I were checking which male grouse were attending their drumming logs. We heard resident male 1424 drumming at his primary log and sat down to take notes on the length of time between drums. Eight minutes into 1424's performance, we heard another bird drumming nearby, to our south. The two birds continued to drum back and forth at two-and-a-half- to three-minute intervals for the next forty minutes. For the most part, the challenging male duplicated male 1424's intervals. Finally, the challenger answered male 1424's drum with silence, letting the dominant bird have the last word. The drumming duel had ended.

We flushed 1424 near his log, close enough that we could hear the jingling of his leg bands as he exploded into flight. A thorough search of the area to the south revealed no other bird, no other log with telltale fecal droppings. The only known established drummer south of male 1424's activity center was male 605. Possibly it was this bird who had found a challenge site between their usual drumming logs and had made his stand.

–R. Scott McBurney

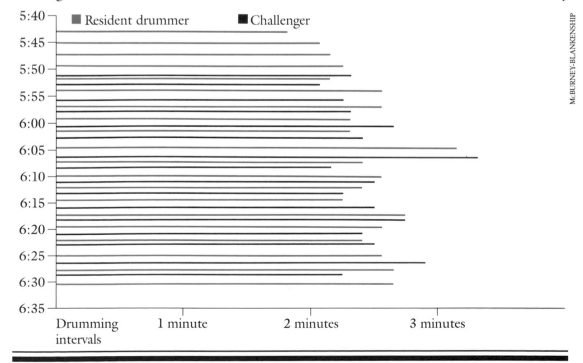

The resident bird's morning performance became a duel when a challenger answered his drums. The challenger closely matched the intervals between the drums of the defender.

McBURNEY-BLANKENSHIP

In the South

*T*he spring drumming season in the southern Appalachians extends from late March to late May, according to studies by Servello and by Hale and his colleagues. If southern grouse follow the patterns of their northern relatives, as many as 85 percent to 90 percent of the males may be active on a given morning during the approximately five-day peak. In North Carolina, Stafford has reported, the drumming peak occurs from about April 6 through April 10. These dates coincide closely with those reported by Mc-Burney for Iowa but are at least two to three weeks earlier than the peak in northern Minnesota.

During the peak period, Stafford found, the most intense drumming is associated with chilly mornings—temperatures approaching 25° F. and rising rapidly. If the morning air is warmer than 42° F., fewer males are likely to be drumming.

As drumming activity subsides in late April, a secondary peak begins. The drummers now are the late bloomers, usually smaller or younger males that failed to find suitable logs the previous fall. Their drumming is sporadic and never reaches the intensity of the first peak.

—Steven K. Stafford

THE PEAK OF DRUMMING

The density of the forest habitat and the cryptic coloration and secretive habits of ruffed grouse combine to make direct observation of their behavior a difficult task. But the male advertises his presence by drumming and therefore is a logical focus for state game managers, who have used annual drumming censuses to keep tabs on grouse populations.

The actual drumming performance, however, is not that easy to witness. The mere presence of a blind near a drumming log is enough to cause many birds to switch to their alternate or secondary logs. More than once has a researcher sat in a blind in the chilly morning darkness, only to hear his subject drum on some log just out of sight. Despite all that has been learned about drumming behavior the last two decades, much about this bird's activities still is unknown. And very little information has been published concerning the external factors that influence drumming activity. It is clear from a 1966 report by Gullion that weather conditions do affect grouse, at least in Minnesota.

The birds' participation in drumming each spring appears to be governed by the severity of the preceding winter. Mild winters introduce higher levels of drumming activity; severely cold winters, especially those with inadequate snow cover for overnight roosting, precede lower drumming activity levels. The timing of the snow melt likewise affects the intensity of drumming each spring: the later the snow melt, the less the birds drum. Once the drumming season is under way, however, subsequent snowfalls have only minor effects on drumming activity.

Grouse prefer to drum when air temperatures range from 26° to 36° F. Temperatures either lower or higher seem to discourage daily drumming. But it is rain, especially downpour, that puts the biggest damper on daily drumming. Strong winds, according to Gullion, do not discourage drumming.

In Alberta, Sumanik found that maximum drumming activity occurs at temperatures between 44° and 52° F., well above Gullion's figures. He also reported that strong winds discourage drumming and cause birds to seek shelter. Sumanik found that a specific light intensity value stimulated peak drumming activity in both morning and evening. Drumming activity tended to increase as light intensities approached this value and to decrease as light intensities receded from it.

The drumming peak for a particular season has been defined in two ways. Gullion con-

siders it the single morning when the highest percentage of birds are drumming. In northern Minnesota, this peak falls within three days of April 29 each year. On the Cedar Creek Natural History Area, farther south in Minnesota, Archibald considered the drumming peak to be the dates on which the average number of drums per grouse was highest. By studying individual grouse equipped with radio transmitters, he found that two such peaks occurred in 1970—one in late April, the other in late May.

Gullion's definition, the more widely used, is a measure of drumming participation; Archibald's measures drumming frequency. As such, the two are not comparable.

Data at Cloquet, Minnesota, indicate that the drumming peak is independent of plant phenology, such as the appearance of catkins on willows or the shedding of alder pollen. To Gullion this suggests photoperiodic control over drumming behavior. Archibald has noted, in addition, that increased drumming during the day is associated with moonlight at night. Both the April and May peaks in 1970 drumming occurred during a full moon, although nocturnal drumming was prevalent only in April.

Most of the male grouse that contribute to the April drumming peak were established on logs the previous fall. Gullion believes it is these birds that do most of the breeding. The April peak past, drummers show so little interest in attending their logs and drumming in early May that the Cloquet researchers regularly close down mirror-trapping operations until about May 15 each year. In May, when the previously established males are drumming less frequently, another group of drummers can be heard. These tend to be smaller males that presumably were unable to compete during the main breeding season. Their drumming is more sporadic and as likely to occur in late afternoon and evening as in the morning, Gullion has observed.

In Iowa, most birds on my study area drummed primarily in the morning. Of two primarily late-afternoon drummers captured in June, one was so small that it could easily have been mistaken for a female.

Temperature, precipitation, wind speed, light intensity—all affect the timing and frequency of drumming. But exactly how, researchers cannot yet say.

In Missouri, ruffed grouse spend the least amount of time on their drumming logs in June.

Percentage of time at drumming site

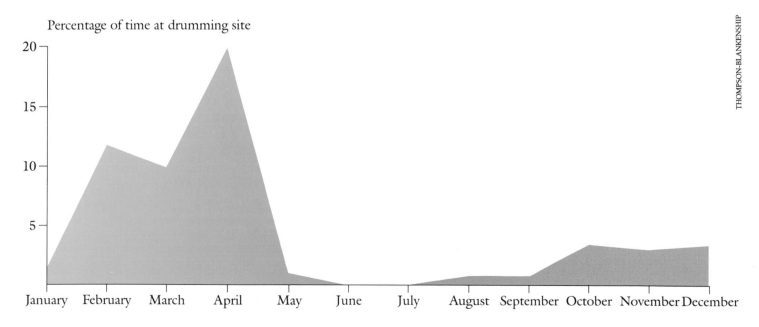

Drumming activity and mating

It is known that the hen ruffed grouse is attracted to the site of the male's drumming performance, that only a brief pair-bond is formed, that the tendency for the male to continue drumming apparently indicates a promiscuous mating habit. At the peak of drumming activity in April 1969, Lee Gladfelter and I witnessed a mating performance, something very few people have ever seen.

When we entered male 603's activity center at 4:55 A.M., the bird flushed out of a mirror trap placed open and unset on one of the five drumming logs that he used. Shortly afterward, we heard him drumming at rapid, forty-five- to sixty-second intervals. Gullion has stated that very short drumming intervals can occur when a male is stimulated by the presence of a female, and it is quite plausible that this male already knew that a hen was nearby. Brander, too, reported a radio-transmitter-fitted hen who had stayed overnight in a drummer's activity center immediately before assumed copulation.

After a few minutes of this rapid drumming, the male moved to a log 50 or 60 feet from our blind and drummed four times at intervals of 45 to 110 seconds. At 5:20 he bobbed his head up and down, jumped off the log, and hurriedly proceeded toward our blind. A female, whose presence we had not previously detected, approached from the side. He intercepted her and copulation occurred immediately. The hen did not leave after this, and the male remained with her in full courtship display for the next twenty-three minutes. Some of this courtship was obscured from view, and it is possible that copulation occurred again. Finally, the female flew away, and less than three minutes later the male drummed once from a nearby log. He then moved to the log with the mirror trap. For the next seventy-five minutes, he alternately attacked his image in the mirror, drummed on a nearby log at two- to three-minute intervals, and engaged in brief ground feeding. At 7:04 we left the blind, forcing the bird to another log where he again drummed. We advanced and he moved to a position just out of sight. At 7:20 A.M. we heard him drum again from that area. Later in the day we captured him in the mirror trap.

The interval of time between drums is shortest before sunrise. The pattern of intervals may be a mechanism by which each bird identifies himself.

Had the female been attracted by drumming to male 603's activity center for the first time on this morning? Or, if she had been nearby overnight, had male 603's pattern of drumming intervals initiated their courtship? We couldn't know; but our observations did coincide with what is generally known about ruffed grouse courtship and mating. The presence of the female indeed seemed to stimulate the male to drum initially at very rapid intervals. The male expended considerable nervous energy following courtship, and his reluctance to cease drumming or leave the vicinity of his logs indicated promiscuous mating behavior.

The drumming interval

The drumming interval—the length of time between two consecutive drums of one grouse—is of more than passing interest to ruffed grouse researchers. The frequency with which birds drum can affect the results of roadside drumming counts, skewing them high if the grouse drum frequently, low if infrequently. In Iowa, direct field observations and audio recordings of drumming were used in the spring of 1969 to secure 314 intervals from four birds drumming in the morning and 25 intervals from two birds drumming in late afternoon. This moderate sampling on a small, 500-acre area produced some interesting data.

• The mean morning drumming interval was 2.50 minutes (the range was 0.75 to 6.92 minutes). The mean late-afternoon

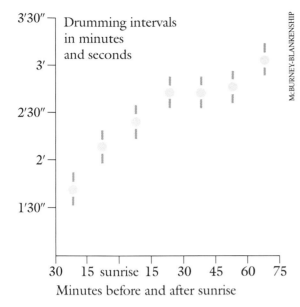

Drumming intervals in minutes and seconds

Minutes before and after sunrise

drumming interval was not significantly different from that of the morning.

• The mean drumming interval fluctuated each week but was shortest during April 19 to 20 and again May 17 to 19. The short intervals in May coincided with an increase in drumming, especially in the afternoon.

• The early-morning drumming intervals were shortest thirty minutes before sunrise, with a trend toward longer intervals as morning progressed.

Palmer's data showed a similar pattern, although he determined that the mean drumming interval of eleven birds was 4 minutes plus or minus 0.28 minute. He found that the greatest variation occurred after sunrise, when there were relatively few long intervals. In Iowa, observations of two drumming birds showed that after sunrise grouse occasionally interrupted their drumming to feed or move to other logs. When this was the case, the resulting long intervals were not included in the data.

It has generally been accepted that the average drumming interval of ruffed grouse is about four minutes. However, I believe that the mean interval of two and a half minutes was representative of birds on the Little Paint Creek study area. Sumanik noted in 1966 that activity on his study areas in southwestern Alberta was higher than one sound per bird per four-minute interval.

Of course, using study areas smaller than 1,000 acres to census drumming males is a risky business. The waxing or waning of one

or two male activity clusters, if present on such areas, could be independent of the general grouse population trends. A clustering of males in one area could result in increased drumming frequency as neighboring grouse constantly challenge one another. In Iowa, topography rules out any obvious clusters of activity centers; under average conditions, drumming sounds are quickly absorbed by the forest and are lost beyond a quarter-mile or even less. When I listened to a drumming bird, as a rule I was unable to hear his nearest neighbors. Occasionally, on a still morning, I heard the drumming of a grouse across a steep valley from the bird under observation but did not note any obvious responses to the sound. Here, unimpeded by the forest, drumming sounds could travel farther, and on calm mornings birds could hear each other from their blufftop positions.

Male grouse can influence their neighbors' drumming patterns. Aubin suggested in 1972 that grouse answer drumming sounds by drumming in turn. Archibald in 1976 identified two possible forms of communication between adjacent males: drumming shortly after the start of a neighbor's drum, and duplicating the interval between successive drums of a neighbor (called *interval copying*).

Archibald also noted that male grouse can duplicate their own drumming intervals as well as those of their neighbors. He has called interval copying "an indication of a truly remarkable timing mechanism." Perhaps this is like a personal song. The actual drumming sound of one male grouse is much like that of any other grouse. But, by varying or repeating his own drumming frequency, or by duplicating the drumming intervals of other grouse, a bird might be able both to identify himself to others and to challenge nearby rival males.

Challenges between drumming birds should not be considered unusual. They are probably a part of the lives of most male grouse. During years of high grouse populations or intense drumming activity in good, continuous habitat, such competition might be frequent. But where grouse populations remain fairly stable, a bird's daily drumming performance is often a solitary one.

—R. Scott McBurney

MARTINSON

*Population
dynamics*

To tally the grouse

————————

*H*uman beings are easy to count. The government sends out an army of census takers, or drops tons of forms into the mail; citizens, being a generally cooperative species, reveal their ages and count their broods and give the government number-crunchers great quantities of data to feed into the computers.

It is more difficult to take a census of those wary masters of camouflage, ruffed grouse. Most attempts to count these secretive birds are by indices, that is, counts or estimates of certain parts of the population, such as the number heard drumming in the spring, or seen per mile of road, or flushed per hour, or bagged per hunting season. Assuming this and extrapolating that and hoping all their assumptions and extrapolations are correct, wildlife number-crunchers calculate the number of grouse in the woods.

Some estimates of density are based on long-term studies, like those by Bump in New York; by King, Eng, and Gullion and Marshall in Minnesota; by Rusch and Keith in Alberta; by Rusch in Manitoba; and by Kubisiak, Dorney and Kabat, and Thompson and Moulton in Wisconsin. These estimates are the most precise available. Since it is difficult to gather information of this quality and intensity over large areas, most estimates are based on samples of small areas. But if the numbers fluctuate similarly across several areas, even these estimates may be considered good indicators of trends in

Drummers, the more conspicuous of the sexes, are most frequently counted. For each drummer, researchers assume one hen.

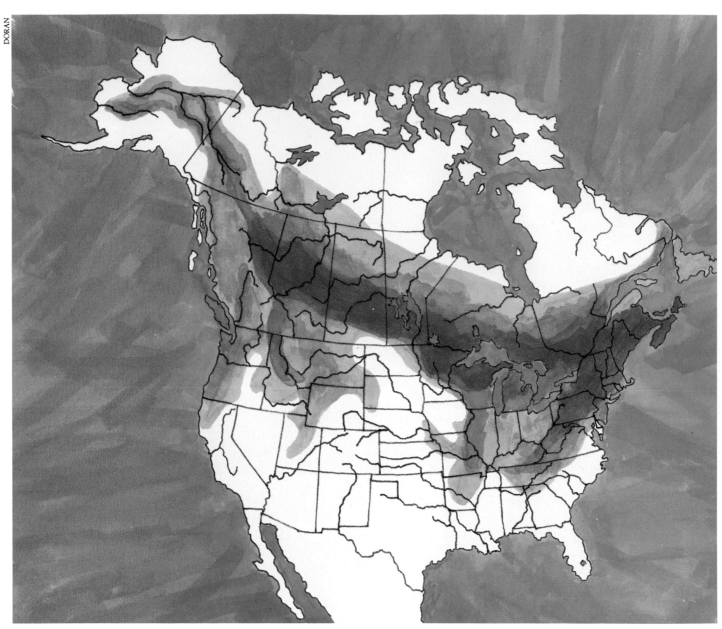

DORAN

Range and population density: orange indicates the historical range of ruffed grouse. Current populations are densest where the color is deepest.

ruffed grouse numbers over large areas.

The most common index of numbers of grouse is the drumming count. Each spring, just about the time the willows begin to leaf out, a researcher drives along a fixed route on quiet mornings and stops every half-mile to tally the number of drumming displays heard in a four-minute period. Drumming counts have been conducted for many years in the Lake States, the provinces of Manitoba and Ontario, and in some New England states. If the researchers' routes are well distributed throughout the grouse range, the drumming count can be a good index to grouse population trends, but there are a few pitfalls. Poor weather (especially high winds), topography, changes in routes, and

observers with differing abilities to hear the low-frequency drumming sound can all disrupt the index. So do changes in the proportion of drummers. Studies in Alberta and Minnesota suggest that 10 percent to 30 percent of males (mainly young cocks) do not drum in any one spring. Nevertheless, most researchers have found that drumming frequency is well correlated with other indices to grouse numbers.

Where the ruffed grouse is an important game bird, the annual fall harvest is another index to population size. But these estimates, based on questionnaires, suffer from a variety of sampling problems and biases that affect their interpretation: it is difficult, for example, to obtain a random sample of

202

RUFFED GROUSE

Minnesota Department of Natural Resources
Small Game Hunter Report 1986

Please indicate the number of days you hunted each species, and the county hunted in for each species, even if none was bagged. Report only game **you personally** killed and retrieved in Minnesota.
If you did not hunt small
game in Minnesota, check here ☐ .

		Number **You Bagged** All Season	Number of Days You Hunted All Season	County **You Hunted** In Mostly
Ducks (all species)	001			
Coots (mud hens)	050			
Canada Geese	040			
Other Geese	041			
Snipe (jacksnipe)	051			
Rails and gallinules	052			
Woodcock	060			
Pheasant	070			
Ruffed grouse (partridge)	071			
Spruce grouse	072			
Sharp-tailed grouse	073			
Hungarian partridge	074			
Fox squirrel	089			
Gray squirrel	090			
Cottontail rabbit	091			
Jackrabbit	092			
Snowshoe hare	093			
Badger	035			
Raccoon	094			
Red Fox	095			
Gray Fox	096			
Coyote (brush wolf)	097			

In addition to a small game license, did you buy (check)
A 1986 Firearms Deer License? ☐ Yes ☐ No
A 1986 Archery Deer License? ☐ Yes ☐ No

Game commissions and departments of natural resources use forms like Minnesota's to keep tabs on populations of game species. Accuracy depends on the willingness of hunters to cooperate.

hunters; hunters may not accurately recall grouse-hunting experiences; successful hunters tend to respond more than disappointed hunters; and some enthusiasts may exaggerate. Changes in hunters' efforts may also have a large impact on estimates of grouse harvests: reports that the birds are plentiful attract more hunters who hunt more often during the season.

Despite the difficulties of assessing numbers of grouse, thirty-one states and all thirteen Canadian provinces and territories believe they have enough ruffed grouse to allow hunting seasons. Some ruffed grouse are found in Illinois, Arkansas, Alabama, and Kansas but are not currently hunted; grouse once inhabited Nebraska but are now absent from that state. Most areas do not have population estimates, but harvest estimates suggest that the highest densities occur in Maine, New York, Pennsylvania, West Virginia, Michigan, Minnesota, Wisconsin, Alberta, and New Brunswick.

In the northeastern states, harvests of ruffed grouse have generally been increasing since 1940. Data on grouse are scarce, but harvests suggest that a general increase in the bird's population has occurred in this region over the past four decades.

In the Northeast and the Midwest, five states report that grouse habitat has increased in the past forty years; one state reports no trend. The three Lake States all report a probable decrease in grouse habitat due to natural forest succession from aspen to more shade-tolerant trees and to the maturation of these climax forests.

Ruffed grouse are not major game birds in the southern and western portions of their range, and population trends here are in general poorly documented. The southeastern states are the southern fringe of ruffed grouse range. Harvests are high just south of the Mason-Dixon line, in West Virginia and Virginia, but low in South Carolina and Georgia. Populations are thought to have declined in West Virginia since the 1940s.

Estimates and reports from biologists in the Midwest suggest that ruffed grouse numbers are generally stable or increasing in Indiana, Iowa, Kentucky, and Tennessee. In Indiana, Iowa, southeastern Minnesota, and southwestern Wisconsin, grouse populations seem to have undergone no major trends over the relatively short period—twenty-five years—for which drumming counts are available. If anything, counts may have increased slightly in southeastern Minnesota and declined somewhat in southwestern Wisconsin.

Ruffed grouse disappeared from Illinois near the turn of the century. Several releases of transplanted grouse have been made in an effort to reestablish the bird.

In Missouri, ruffed grouse were reduced to small remnant populations near the turn of the century but have been restored to some parts of the state, encouraged by protection, habitat management, and transplants of grouse from other states. Missouri held its first grouse season of modern times in 1983.

Although harvests exceed 100,000 in Idaho and Washington, the ruffed grouse is not the major game bird here or in any other western state. Ruffed grouse populations are very small and isolated in California, Nevada, and South Dakota. Ruffed grouse were not even known in Nevada until introduced

Scarcity in the South

*T*he Sunbelt, focus of America's population shift during the 1960s and 1970s, holds few attractions for ruffed grouse. At least, few of the birds choose to live there. No ruffed grouse at all inhabit the wildlands around such favorite human habitats as Tucson, Dallas, or San Diego. And in the southeastern United States, ruffed grouse population densities are but a fraction of those in the northern part of the continent.

In 1963 Weber and Barick reported fall and spring densities of 3 to 4 grouse per 100 acres in North Carolina and Georgia; Harris's 1981 paper confirmed those numbers. Hale et al. reported 1.8 to 2.6 drumming males per 100 acres in Georgia in 1982, figures three to four times lower than some densities in the North. In any case, there are far fewer grouse in the South than in the North.

One reason is that the Southeast lacks the extensive areas of suitable habitat common to the North. Without high-quality cover, southeastern grouse probably are more susceptible to predation and may not have access to adequate food. These factors may be the cause of the apparent low success of grouse in the South. The percentage of juvenile grouse in the fall harvest is lower in the South than in the North, according to figures published by Davis and Stoll in 1973: generally, 65 percent to 75 percent in the North, 45 percent to 55 percent in the South.

This difference is thought to indicate poor breeding success, but it may be due at least partly to the late hunting season in the South. In the North, most grouse are taken from October to December; in the South, most are harvested from December to February. Before the southern hunting season even begins, nonhuman hunters—both avian and mammalian predators—have had their chance to pick off the less wary and inexperienced juveniles, and this possibly accounts for the lower age ratios in the harvest.

Food is another problem for the southern ruffed grouse. In spring, summer, and fall, its diet is adequate: leaves of herbaceous plants and fruits, as in the rest of the bird's range. But during winter the southern ruffed grouse does not have available the buds, twigs, and catkins that its northern cousins prefer, and it resorts to evergreen leaves and ferns.

Such a diet is low in protein, and it has been shown in captive grouse that such diets result in smaller clutches, eggs less likely to hatch, and chicks less likely to survive. What little protein those evergreens and ferns offer may not even be available to the birds, for these plants contain relatively high levels of tannins and other potentially harmful compounds—and tannins partially prevent the digestion of protein.

The scarcity of nutritionally adequate foods, then, may also be limiting grouse members in the Southeast.

—Frederick A. Servello and
Roy Kirkpatrick

in 1970. Harvests in the West are generally stable or increasing.

In North Dakota, ruffed grouse are found mainly in the Turtle Mountains, adjacent to the Canadian border. Drumming counts in this area, which have been conducted since 1951, show a pronounced and regular fluctuation, reaching peaks and lows about every nine to ten years, and an overall slight decrease.

The ruffed grouse is the number one game bird in the Lake States, where it has been intensively studied for many years. The longest series of grouse population estimates comes from Cloquet, Minnesota, where Ralph King, Robert Eng, Gordon Gullion, and others have tracked grouse populations almost continuously since 1932. Drumming counts in northern Minnesota have been conducted since 1949. Estimates of annual harvests often exceed 500,000 each in Michigan, Minnesota, and Wisconsin. As in

Western numbers

Compared with populations in prime habitats of the upper Midwest, the North, and the Northeast, grouse numbers in the West tend to be relatively low. In western Washington, one study found an average density of about 34 birds per square mile. In Alberta, in an area of mixed aspen, spruce, and bog habitats, estimates of densities ranged from 28 per square mile in April to 90 to 100 per square mile in August. Density of drumming grouse has been reported at 35 per square mile in northern Idaho, and in southeastern Idaho there may be only 1 to 15 grouse per square mile of suitable habitat.

In western Washington, Brewer found that the survival of adult grouse into the next year ranges from 75 to 83 percent. This is substantially higher than the 27 to 30 percent survival rates noted in Alberta by Rusch and Keith: 21 to 34 percent for young grouse from hatching to the next spring, and 41 to 42 percent for drumming males.

Most of the birds that fail to see their second summer are victims of predators: 25 percent of the annual mortality and 80 percent of the fall-to-spring mortality in Alberta were caused by great horned owls, goshawks, and lynx. Juveniles suffer higher mortality than adults in the fall, at least in Alberta. Certainly there are more juveniles at that time for predators to make a meal of. According to various studies, in northern Idaho 71 percent of all fall birds are juveniles; in western Washington, 64 to 75 percent; and in Alberta, 76 to 84 percent.

In many areas of their range, ruffed grouse ride a ten-year roller coaster of population highs and lows. This cycle is not consistent throughout the West. In Alberta it is evident and may be tied to the lynx–snowshoe hare cycle. In western Washington, Idaho, and Utah, however, there is no conclusive evidence for cyclic ups and downs.

In the late 1970s more than 400,000 ruffed grouse were harvested each year by hunters; about 50 percent of the total came from Washington state. This kill represented about 11 percent of the total for the United States. Including the harvest in Yukon, Northwest Territories, British Columbia, and Alberta, about 16 percent of all ruffed grouse shot were harvested in the West.

Success for hunters in Washington has averaged 3.19 to 3.78 birds each. Not all the birds were ruffed grouse, however: 37 percent were other grouse species. The kill was about 11 to 16 percent of the total fall population. In Alberta, hunters took about 9 percent of the total fall population.

Western ruffed grouse populations could easily sustain substantially higher harvests. The bird is not heavily promoted as game in most western states and provinces, and hunting regulations usually lump all "forest grouse" together and set bag limits for ruffed, spruce, and blue grouse combined. It is likely that the majority of ruffed grouse harvested in this region are taken incidentally by big-game hunters.

—*Dean F. Stauffer*

North Dakota, harvests here tend to fluctuate widely, reaching peaks about every nine to ten years, but the harvests have generally increased over the past forty years.

Ruffed grouse are important game birds in Alaska and the Canadian provinces. Recent harvests in Alberta, British Columbia, Manitoba, and New Brunswick exceed 100,000 each. Few data are available from Alaska, but responses to twelve years of questionnaires show a peak in 1968. A high in 1968 also occurred in Alberta, where a population study was conducted from 1965 to 1975. Trappers throughout Alberta reported similar trends on their circuits, according to a compilation by Keith and Rusch.

Manitoba's harvest estimates have a general upward trend, but every eight to ten years there have been closed seasons or very low harvests. Peaks occurred in 1933, 1941, 1952, 1961, and 1971; no estimates are available for the 1980s.

Like many other species of North American wildlife, ruffed grouse were not native to Newfoundland. Introduced in the 1960s, they have now spread to the most suitable forest habitats on the island. Although overall numbers have increased with this expansion of range, the number of grouse per square mile has fluctuated in the same way as in the mainland Canadian provinces: peaks in the early 1970s and 1980s, preceded and followed by declines. It appears that these transplanted grouse may be following the pattern of cyclic fluctuation common among grouse throughout most of Canada and the Lake States.

In most places throughout their range, ruffed grouse seem to have held their own in the past forty years; in many places their numbers seem to be increasing. Moreover, where ruffed grouse had disappeared (Illinois, Arkansas), been reduced to remnant populations (Missouri), or never been native (Nevada, Newfoundland), transplanted birds appear to be doing well. All in all, the continental trend for ruffed grouse is that populations, having decreased in the late 1800s and early 1900s and stabilized during the 1930s and 1940s, have been growing.

—Donald H. Rusch and
Stephen DeStefano

Trapping males

Research into populations and territorial interactions of male ruffed grouse has largely been based on two field techniques. One is the intensive search for drumming logs on study areas. Researchers attempt to locate all drumming birds by looking for such signs as droppings and molted feathers at drumming sites. The second technique involves capturing and marking individual grouse.

The means for trapping males on drumming logs is the mirror trap, a simple, wire-covered box trap with a falling gate at one end and a mirror at the other. When the trap is placed on a log a few feet from the drumming stage, the grouse sees his image and attacks it. Presumably, he believes his reflection is another male trespassing on his log. When the bird steps on a treadle within the trap, the gate is released and he is caught. On large study areas, it is not possible to fool every territorial male with a mirror trap, but success is usually high, often exceeding 90 percent of all known drummers.

Setting traps on drumming logs sometimes prompts especially wary birds to use other logs within their activity centers more frequently. Setting traps on these alternate logs often helps in capturing such birds. Some males can be caught only once: in subsequent seasons, these trap-wise survivors continue to use their activity centers and drum on their same logs, but ignore the mirror traps.

To allow a bird to get used to a trap on his log, researchers leave the trap open and unset, with the gate removed. Very often, the grouse will begin roosting in the trap and can then be easily caught. This brings up a curious aspect of grouse behavior: the original aggressiveness in attacking an intruder—the image in the mirror—seems to give way to a recognition that the image is actually the bird's own. I once recorded a bird in an unset trap. The cooing sounds on the tape left me convinced that the grouse either recognized his reflection or at least accepted it as a friendly companion. This same bird, male 603, also realized that the trap had a back.

On one occasion, he left the unset trap, circled to the rear, and then pecked at the backside of the mirror in an attempt to reach the image. We set the trap and caught him later that day. I could not catch a bird in this activity center the following year. Had male 603 figured it out?

Of concern to researchers are the injuries grouse sustain when caught in mirror traps. I captured several birds that had lost most or all of their rectrices (tail feathers) and scalped themselves down to the bare tops of their skulls. All of these birds survived and returned to their drumming logs. Such injuries usually are superficial, but they can be minimized if the wire trap sides are covered with burlap, which usually prevents birds from attempting to flush against the wire. Prompt checking of traps is equally important. Predators can discover confined birds and frighten them badly enough that they injure themselves. Once, while I was banding a trapped drummer, the grouse emitted a distress call. This vocalization brought an immediate response: crashing through the brush, a red fox appeared. I can't say which of us was startled the most. The grouse flinched; I yelled; the fox bolted. The grouse was unhurt but very frightened.

In the Iowa studies, we marked grouse with colored, anodized aluminum leg bands. Each bird wore two bands per leg. The lower right leg band bore the bird's identifying number, but we didn't have to get close enough to read it to identify the bird, since no two grouse wore the same color combination. With eight band colors and four positions (upper and lower on each leg), more than 4,000 combinations were possible ($8^4 = 4,096$). Using binoculars and a powerful flashlight for low-light conditions, researchers can recognize individual birds from their leg-band colors, at least in forest habitat with good road access. In northeastern Iowa's rugged topography, this sight identification technique was less useful, but marked birds were easily recognized when they flushed reasonably close to an observer. The jingling of the aluminum bands, along with observation of the bird's color phase, red or gray, was sufficient to identify grouse flushed near known drumming logs.
—R. Scott McBurney

Mirror trap: the drummer, seeing his reflection, believes it is an intruder and enters to challenge it. Some grouse avoid such traps after being caught only once.

A captured ruffed grouse is weighed. Feather samples may be plucked while the bird is in the hand.

Still immobilized in its drawstring bag, the grouse is banded. Researchers will determine its sex and age before releasing it.

When the grouse is taken during the hunting season, or its remains are found on the forest floor, researchers will close the book on this bird's life story.

Roadside drumming counts

Spring roadside drumming counts have been widely used as indices to regional trends in ruffed grouse breeding populations. Road transects through known grouse habitat are established and surveyed annually, usually on calm mornings from thirty to forty-five minutes before sunrise to one to two hours after. The total number of drums heard during a four-minute period is recorded at each of a prescribed number of stops along a transect. The basis for the four-minute listening period per stop is the generally accepted belief that grouse drum at an average interval of four minutes. The mean number of drums per stop is the drumming index for a particular transect. Indices can be averaged to arrive at a single drumming index for a certain region.

A number of factors—weather, topography, design of transects, consistency of technique—can affect drumming count results. But the grouse themselves can also influence the index values. Not all the males may decide to drum on a particular morning, for example. Drumming participation, the number of males heard along a given transect compared with the actual number of males occupying activity centers within hearing range, can thus affect the results. And since some birds may drum at intervals much longer—or shorter—than four minutes, drumming frequency, the ratio of the number of drums heard to grouse producing the sounds, is another consideration.

Such variables can play havoc with the data

wildlife managers need. In southwestern Wisconsin, Rodgers has reported that drumming counts, unusually low in the spring of 1976, increased 2.7 times in 1977. Yet numbers of territorial male grouse on five study areas located along one of the transects increased only 29 percent. The difference was due to greater drumming participation by males in 1977. Rodgers believed that birds in this habitat, limited by steep topography and agriculture, were responding to increased competition for drumming sites.

Competition also can cause certain grouse to drum more frequently. This might be especially true in forest areas where activity centers are clustered. It has already been shown that two or more male grouse can influence one another's drumming intervals. If a drumming survey route transects such an activity cluster, not only can more grouse be heard drumming, but certain birds may drum more than once during the prescribed four-minute stop as they respond to one another's territorial claims. Is the four-minute listening period too long? Not necessarily—so long as all surveyers use the same period on all surveys. It is important, however, that enough survey routes exist to produce a drumming index representative of the overall drumming activity of a region.

The frequency with which grouse drum also depends on the time of day. Birds drum at the shortest intervals about a half-hour before sunrise. Progressively longer intervals occur after sunrise. Palmer has recom-

PRATT

mended that drumming censuses begin one hour before sunrise. Routes surveyed later than one hour after sunrise could provide noticeably lower drumming index values than routes surveyed earlier. Not only do birds tend to drum less frequently as morning progresses, but drumming participation often decreases as some grouse leave their logs to feed. Obviously, if a limited number of people are available, surveying all routes simultaneously becomes difficult.

Roadside drumming counts, then, are imprecise methods affected by such variables as weather, topography, forest type, and the drumming behavior of the grouse themselves, not to mention the finances of the census-takers. Are such indices worth the

effort spent to achieve them? The answer is usually yes. They need to be interpreted correctly, however. Gullion has stated that drumming counts are misleading indicators of the numbers of male grouse living in forest areas because of the variation in drumming activity from year to year. But because the same factors that affect drumming activity also affect breeding activity and reproductive success, he concluded that roadside drumming counts can provide rough forecasts of the populations of grouse available for fall hunting. And in both northern Minnesota and Wisconsin, roadside drumming counts have indeed significantly correlated with subsequent fall harvest.

—*R. Scott McBurney*

Even a recognized index like the drumming count may be imprecise. This researcher hears only one of the drummers in the area. A second is downwind and inaudible, and in the distance, a third is momentarily silent.

The grouse cycle

*I*t is variously known as the rabbit cycle, the grouse cycle, the game cycle, the ten-year cycle. It brings drastic fluctuations in animal populations, from abundance to seeming extinction. It has a marked effect on the success of grouse hunters. But just what is this phenomenon, and what causes it?

The existence of a cycle in some species of wildlife has long been recognized. In the late nineteenth century, Ernest Thompson Seton observed that the hare population in Manitoba "goes in cycles of multiplication." He related the following account:

"In the spring of 1882, when first I lived at Carberry, Manitoba, I could find, perhaps, 2 rabbits in three or four hours' tramping through the woods. In 1883, they seemed no more plentiful; in 1884, one might see a dozen or more in a morning's walk; in 1885, they were perceptibly more numerous. But 1886, though not a rabbit year at Lake of the Woods, was the greatest ever recorded in the Western country . . . Near the Spruce Hill, at the edge of the poplar woods, Carberry, Manitoba, I stood; and looking around, counted the rabbits within a radius of 30 yards. They numbered 11, and there must have been many that I did not see; so that 20 would be a safe number at which to put them; that is, 20 to the acre. But dividing it by 2 to allow for the sparser places, it would easily total 5,000 to the square mile

The grouse is one of several species whose population appears to fluctuate in ten-year cycles, at least in its northern range.

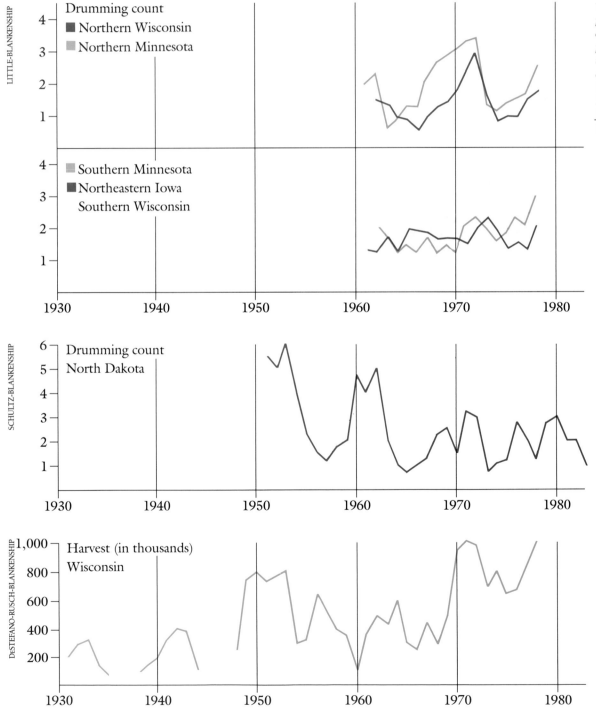

The indices used to estimate population levels differ in each case, but the data show that peaks and dips occur consistently across the northern tier of the United States. In the Turtle Mountains of North Dakota, grouse have recovered from each dip but at ever-lower levels.

. . . The summer and fall of 1892, I spent in the same region, and did not see a single snowshoe."

In the twentieth century, biologists began debating the length, the causes, and even the existence of the ten-year cycle, but relatively little effort was devoted to field studies. In New York, Bump and his associates conducted a comprehensive investigation; their work was inspired by concerns for grouse populations after a cyclic low was identified in 1928, prompting a closed season in 1929. They sought to determine the factor or factors responsible for major cyclic declines in grouse abundance and to recommend management strategies to forestall or reverse them. Ironically, despite the wealth of knowledge they acquired—still a very important source of information on the species—they failed to find any major cyclic changes in grouse numbers. On both the Connecticut Hill and the Adirondack areas, fall populations varied about threefold between 1930 and 1942 without any clear pattern that could be called a cycle.

Yet major fluctuations have been documented elsewhere at sufficiently regular intervals that they may safely be termed cycles. Many theories have been advanced in an attempt to explain them, implicating disease, weather, forest fires, sunspots, starvation, crowding, predators, genetic changes, and chance.

In his book, *The Ten-Year Cycle*, Lloyd B. Keith reviewed the evidence for regular fluctuations in the wildlife of North America. Among his conclusions:

• Cyclic fluctuations in numbers of snowshoe hares, lynx, red fox, prairie grouse, and ruffed grouse do exist.

• Mean intervals between peaks are about ten years.

• Fluctuations tend to be synchronous among species and areas.

• The ten-year cycle is primarily a phenomenon of the northern coniferous forests and the aspen parklands.

Annual changes in numbers occur in virtually every wildlife species: densities are seldom constant. Even animals whose populations are stationary over the long term may undergo large variations in year-to-year numbers. But only large fluctuations that occur at more or less regular intervals are considered cycles.

No one explanation for the ruffed grouse cycle is universally accepted, and some theories are downright controversial. The synthesis presented here is based largely on the results of Keith's long-term studies in Alberta, begun in 1961, and on the work and analyses of Phil Doerr, Charles Fischer, Robert Small, James Holzwart, and Donald Rusch, as well as on interpretations of the major studies by Bump, Gordon Gullion, and their associates.

Population change, whether a long-term trend or a short-term variation, occurs in response to changes in rates of movement, reproduction, and mortality. If those rates do not change, population trends do not change. Since most ruffed grouse populations persist over long periods of time, becoming neither extinct nor abundant, the average growth rate must approach zero, and these birds must have characteristic or average rates of movement, reproduction, and mortality. The explanation for the ruffed grouse's ten-year cycle must lie in one or more of those variables.

MOVEMENT

If all the grouse in your favorite oak wood-lot move to a pine plantation during a winter storm, grouse numbers in both the oak and the pine habitats will definitely be affected. But such changes in domicile have negligible effects on large areas. Moreover, grouse are not migratory. Although some birds undoubtedly disperse from Wisconsin to Minnesota each year, for example, they form a very small percentage of the Wisconsin grouse population, and their departure tends to be offset by grouse coming from Minnesota into Wisconsin. In assessing general population trends and cycles, then, it is safe to ignore the effect of movement and concentrate instead on changes in reproduction or mortality.

REPRODUCTION

How many hens lay eggs? How many eggs do they lay? And how many of those eggs hatch? The answers to these questions determine the rate of reproduction.

About half the grouse in spring are hens, and the average number of eggs in a nest—a clutch—is eleven. A hen whose first nest is destroyed may renest, but ruffed grouse are not known to hatch two clutches per year in the wild. So if all hens nested and all eggs hatched, each hen would produce eleven chicks, or five and a half chicks for each spring grouse, male and female.

In natural populations, however, this reproductive potential is seldom, if ever, attained. Although hunters may bag six or seven or even nine young for every adult in the fall, remember that the young are more vulnerable to the gun than their wiser elders and are thus overrepresented. The fall ratio is also affected by the mortality of chicks and adults during summer: chicks are more vulnerable to predators, weather, and food scarcities. So the age ratio in the harvest may not be a good estimate of the reproduction rate. Nevertheless, it is one of the few measurements we have that gives clues to the variation of that rate from year to year.

The percentage of hens that lay eggs is a potentially important component of the reproductive rate: it limits the effects of the rates that follow. If only 10 percent of the hens lay eggs, there won't be many chicks, and even big clutches and high hatching rates cannot compensate. Few estimates of the proportion of hens that lay eggs are available, but it seems reasonable to assume that hens in poor condition might not nest.

The dramatic response of grouse numbers to proper food and cover is ample testimony to the overwhelming importance of habitat. But habitat *per se* does not influence ruffed grouse populations; habitat must influence either the reproductive rate or the mortality rate. Gordon Gullion and his associates have clearly demonstrated the significance of aspen in the ecology and distribution of the ruffed grouse, and aspen husbandry has become the keystone of ruffed grouse management. Lack of food would probably prevent grouse from selecting an area in the first place, but a sudden, widespread failure of food supplies might influence grouse condition and subsequent mortality or reproduction.

There is, however, no strong evidence of

MARTINSON

The number of laying hens and the number of eggs in their clutches appear to be relatively constant and thus unconnected with cyclical changes.

dramatic variation in grouse condition. In Alberta, grouse in declining and low populations actually weighed slightly more than grouse in increasing or high populations. Weights of grouse in Bump's New York study were unrelated to population level. But lack of evidence does not rule out the hypothesis. As Gullion has pointed out, researchers can weigh and measure only surviving grouse: the dead tell no tales.

Grouse and other gallinaceous birds are notorious egg factories, often producing eggs far in excess of their reproductive needs. Consider, for example, the domestic chicken. Pheasants and gray partridge even dump their extra eggs in the nests of other birds. But do ruffed grouse in poor condition not lay eggs? Perhaps. Again, the evidence is weak. And since female grouse in poor condition have not yet been identified, it's difficult to know.

In recent years the technology of telemetry, or radio-tracking, has enabled researchers to follow young grouse for a year or more. Near Wautoma, Wisconsin, Small and Holzwart began radio-marking young and adult hens in 1982. Of the more than one hundred marked hens, twenty survived to the nesting season with working radios. All twenty laid eggs. That is, of course, a relatively small sampling of birds, but it does suggest that all hens may breed each spring, and we are unaware of evidence to the contrary.

The number of eggs per nest is another variable to consider. Clearly, it would have a direct influence on population. And even though ruffed grouse nests are difficult to

find, clutch size is the best documented component of the reproduction rate in ruffed grouse.

In an outstanding effort in New York State, Bump and his researchers located 1,473 nests between 1931 and 1941. At Rochester, Alberta, Rusch et al. found only 43 nests between 1966 and 1975. Bump reported an average of 11.5 eggs per nest; thousands of miles away and thirty years later, Rusch got 11. Bump's mean annual clutch size varied from 11.1 to 12.1 eggs; Rusch's annual averages ranged from 10.1 to 12 eggs.

Compared with some birds, then, clutch sizes in ruffed grouse seem remarkably constant. The small variation in numbers of eggs per nest seems insufficient to account for the major changes in population that shape the ruffed grouse's ten-year cycle.

Predation is a factor to look at. Ruffed grouse nests are sometimes destroyed by skunks, raccoons, foxes, and other predators. Because entire clutches rather than individual eggs tend to be lost, the figure is usually reported as nest success rather than egg success or hatch success.

Nest success appears to be more variable than numbers of breeding hens or clutch sizes. Bump reported that in New York the percentage of destroyed nests varied from 24 percent to 52 percent, with an average of 39 percent; predators were usually responsible. His was a large sample—1,431 nests. In

HERTLING

Alberta 10 of 43 nests, or 23 percent, were destroyed by predators. In Wisconsin, Holzwart found that fewer than half of the radio-marked hens were able to hatch chicks.

But in general, data on nest success in grouse suggest that at least half the eggs laid eventually hatch. Yet Bump found no relationship between the percentage of destroyed nests and the percentage of young in fall populations or the year-to-year changes in grouse numbers. In other areas not enough nests have been found to test for such relationships.

Theories that relate grouse abundance to food supplies (Gullion and Svoboba 1972), competition or genetics (Page and Bergerud 1984), or weather (Larsen and Lahey 1958) all assume considerable variation in the reproductive rate. Unfortunately, too few female grouse have been intensively monitored and too few grouse nests have been found in too few places to conclusively rule out major differences in reproduction rates. In general, there is no strong evidence that changes in grouse numbers are related to differences in reproduction.

Fall ratios of young to old do not usually vary so much for ruffed grouse as for other game birds, where almost complete reproductive failures, or "busts," sometimes occur. But they do vary. Between 1950 and 1982 the percentage of immatures among grouse killed in North Dakota varied from

The adult birds suffer losses, too. Through autumn and winter, predation, hunting, exposure, and inadequate nutrition continue to reduce the number of grouse. By the time spring has returned, there are again only two breeding pairs.

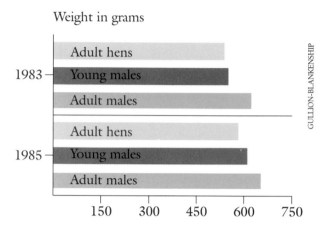

Weight in grams

	1983	
Adult hens		
Young males		
Adult males		

	1985	
Adult hens		
Young males		
Adult males		

150   300   450   600   750

Generation gap

*O*ccasionally, young birds from one cohort may average larger than their parents, depending on the severity of the winter.

For example, consider the weights of grouse bagged during the National Grouse and Woodcock Hunt at Grand Rapids, Minnesota. In 1983 the grouse population was in a cyclic decline, and the birds—adult hens, young males, and adult males—were small. Apparently, the previous winters had been harsh and had stressed the hens, who then produced chicks that were small and weak and never caught up. Two years later, following a more favorable winter, when food supplies and roosting snow were more satisfactory, nesting hens were in better condition and produced larger, more vigorous chicks. These chicks were able to survive better and provided the basis for a recovery in the population. Consequently, the weights in each category were higher that year.

—*Gordon W. Gullion*

40 percent to 86 percent, with an average of 67 percent. In only seven of twenty-three years did immatures constitute less than 58 percent or more than 76 percent, according to Schultz. In Manitoba, immatures ranged from 40 percent to 83 percent, averaging 69 percent.

In North Dakota there was not much of a relationship between age ratios and cyclic population trends. Data from Manitoba, although less complete, suggest a similar non-correspondence. The provincial bag was only 40 percent immatures during 1968, a year of stable or slightly increasing population, but 83 percent immatures during 1963, a year of decline. Studying grouse during a cyclic decline in Manitoba's Interlake region, Rusch, Gillespie, and McKay found that the number of drumming males on some 2,000 acres varied from 100 in 1971 to only 3 in 1972. The average bag of hunters likewise decreased, from 1.1 grouse per hunter in 1970 to only 0.1 in 1972. Fall age ratios changed little; only 62 to 66 percent of the bag in each of those years consisted of immature grouse.

The studies of Rusch, Doerr, Fischer, and Keith suggest a strong relationship between the grouse cycle and the percentage of immatures in the population near Rochester, Alberta, from 1966 to 1975. Growing populations comprised 84 to 88 percent immatures in the fall; declining populations had only 68 to 79 percent immatures. Yet clutch size, hatching success, and brood size all remained constant through the cycle. The researchers therefore concluded that the fluctuations in fall age ratios and the cyclic changes in numbers were probably not caused by any changes in the rate of reproduction.

MORTALITY

Death in ruffed grouse is somewhat easier to study than birth. The remains of grouse that died in winter are often found in spring on the forest floor, much more easily than hens on nests. Drummers tend to use the same log or territory throughout their lives, and their drumming sounds make them easy to find, too. The failure of a marked or banded male to return to his territory the following year can safely be attributed to mortality.

Small, lightweight, long-lasting radio transmitters mounted on bibs or ponchos have worked well on ruffed grouse chicks and juveniles, providing an exciting new source of information on grouse mortality. Disease, parasites, exposure, and starvation are all causes of death, but the overwhelming cause in ruffed grouse throughout their range is predation by raptors, such as great horned owls, sharp-shinned hawks, red-tailed hawks, broad-winged hawks, goshawks, and Cooper's hawks; by furbearers, such as lynx, coyotes, foxes, and weasels; and by man.

Bump's investigators in New York concluded that about half the usual brood mortality was due to predation but acknowledged the difficulty of distinguishing between primary and secondary causes of death. A chick weakened by malnutrition or exposure, for example, is easy prey for a fox or great horned owl. Various other studies also suggest that slightly more than half the chicks are lost by the time the brood disperses in early September.

When they disperse, the juvenile grouse are almost as large as adults; by early or mid-October, they are nearly indistinguishable from adults in size and behavior and are ap-

Toxic plants

Self-defense by plants is a newcomer to the list of possible causes for the periodic fluctuations in grouse population levels. The theory was prompted by the discovery that many species of plants defend themselves against attack by producing chemicals that make them toxic to certain insects. There is evidence that individual plants being attacked by insects can somehow communicate their distress to nearby plants and warn them to prepare their defenses.

What has this silent strife in the forest to do with ruffed grouse? The grouse of northern woods depend heavily on aspen buds in winter. Aspen buds are relatively large in size, which enables a grouse to complete its morning or evening feeding period in fifteen or twenty minutes, and they are highly nutritious. But under certain conditions, the aspens and many other plants produce phe- nols and tannins that make them less palatable to wildlife, and possibly less digestible. If deprived of aspen buds, grouse must rely on other foods, such as catkins. To eat these less-desirable foods, the birds need to go farther and spend more time feeding, thus expending more energy and increasing their exposure to predators: fewer grouse survive the winter, fewer broods are produced the following spring.

Gullion has therefore suggested that there may be a relationship between the northern grouse cycles and chemical changes in their foods. In the South, when aspen buds are not of great importance, grouse cycles have not been recorded. Basic research is yet to be carried out, however, and at present the cause of grouse cycles must still be recorded as unknown.

— *Harold L. Barber*

Grouse tracks lead into a dense thicket of hazel. The birds eat the catkins of this species, but if their preferred foods contain high amounts of tannins and other indigestible substances, they may seek alternatives. Such a dietary change can affect their survival.

proaching adults in skill at avoiding predation. Among full-sized birds, death from disease, exposure, or malnutrition is rarely encountered in grouse. Rather, predation is responsible for virtually all the mortality that typically eliminates about 50 percent to 60 percent of the population from one fall to the next.

In nature, however, there is little that is typical or constant except change. And having discounted movement and reproduction rates as causes of the ten-year ruffed grouse cycle, as well as noncyclic fluctuations in populations, we come down to grouse mortality. What factors, then, cause changes in rates of mortality?

Habitat and mortality. The grouse's preference for forests with leafy canopy and overhead cover and a thick understory of shrubs, saplings, and seedlings is for good reason: the bird survives better in good habitat. In the Lake States and Canada, aspen forests ten to twenty-five years old normally provide this type of cover, and the highest grouse densities are found there. Grouse that select these habitats have a survival advantage over grouse that select other forest types. In 1970 Gullion reported that Minnesota drummers in just the right sort of aspen stand lived about twice as long as drummers in other forest types or aspen plus scattered high pines. He suggested that the high pines provided sites from which raptors could readily ambush ruffed grouse. The relationship between thick forest understory, high grouse survival, and consequent high grouse density has been documented in Alberta, Manitoba, Ontario, New York, and Pennsylvania, among other areas, and has been firmly established as a principle of ruffed grouse ecology.

The operation of this principle is responsible for many of the increasing ruffed grouse populations. In parts of the Northeast, Midwest, and Lake States, for example, forest composition has changed in favor of ruffed grouse in the past forty to fifty years. The latter half of the nineteenth century and first part of the twentieth were periods of rapid expansion of exploitive agriculture and forestry. The plow and the saw took a heavy toll on ruffed grouse habitats, and grouse dwindled and even disappeared from some parts of their range. But the economic depression of the 1930s put many marginal farms and cut-and-run forestry operations out of business. The subsequent healing of the land and integrated forest management practices have led to major increases in forest habitats for grouse.

Changes in habitat can prompt changes in numbers of grouse, and periodic forest fires, a sort of natural habitat management, may even result in fluctuations that resemble cycles. But cycles usually occur in the absence of major habitat change. Habitat can account for long-term trends in grouse numbers, not cycles.

Hunting and mortality. Hunting, like other forms of predation, is an obvious cause of death among ruffed grouse. Indeed, market hunting and unregulated sport hunting were a major cause of the low grouse populations near the start of the twentieth century. The beginning of the conservation era and the 1900 passage of the Lacey Act, which prohibited interstate commerce in illegally taken game, led to the end of market gunning and the beginning of restricted or closed seasons for ruffed grouse in many states. With the advent of modern game management and regulated sport hunting, grouse populations have prospered throughout their range. In fact, grouse now occupy many areas where they were formerly absent from 1880 to 1920.

But does this form of mortality substitute for other forms of predation, or is hunting additive to other deaths? In other words, is regulated sport hunting of sufficient magnitude and impact to influence grouse numbers?

As grouse numbers rebounded, closed seasons on grouse hunting were reopened, and open seasons were lengthened. Between 1946 and 1986 thirty of forty-one states and provinces lengthened their seasons; no state or province has shortened its hunting season over the past four decades. And longer seasons usually mean more hunters and larger harvests. Ten states and provinces have reported increases in the number of ruffed grouse taken by hunters in the last forty years. Are these increased harvests affecting grouse population trends?

If, as estimates indicate, harvests of grouse

One less bird to breed next spring: although hunters affect grouse numbers, they are an unlikely cause of population swings.

are still increasing in most places, then the answer might seem to be no, at least over large areas. However, if harvest *rates* (the proportion of the population taken) are also increasing, these harvest estimates may not reflect grouse numbers. Grouse numbers are unknown in any case, and we cannot know how grouse numbers might have grown without hunting losses. Moreover, on some heavily hunted public lands in Wisconsin and Minnesota, where hunters bag half or more of the fall grouse populations, hunting does indeed have a negative impact on numbers in the following spring. There is no strong evidence that hunting is depressing grouse numbers over wide areas, but data are sparse, and more studies of the magnitude and effect of harvest rates are needed; we cannot continue to blithely assume that hunting has no effect. Recall Gordon Gullion's summary in *Ruffed Grouse Management: State of the Art in the Early 1980s:*

"Perhaps we have too long, too conveniently blamed scarce grouse populations upon inadequate habitats. While insufficient habitat surely compounds this problem and is the problem in many areas, we must be careful about where we lay the blame in areas where habitats are adequate. Too much hunting can suppress ruffed grouse populations in even the best coverts."

Whatever their effect, hunters are relatively few. And although their numbers and efforts do change in response to reports of grouse numbers, hunters are not cyclic; on the contrary, they are determinedly annual. And that leaves nonhuman predation as a possible cause of the ten-year cycle.

Predation and mortality. Of the animals involved in the ten-year cycle, the ruffed grouse, sharp-tailed grouse, and snowshoe hare are the major prey species; the lynx, great horned owl, and goshawk are the main predators. Observing the demographic and behavioral interactions of the predators with their prey, Keith formulated his 1974 model of the cycle.

1. Hares, like their relatives the rabbits, can breed several times each season. As their numbers reach peak densities, hares begin to run short of food, mainly woody browse species. Food shortages lower reproduction and survival rates of hares, and their numbers begin to decline.

2. Populations of lynx, horned owls, and goshawks, which depend primarily on hares for food, had increased with the hares. Since, however, the hare produces more young than its predators, hare numbers increased at a faster rate. Thus the ratio of hares per predator also increased. But when hare populations begin to decline, the ratio of hares per predator decreases, and the predators consume a larger fraction of the hare population, thus accelerating and lengthening the hare decline.

3. Grouse populations had increased because as hare populations were increasing, the few predators had fed mainly on hares. But as hares become less abundant, predators begin to take more grouse, even though grouse were never abundant enough to provide a staple source of food. The grouse population cannot sustain the predation rate and begins to decline.

4. Now the number of predators begins to decline because of the shortage of hares and grouse.

5. At this point—the low point of the cycle—the stage is set for recovery of both prey and predator populations. The woody vegetation browsed by the hares has regenerated. With ample food and few predators, hare and grouse populations are once again able to increase.

This model was the most comprehensive and compelling explanation for the cycle yet developed. Do the current data support it?

Two studies in Canada have attempted to estimate mortality and predation rates in ruffed grouse during cyclic fluctuations. At Rochester, Alberta, a cyclic high occurred in 1968, when an average of sixty-one grouse inhabited every 100 hectares of upland forest; in 1974 there were only fourteen grouse per 100 hectares. The rate of population decrease was correlated with the percentage of juveniles in the fall population, the rate of loss between summer and fall numbers, and the overwinter loss. The changes were attributed to mortality of young grouse in summer and fall, and overwinter losses of both young and adults. Grouse chicks were found to be especially vulnerable to red-tailed hawks in June and July, although goshawks,

Counts taken during deer drives in late April through early May show that the hare population dips lower than the grouse population, almost to extinction, but recovers faster and peaks higher.

The fortunes of the lynx rise and fall with the population of its prey, as these Manitoba harvest statistics indicate.

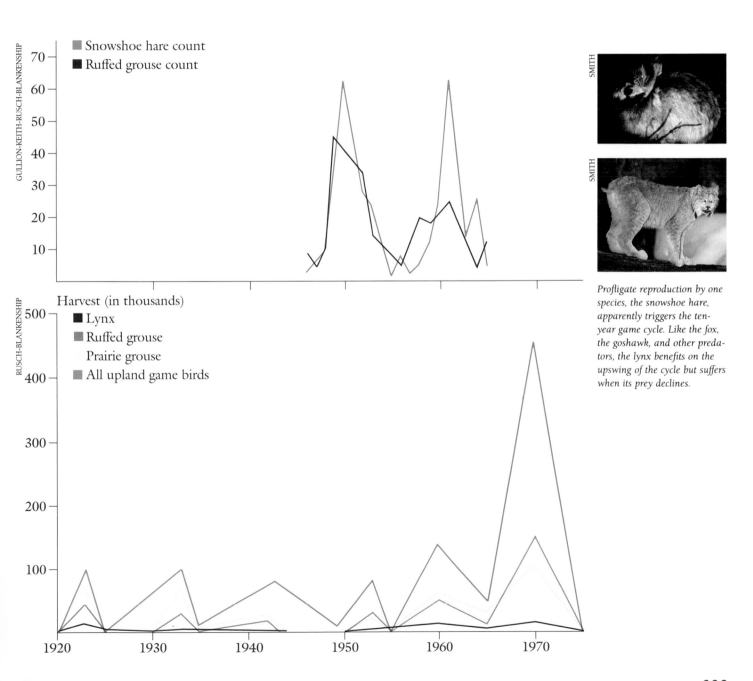

Profligate reproduction by one species, the snowshoe hare, apparently triggers the ten-year game cycle. Like the fox, the goshawk, and other predators, the lynx benefits on the upswing of the cycle but suffers when its prey declines.

Snowshoe hare populations increase dramatically when food is abundant and predators are scarce. The prolific hares, however, deplete their food supply, and large numbers of undernourished snowshoes present an easy target for lynx, goshawks, and foxes.

great horned owls, broad-winged hawks, coyotes, and lynx were also important grouse predators.

But estimated predation rates by red-tailed hawks in May through July and by great horned owls in April through June were more closely related to hare densities than to those of grouse. That is, raptors killed an increasing number of grouse as the hare population grew; when it declined, the avian predation rate on grouse declined, too, irrespective of the grouse densities. But the rate of overwinter loss, which was primarily due to raptors, also had a lot to do with rates of change in grouse numbers.

At Chatfield, Manitoba, grouse populations were near a cyclic high in 1971, with

forty-four grouse per 100 hectares of upland forest; in 1973 only three grouse were counted. The dramatic decrease was associated with high mortality of drumming males and chicks and high losses during winter. Data on raptors and their food habits suggest that horned owls and red-tailed hawks together were major sources of mortality of ruffed grouse chicks in June and July of 1971 and 1972. Trends in predation rates at Chatfield are unknown, but the rates during the ruffed grouse decline of 1971 to 1973 were at least as high as the highest rates for the same predator-prey species at Rochester, Alberta.

Evidence at remains of grouse that died overwinter suggested that avian predators ac-

PRATT

counted for about 70 percent to 75 percent of the overwinter mortality at Rochester and Chatfield. The culprits: great horned owls and goshawks, the only raptors commonly wintering in these areas.

The longest study of grouse populations in the Lake States was conducted at Cloquet, Minnesota, where Eng, Gullion, and Marshall have monitored survival of drumming males and population densities since 1956. Mortality of breeding male grouse was 69 percent in the winter of 1972–1973 but a more moderate 54 percent in 1982–1983; in both those winter seasons great numbers of goshawks were observed and were assumed to be the main predators. However, drumming counts indicated that the area's grouse numbers changed little during either 1972–1973 or 1982–1983.

In central Minnesota Richard Huemphner monitored predation on sixty-five radio-marked grouse at Cedar Creek from October 1970 through May 1973. Mortality estimates from radio-marked birds are considerably more reliable than those developed from population statistics. Forty-seven of the marked grouse, or 72 percent, were killed by raptors that Huemphner believed were owls or goshawks. Predation rates were highest in January and February and were always higher from October through March than from April through September. The highest predation rate of the study—94 percent—occurred during the winter of

As the number of hares crashes, the predators, themselves now numerous, seek other prey. Grouse are not plentiful enough to sustain heavy predation; a decline in both predator and prey populations ensues. Low numbers of all species allow regeneration of the food supply, and the stage is set for the cycle to begin again.

1972–1973, when many goshawks are known to have moved into the area. Nine years later another goshawk invasion was observed, and the drumming count declined 55 percent.

Goshawks were implicated again in an unpublished study by DeStefano, Small, Holzwart, and Rusch, who monitored banded and radio-marked drummers near Navarino and Wautoma in central Wisconsin from 1979 to 1986. Mortality was high—80 percent—in the winter of 1981–1982, and grouse numbers declined in two of the three following years. Goshawk populations were high. However, there was no significant correlation between lower mortality rates of drumming males and annual rates of population increase.

Following 188 radio-marked ruffed grouse near Wautoma, Wisconsin, from August 1982 through May 1986, Small and Holzwart reported that predation accounted for sixty-one mortalities, hunting for thirty-seven, and other factors for thirty-five. Goshawks and owls were the main avian predators. Predation rates were generally higher from October through March than from April through September, with winter predation rates varying from 68 percent in 1983–1984 to 42 percent in 1985–1986. Yet numbers of drummers in central Wisconsin remained low and varied only slightly during the entire period.

What are we to make of all these data? It's clear that raptors are the big cause of grouse mortality. But whether grouse populations rise and fall in synch with other prey species and with their predators, according to Keith's model, is more complicated.

In 1977 Keith and his researchers showed that the May through July raptor predation on ruffed grouse at Rochester, Alberta, generally varied in inverse and delayed manner with the density of snowshoe hares. That is, as long as hares were plentiful, grouse were safe; once hares became scarce, grouse were preyed upon. As in other cycles and other parts of Canada, the grouse at Rochester declined before the hares. We believe the grouse decline resulted from high predation in both winter (for which rates have been documented) and late summer and early fall

(for which rates are largely unmeasured). If predators are catching more grouse before a hare decline, it may be that grouse are either more attractive or more vulnerable than hares, or that predator numbers are increasing faster than grouse numbers. In the Lake States, grouse populations often begin their decline after the hares. Higher predation rates on grouse *after* a hare decline may be attributed to invasions of raptors from Canada. The buffering effects of a larger and more diverse prey base in the Lake States may also give grouse a short reprieve as predators consume alternatives.

In a 1988 review of the role of predation in the ruffed grouse cycle, Keith and Rusch drew the following conclusions:

1. Predation on young grouse through September largely determines annual rates of increase and hence the cyclic trend in grouse populations. We suggest that the intensity of such predation varies with the snowshoe hare cycle: low when both hares and their predators are scarce, increasing just enough to prevent further grouse population growth before the hare peak, and increasing greatly as hares decline.

2. The abrupt cyclic declines in Minnesota and Wisconsin ruffed grouse are consistently associated with the influx of raptors, whose invasions are apparently triggered by the cyclic declines of snowshoe hares in Canada.

3. Overwinter losses of grouse in two areas of the Lake States were highest during invasions of raptors, primarily goshawks and owls. These losses, due to predation, were followed by several years of declining or low ruffed grouse populations.

4. The association between influx of raptors and decline of grouse suggests that in Minnesota and Wisconsin, grouse cycles are triggered by invading goshawks and great horned owls.

Keith's original model, then, seems to be a valid explanation for the ten-year cycle in Canada. In the northern tier of the United States, however, the fluctuations in grouse numbers are more a side effect of the snowshoe hare cycle in Canada, which drives hungry goshawks and other raptors across the border in search of food.

—*Donald H. Rusch*

The goshawk becomes a major cause of ruffed grouse mortality when a decline in the number of hares in Canada drives raptors south in search of food.

The role of diseases and parasites

*B*oth diseases and parasites have been suggested as important factors involved in the periodic or cyclic fluctuations in the numbers of ruffed grouse. Shillinger and Morley (1937) indicated that certain characteristics of cyclic changes—several years of scarcity with a subsequent gradual increase to abundant levels followed by a sharp decline—pointed strongly to disease as an important consideration. Also, the ease of transmission and the increase in virulence of diseases often associated with abundant animal populations supported the theory that disease was responsible for sudden declines in game populations. The authors noted that because ruffed grouse are susceptible to infection by ulcerative enteritis, this bacterial disease might be responsible for these periodic fluctuations. Ulcerative enteritis is an acute disease of galliform birds and is caused by the bacterium *Clostridium colini*. Primary lesions are found in the intestines and the ceca, which become inflamed and ulcerated. Primarily a disease of confinement, ulcerative enteritis is very rare among wild birds and has been reported only in pen-raised ruffed grouse.

Green (1931) encouraged further investigation of tularemia as a cause of die-offs in ruffed grouse and snowshoe hares *(Lepus americanus)*. This disease was known to occur in hares as well as in upland game birds and was transmitted by the rabbit tick *(Haemaphysalis leporispalustris)*, a common parasite of both ruffed grouse and snowshoe hares. Green suggested that fluctuations in both the virulence of tularemia and the levels of tick infestation on these animals might be related to the periodic population

changes. Birds infected with tularemia grow progressively weaker and, consequently, more susceptible to other forms of mortality, such as predation.

O'Roke (1940) postulated that the blood protozoan *Leucocytozoon bonasae* might be responsible for die-offs of young ruffed grouse. He based his theory on field evidence indicating that this parasite caused sickness and death of young wild grouse. This parasite lives in the bird's white blood cells and is transmitted by biting insects such as mosquitoes, blackflies, and midges. Later studies, however, failed to corroborate this theory. Erikson (1953) found equivalent infection rates of *L. bonasae* in grouse during periods of increase and decline. As a result of field observations, he concluded that the blood protozoan was not responsible for substantial mortality in wild grouse. Dorney and Todd (1960) also found no evidence of heavy mortality resulting from blood protozoans, although such parasites might act as additional stressors, especially at high grouse population densities.

During their long-term study of ruffed grouse, Bump and his colleagues (1947) examined birds during periods of increase and decrease in the population cycle. They encountered a great variety of grouse diseases and parasites but found no evidence that any such agent was responsible for widespread population fluctuations.

In contrast to the idea that parasites might cause population fluctuations, the stomach worm, *Dispharynx nasuta*, has been credited as a possible stabilizing influence (Marquenski 1986). This roundworm attaches to the wall of the glandular stomach and frequently causes damage and sloughing of mucosal tissue that may block the passage of food. Although the stomach worm can cause death directly or increase susceptibility to other mortality factors, this parasite has not been proven to cause cyclic fluctuations. Marquenski's hypothesis of the stabilizing effect of *D. nasuta* was based on observations made earlier by Bendell (1955) during a four-year study of blue grouse *(Dendragapus obscurus)* on Vancouver Island. Bendell presented evidence that the stomach worm suppressed juvenile survival to such a low level that the population did not increase sufficiently to trigger population crashes from, presumably, other causes. An equilibrium between death of older birds and replacement by surviving younger birds reduced extreme changes in the size of the population.

Thus, parasites and diseases may cause death in ruffed grouse and may influence population levels. These limiting factors, however, have not been confirmed or refuted as primary causes or deterrents of periodic fluctuations. Although further investigation may reveal that disease is the driving force in grouse population cycles, it is more likely that cycles are the result of a complex set of factors and that disease is but one of them. Furthermore, if various factors interact to produce cycles, it also is likely that their relative importance may not always be constant. For example, disease might be an important part of a decline during one cyclic fluctuation, but predation or poor nesting success might be more important during another.

—Emily Jo Wentworth and
William R. Davidson

Even a nonfatal disease may influence population levels if it weakens the grouse enough to give a predator the edge.

Predators on foot

The thumping beat of the grouse's wings breaks the morning silence. In a blinding whir too fast for any eye to follow, the amorous male sends his love call over the forest airwaves. On a nearby ridge, a female grouse hears the matrimonial summons and begins to move toward the sound.

But another creature also hears. A quarter-mile from the rotting log where the male grouse now struts and preens, a bobcat lies curled beneath the low-hanging boughs of a cedar. The night's hunt did not go well, and the cat is hungry. When the second staccato burst of drumming trails off again to silence, the bobcat arises.

At a trot, the cat follows the drumming beacon to its source. But experience has taught the feline that ruffed grouse are wary prey, ready to explode in flight at any moment. As it draws near, the bobcat slows its pace.

Moving now just an inch at a time, it creeps unseen through the trees until it crouches a few scant feet behind the bird. In a rare stroke of luck for the bobcat, the drummer remains oblivious to the danger, and in the next flurry of wingbeats the predator pounces. Minutes later, a few feathers are all that remain of the encounter.

Ruffed grouse occasionally provide meals for cougars, foxes, coyotes, mink, lynx, weasels, raccoons, and skunks as well as bobcats. The *modus operandi* does not vary a great deal

Leg bands, feathers, and other indigestible parts on the forest floor: a red-phase adult female fell prey to a carnivore.

Red and gray foxes, which plunder nests and stalk the birds, are probably the most common mammalian predators of the ruffed grouse. Yet even foxes take grouse only occasionally.

from predator to predator. Most of these mammals are nocturnal or crepuscular, and most hunt alone, although coyotes often work in pairs. Canines use their keen sense of smell to locate prey; cats often rely on their eyes to find game. Both have excellent hearing. The mustelids (weasels, mink, and skunks) put their insatiable curiosity to good use by investigating every possible place where prey might hide.

For most predators, the challenge lies in getting near enough to the bird so that a final pounce or rush can be successful. Once the grouse is in its grasp, the predator quickly finishes the job with strong jaws and rapierlike canine teeth. Wild cats also possess razor-sharp claws that can rip even large game to shreds.

For a variety of reasons, however, grouse are not severely threatened by any predator species. Tipping the scales at perhaps half a pound, a weasel may have a tough time killing a grouse that weighs three times as much. The mink, being a larger animal, does not have that difficulty, but because it rarely ranges far from stream or lakeshore, it encounters relatively few grouse. Skunks and raccoons probably move too slowly to be much of a threat to explosive adult birds. Cougars generally prey on larger animals, such as deer. Coyotes usually prefer the open prairies and meadows that grouse avoid. Bobcats appear to have little trouble taking grouse, but they are not nearly so numerous as other predators.

This leaves the foxes—both red and gray— as the chief mammalian predators of ruffed grouse. Their 8- to 12-pound heft gives them the size to dispatch quickly any grouse they can get their paws on, and the brushy woodland that grouse prefer suits them just fine.

At twilight, the fox leaves its den or day-bed to begin a peripatetic reconnaissance of its home range. From experience it has learned which weed patches, fencerows, and woodlots are most likely to produce a meal. With typically keen canine ears and nose, it strains to catch the cluck of a grouse, the spectral squeak of a mouse, or the smell of anything edible.

Like the fine hunting dog that it is, the fox keeps moving until its senses alert it to game. The fox then freezes in midstride until the prey betrays itself by movement, sound, or odor. After stalking within a few feet of the usually unsuspecting victim, the fox executes a graceful leap that ends with the prey pinned to the ground beneath its feet. A quick bite to the head concludes the encounter.

If a fox is hungry, it may consume a slain grouse on the spot, leaving only feathers and large bones as evidence. If its belly is full, however, a fox may choose to stash a grouse corpse in a shallow grave and eat it later when hunting has not been so good. In the spring, adult foxes often carry prey back to the den, so that the pups can feed themselves and become familiar with the creatures

that will sustain them for the rest of their lives.

Because of their generally stealthy nature, grouse predators almost always do their work unseen by human eyes. On one occasion, in the 1930s, however, a researcher in the New York woods had the opportunity to watch as a fox plied its trade. As part of Gardiner Bump's scientific team keeping a twenty-four-hour eye on a nesting female grouse, the man was perched high in a nearby tree when the fox approached just after dawn. Working back and forth through the woods, the predator eventually came within a few feet of the hen, and she flushed from the nest.

The fox leaped at the bird but missed, then followed her through the trees. Soon, however, the predator gave up the pointless chase and returned to search out the nest that experience said must be there. Moments later, the fox left the area, its belly full of grouse eggs.

But the predators don't always win. According to biologist Frank Edminster, one hen hatched and brought off her brood from a nest that lay barely 50 feet from an active fox den. The fox pups, he reported, tussled and played within 20 feet of the incubating hen.

Because of their reluctance to flee, nesting grouse hens are particularly vulnerable to predation. And once a predator discovers a nest, the eggs are almost certain to disappear. In addition to the animals that prey on

Left: Preoccupied with his courtship display, the drummer exposes himself to danger. Right: If her threats fail, the hen will attempt to lure the intruder away from the nest. But having revealed its contents, she may return to find the eggs eaten.

adult birds, porcupines, squirrels, woodchucks, and chipmunks have also been known to make a meal of grouse eggs. In one study in Tennessee, biologists found that wild hogs were destroyers of grouse nests.

Again, however, foxes get blamed for the lion's share of destroyed nests. Surprisingly, there have been reports that foxes at least occasionally eat only a few of the eggs in a raided nest. They may intend to come back later for the rest, but no one knows for sure. In most cases, however, a fox that stumbles upon a clutch of grouse eggs will consume them all.

Each species of predator has evolved a particular technique for opening grouse eggs

Lynx rufus
bobcat

Mustela erminea
short-tailed weasel

Canis latrans
coyote

Mephitis mephitis
striped skunk

and removing the tasty treat inside. What's left behind can act as a sort of fingerprint to identify the raider. Typically, foxes bite into the side of the egg, destroying perhaps half of that surface; the rest of the shell remains intact. Weasels, with their smaller teeth, finely shred almost the entire shell. Skunks, not known for their daintiness, virtually crush the shell. Raccoons often bite off the end of the egg. Storage-minded chipmunks occasionally roll the eggs away intact and hide them elsewhere.

Because of the predators' almost universal appetite for eggs, spring is probably the toughest time for grouse—that is, potential grouse. In winter, however, more carnivores have a difficult time finding food and may turn their attention to adult birds. Prying predator eyes can spot a grouse more quickly against a white background than against mottled summer underbrush. And tracks in the snow may lead a fox or other meat-eater directly to a roosting bird.

Despite the predatory world's appetite for grouse—both eggs and birds—the ruffed grouse has little to worry about, as a species. Skunks find it much easier to dine on grubs, grasshoppers, carrion, and vegetable matter than to catch grouse. Mink feed largely on crustaceans and other creatures in their lake-shore habitat. Weasels usually go after smaller birds and mice. For most of these animals, a grouse dinner is a rare treat indeed.

Even foxes don't eat many grouse. Figures vary, but researchers examining fox stomachs generally find grouse remains in only 2 percent to 8 percent of the animals. One biologist guesses that an average fox may eat no more than two grouse per year.

Consequently, the assumption that fewer predators means more grouse is not necessarily true. Grouse evolved amid their carnivorous enemies, and as a species the birds are capable of dealing with the problem, or they would never have survived. If foxes and their meat-eating kin don't hold grouse numbers in check, something else will. The real key to maintaining healthy grouse populations is not predator control, but habitat enhancement.

—Gary Turbak

RUFFED GROUSE

Friends of the ruffed grouse

Ruffed grouse do not live alone in their woodland home. Since grouse may be found in oak woods, northern hardwoods and conifers, and aspen forests from coast to coast and from northern Canada and Alaska south into Missouri, there are numerous animals to be found in these varied habitats. Most authorities, however, agree that the ruffed grouse is primarily a bird of young, early successional forests and is most abundant in association with aspen. Thus we will primarily look at the wildlife of this habitat type.

The most important friend of the ruffed grouse is undoubtedly the snowshoe hare, even though this association is entirely inadvertent. The range of the 13- to 18-inch, 2- to 4-pound hare overlaps almost all of the range of ruffed grouse except along its southern edges. Hares also extend farther north than do grouse. No one should find the snowshoe hare difficult to identify. It is brownish gray during summer, molting to snow white for the winter months.

The hare is the primary prey species for many animals—great horned owls, goshawks, lynx, and others—that also prey on grouse. When hares are abundant, grouse populations are buffered against predation as the predators concentrate on the numerous hares. However, as hare populations decline, predators shift their attention more to grouse, and grouse populations decline. So goes one theory on the game cycle.

The game cycle, and the dramatic fluctuations in the number of snowshoe hares, is also of great importance to the habitat. During the peak of the hare population, these browsers gnaw their way through great quantities of woody vegetation, which retards the forest succession that would otherwise convert some aspen communities to white spruce. Thanks in part to the snowshoe hare, better grouse habitat is maintained for a longer period of time.

In southern parts of grouse range the snowshoe hare gives way to the cottontail rabbit. Here, neither the cottontail nor the grouse is so cyclic as in the North, partly because predators in southern coverts have a wider choice of prey. Cottontails, chipmunks, numerous squirrels, other small mammals, reptiles, and amphibians—all are

As long as snowshoe hares are plentiful, the snowy owl is likely not to prey on ruffed grouse.

Alces americana
moose

Odocoileus virginianus
white-tailed deer

Castor canadensis
beaver

Lepus americanus
snowshoe hare *(left);*
Sylvilagus floridanus
cottontail rabbit *(right)*

Rana pipiens
leopard frog *(left);*
Thamnophis sirtalis
garter snake *(right)*

Philohela minor
woodcock

available to a hungry predator. Because the rabbit population is both lower and more stable than that of the hare, and the vegetation is different, the rabbit is less effective in modifying the habitat for the ruffed grouse's benefit.

Two other mammals have the ability to modify grouse habitat, also to a lesser extent than the hare. The white-tailed deer–the number one big game animal in North America–is also a browsing animal. Dense populations can affect the habitat by slowing forest regeneration, creating multiple stems on woody plants, creating a "browse line" below which edible vegetation has been eaten, and virtually eliminating some highly palatable plant species. In the northern part of grouse range the moose, a relative of the white-tail, fulfills these functions.

The beaver, too, can change habitat–only faster. Many of the trees important to grouse, such as aspen, birch, alder, and maple, are on the beavers' preferred menu and may be cut down altogether. Moreover, a beaver dam can quickly flood a low-lying forest stand and drive all residents to higher ground. Beavers are well distributed along streams and lakes throughout ruffed grouse range.

Of the numerous birds that occupy ruffed grouse habitat–some found in several habitat types, others found only along the forest edges–most migrate for the winter and leave the habitat to the grouse and a few hardy resident species. One of these migratory birds, the woodcock, is an important avian friend of the grouse, for indirect reasons. The woodcock is a stocky, quail-sized bird with large, dark, bulging eyes and beautiful "dead-leaf" camouflage. Its most notable feature is its long bill with a prehensile tip for grabbing worms as it probes for food in moist soil. The woodcock is also noted for its fascinating courtship flight and nasal call (called *peenting*) during the spring. It is a very popular upland game bird, and herein lies the reason it can be considered a friend of the ruffed grouse.

Many woodcock hunters are also grouse hunters, especially in the populous eastern states where woodcock are abundant. Those who support management and research for one species tend to support programs for the

236

HERTLING

other. Frequently, habitat manipulation for grouse is beneficial for woodcock, and vice versa, with alder habitat and woodland openings being especially important.

The benefits or costs of grouse habitat management for other birds are not so clear. As more habitat is altered for grouse, the impact of timber harvest and the subsequent fragmentation of forest habitat have made habitat management a controversial issue.

In Pennsylvania, Yahner studied the impact of timber harvest for grouse management in small even-age stands of aspen and mixed-oak cover. In 1986 he reported finding thirteen bird species in these habitats during winter and sixty-nine species during the breeding season. The black-capped chickadee was the most common winter bird and the rufous-sided towhee was the most common breeding bird. The gray catbird, golden-winged warbler, chestnut-sided warbler, ovenbird, yellowthroat, and field sparrow frequently used young clear-cuts. Yahner concluded that species adapted to early successional habitats benefited from projects to improve grouse habitat.

As one proceeds south from ruffed grouse range, the number of reptiles and amphibians greatly increases in both species and abundance. The shorter winters and longer summers are more suitable for most cold-blooded "herps." Ruffed grouse occasionally eat a just-hatched snake, or a small frog or salamander, and conversely, a large snake may dine on grouse eggs or chicks. Beyond

that, there is little association between grouse and "herps."

The common garter snake is the most likely snake species the grouse encounters across a broad part of its range. In the southern and eastern regions, northern ring-necked snakes, tiny red-bellied snakes, and black rat snakes share grouse habitat. Around the Great Lakes, a few hog-nosed snakes and perhaps a bull snake might be encountered. The preferred habitats of most other snakes within grouse range do not overlap with that of grouse.

Several amphibians are frequently found in grouse habitat. In the leaf litter of moist eastern woodlands, the terrestrial "red eft" stage of the eastern newt is common. In the same habitat, the large spotted salamander is common but spends much of its time underground. The red-backed salamander frequents leaf litter and decaying logs in cool hardwood forests.

A few frogs also share grouse habitat for a short period during the summer. The wood frog sings from temporary woodland pools during the very first days of spring. This small, brown frog with its dark, raccoonlike mask can be found throughout grouse range even into Alaska and northern Canada. The common toad's dry skin allows it to inhabit a wide range of forest types over the eastern half of grouse range. A visitor to a grouse covert might also encounter a chorus frog, gray tree frog, or leopard frog.

—*Scott R. Craven*

The young forests that are grouse's preferred habitat mature quickly. Deer, hares, and rabbits slow forest succession by browsing woody vegetation. Beavers harvest maturing trees, thereby encouraging seedlings and saplings.

Habitat management that benefits the woodcock often improves cover for ruffed grouse as well.

MICH. DEPT. OF NATURAL RESOURCES

Death from the sky

Something had died, there in the snow. On the freshly whitened ground beneath the naked aspens, scattered feathers indicate the identity of the victim: a ruffed grouse. On either side of the trampled spot are the killer's distinctive wing prints, tips pressed downward and spread: a goshawk. The only sound is a swish of branches as a sparkling cascade of sun-loosened snow slides off the surrounding pines.

Just the bare wingbeat of the event is recorded—not the drama, the abruptness of the kill. But if this was a typical encounter, the scenario probably went something like this:

Toward evening, the grouse, a male, ventures out from the security of a clump of young pines to feed. Its usual ground food covered with snow, the bird flies to an aspen branch and begins to pick at the buds. Unseen by the feeding grouse, a black-and-white goshawk hurls itself among the aspens like a dodging, dipping missile. Its keen eyes reflexively gauging distance, obstacles, and speed, the hurtling predator spots the unsuspecting grouse. Then, at 50 miles an hour, the goshawk flicks its tail to make a slight midcourse correction and twists its body to strike, outstretched talons first. The impact drives the talons home and tears the grouse from the branch, literally pounding it down to the ground.

On the snow, the grouse's death struggle lasts only a few moments. The goshawk,

A deadly accurate missile, the goshawk dives for its prey. The speed of its stoop gives the grouse little chance to escape.

POPULATION DYNAMICS

The goshawk is an efficient carnivore. Its talons are sharp, and its beak is built for tearing flesh and disjointing bones.

head up and back to keep out of the way of the flailing grouse, retains its viselike grip. The struggles stop. The larger bird now methodically plucks its prey by locking on with needle-sharp talons and tearing out clumps of feathers with its powerful hooked beak. When the carcass is neatly plucked, the bird catapults itself upward with a single beat of its wings, leaving the telltale impression in the snow.

Without relinquishing its hold, the predator flies to a tall lightning-blasted pine and eats. Gripping its perch with one foot, its meal with the other, the goshawk tears out bites. Entrails and other soft parts are quickly devoured. The stout beak has a toothlike projection in its upper mandible that is then used to disjoint bones, freeing head, breast, back, and legs. Very few scraps remain. Undigested bits of bone and feather will later be expelled through the goshawk's beak as compacted pellets.

Once described by conservation writer John Madson as the ultimate grouse-killing machine, the goshawk is one of those predatory birds we call raptors—which is somewhat redundant, since, in Latin, *praedator* and *raptor* both mean "plunderer." To carry it one step further, the participle *raptus* comes from a verb meaning "to snatch forcibly"— as, indeed, the feeding grouse was violently taken.

Like an eagle, the goshawk has sharp talons for tearing apart its prey, plus the strong beak and well-developed eyes for the hunt.

These adaptations for a carnivorous diet characterize all raptors that prey on ruffed grouse.

Keen vision is essential, both to scout from on high and to judge distance between branches. A raptor's eye is extremely well developed and has about eight times the resolution, or image sharpness, of a human eye: a soaring eagle can see a rabbit at 2 miles. If a human eye were developed in the same proportion to body weight as the eye of a peregrine falcon, it would be several inches across and weigh 3 pounds or more.

Eye position alone gives many raptors a tremendous advantage. The golden eagle, for example, has eyes positioned farther forward than a kestrel; the two fields of vision partially overlap, which gives the eagle a three-dimensional image and the ability to gauge distances as it drives its body downward, talons set to snatch or strike.

Evolution has exacted a price for the eagle's advantages of sight, however. A ruffed grouse can keep watch on both sides at once, but its predator, though blessed with binocular vision, must turn its head for increased side vision.

Among the birds of prey, each family and genus has its special adaptations for finding, killing, and eating prey. Aside from vultures, which do not have strong enough feet to kill effectively, and the osprey, which is a fish-eater and the only North American raptor that dives into water, those groups are hawks, falcons, owls, and eagles.

The ruffed grouse has keen vision, but the even greater visual acuity of raptors gives them an advantage. Note the size of the goshawk's eye.

KUBISIAK

HERTLING

Accipiter cooperii
Cooper's hawk

Accipiter gentilis
goshawk

Accipiter striatus
sharp-shinned hawk

Buteo lineatus
red-shouldered hawk

Buteo jamaicensis
red-tailed hawk

Buteo lagopus
rough-legged hawk

THE HAWKS

Accipiters are hawks having short, rounded wings and long, barred tails. These include the goshawk, Cooper's hawk, and sharp-shinned hawk. The goshawk is a secretive bird and—luckily for the ruffed grouse—is uncommon, though it ranges from as far north as the subarctic tree line across most of the northern United States and migrates south from there. It is about 24 inches long, with a 42-inch wingspan. The Cooper's hawk is 3 or 4 inches shorter than the goshawk, with correspondingly shorter wings. It is most abundant in New England and Canada, but can be found across most of the continent. The sharp-shinned hawk is a mere 10 inches long, with a 20-inch wingspan, and would appear to be too small to pose much danger to a ruffed grouse. But appearances are deceiving. Sharpshins have been known to attack birds much larger than themselves—including, as recorded by A.C. Bent in 1937, a full-grown night heron.

These hawks generally hunt forestland by flying below the canopy or perching in treetops, watching for movement below. They are not soaring birds, but because of their broad wings, they are good gliders. They often alternately fly and glide until prey is sighted. Then they pounce with a burst of speed, steering with their long tails.

Buteos include larger hawks having broad wings and short tails that can be fanned out. Representatives are the red-shouldered, rough-legged, red-tailed, broad-winged, Harlan's, ferruginous, and Swainson's hawks. Most of these species overlap the ruffed grouse's range to some extent, in both Canada and the United States. Buteos do most of their hunting by circling over mixed open farmland and woods or—in the case of the broad-winged hawk—forest clearings.

All are adapted for soaring. The wingtip feathers spread to form layered winglets. Though these are not as pronounced as in the golden and bald eagles, they enable the birds to soar on air currents for long periods, getting the most ride for the least expenditure of energy, while scanning the ground for prey. When prey is sighted, the buteo may circle, then stalk by taking advantage of concealing trees and hills to approach its victim undetected. Buteos may just as often hunt by sitting and waiting. The broad-winged hawk, which nests in forests, is a master at this technique. Brown and Amadon, in *Eagles, Hawks and Falcons of the World,* describe a broad-winged hawk's hunting method: "It usually seeks its food from a low perch. When it suspects prey is about to appear the eyes dilate, the tail twitches cat-like and with swaying body it launches itself downward at the proper moment."

The hen harrier—or marsh hawk or northern harrier, as it is known in the North American part of its globe-spanning range (from the whole of Eurasia to all of North America)—is about 20 inches long with a 40-inch wingspan. A nimble flyer, it has long, narrow wings and a long, blunt-ended tail. Though it is not especially fast, it can soar at 300 feet or course low to the ground with its wings cocked above horizontal. When it hunts, it often flies as low as 10 feet above the vegetation of marshes and open fields, following the contours of the terrain in search of prey. Generally, its kill method is swoop-and-snatch, using the element of surprise. Its diet consists of birds and small mammals, up to and including rabbits.

THE FALCONS

Falcons are built for speed as well as for killing: the wings are long and pointed, and the tail is narrow and short in proportion to the relatively stout body. These birds fly with a pulling motion, and they chase their prey, closing with a tremendous burst of speed. When the prey is a bird, the falcon dives on it, talons extended, and kills the victim in midair—often with an explosion of feathers. Falcons are endowed with a "killing toe"—a long rear talon that, just before impact, can be pointed outward like a spear.

The fastest-flying falcon is the peregrine, a medium-sized raptor measuring about 15 inches, with a wingspan of 40 inches. This bird has been clocked in its dive, or stoop, at nearly 200 miles per hour. Other falcons include the gyrfalcon, merlin (pigeon hawk), and American kestrel (sparrow hawk).

The gyrfalcon is larger than a peregrine (about 22 inches long, with a 48-inch wingspan) and is primarily an arctic bird that feeds on lemmings, waterfowl, and shore-

HERTLING

Falco peregrinus
peregrine falcon

Falco rusticolus
gyrfalcon

Bubo virginianus
great horned owl

Surnia ulula
hawk owl

Asio flammeus
short-eared owl

Nyctea scandiaca
snowy owl

birds. When the lemming supply runs low, however, gyrfalcons move into southern Canada and the northern United States, preying on rodents, upland birds, and waterfowl.

Merlins and kestrels, also of the falcon family, feed primarily on insects, such as grasshoppers, crickets, butterflies, and dragonflies. Their diet is supplemented by rodents, small birds, and the young of larger birds.

Kites have long tails that are notched or forked at the ends, and their wings are pointed like those of falcon. They have weak feet, for raptors, and their diet consists mostly of insects, amphibians, and snails, but also being opportunists, they will occasionally take a ruffed grouse. There are four species considered resident north of Mexico: swallow-tailed, white-tailed, Mississippi, and Everglades (snail). All live in the southern United States, but a few individual swallowtails and whitetails have been seen as far north as Wisconsin, and the Mississippi kite ranges as far north as southern Iowa.

THE OWLS

Most people think of owls as night hunters, but some, like the great horned owl, hunt at dusk as well as at night; others, including the hawk owl, short-eared owl, and snowy owl, hunt entirely by day. Owls prey on rodents, amphibians, reptiles, and birds. The great horned owl, 2 feet or more in length, with a wingspan of 4 feet or more, can feed on prey as large as a skunk.

Owls evolved independently from hawks and their kin and, as a result, have some unique adaptations for getting their prey. The eyes are positioned side by side, which affords true binocular vision—the ability to focus both eyes entirely on one object. Side vision is poor, but the owl can compensate somewhat for this by being able to rotate its head nearly completely around. Although owls have large eyes, they can contract the size of the large pupil to an astonishing degree in daylight.

Although the tufts on the heads of certain species are not ears, owls do have a good sense of hearing and rely heavily on it to locate their prey. The bird is cock-eared: one ear is lower on the head than the other, each with a different internal structure. This enables the bird to locate prey precisely by balancing out the differences in sound. A facial disk of fluffed-out feathers helps focus incoming sound waves. Some owls emit ultrasonic noises that bounce back like radar.

The great horned owl, which ranges across all of the United States and Canada, and the slightly smaller barred owl, of the eastern two-thirds of the United States and much of Canada, are both forest hunters. Such a large bird flying through the trees would surely attract its prey's attention—the sound of feathers flopping the air alone would betray its presence. But owls have unique feathers and can forage by flying noiselessly, taking their prey unaware, and striking it with sharp talons. The feathers are designed in a way that muffles sound while the bird flaps its wings or glides: the primary feathers have soft barbules on the leading edges, which gives a feather-duster effect, diffusing the airflow and preventing the whistling wingbeats so noticeable in some birds.

THE EAGLES

The mature bald eagle, with its white head and tail, is common currency in American culture—quite an honor for a species that is part scavenger, part predator. Its preferred diet is fish, though it often feeds on carrion and has been known to flock around garbage dumps. These habits earned it the enmity of Benjamin Franklin, who much favored the wild turkey as a national emblem. Immature balds, younger than four years, lack the stark white head and tail and blackish body. They are much less distinctively marked: dark brown, tan or mottled, and can be mistaken for golden eagles.

Golden eagles are more versatile predators than balds, feeding mostly on rodents and ducks—but in the western United States, livestock growers often accuse them of killing lambs. Like the bald, the golden eagle is a soaring raptor, but it often hunts by flying and gliding low to the ground, taking advantage of the terrain to surprise its prey. The species is found over much of Canada and in the western United States; some goldens winter in the Appalachians. Mature golden eagles are 3 feet or more with wingspans of 7½ feet; balds are slightly smaller.

Aquila chrysaetos
golden eagle

Haliaeetus leucocephalus
bald eagle

THE IMPACT ON GROUSE

Ruffed grouse are not the mainstay in the diet of any of these raptors. All tend to concentrate instead on mice, rabbits, and even insects. Yet unquestionably, raptors do kill ruffed grouse. Evidence has been found in goshawk stomachs, in the pellets of undigested matter expelled by great horned owls, and through observation of several kinds of hawks. The victims are often sick, infirm, or injured birds, however, and thus raptors can actually benefit a population of prey species, keeping it healthy by weeding out the misfits.

At certain times, though, even healthy grouse are vulnerable. When, for example, a grouse's ground food is buried by snow, it

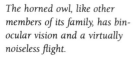

The horned owl, like other members of its family, has binocular vision and a virtually noiseless flight.

MAXSON

must take to the trees to forage on buds. And in spring, when the male grouse is actually advertising his whereabouts by drumming, raptors get an assist. A 1972 study in Alberta by Rusch, Meslow, Doerr, and Keith found that more adult male ruffed grouse than females were killed by owls, apparently because the displaying males were more visible—or audible. Other research, in the Cloquet Forest Research Center in Minnesota, has shown that grouse in hardwood forests are less vulnerable to predation by raptors than grouse in stands of evergreens with a dense canopy and shade-thinned understory. In the conifers, the grouse are more visible and the raptors can strike from concealment.

Landmark research done in the 1930s in Pennsylvania and in the late 1940s and early 1950s in Michigan has given some idea of the extent of predation on ruffed grouse by raptors. In a study that could never be duplicated today for fear of reducing already declining raptor populations, 2,817 hawk stomachs were examined over 13 years in Pennsylvania. Luttringer reported in 1938 that only sharp-shinned, Cooper's, and goshawks had eaten ruffed grouse and pheasant. Among all these specimens and species, only 89 stomachs contained remains of ruffed grouse or pheasants.

The Michigan research, conducted by F.C. and J.J. Craighead, focused on a 36-square-mile area; populations, movement, and mortality of hawks and owls and their prey were recorded. Predation alone, the researchers concluded, could not seriously depress populations of grouse and other prey.

Like most predators, raptors are opportunists—discounting such species as the extremely specialized Everglades kite, which feeds on only one genus of snail. Where their ranges and habitats overlap those of ruffed grouse, raptors can be considered potential predators. On occasion, an individual bird might even specialize in hunting ruffed grouse. And a raptor not usually associated with grouse may move from its normal range and penetrate ruffed grouse country. The snowy owl, for example, may react to a shortage of lemmings, its preferred food, and move south of its arctic range to become a potential predator on ruffed grouse. Regardless of food preference or range, raptors do not have the best of reputations; more than one has been shot by a vengeful hunter who, perhaps remembering evidence seen in snow of a raptor's kill, believes he or she is protecting the ruffed grouse population.

Research shows quite the opposite: elimination of one cause of mortality does not tend to increase the grouse population. Instead, any population gains that might be realized tend to be compensated for by losses from other causes.

The classic study on compensatory mortality was Edminster's, in New York, in 1931–1935. During one period grouse were declining in numbers, and during another their numbers were increasing. Three test areas were used. In one area, all predators were killed, in another they were selectively thinned, and in a third, left alone. Removal of predators did not help the grouse one bit. In fact, regardless of the statewide trend in grouse populations—decline or increase—the test areas in which predators were eliminated wound up having fewer grouse than did areas having predators. The implication was that whatever undetermined factor was causing grouse to decline, predators seemed to reduce those losses—perhaps by removing the less healthy birds.

Ruffed grouse populations, at least in the northern parts of their range, tend to fluctuate in cycles. The reasons for this appear to be a complex combination of environmental factors that have never been fully explained. Populations of mice and other prey in a raptor's diet follow a similar pattern. In turn, populations of raptors and other predators tend to rise and fall accordingly—generally, the more prey, the more predators. And as prey populations decline, predators often shift to alternative foods, move to other areas, or fail to produce as many young.

One example of how predators may shift to alternative foods occurred in 1972, in the study by Rusch et al. in Alberta. The focus of the research was great horned owls and their predation on ruffed grouse and snowshoe hares on a 52-acre tract. In the study area, the owls, which killed up to about 4 percent of the snowshoe hares, then supplemented their diet with up to 5.1 percent of the grouse population. In early summer the ruffed grouse chicks blend so closely with the forest floor that they are much more vulnerable to such ground predators as feral cats and skunks than they are to raptors. But in late summer, it was the female grouse that suffered the most losses to great horned owls—apparently because of her activity in caring for her brood. The motherless chicks, of course, soon died also.

When the days become shorter and the hunt less productive, some species of raptors migrate—often in large numbers. "Formerly, great flocks of red-tailed, Swainson's and rough-legged hawks could be seen wheeling majestically across the sky in the Plains States," writes Steven Peterson in his recent update of Frederick Lincoln's *Migration of*

KUBISIAK

The red-tailed hawk and other buteos may launch their attacks from perches rather than search for prey by soaring.

Birds. "In the East, good flights of broad-winged, Cooper's, and sharp-shinned hawks are still often seen, particularly along the Appalachian ridges." Two major viewing spots favored by bird-watchers and biologists are Hawk Mountain, in Pennsylvania, and Cape May Point on the Delmarva Peninsula. Most spectacular are the hawks, which wheel in great "kettles," as such groups are called. Some, like the peregrine falcon, head deep into South America to winter. Others, such as the goshawk and snowy owl, pushed south by lack of prey, infilter rather than flock into the northern United States.

But all of this shifting has little impact on ruffed grouse. As some predators move out, others—sometimes members of the same species—move in to spend the winter. Or, like the great horned owl, they stay put. And the current major migration routes pass through some prime grouse range.

The bottom line, then, is that some raptors do indeed kill ruffed grouse, but not normally in numbers that will significantly reduce the population. Biologists agree that ruffed grouse in good habitat generally will maintain good populations despite—or even because of—predation by raptors, barring cyclic decline, climatic changes, disease, or habitat change. Our magnificent birds of prey are more to be watched and admired than condemned as wholesale destroyers of ruffed grouse, or judged less worthy than even a prized game bird.

—Bill Vogt

Tipping the balance

"There are two kinds of hunting," said Aldo Leopold: "ordinary hunting, and ruffed grouse hunting." Over the past several centuries the ruffed grouse has been the ultimate test of the hunter of upland game birds, and countless millions of this palatable species have been brought home for special feasts. Although the bird endured threats to its existence in the millennia before the first shotgun blast, the human hunter has introduced a new cause of mortality. Yet ruffed grouse always show up in the spring, no matter how many hunters took to the woods the previous fall. Should we then even worry about the impact of hunting on grouse populations and distribution?

For more than 250 years, people have indeed been concerned. Early regulations to limit the number of ruffed grouse taken by hunters included abolishing the use of nets, traps, and snares to capture grouse, making the sale of grouse illegal, and establishing bag limits and abbreviated seasons. Ruffed grouse numbers continued to fluctuate, however, and any decline in numbers was usually blamed on hunting. Hence, hunting seasons were often closed, sometimes for two or three years, and when hunters were allowed to return to the woods, they would have a much shorter season to pursue their quarry. This pattern—low numbers of birds, prompting reduced or closed hunting seasons, followed by higher numbers and more

The human hunter and his bird dog have added to the number of grouse predators. But the impact is not additive if hunting merely substitutes for some other form of mortality.

248

What impact does hunting have on ruffed grouse numbers and distribution?

Starting in the 1930s, findings from studies on a variety of game animals were beginning to suggest a general principle: the principle of compensatory mortality. Researchers knew that any one of numerous mortality factors could affect the population of a species. The magnitude of these factors might vary, but the overall mortality rate never seemed to change significantly. Apparently, if a horde of avid hunters pursued a population of ruffed grouse, other mortality factors, such as natural predation and disease, would decrease, and the overall mortality rate would stay the same. According to this theory, the animals not taken by hunters would otherwise die from natural causes. The principle of compensatory mortality became widely accepted, and hunters and wildlife managers began to question the notion that hunting limited ruffed grouse populations. The new idea was that hunting had little or no impact. Harvest regulations have become more liberal ever since.

But the population dynamics of any animal involve a complex association of numerous factors, all of them difficult to monitor. Explaining how any one of those factors affects ruffed grouse populations is no small challenge. Consider one of the most basic components: the number of birds in a particular area. To get an index to any change in numbers, density estimates must be obtained before the hunting season begins and again after the season closes. Young birds will be moving in and out of the area during the fall dispersal, however, and the entire population is subject to other mortality factors all the while. It is possible to try to measure the hunting mortality rate more directly by banding the legs of captured birds, some of which will then be reported killed by hunters. Yet adjustments must then be made for other causes of mortality, crippled but unrecovered birds, lost bands, hunters who forget to make their reports, and the fluctuation in density due to dispersal. Another way to estimate hunting mortality involves marking a sample of the population with radio-transmitters, which can then be monitored throughout the hunting season. This method provides a more direct

This red-phase adult male was shot but not recovered by the hunter. Harvest statistics do not include such crippled birds, which may be at least 10 percent of the reported kill.

liberal regulations—continued through the late 1940s.

Just about the same time, studies on ruffed grouse populations began to suggest a new idea, that ruffed grouse numbers fluctuate naturally, regardless of the number of hunters and the birds they kill. As De-Stefano and Rusch noted in 1982, many biologists now believe the fluctuations in numbers of hunters and grouse harvests are a result rather than a cause of fluctuations in game abundance. So when wildlife managers predict a good season, or when fellow hunters report success, more hunters set out for the woods and more grouse are taken. Studies in the past twenty to thirty years have since provided strong support for the concept that ruffed grouse populations fluctuate, or cycle, approximately every ten years. There are several theories as to why grouse numbers rise and fall so regularly, but hunting is not a likely explanation. That brings us back to our original question:

estimate of hunting mortality, and fewer adjustments are needed, but to obtain a large enough sample, researchers must spend a great deal of time and money to monitor the individual grouse throughout the course of the hunting season.

There is yet another variable. Because of the cyclic nature of the ruffed grouse, the magnitude of the mortality factors affecting a population varies over a ten-year period, and hence any index, any estimate must be monitored for at least a decade. Since the number of hunters and the number of ruffed grouse they kill each year are probably results of the cycle, we cannot assume that the kill rate is static from year to year. In other words, the number of hunters is likely to vary through the cycle, as is the number of birds shot, as is the time of year when they perish.

Given the difficulty of obtaining accurate estimates of hunting mortality on ruffed grouse populations, just what information is available? A large proportion—50 percent to 75 percent—of the kill is usually taken in the first four to six weeks of a three- to four-month season. Thereafter, the harvest slows, as does hunter effort. The percentage of the total population killed by hunters varies tremendously, with reports ranging from 10 percent to even 42 percent. Such a wide range should not be surprising, given differences like hunter access, in terms of roads and trails. Who owns the land matters, too: in 1985 Small reported that in central Wisconsin, the hunting mortality rate on state land was 92 percent versus 19 percent on private property.

Male and female grouse appear equally susceptible to the gun, but juveniles have been reported more vulnerable than adults in some studies. The difference may be that juveniles travel over a greater area than established adults during the fall dispersal, which coincides with most hunting seasons, and they therefore encounter hunters more often. Where good access allows hunters an equal chance at *all* birds, however, hunters may flush adult and juvenile grouse in proportion to their numbers in the population, and DeStefano and Rusch believe that no difference in vulnerability between age classes would then occur.

So what should the grouse hunter's limit be? Should researchers determine the number of natural overwinter losses, without hunting, and then, applying the idea of compensatory mortality, conclude that this number of birds could be shot instead? Should we worry that with the increasing number of ruffed grouse hunters, and their increased use of public hunting grounds, hunting may go beyond compensating for other kinds of losses and become an additive form of mortality? Although other mortality factors may decrease as hunting mortality increases, is there a threshold beyond which an increase in hunting mortality would raise the total loss of birds and lower subsequent populations? If so, what is the threshold for ruffed grouse in each region throughout its extensive range? Is late-season hunting removing birds that would otherwise breed in spring and later provide more targets for early-season hunting? Evidence here is contradictory: some studies indicate high survival rates over winter; others have found high mortality rates. What about spring dispersal? Are the grouse moving from areas of high density to places that suffered high mortality from both hunting and natural causes? Information here is slight.

As researchers pursue the answers, the ruffed grouse continues to enrich our experience, not just for hunters but for everyone with an interest in the outdoors. It is a precarious balance in which ruffed grouse exist, and we must learn how to keep it.

—*Robert J. Small*

The effort—and thus the success—of hunters peaks in fine fall weather. Come January, grouse are more susceptible to death from other causes.

Unwary birds

*T*he ruffed grouse in Alaska, like most of its western relatives, "is comparatively tame and unsuspicious, and its behavior bears little resemblance when hunted to the thunder-winged flight that gives this species a reputation as king of all game birds in the northern and eastern United States. In Alaska it is usually possible to walk up on them with about the same ease as with the ptarmigan and spruce grouse. Perhaps if they were hunted more aggressively the survivors would develop the same wary habits that are so conspicuous in their New England cousins."

—Gabrielson, Ira N., and Lincoln, Frederick C.
Birds of Alaska: *A Wildlife Management Institute Publication (Harrisburg, Pa.: The Stackpole Company), 1959*

Harvest statistics

Below are representative statistics on the numbers of ruffed grouse taken by hunters in recent years. In some states and provinces, the length of the season and the bag limit may vary by locale. Note that where grouse hunting is popular, the number of hunters approximates and, in certain cases, even exceeds the number of grouse they bagged. The data were compiled by Rusch.

	Estimated harvest	Hunters	Bag limit	Season length (days)
Maine (1982)	644,000	134,000	4	92
New York (1982)	562,000	172,000	4	127
Michigan (1982)	522,000	193,000	5	61–93
Pennsylvania (1984)	500,000	550,000	2	53–67
Wisconsin (1982)	400,000	185,000	5	91–122
New Brunswick (1982)	389,000	–	none	46
Minnesota (1982)	339,000	316,000	5	105
Alberta (1982)	327,000	100,000	10	74–88
West Virginia (1982)	240,000	90,000	4	136
Idaho (1983)	170,000	35,000	4	72
Washington (1979)	153,000	64,000	3	103
British Columbia (1982)	134,000	27,000	5	60–120
Massachusetts (1981)	79,000	45,000	3	85
Oregon (1982)	57,000	28,000	3	30–110
Newfoundland (1980)	54,000	28,000	6	77
Tennessee (1978)	38,000	19,000	–	143
North Carolina (1977)	33,000	13,000	3	134
Montana (1982)	23,000	37,000	4	79
Saskatchewan (1982)	17,000	10,000	5	68
Utah (1981)	14,000	9,000	4	73
Iowa (1982)	9,000	8,000	3	86
Maryland (1983)	9,000	9,000	2	119
Yukon (1978)	4,300	4,600	10	91
North Dakota (1982)	4,000	2,200	4	108
Rhode Island (1982)	2,500	13,500	2	129
Northwest Territories (1982)	700	–	5–10	242
Labrador (1981)	500	2,500	10	210
California (1983)	100	–	2	31
Manitoba (1982)	–	25,000	6	120–240
Alaska (1983)	–	–	5–15	203–288

The tangled web
of mortality

Despite all the attention that biologists and wildlife managers have devoted to ruffed grouse over several centuries, little is known about one of the most important aspects of ruffed grouse biology: the specific causes and timing of mortality throughout the year. This is especially true for juveniles during the first two months after hatch, June and July, and during the fall dispersal period, late September and October.

The great majority of the mortality rates determined in the past have been estimated indirectly, through changes in population estimates, rather than by a direct account of actual deaths. These rates are usually calculated for the brood period, from hatch to brood breakup, and for the overwinter period, fall to spring. Take a species with a geographic range as extensive as that of the ruffed grouse, add the subject's typical fluctuations in population, and you will not be surprised that variation in mortality rates is large. In New York, for example, Bump and his colleagues estimated mortality during the brood period at 33 percent; in Wisconsin, for the same period, Dorney and Kabat came up with an estimate of 62 percent. For the overwinter period, a longer span of time, the figures vary even more widely, from King's estimate of 17 percent to Dorney and Kabat's 87 percent.

Such discrepancies could be a result of cyclic changes in ruffed grouse populations,

For adult birds, like this flushing hen, mortality is lowest in summer.

or of geographic differences that affect the timing and causes of mortality. Perhaps extrinsic factors like food, weather, and predation are at work, or intrinsic factors like territoriality and genotypic polymorphism. Whatever the reasons, however, we need to know more.

Understanding when and by what causes ruffed grouse perish may also help us figure out whether hunting mortality is primarily additive or compensatory. If we can determine the percentage of grouse killed by predators during winter *after* hunters have put their shotguns away for the year, we may be able to solve part of the puzzle of why ruffed grouse populations fluctuate.

The use of radiotelemetry has helped researchers obtain more detailed information. But because of the high costs of such studies—not only in equipment but also in manpower—only a few have been performed. Through the work of Huempfner and his colleagues, as yet unpublished, and Rusch and his students, some data on the specific

Hunters, predators, and the elements conspire against the birds in winter. The grouse that occupied this snow roost has—for the moment—escaped the dangers.

SMITH

causes and timing of ruffed grouse mortality now exist.

In central Wisconsin, Small radiomarked 171 ruffed grouse in 1982–1985, a period when grouse numbers were low throughout many of the Lake States and Canada. Monitoring the birds at least every other day, he recorded a total of 88 mortalities. Estimates of mortality were then computed for each of the four seasons, based on the number of grouse marked and the number of mortalities recorded during each season. Adult mortality was lowest in spring, at 9 percent, but gradually increased through the rest of the year, with estimates of 17 percent in summer, 28 percent in fall, and up to 50 percent in winter. Combining these seasonal estimates, Small found an average annual mortality rate of 73 percent for adult grouse. Roughly speaking, then, only one of every four adult grouse would survive to breed again the following spring.

Just surviving long enough to breed once is even more chancy: most juveniles don't ever get the opportunity. In Small's studies, each season nearly half the young birds perished. Even during summer, when the chicks enjoyed the protection of the hen, one-third of the juveniles did not survive. It appears that the main culprits throughout the year are the avian predators, primarily the great horned owl and the goshawk. There is some evidence that foxes and other predators may take juvenile grouse during early summer, but there have been no studies on the specific causes and timing of mortality of grouse younger than two months, given the difficulty of marking and monitoring the chicks when they are so small. With nearly half the juveniles dying each season, the probability that a young bird will survive its first year is low. Nine of every ten young grouse died before reaching their first birthday in the central Wisconsin study.

With high mortality for juvenile grouse throughout the entire year, the portion of deaths due to hunting is relatively small, since hunters pursue the birds for only a few months in fall and winter. It appears that for central Wisconsin, of the nine deaths among every ten juveniles, hunters got one, predators eight. The proportion of adults lost to the gun is greater than for juveniles, as about four of every ten adults that perish each year were taken home by hunters. This does not mean that more adults were shot, only that the *proportion* attributable to hunting was higher for adults. In Small's studies in central Wisconsin, nonhuman predators took a smaller proportion of adults (six of ten) than juveniles (eight of nine).

The above figures may suggest to some that predators kill a great number of grouse each year, and that hunters should be able to take more for themselves, since it appears the birds will die from predation anyway. Maybe yes, maybe no. This idea has been the subject of much debate. Let's start with the assumption that we wish to manage grouse populations so that fall hunters can take the maximum number in fall yet leave enough birds to reproduce in spring that the same maximum number will be available for hunters the next fall. If they want the highest number of birds flushing in front of them each fall, hunters will not want to reduce the population below that level. This type of management plan is often called maintaining the population at its *maximum sustainable yield,* or MSY.

The key to solving the problem then lies in determining how predators will behave after hunters have taken their harvest. If hunters reduce the grouse population just to the level of MSY, and if predators kill no grouse but switch to alternative prey, then hunters will have left enough birds overwintering to reproduce the maximum number for the next fall: the MSY is intact. But if (and this is the much more likely scenario) predators kill some grouse in addition, hunters will have, in effect, reduced the population of grouse below the MSY. Next fall there will most likely be fewer birds.

Not let's assume that hunters leave the grouse population at a level *above* the maximum sustainable yield. If predators further reduce the population just to the MSY level, then hunters will have taken the optimum number. But if predators reduce the population *below* the MSY level, then hunters will once again have reduced the population such that a maximum sustainable yield cannot be maintained.

It may not be appealing to discuss the mortality of ruffed grouse in such technical, abstract, perhaps even unrealistic terms. But it is necessary to consider the interactions between hunters and predators, and their effects on grouse numbers throughout the seasons. So the answer to the hunter's question—"If I don't shoot the grouse, won't the hawks and owls get them?"—depends on the level of the grouse population after the guns have become silent, and how many grouse the hawks and owls need to survive.

Even if biologists believe they understand the theoretical interactions between hunting mortality on the one hand and natural mortality on the other, obtaining the data to determine how these two factors interact is extremely difficult. There are numerous reasons why, and they are worth repeating.

First is the grouse's extensive range and the wide array of habitats it encompasses. Surely the local predator populations vary accordingly, and it is known that some avian predators, like the goshawk, periodically make massive invasions from north to south. Second, there is the cyclic nature of grouse populations, which is strong evidence that mortality, and possibly reproduction as well, is not stable throughout the cycle. Third, hunting mortality has varied greatly in the past; it is difficult to predict in general, and the issue is complicated further by higher hunting mortality on some public lands than on private lands.

Finally, there is the question of just how vulnerable the juveniles are during dispersal. In studies of the greater prairie chicken, Bowman and Robel found high juvenile mortality as the birds were dispersing; but Keppie, working on spruce grouse, reported, "Clearly, dispersing birds did not suffer extraordinary mortality." Which is the case for ruffed grouse? There are conflicting reports. In the only dispersal study to date using radiotelemetry, Small concluded that juvenile ruffed grouse did not appear to suffer from increased mortality during the fall dispersal period.

Trying to understand the interactions between the different factors that contribute to seasonal mortality rates is a challenge for wildlife biologists. The bits of data that are reliable are difficult to piece together; hence studies must continue.

—Robert J. Small

The human hunter

To say that the impact of hunting on the ruffed grouse is difficult to measure is to put it mildly. Consider all the factors that themselves are hard to quantify, and how they vary during the hunting season and throughout the range of the bird: the amount and distribution of cover; the behavior of ruffed grouse; the huntability of the area, its size and accessibility and terrain; plus the nature of the hunters and their efforts—whether with or without dogs, in brush or along roads—not to mention their skill. Yet game managers are expected to provide a reasonably accurate appraisal of how grouse are faring.

Fall favors the hunter. From mid-September through mid-October young birds are dispersing from their juvenile range. One might speculate that these birds, which constitute about 65 percent to 80 percent of the fall population in Wisconsin, would be temporarily more vulnerable to hunters as they pass through marginal, less secure habitats in their search for new homes. And indeed, the proportion of juveniles shot along roads has been 85 percent, versus 77 percent for grouse taken in brush in Wisconsin from 1953 to 1957, Dorney and Kabat reported.

For the ruffed grouse, there is no safety in numbers. When two or more members of a brood move together, or juveniles of different broods meet up, the advantage goes clearly to the hunter: multiple flushes mean more shooting opportunities. The

With the deciduous cover lying on the forest floor, the hunter and his dog enjoy an advantage over the ruffed grouse. Birds in coverts close to roads are the most vulnerable.

Left: In late summer the inexperienced juvenile grouse are protected by vegetation as they seek suitable cover. Right: When the leaves have fallen, evergreens and other dense thickets may provide security.

birds also become more vulnerable when they flush at short intervals, allowing hunters to anticipate them. Any unwary birds that flush to the nearest tree may provide easy targets. Reflushes of birds within shooting range are also more likely before juveniles learn what their pursuers are up to.

Yet even these inexperienced, wandering juveniles are not wholly defenseless. The dense foliage of deciduous trees, shrubs, and vines provides good camouflage into late October. In some areas, low-growing shrubs, ferns, and other herbaceous plants may provide protection at ground level. The warm temperatures prevalent during much of September and October keep some hunters home and limit the time afield for others. And interest in hunting waterfowl, deer, and other species may distract hunters from pursuing upland game birds.

Whatever the level of hunter effort and grouse mortality, researchers generally agree that early-season hunting does not have a negative impact on grouse populations. Many birds that would otherwise be lost to natural causes of death find their way into the recreational hunter's gamebag.

By late October the fall dispersal of juvenile grouse is complete, and most birds occupy the best habitat they can find. Forests of aspen, maple, and other hardwoods become more open as the last leaves flutter to the ground, but as the temperature dips below freezing, grouse seek out thickets of conifers and oaks, particularly those that re-

tain most of their leaves through late winter. Here, the cover offers insulation from the bite of winter. Where such stands of evergreens and oaks are few and far between, or accessible to hunters, grouse may be more vulnerable, particularly if the hunters are dedicated and skilled. Some accessible public lands that fit this description are especially well hunted: the Sandhill Wildlife Area in Wisconsin, the Mille Lacs Wildlife Area in Minnesota, and east-central Wisconsin.

Interest in grouse hunting falls off considerably when the gun deer season opens, in mid-November in Wisconsin. By early winter, ruffed grouse are less vulnerable to hunting for another reason: there are fewer of them, the bulk of the summer population having succumbed to either fall hunters or natural predators. The remaining birds live at much lower densities than they did in September and October. These survivors are often in coverts so isolated or remote that the hunter must expend considerable effort just getting to them. Grouse that have survived to this stage of the hunting season are often very wary and flush out of shooting range. They may also flush in unanticipated directions or from unexpected roosts, like the canopy of standing trees or the blind side of a dense thicket. Once flushed, the birds are usually difficult to approach within range again.

The first snowfalls of the season leave the birds at a disadvantage. Grouse cannot burrow in to snow-roost until the snow is at

260

least 18 to 20 centimeters (7 to 8 inches) deep, and if they roost or feed on the white cover, they are easily detected. Although crusted snow also prevents grouse from snow-roosting, it crunches underfoot and alerts birds to approaching intruders. Deep, fluffy snow favors the birds by providing good roosting cover and concealment. But birds that are not in burrows may also be difficult to locate, since they may roost in either sparse or dense cover. Although winter roosts are usually near a food supply, such as mature aspen, the net effect is that the hunter is discouraged, and fewer grouse are killed in winter.

The white blanket of snow exposes the grouse to predators, including humans. But because snow and cold discourage many hunters, late-season hunting does not appear to be harmful, except in small, easily accessible woodlands.

REFUGES

Most hunters concentrate their grouse hunting within 400 meters of drivable roads. Where roads are limited and hunters must walk in to hunt, suitable grouse habitats become de facto grouse refuges. Relatively large blocks of such inaccessible land occur throughout central and northern Wisconsin, for example.

Natural refuges also exist where blocks of suitable grouse habitat are surrounded by marsh, open water, large crop fields, other woodlands with extensive parklike cover, or grasslands with inadequate woody cover—all of which may create effective barriers against hunters. Juveniles dispersing from these areas can replenish the grouse population in habitats accessible to hunters. Recent studies by Small in east-central Wisconsin indicate

Most birds are taken in fall, before cold, hunger, and natural predators have had their turn. Juveniles are often less wary than their elders, and they may be relegated to less secure coverts.

that adult hens may travel as far as 1,600 meters in spring. Movements of this magnitude mean that adult hens and their offspring can easily colonize local coverts that may have been overhunted.

Man-made refuges exist where grouse hunting is restricted by the landowners, or by the proximity of residences or other developments, which can reduce or eliminate opportunities for hunting. Refuges designated for waterfowl may also favor grouse if suitable grouse habitat is available. So may parks, military compounds, and safety zones. The net impact of refuges on grouse populations varies by region, however, and may be minor, particularly where grouse habitat is fragmented. In these areas, hunters usually have easy access, and the cumulative long-term effect of extensive hunting may be depression of grouse populations.

CYCLES

Each year hunters go afield with different expectations and resolve. If word is that the grouse are plentiful, flushing at every turn and filling gamebags, hunters are likely to spend more days afield and pursue birds more aggressively. At Sandhill, both the number of hunting trips and the number of birds bagged have been greater during high years of the grouse cycle: 64 percent of the hunters went out twice or more and took an average of 0.35 grouse per trip, compared with 55 percent and 0.24 grouse in low years. Hunters also reported more flushes

during high years of the grouse cycle, an average 1.1 birds per hour, compared with 0.5 birds per hour in low years. Given the same season length, it appears that grouse populations can withstand greater hunter exploitation during cyclic highs.

At lower densities of grouse during the low years of the cycle, hunters must work harder to find their birds. Discouraged hunters may make fewer trips per season, and many pursue other game species.

LATE-SEASON HUNTING

Most of the grouse to be killed by hunters will have been taken before December 1. Yet the potential impact on breeding grouse populations is high in certain areas, and some researchers have expressed concerns that heavily hunted coverts may not be adequately repopulated with grouse the following year. Their fears may be realized in accessible coverts, particularly on public lands in southern Wisconsin, where the hunting season does not close until January 31. Such extended hunting seasons may indeed represent a threat to maintaining higher grouse densities where suitable grouse habitat is either fragmented or isolated. Although extended hunting seasons have been in effect for several years with no detectable, widespread negative impact on grouse populations, it is quite likely that grouse numbers may be suppressed either locally or within portions of this region. This has been demonstrated by grouse research and hunter surveys on public lands in southern Wisconsin, where hunting pressure has been high and grouse survival low. But it is worth noting that public lands constitute only 5 percent of this area.

The question remains, however, whether the harvest rate–the proportion of the fall population taken by hunting–is within acceptable limits. Studies in central Wisconsin indicate that if harvest rates exceeding 40 percent are sustained over large areas for two or more years, breeding grouse densities may be depressed.

Yet on the Navarino Wildlife Area in northeastern Wisconsin, DeStefano and Rusch have reported an estimated mean harvest rate of 40 percent from 1978 to 1981, with no detectable adverse impact on breeding grouse populations. Dorney and Kabat concluded that 30 percent to 35 percent was an acceptable harvest rate in areas without the buffering effect of unhunted coverts nearby. Recent regional estimates of grouse harvest rates in Wisconsin do not exceed 25 percent of the fall population, suggesting minimal overall impact from hunting. Thus, although grouse numbers may be depleted on local areas, the overall impact appears to be within acceptable limits.

Hunted and unhunted areas

It stands to reason, and it has been confirmed by drumming surveys: grouse populations are lower in hunted than in unhunted areas. At Sandhill, for example, Kubisiak found that from 1971 to 1982, drummer densities averaged 4.7 cocks per 100 hectares in the 818-hectare hunted area, compared with 9.3 in the 1,037-hectare unhunted area. Breeding birds may have moved after the hunting season, and differences in mortality rates and habitat quality could also have skewed the results, but certain other bits of data suggest that hunting made the difference.

Before hunting was allowed at Sandhill in 1971, drummer densities were nearly the same on both the to-be-hunted and the not-to-be-hunted areas. In fact, there were a few more drummers in the area that was about to be opened to hunters: 9.3 per 100 hectares compared with 7.6 per 100 hectares. After hunting began, with moderate to high

harvests, populations either declined or remained at considerably lower densities in the hunted area, even though both areas were similarly managed. Since 1983, the number of hunters has been reduced and fewer grouse have been killed.

Hunting, then, goes beyond compensating for other kinds of mortality. Or does it? In Wisconsin, hunting has been allowed on a 482-hectare portion of the 7,290-hectare Wood County Wildlife Area. The habitat resembles that of the unhunted Sandhill area, and survey results indicate that drummer densities were nearly the same: an average of 4.2 cocks per 100 hectares on the Wood County hunted area versus 4.7 on the Sandhill unhunted area. This, despite a hunting season that stretched from mid-September to January 31. The preliminary results suggest that given the current level of hunting effort, grouse populations were not depressed because of hunting.

Most of the 529 banded grouse recovered by hunters at both Sandhill and Wood County were shot within 800 meters of drivable roads–more than 95 percent. Within 400 meters of drivable roads, a greater proportion of banded birds were recovered on the Wood County area than at Sandhill.

Few birds survive more than one year; this provides further justification for cropping the annual surplus by hunting. Of 712 birds banded on areas open to hunting at Sandhill and Wood County, 333 (47 percent) were either shot or found dead of crippling injuries. Of these, 291 were recovered the same year they had been banded. Another 32 were shot the following year, 6 were taken in the third, and 2 in the fourth. Of 428 birds banded on the Sandhill unhunted area, only 55 (13 percent) were recovered, most of them by hunters on lands open to hunting. Only 22 were recaptured in live-traps the following year, and 7 the second year.

But one juvenile male banded in 1978 lived at least until 1981, when he was recaptured on the hunted area. And an adult male banded in 1979 was shot in 1982, and an adult female banded in 1979 was recaptured in 1981.

The number of grouse hit but unrecovered on the Sandhill–Wood County areas was 10 percent of the total kill during the 1981–

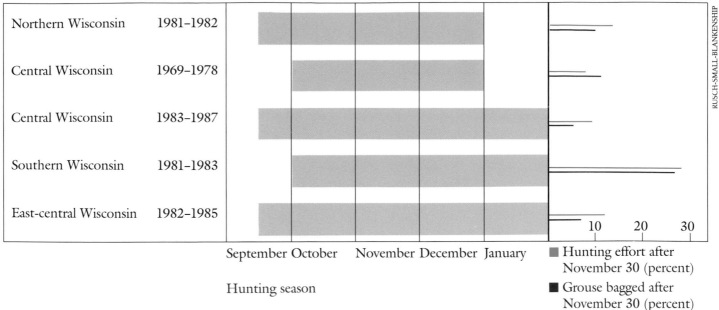

		September	October	November	December	January	
Northern Wisconsin	1981–1982						
Central Wisconsin	1969–1978						
Central Wisconsin	1983–1987						
Southern Wisconsin	1981–1983						
East-central Wisconsin	1982–1985						10 20 30

Hunting season

■ Hunting effort after November 30 (percent)

■ Grouse bagged after November 30 (percent)

The long hunting season in some areas is controversial. One concern: even though overall numbers of grouse remain stable, high harvest levels in convenient coverts may reduce local breeding populations.

1986 hunting seasons. In comparison, the mean crippling rate was 13 percent at Navarino, according to DeStafano and Rusch in 1986, and 11 percent in New York, according to Bump and his colleagues in 1947. These estimates represent a minimum since hunters are likely to underestimate the number of birds that they cripple: some birds that are hit do not appear to be injured and continue in flight for some distance; others may be hit but obscured by dense foliage or the terrain.

Sandhill has provided a unique opportunity to see how hunters affect grouse populations. The birds in the area to be hunted were monitored in spring with complete counts of drummers from 1971 to 1982. Fall populations on the opening day of the hunting season were estimated by applying an expansion factor to the spring counts. Figures on grouse kills were obtained from hunters, who reported daily effort, success, and dog use.

Given this information, it was possible to determine the percentage of the estimated fall population that was shot with various levels of known hunter effort (cumulative hunter days per kilometer). These results suggest that cumulative hunter days per kilometer should be kept at about 30 to 32 to achieve a 35 percent to 40 percent harvest rate. So if hunter effort can be estimated, the grouse kill can be predicted with reasonable accuracy, at least in habitat comparable to that of Sandhill.

Other factors, too, may differ from those observed at Sandhill: the size and accessibility of the area, the proportion of hunters making repeat trips to an area, the hunters' knowledge of an area, the time they spend road or brush hunting, their use of dogs, their skill . . . all of which brings us back to the starting point of this article, that the impact of hunting on the ruffed grouse is indeed difficult to measure.

—John Kubisiak

Opportunity in the South

Ruffed grouse of the Appalachian hill country inhabit dense cover and rugged terrain where hunting is difficult. As one hunter expressed it: "You must be able to walk for hours on steep slopes, holding a gun with one hand and a sapling with the other, yet maintain enough energy to run the last hundred yards when your dog points. Then you have to be able to laugh it off—and come up with a suitable excuse—when the grouse makes a clean getaway."

Such conditions can lead to a low rate of hunter success even where grouse are plentiful, and they are probably more plentiful throughout the southern region than people realize. Numbers are limited more by habitat quality than by hunting, and much of the region could support an increase in hunting pressure.

Spring breeding population densities among southern grouse vary from one to five birds per 40 hectares (100 acres). The rate of recruitment—the annual contribution to the grouse population that comes when the chicks hatched in spring survive their first summer and, as hunting season opens, become fair game—is lower than that of northern grouse. Fall and winter populations in the South, determined from hunter harvests, have averaged two to five juveniles per adult hen. During average years, Robinson has reported, the hunting season flush rate is slightly more than one bird per hunter hour.

Grouse are not nearly so plentiful in the South as they are during peak population years in the northern regions, but neither do they experience drastic fluctuations in population levels. Although the numbers of ruffed grouse do vary from year to year, depending on the weather, food supply, and rate of predation during the reproductive season, cycles have not been reported.

Nor are grouse so plentiful as they once were, when they inhabited a much more extensive region in the South. Even after the early settlers arrived, the birds survived in much of Arkansas, most of Missouri, and all of Kentucky, Illinois, Indiana, and Ohio. They thrived for a time after land-clearing operations had created small forest openings and brushy coverts, but they were decimated by forest removal as the region was settled and cleared for agriculture. Their numbers reached a low ebb during the Depression, when extensive tracts of agriculturally submarginal hill lands were cleared and farmed.

An exodus of people from the hill farms of Appalachia to cities and industrial centers was well under way by 1940. Once abandoned, this farmland became highly suitable grouse habitat. Grouse increased in numbers and expanded their range, and in places they continue to do so. Near the western edge of their southern range, they inhabit many areas from which they were absent twenty or thirty years ago.

A number of states have attempted to reestablish the ruffed grouse in its old range, but most efforts have been unsuccessful, probably because of habitat deficiencies. The main exceptions are in Indiana, where the range has been expanded by relocating trapped native birds, and in Missouri, where limited success has been achieved by introducing grouse from other states. Restoration efforts continue in portions of Arkansas and western Kentucky.

Because drastic declines in quail and rabbit numbers have left hunters with less to hunt, creating a greater demand for grouse, state wildlife agencies that have long ignored the ruffed grouse have recently focused more attention on this species. Modern clear-cut logging methods often benefit grouse by encouraging young trees, shrubs, and vines. The future outlook for the king of game birds is optimistic in the southern and Appalachian range—good news, for those who value the quality of their hunting experience would really rather hunt ruffed grouse.

—Harold L. Barber

MARTINSON

The kingdom
of the ruffed grouse

Food

Ruffed grouse feed primarily on the leaves, buds, and fruits of forest plants. They have been called browsers—an accurate description, given the wide variety of plant foods they select. They are almost exclusively vegetarians for most of the year, but insects and other small invertebrates make up a major portion of the foods consumed by young chicks.

Like most other gallinaceous birds, grouse are able to satisfy their water requirements from dew and succulent foods, and they have no need to seek out pools and streams. Partly because they are woodland inhabitants, seldom venturing more than a few feet from woody cover, they normally make little use of cultivated grains or other agricultural crops. Servello and Kirkpatrick have found, however, that if ruffed grouse have access to corn along woodland or field edges, they will consume it: corn constituted 11 percent of the dry weight of crop contents of twenty-three grouse collected in New York in 1987, and it was also found in a few crops of Wisconsin grouse.

Grit, which helps the grouse grind food in its gizzard, is routinely consumed when it is available. When the ground is covered with snow, however, its absence from the diet seems to cause no problem. Hard seeds, such as those produced by dogwood, cherry, and sumac, then serve the same purpose. Only the pulpy portions of such fruits contribute to grouse nutrition. The seeds of

In the northern part of its range, the ruffed grouse survives the winter largely by eating tree buds, but in the South, it turns to other foods.

THE KINGDOM OF THE RUFFED GROUSE

plants such as dogwood and mountain ash remain undigested: they are still recognizable after they have passed through the bird's digestive tract, and they are still capable of germinating.

Various species of forest herbs, vines, shrubs, and trees contribute grouse foods. In a study of grouse food habits in just one state, Stoll and his coworkers identified more than 100 species of plants and a variety of insect remains from digestive tracts and droppings. The oak-hickory forests of Missouri do not have many of the foods that are important to the ruffed grouse in its northern and eastern ranges, like aspen, birch, and cherry. Mountain laurel, a common shrub and grouse food in the Southeast, is also absent. Yet the ruffed grouse survives in Missouri. When the entire range of the ruffed grouse is considered, from the northern to the southern boundaries, it becomes apparent that grouse consume a great variety of foods.

The ruffed grouse is the most widely distributed nonmigratory game bird in North America. Its northern limit coincides very closely with the tree line that marks the extent of the boreal forest across Canada and part of Alaska and into high mountain elevations in portions of the Northeast and the Rocky Mountains. The southernmost portion of the inhabited grouse range extends from the Lake States southward to western North and South Carolina, northern Georgia, and eastern Tennessee.

These different zones provide vastly different habitats for ruffed grouse: in the North, evergreen trees (which contribute little or nothing to the grouse diet), aspen and paper birch, and a few other kinds of trees and shrubs; south of the boreal forest, conifers mixed with sugar maple, red maple, black cherry, and other hardwoods, plus many shrubs; in the South, an immense variety of forest vegetation, including most of the trees and shrubs that occur farther north, along with yellow poplar, American holly, blackgum, and several oak species.

The wide range of climatic conditions also influences feeding habits. Deep snows blanket the northern forests and mountains throughout the winter months, severely limiting the resident birds' choice of food, while southern grouse continue to feed on fruits, seeds, and even green leaves.

Beginning in April, northern grouse feed on the catkins, or flowers, of mature male aspens.

KUBISIAK

SPRING

For the ruffed grouse, this is a period of transition from the winter diet of buds, twigs, catkins, acorns, and last year's leaves to the new growth—flowers and fruits and leaves—of spring. Wherever the bird lives, food resources are at a minimum in early spring. The flower buds and catkins of trees and shrubs have been subject to winter-long foraging by grouse and other wildlife, and the green foods of spring have not yet made their appearance.

Male aspens begin flowering in early April in the northern region; the catkins are a choice and nutritious grouse food. Throughout the remainder of April and early May—the breeding season—these catkins sometimes constitute almost the only food of grouse in the boreal zone. An abundance of spring greenery appears about the middle of May, and grouse then turn from their diet of buds and catkins to the leaves of herbaceous plants: strawberry, bunchberry, gold-thread. Aspen and wintergreen leaves, shield fern fiddleheads, willow and beaked hazel catkins, and the buds of apple, birch, and cherry also contribute to the grouse diet in early spring.

The buds and catkins of male aspen are a principal spring food of grouse in New York, Missouri, Maine, and Minnesota—and are probably favored wherever they can be found. Grouse prefer these foods so much that where mature aspens were cut down in Minnesota, drumming sites were soon vacated. These Minnesota birds are not satisfied with any old aspen, either: their preference is for trembling aspen over large-toothed aspen.

Where aspen is common (mostly in the North), most drumming sites are close by. Of 727 primary logs in Minnesota, 82 percent had aspen either overhead or within 30 meters. In central Wisconsin, 60 percent of 465 primary logs in aspen habitats were within 30 meters of a good supply of mature aspen, whereas in oak habitats only 28 percent of 65 logs were within 30 meters of aspens. Although aspen catkins are a major food item in southeastern Ohio, Stoll and his colleagues found that drumming logs were not near aspen clones, suggesting that the birds move some distance from their drumming sites to feed. In western Washington, Brewer found that black cottonwood, a close relative of aspen, was important in the grouse's spring diet. At nearly every site he studied, the nearest cottonwood tree was not far from the drumming log, an average of 46 meters away.

The importance of other foods during

Where aspens are unavailable, the buds, twigs, and catkins of hazel and other related tree species offer a substitute. Birch and cherry are also used.

KUBISIAK

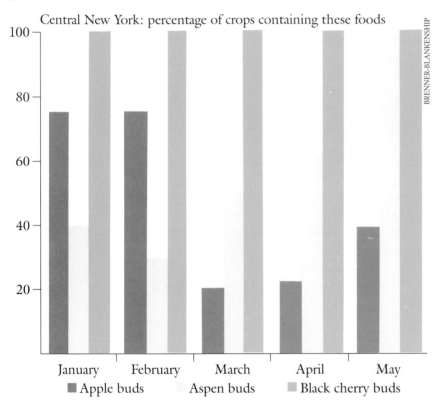

Central New York: percentage of crops containing these foods

January February March April May

■ Apple buds   Aspen buds   ■ Black cherry buds

BRENNER-BLANKENSHIP

spring varies throughout the birds' range. Sources include oak, birch, hazel, cherry, ironwood, dogwood, viburnum, and sumac, which furnish mature fruits, seeds, buds, twigs, and catkins. Grouse also relish the leaves, seeds, and flowers of frost-resistant herbaceous plants, but use of these foods does not appear to be appreciable in the North until male aspen flower buds have shed their pollen, according to Gullion. In addition to aspen buds and catkins, green plant material constitutes an important item in the spring diet of grouse in central Wisconsin. The evidence lies in droppings at most drumming sites. Principal herbaceous species available in this area include wild strawberry, wintergreen, dewberry, and bunchberry, in addition to the emerging leaves of aspen and various other trees, shrubs, and ground layer plants. Considerable use of green plants in spring has also been observed in Maine and Washington.

KUBISIAK

KUBISIAK

In Missouri, grouse continue to feed on acorns and catkins while they await the arrival of spring and fresh foods. Young, newly sprouted vegetation is high in protein and other nutrients needed for the physiologically stressful period of mating and egg laying. By the end of spring up to 80 percent of the diet may be green leafy vegetation. Early-ripening fruits and seeds are also of major importance.

Farther east, in Ohio, aspen catkins are less abundant but still constitute a large part of the early spring diet. Green leafy plant material is also used heavily in Ohio, along with lesser amounts of fruits that have remained intact through the winter, such as greenbrier and sumac.

In the southern portions of the grouse range, berries, grapes, and other soft foods have been eaten or have decayed over the winter, and most of the durable foods, such as beechnuts and acorns, have been con-

sumed by squirrels, deer, and other wild creatures. Avens and Christmas fern fronds, however, have remained green throughout the winter, and their leaves continue to provide a source of food except when covered with snow.

Spring greenery begins to appear about the middle of April in the South. Grouse now eat the swelling buds and emerging young leaves of many kinds of trees and shrubs. In Virginia, grouse also eat coltsfoot flowers, dandelion, and cinquefoil, plus the leaves of many other herbaceous plants. The seeds of red maple are occasionally eaten when they mature in spring; they are not a main food source, and they are low in nutritional value.

Grouse broods begin hatching in May: the first half of the month in the southern grouse range, and the latter part in the northern range. Hatch dates coincide with the appearance of insects. Bugs both winged and terrestrial are easily captured and consumed by the very young grouse chick, which is not physically capable of browsing on plants. Insects are also high in protein and easily digested, providing the necessary nutrients for rapid growth and development of the young bird. The chicks are opportunistic and seem to take anything that moves. Insects and other small invertebrate animals—leafhoppers, ants, flies, aphids, spiders, mosquitoes, crickets, caterpillars, moths, grasshoppers, earthworms, grubs, snails—provide 90 percent to 95 percent of the chick's diet until about one month of age, Robinson has calculated.

Adult grouse, too, eat animal foods year-round, but the proportion peaks during the summer and fall, when these foods account for up to 5 percent of their diet.

Coltsfoot, one of the first plants to flower in the Southeast, is common along roadsides as well as stream banks and other moist places. As early as mid-March, ruffed grouse stuff their crops to capacity with this spring forage.

Left: *Invertebrates are known to be the staple of young chicks, but adults, too, take advantage of the abundance of animal foods in late spring. This crop was full of caterpillars.* Below: *Pulpy fruits, such as crab apple, and soft fruits like blackberries constitute a major part of the grouse's summer diet.*

SUMMER

Of all the seasonal diets of the ruffed grouse, least is known about summer foods. Leaves, fruits, and seeds of aspen, blackberry, raspberry, blueberry, elderberry, strawberry, clover, dandelion, salal, and sedge are common foods in northern regions like New York, Minnesota, and Vancouver. In Ohio, grouse eat the fruits of blackberry, raspberry, smartweed, avens, dock, bulrush, and buttercup, plus the leaves of woody and herbaceous plants. In Virginia, leaves of herbaceous plants make up two thirds of the summer diet of grouse.

Across its range, the ruffed grouse seems to prefer blueberries, blackberries, strawberries, wintergreen berries, elderberries, and similar soft foods. The pulpy fruits of wild cherry, hawthorn, crabapple, and mountain ash also rank high on the list.

The percentage of animal foods in the diet declines as juvenile grouse mature. Between one and two months of age, the proportion falls to 30 percent. Plant foods—tender green leaves, ripe blackberries, grass seeds, sometimes even mushrooms—make up the difference. Fruits, seeds, and leaves predominate by week 7, and by two months of age the juveniles have become primarily plant eaters. The timing of this changeover from carnivore to omnivore to herbivore appears to be consistent throughout the grouse's range. Still, adult birds continue to consume small quantities of animal foods and have been known to occasionally eat salamanders, frogs, and even small snakes.

Fall fruits and seeds

The autumn diet of the ruffed grouse varies by region. Grapes – so important to the bird in the South – are relatively unimportant in the North.

High use is defined as constituting more than 10 percent of the bird's diet in at least one study; *low to moderate use,* less than 10 percent. The information is based on studies by Kittams, Brown, Bump et al., Phillips, Vanderschaegan, Schulz et al., and Servello for the North, and Korschgen, Snyder, Stoll et al., Seehorn et al., and Servello for the South.

NORTHERN REGION (Alaska, New York, Maine, Minnesota, North Dakota, and Utah)

High use
acorn (*Quercus* sp.)
hawthorn (*Crataegus* sp.)
meadow rue *(Thalictrum fendleri)*
rose *(Rosa woodsei, R. acicularis)*
apple (*Malus* sp.)
highbush cranberry *(Viburnum edule, V. trilobum)*
arrow-wood *(Viburnum* sp.)
wild lily of the valley *(Maianthemum canadense)*
kinnikinnick *(Arctostaphylos uva-ursi)*

Low to moderate use
grape (*Vitis* sp.)
cherry (*Prunus* sp.)
raspberry (*Rubus* sp.)
sedges (*Carex* sp.)
bearberry *(Arctostaphylos alpina)*
maple (*Acer* sp.)
serviceberry (*Amelanchier* sp.)
mountain ash *(Sorbus decora)*
blueberry (*Vaccinium* sp.)
bunchberry *(Cornus canadensis)*
elderberry (*Sambucus* sp.)
dwarf corral *(Cornus canadensis)*
lingonberry *(Vaccinium vitis-idaea)*
staghorn sumac *(Rhus typhina)*
smooth sumac *(Rhus glabra)*
poison ivy *(Rhus radicans)*
chokeberry (*Pyrus* sp.)
nannyberry *(Viburnum lentago)*
huckleberry *(Gaylussacia buccata)*
beech *(Fagus grandifolia)*
baneberry *(Actaea arguta)*
wolfberry *(Symphoricarpos occidentalis)*
corn

SOUTHERN REGION (North Carolina, Virginia, Georgia, West Virginia, southeastern Ohio, southwestern Pennsylvania, and Missouri)

High use
grape
acorn
multifora rose *(Rosa multifora)*
greenbrier (*Smilax* sp.)
dogwood *(Cornus florida)*
blackgum *(Nyssa sylvatica)*
honeysuckle *(Lonicera japonica)*
staghorn sumac

Low to moderate use
beech
hawthorn
viburnums
white avens *(Geum canadense)*
fragrant sumac *(Rhus aromatica)*
smooth sumac
poison ivy
blueberry
common privet *(Ligustrum vulgare)*
wintergreen *(Gaultheria procumbens)*
mountain ash (*Sorbus* sp.)
maple
bittersweet *(Celastrus scandens)*
tick trefoil (*Desmodium* sp.)
cherry *(Prunus serotina)*
holly (*Ilex* sp.)
Korean lespedeza *(Lespedeza stipulacea)*
bush clovers (*Lespedeza* sp.)

Serviceberry and wild grapes are among the most important fall foods. Grouse do not fatten themselves in preparation for the scarcities of winter, as do many migratory species, but with the abundance of nutritious foods, the birds attain their heaviest weights of the year in autumn.

Autumn

Fall is a time of food abundance in the year of the ruffed grouse. Choice fruits and seeds are present in quantity, and they are readily available both on the bare ground and in bushes and trees.

Across Canada and the northern United States, the fruits of mountain ash, cherry, hawthorn, and rose provide sustenance.

In the northern hardwoods zone of the Lakes States and the Northeast, the fruits of dogwood, viburnum, apple, crabapple, hawthorn, bittersweet, and partridge berry are important fall foods. These fruits are often covered with leaves and grass after they fall to the ground, and thus protected, many remain sound until the following spring. Although sometimes unavailable because of snow cover, they contribute to the winter diet.

Grapes are a favorite autumn food wherever grouse can find them, and grouse are often concentrated in grapevines until sometime in late November, when the fruits fall to the ground. During the occasional years when beechnuts are abundant, grouse rely heavily on this highly nutritious food during late fall, winter, and early spring.

Acorns and the fruits of greenbrier, grape, and dogwood are important to grouse in the Southeast. Although these fruits typically form the bulk of the fall diet throughout the birds' range, grouse are opportunistic and will eat whatever soft fruits are available. Even the fruits of common poison ivy are eaten. This early fall diet is usually supplemented with leaves from a variety of herbaceous and woody plants, including cinque-foils, avens, and clovers.

For ruffed grouse in the Midwest, the most important fall foods are soft fruits, followed by acorns, green leafy plant material, and buds and catkins. In Missouri, grouse eat the fruits of wild grapes, multiflora rose, poison ivy, and flowering dogwood. Here grapes constitute about 30 percent of their fall diet. Multiflora rose fruit, their next favorite, accounts for about 10 percent. One of the most important wildlife foods in oak-hickory forests is mast. Oaks are not common in northern hardwood forests but are the dominant tree in midwestern forests. Although grouse can swallow whole acorns, they frequently feed on pieces left by other wildlife—deer, wild turkeys, and especially squirrels. Acorns constitute 15 percent to 30 percent of an average grouse's fall diet. The leaves of white avens and ladies'-tobacco are two important green plant foods. Other plants eaten by grouse in the Midwest are phlox, violets, clover, bush clovers, and ferns. During the fall, about 5 percent of a Missouri grouse's diet consists of buds and catkins. Catkins from hop hornbeam, hazel, and fragrant sumac are the most common.

Acorns are common grouse foods in Maine, Wisconsin, and the Southeast, as well as in the Midwest. Beechnuts, too, are highly preferred, but grouse can find them only in northern regions. When there is a bumper crop of acorns in the Southeast, grouse have been known to feed heavily on them until as late as the following March and April.

Fall and winter foods

The ruffed grouse has adapted to the varied sources of food throughout its range. Those listed below are known to be part of the bird's diet because of crop and fecal analysis or observation by McDowell, Schemnitz, Woehr and Chambers, Stoll et al., the Pennsylvania Game Commission, and Stafford and Dimmick.

Connecticut
oaks (*Quercus* sp.)
grape (*Vitus* sp.)
birches (*Betula* sp.)
hawthorn (*Crataegus* sp.)
hazelnut (*Corylus* sp.)
witch hazel (*Hamamelis virginiana*)
dogwood (*Cornus* sp.)
partridgeberry (*Mitchella repens*)
blackberry (*Rubus* sp.)
apple (*Malus* sp.)
poison ivy (*Rhus radicans*)
viburnum
cherry (*Prunus* sp.)
barberry (*Berberis* sp.)
cinquefoil (*Potentilla fructicosa*)

Maine
apple
clover (*Trifolium* sp.)
quaking aspen (*P. tremuloides*)
hawthorn
strawberry (*Fragaria* sp.)
hazel (*Hamamelis* sp.)
white birch (*B. papyrifera*)
willow (*Salix* sp.)
beech (*Fagus grandifolia*)
yellow birch (*B. lutea*)
blueberry (*Vaccinium* sp.)
hawkweed (*Hieracium* sp.)
geum (*Geum* sp.)
viburnum
wintergreen (*Pyrola* sp.)
oaks

New York
black cherry (*Prunus serotina*)
apple
aspen
hop hornbeam (*Ostrya virginiana*)
gray birch (*B. populifolia*)

Northeastern Ohio
aspen
hop hornbeam
poison ivy
greenbrier (*Similax* sp.)
grape
cherry
hawthorn
black gum (*Nyssa sylvatica*)
avens
beech
oaks
dogwood
sumac (*Rhus* sp.)
hazelnut
rose

East-central Ohio
grape
aspen
poison ivy
dogwood

(East-central Ohio continued)
ferns
bittersweet (*Celastrus scandens*)
cherry
rose
avens
hop hornbeam
bedstraw
tick clover (*Desmodium* sp.)
sumacs
viburnum
hawthorn

Southeastern Ohio
greenbrier
sumac
dogwood
oaks
grape
ferns
aspen
honeysuckle
viburnum
avens
bittersweet
rose
poison ivy
lespedeza
cherry

Pennsylvania
grape
rose
cherry
greenbrier
viburnum
blueberry
hop hornbeam
privet
white oak (*Q. alba*)
blackberry (*Rubus* sp.)
teaberry (*Gaultheria procumbens*)
dogwood
hazel
aspen
skunk cabbage (*Symplocarpus foetidus*)

Southern Appalachians
greenbrier
mountain laurel (*Kalmia latifolia*)
Christmas fern (*Polystichum acrostichoides*)
dogwood
cinquefoil
black birch (*B. lenta*)
avens
honeysuckle
aster
grape
alumroot (*Heuchera villosa*)
sheep sorrel (*Rumex acetosella*)
hawkweed
blueberry
ferns

MARTINSON

In winter the ruffed grouse prefers aspen buds; substitutes, including the twigs and buds of other tree species, are eaten only if the bird cannot find aspens.

The diet in winter

Only in the southern portions of its range can the ruffed grouse continue to feed on green leaves and the now-decaying fruits of grapevines and wild roses; elsewhere it resorts to tree buds and catkins.

	Tree buds and catkins	Fruits	Green leaves and ferns
Alaska	quaking aspen willow		
Minnesota	aspen sp. beaked hazel		
Maine	aspen sp. yellow birch hop hornbeam		
New York	quaking aspen birch sp. hop hornbeam cherry sp.		
Utah	quaking aspen		
Ohio	aspen sp. hop hornbeam	grape greenbrier multiflora rose honeysuckle	greenbrier ferns
Missouri	hop hornbeam	multiflora rose acorns	
Virginia		greenbrier rose grape	greenbrier mountain laurel
Tennessee			mountain laurel Christmas fern greenbrier honeysuckle
North Carolina		grape dogwood	mountain laurel Christmas fern
Georgia		acorns	mountain laurel greenbrier Christmas fern

Left: With the foods of the forest floor now covered by snow or locked in ice, the ruffed grouse resorts to the flower buds of the male aspen. Right: Reluctant to expose themselves to the twin dangers of predation and cold, northern grouse leave the security of their roosts to feed only once or twice a day.

Winter

Many species of birds take advantage of autumn's plentitude to fatten themselves in preparation for migration and the leanness of winter. The ruffed grouse, however, usually stores very little fat and must feed on a daily basis throughout the year. In their northern range, the birds usually feed twice a day during the winter—once at about the time of sunrise and again at sunset. During periods of extremely cold weather they may forgo the morning period and feed only in midafternoon. Farther south, where temperatures are seldom low enough to keep them on their roosts, grouse are likely to feed at nearly any time during the daylight hours, although Servello and Kirkpatrick report that their captive birds feed in early morning and late afternoon, whatever the weather.

The timing of the change from fall to winter diet varies with the onset of winter. Snows come early to the North. In Alaska and other high latitudes, grouse cannot eat much fruit after September. Farther south, around the Great Lakes and in New England, the changeover occurs in October or early November. Given good weather during the growing season, fruits are the major part of the diet in Virginia, North Carolina, and Georgia through January.

When grouse in the North can no longer depend on fruits and seeds, they switch to a diet consisting mainly of buds and catkins. The bird must now find foods above the snow, in trees and shrubs. The winter menu contracts to perhaps three, two, or even just one item. For five to six months the male flower buds of quaking aspen and bigtooth aspen may constitute the northern birds' sole food. The buds and catkins of birch, ironwood, hazelnut, and willow appear to be only a supplement as long as aspen buds are available.

Although not so vital as in the boreal zone, aspen buds are an important winter food in the northern hardwood forests. In some years, it is not uncommon for grouse to feed on the buds, twigs, and catkins of yellow birch, black cherry, hop hornbeam, and hazelnut. Greenbrier fruits and leaves, sumac seeds, and the catkins of hazelnut and ironwood are also heavily used.

The winter grouse menu in the deciduous forests of the southern region offers a much greater variety than that of the northern mixed evergreen-deciduous zone. At least fifty plant species have been identified in the winter diet, and only fourteen of those accounted for more than 1 percent of the total volume of foods consumed. Greenbrier fruits and leaves, mountain laurel leaves, and ferns are of primary importance. The fruits of dogwood, cherry, and American holly are also consumed, along with the leaves and fruits of Japanese honeysuckle and wintergreen, and the catkins of hazelnut and ironwood.

In the West, the choice of winter foods is largely a function of snow depth. In western

Washington, where there is little snow, primary winter foods are black cottonwood buds and stems, and the leaves of evergreen plants like the buttercup. But where snowfall is substantial, buds and twigs of woody trees and shrubs are critical for grouse survival. Where available, aspen and willow buds are important. In Alberta, grouse tend to select aspen buds that have particularly high levels of protein. Throughout the West, numerous other deciduous woody plants provide winter food: buds and twigs of serviceberry, chokecherry, maple, rose, and mountain ash.

Grouse in the Midwest eat fruits and acorns as long as they are available. Fragrant sumac and hazel catkins are used less often, but persistent fruits, such as multiflora rose hips and bittersweet, are eaten throughout the winter. Seeds from tick trefoils, bush clovers, and white avens may make up about 10 percent of the diet. Eventually, however, catkins and the buds of hop hornbeam become the most important winter food.

In the southern portions of the grouse range, where tree species suitable for budding are uncommon and the winter snow cover is normally of short duration, the grouse continues to find its food on the forest floor. From October through January, fruits account for 50 percent to 70 percent of the bird's diet in each month; by February, leaves constitute more than one-half. In the South, buds and catkins account for less than one-tenth. Animal foods make up only 1 percent of the diet of southern grouse during the winter months.

Mountain laurel, Christmas fern, greenbrier, and honeysuckle are the most commonly eaten foods in late winter in the South. The leaves of golden ragwort, a low-growing herb that remains green all winter, may be an important winter food in some portions of the grouse's southern range. Cinquefoils, avens, clovers, foam flowers, strawberry, geranium, and violet contribute to the herbaceous food variety.

Despite this variety, the southern grouse's winter diet may be poor in nutritional quality. During winter, evergreen leaves and ferns are the primary foods in the Southeast, in contrast to the northern birds' diet of buds, twigs, and catkins. This evergreen leaf diet is low in protein and contains relatively high levels of tannins and other potentially harmful phenolic compounds. According to some researchers, the scarcity of preferred and nutritionally adequate foods may be one of the factors that limit grouse numbers in the Southeast.

—*Harold L. Barber, Fred J. Brenner,*
Roy Kirkpatrick, Frederick A. Servello,
Dean F. Stauffer, and
Frank R. Thompson III

Plant foods

The ruffed grouse prefers the leaves of some plants, the seeds, fruits, flowers, or buds of others. Choice of food depends on season as well as plant species. The information presented here was compiled by Brenner.

Species	Food item	Species	Food item
Trees and shrubs		**Vines**	
oaks	fruit, buds	blackberry	seeds, fruits
birch	catkins, buds	poison ivy	seeds, fruits
hawthorn	seeds, fruits, leaves, buds	greenbrier	fruit, leaves
hazelnut	catkins, buds	bittersweet	fruit, leaves
witch hazel	seeds, leaves, buds	**Groundcovers**	
dogwoods	seeds, fruits, catkins	cinquefoil	leaves
apple	fruit, buds, seeds, leaves	partridgeberry	seeds, fruits, leaves
cherry	seeds, buds, fruits, leaves	clover	leaves
aspens	buds, catkins	strawberry	leaves, fruit
beech	buds, fruit	geum	leaves
willow	buds, catkins	wintergreen	leaves, fruit
blackgum	fruit	avens	leaves, fruit
sumac	fruit	bedstraw	leaves
rose	fruit, buds	tick clover	fruit, leaves
viburnum	fruits, seeds, buds	lespedeza	fruit, leaves
barberry	fruits, seeds	teaberry	fruit, leaves
blueberry	fruits, leaves, buds, twigs	skunk cabbage	fruit
privet	fruit	alumroot	leaves
mountain laurel	leaves, buds	wintergreen	leaves, fruit

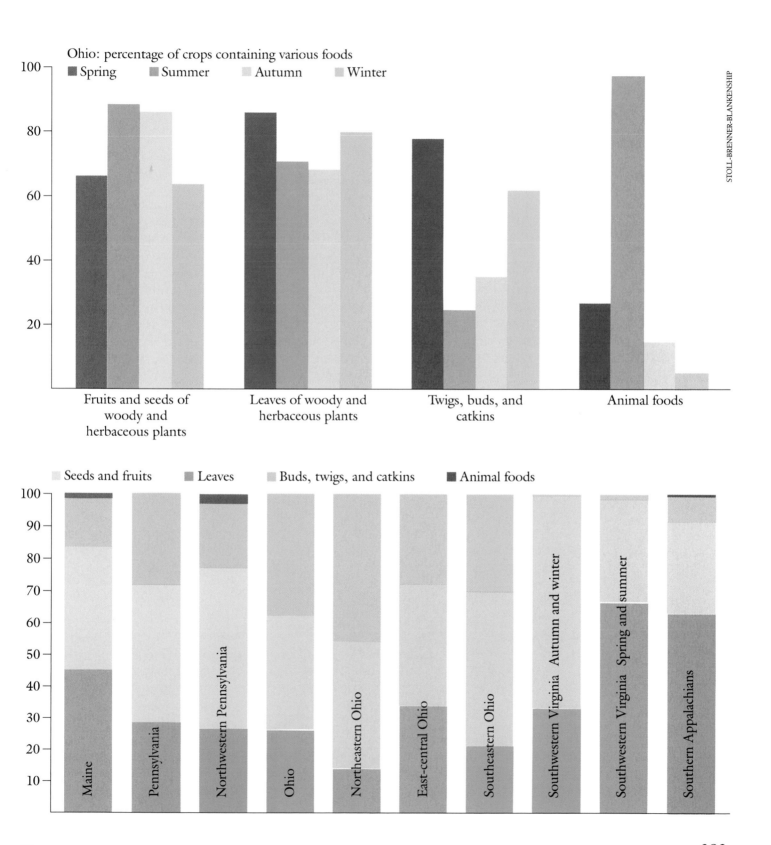

Ohio: percentage of crops containing various foods
■ Spring ■ Summer ■ Autumn ■ Winter

Fruits and seeds of woody and herbaceous plants

Leaves of woody and herbaceous plants

Twigs, buds, and catkins

Animal foods

STOLL-BRENNER-BLANKENSHIP

■ Seeds and fruits   ■ Leaves   ■ Buds, twigs, and catkins   ■ Animal foods

Maine

Pennsylvania

Northwestern Pennsylvania

Ohio

Northeastern Ohio

East-central Ohio

Southeastern Ohio

Southwestern Virginia Autumn and winter

Southwestern Virginia Spring and summer

Southern Appalachians

Nutrition

Just how much food the ruffed grouse eats is not known, at least not for ruffed grouse in the wild. The answer would depend in part on what the bird needs to maintain its body weight, and that depends on the bird's metabolism, which itself is difficult to calculate. On a mild day a perfectly inactive 644-gram grouse—not flying or drumming or feeding or even digesting food—would use up about 46 kilocalories (which are equivalent to the calories cited in human nutrition) per day. This is known as the standard metabolic rate. Animate the bird and put it into a real setting—winter, say—and it might use double the amount of energy. Set the bird to drumming or egg laying and its energy requirements are probably considerably greater.

Captive grouse at Virginia Tech eat 27 to 46 grams of commercial dry feed per day, depending on the nutritional quality of the pellets. But not everything the wild bird eats provides the same amount of useful energy. The ruffed grouse, in fact, survives on an unlikely diet of twigs, buds, and leaves. The part of these foods that is digested and eventually used in daily metabolism is called metabolizable energy, measured as the weight of the food minus whatever exits at the nether end of the bird. This digestible part is nearly the same as something called the neutral detergent soluble content—the nonfibrous sugars, starches, fats, and proteins. The higher the NDS content, the higher the digestibility, and the more usable energy the

grouse gets from its food. Certain types of chemicals, however, lower the nutritional value of some plants. These chemicals, sometimes called plant defensive chemicals, include alkaloids, resins, and phenolics, or tannins. Phenolics and resins reduce the digestibility of protein from plants, and all three chemicals can make plants unpalatable or toxic. Mountain laurel, for example, the most commonly used winter food of grouse in the Southeast, is fatally poisonous to a large number of animals, including humans, when eaten in large quantities. Its effects on grouse are unfortunately not yet known, but some researchers hypothesize that such defensive strategies by plants strongly affect forage preferences and annual changes in the ruffed grouse's diet.

Researchers can use a formula to determine the metabolizable energy content (the ME) of the ruffed grouse's diet:

$$(.87 \times NDS) - \text{total phenols} - 5.76 = ME$$

Acorns and beechnuts offer the ruffed grouse the greatest food value, the highest level of metabolizable energy. Next are the fleshy parts of soft fruits (such as grapes), herbaceous leaves (like clover), deciduous leaves (greenbrier, aspen), evergreen leaves (mountain laurel), and catkins. At the low end are the winter foods, tree buds and twigs, which contain 1.5 kilocalories of metabolizable energy per gram. Including catkins, a northern grouse in winter gets about 1.3 to 2 kilocalories per gram of food.

A great variety of leaves, high in protein, constitute the spring and summer diet of grouse. This crop sample was collected in Virginia.

Fruits, such as the apple pieces from a crop sample collected in Maine (right), are relished by grouse. In early fall, grouse may feed heavily on apples. This grouse had also been feeding on aspen buds (left).

A grouse in the Southeast eating evergreen leaves gets about 2 to 2.4 kilocalories per gram.

The protein content of grouse foods also varies, from the flowers and new leaves of spring (15 percent to 19 percent protein) to the twigs and buds of winter (8 percent to 14 percent protein).

So just when the ruffed grouse needs extra energy to keep warm and to prepare for breeding, its diet is poorest in both caloric and protein content. The winter diet is instead full of roughage. Yet the species is adapted to survive on this diet of fibrous food. Relative to its body size, the ruffed grouse, like other members of the family Tetraonidae, has a larger digestive system than the rest of the galliform birds. To handle all the fiber, a grouse has two large ceca at the junction of the small and large intestines. Although not studied in the ruffed grouse specifically, the function of these blind pouches has been examined in related species. Fine particulates and soluble food material are forced into the ceca by contractions of the intestines. This finer (and presumably more digestible) material is retained in the cecum for six to eight hours of further digestion, while the more fibrous material left in the large intestine is quickly excreted. This separation of food material allows grouse to consume a large amount of high-fiber and low-energy food each day but retain only the most nutritious portions for long-term digestion. And a fair amount of

Where snow blankets the ground, tree buds and catkins are the principal winter foods. This crop sample, collected in February in New York, contains yellow birch buds (left) and catkins (right).

In the Appalachians of the Southeast, evergreen plants, such as leaves of mountain laurel (left) and fronds of Christmas ferns (upper right), and the deciduous leaves of greenbrier (lower right) are the principal late-winter forages. This crop sample was collected in North Carolina.

These forages were from the crop of one grouse, killed in winter. Clockwise from upper left: Acorn meat, greenbrier leaves, Christmas fern fronds, cinquefoil leaves, and laurel leaves. Note that the bird ate only the acorn meat and not the less digestible shells; this is not uncommon.

THE KINGDOM OF THE RUFFED GROUSE

285

the fiber in the ruffed grouse's diet is digested: apparently 10 percent to 20 percent.

Getting every last bit of energy and protein is of special importance to breeding hens. Captive females on high-protein diets lay heavier eggs and have larger clutches, their eggs are more likely to hatch, and their chicks are more likely to survive. The protein required in diets for captive grouse is about 11.5 percent, assuming an otherwise high-energy diet. But breeding hens need 17 percent to 20 percent protein, and even then they lose weight. The diets of wild grouse in Virginia have been found to match these protein requirements.

—Frederick A. Servello and
Roy Kirkpatrick

Feeding in trees like this
wild apple, grouse remain
alert for potential predators.

Nutritional values

A diet of buds and twigs may sound unlikely, but it offers the ruffed grouse sufficient energy and protein to survive the winter. Fall foods, such as acorns and grapes, provide more energy and fewer tannins, the resins and other phenolic compounds that make food less digestible.

Data for protein content are based on Treichler et al., Huff, Doerr et al., and Servello and Kirkpatrick; Servello and Kirkpatrick researched the metabolizable energy and phenolics.

Food	Metabolizable energy	Protein	Tannin phenolics
Buds and twigs			
quaking aspen		11.7–12.9%	3.1–4.3%
yellow birch	31%	11.0–14.4	2.9
black cherry	35	16.4	2.4–3.7
Catkins			
yellow birch	38	11.9	1.8
hop hornbeam	37	14.0	
Leaves of woody plants			
mountain laurel	42	8.1–9.2	6.7
greenbrier	51	10.8–13.1	0.4
apple	55	13.9	1.3
Herbaceous leaves and ferns			
clover	57	29.1	
Rumex acetosella		20.6	
mixed herbaceous leaf samples	54–63	21.0–27.0	
Christmas fern	34	10.3	6.5
Fruits			
acorn meat	78	8.0	
grape (flesh)	60	8.7	1.8
apple	63	4.8	0.2

Fat dynamics

*T*he ruffed grouse's body-fat level varies by season. To determine the amount of fat in a ruffed grouse, researchers freeze-dry the plucked animal, grind it up, and after weighing it, extract it in ether. The ether dissolves the fat, and the defatted sample can then be weighed. The difference between the two samples is the fat.

In Virginia, one study found a low of 4.5 percent body fat in summer and a high of 16.3 percent in the fall, when grouse were consuming large amounts of highly digestible fruits. The finding coincides with a New York study in which ruffed grouse had fat levels of 14 percent to 17 percent in fall and early winter. In the spring, the Virginia hens appeared to accumulate fat before breeding and then lose fat during egg laying. During the breeding season, hens also have a substantially greater fat level than males.

In Ontario, another study determined that grouse had little fat reserves from January to August and concluded from controlled experiments that the birds rely on glycogen reserves and regular feeding rather than stored fat for winter energy metabolism.

The fattest grouse? A New York bird collected in the fall, whose body fat level was all of 35 percent.

*—Frederick A. Servello and
Roy Kirkpatrick*

The southern grouse diet in winter

---

*T*he winter food habits of southern ruffed grouse differ markedly from those of their northern relatives. Grouse in the boreal forests are florivorous; southern Appalachian birds are primarily herbivorous.

Grouse in the northern and midwestern areas of the United States select the most nutritious food available—the male aspen bud—during stressful winters with their deep snows and freezing temperatures. Without this food, the birds' physical condition deteriorates and their survivability is diminished. But in the South, this food is of no consequence, for the simple reason that aspen occurs only sparsely in the southern Appalachians. Although their diet may change during severe winters, southern Appalachian grouse must derive their sustenance not from the buds of trees and shrubs but primarily from green plant material and fruits, many of which would be considered poor sustenance for grouse in the North.

Still, the birds know to select the most nutritious foods available during this period of environmental stress, and as Treichler once stated, the principal grouse foods in this region "are well qualified as sources of energy and other essential nutrients required for maintenance of grouse during the winter." Black birch buds and catkins, and Christmas fern, for example, are higher in overall nutrition than many of the other frequently used foods, and both are important

In the Southeast, second-growth hardwood forests can provide habitat and food resources if the understory is interspersed with mountain laurel. But rhododendron thickets offer poor forage.

THE KINGDOM OF THE RUFFED GROUSE

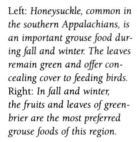

Left: *Honeysuckle, common in the southern Appalachians, is an important grouse food during fall and winter. The leaves remain green and offer concealing cover to feeding birds.* Right: *In fall and winter, the fruits and leaves of greenbrier are the most preferred grouse foods of this region.*

in the fall and winter diets of southern grouse.

The general absence of deep snows in the South allows grouse to select herbaceous foods from the forest floor almost continuously throughout the winter. Feeding on tree buds, commonly known as budding, is not pronounced among southern grouse because of this widespread availability of understory foods. During periods of light snow cover, grouse are able to forage on some herbaceous material. Even when snow accumulations of 5 inches or more persist, grouse can feed on the evergreen foliage of such shrubs and vines as honeysuckle, mountain laurel, and greenbrier, rather than resort to extensive budding in trees. Only during prolonged snow periods do southern grouse eat the leaf and flower buds of certain trees and shrubs.

Grouse in this southern region, then, select foods primarily from plants in the lower strata of vegetation. An analysis of their choices indicates that fall and winter foods are primarily herbaceous plants, shrubs, and vines that produce evergreen foliage. A study in North Carolina and Tennessee by Stafford and Dimmick showed that 75 percent of the fall and winter diet consists of herbaceous annuals and perennials (ferns, cinquefoil, avens); the leaves and fruits of greenbrier, honeysuckle, and grapevines; and the buds and leaves of woody shrubs (mountain laurel, blueberry).

In another study—an examination of 311

grouse crops by Stafford in the Blue Ridge, the Cumberland Plateau, and the Great Valley—leafy plant parts accounted for 63 percent of the volume of food consumed by grouse during the fall and winter. Soft fruits ranked second, at 29 percent. Soft mast from such species as greenbrier, hawthorn, grape, and honeysuckle are predominantly fall foods and rank high in the diet during the period from September through November. By early December, fruit consumption has declined substantially. By late January in most years, fruits may constitute less than 5 percent of the grouse's diet because this favored food group has deteriorated on the ground.

What about acorns? Several oak species are well represented in the Appalachian forests, and some produce acorns annually. Several food habit studies in this region and others indicate that acorns are an important food item. Oak acorns are indeed important to the ruffed grouse throughout most of the hardwood forests of the eastern United States. In the southern Appalachians, however, acorns may be important in some areas and not in others. In Virginia, Nelson and his coworkers ranked acorns second by vol-

Foods of the ruffed grouse

Growth form	Number of foods	% of diet
herbaceous plants	7	29.5
woody vines	3	25.4
shrubs	3	20.3
trees	1	3.3
total	14	78.5

SERVELLO

Sapling and pole-sized hardwood stands with shrubby undergrowth can often supply all a grouse's needs during all seasons in the Appalachians.

ume and sixth in occurrence among all foods consumed. But in Tennessee and North Carolina, Stafford examined 311 grouse crops over a two-year period and found acorns in only 4. Even in the Adirondacks and Catskills of New York, where oaks are prevalent, Bump found that acorns constituted less than 2 percent of the fall and winter diet. Perhaps the variability of acorns in the diet reflects not the ruffed grouse's preferences but the number of oaks in a particular habitat, or the number of acorns they produce, or the availability of other foods. Another factor may be involved: mature, mast-producing oaks commonly occur where the understory is sparse and the cover is unattractive to grouse.

The leaf and flower buds of certain hardwoods and shrubs provide food during the winter in mountainous areas but are seldom used by birds in the Great Valley. Buds and catkins, primarily from black birch and blueberry, contribute only 8 percent of food volume in North Carolina and Tennessee.

In autumn and winter, southern grouse rather naturally seek habitats where they will find their favorite foods. And most of their foods are found in more or less open areas:

in the southern Appalachians

Food item	% of diet
green leafy material	63.1
fruits	28.5
buds and catkins	8.0
animal	0.4
total	100.0

overgrown pastures, abandoned farmlands, and overgrown woodlands that have been mechanically cleared and border second-growth hardwoods. Such sites are reverting to a shrubby state. Ungrazed or rotationally grazed pastures with scattered clumps of black locust, wild rose, greenbrier, yellow pine, and hawthorn appear to be the favored feeding sites throughout the region during the fall and early winter. Cutover woodlands are highly productive feeding sites for the first few years after the overstory has been removed, when grasses and forbs dominate. Bump and his colleagues reported that such openings were very important to grouse throughout the northeastern forests. In colonial times, areas like these were common in the southern Appalachians, and grouse responded favorably to them. During the late winter, open areas interspersed with greenbrier tangles and adjacent to yellow pine and mountain laurel thickets are preferred feeding sites. These cover conditions correspond closely to those described by Bump for New York and Ohio. Openings interspersed among defoliated mature hardwood sites are generally poor feeding areas.

Mountain coves and ridges and foothill valleys that contain evergreen shrubs and trees are other frequently used feeding sites, especially during late winter. Mountain coves generally have sufficient moisture from spring seeps to sustain low-growing herbaceous food items, and the evergreens provide shelter for feeding and prevent deep snow from accumulating at ground level.

Preferred food plants such as mountain laurel, honeysuckle, and greenbrier also protect grouse while they feed. Mountain laurel, widespread in the region, provides feeding grouse with cover that both permits ease of movement and protects them from avian predators. According to Stafford and Dimmick, mountain laurel may be a key to high-quality grouse habitat in the southern Appalachians. Honeysuckle, which is more abundant in the Great Valley than in other areas, may serve as a replacement for laurel there. Rhododendron, whose growth characteristics resemble those of mountain laurel, occurs primarily in the moist ravines and north-facing slopes at higher elevations. Not a food source, rhododendron may nevertheless benefit grouse by providing covered corridors for birds feeding on other understory foods. Food habit studies in Virginia, Tennessee and North Carolina, Pennsylvania, New York, Ohio, and Missouri have all yielded similar results.

Southern ruffed grouse are opportunistic, consuming a wide variety of plant material throughout autumn and winter, no one of which seems to be vital to their overwinter survival. Stafford has listed fall and winter foods in order of importance:

Blue Ridge	Cumberland Plateau	Great Valley
greenbrier	Christmas fern	greenbrier
mountain laurel	flowering dogwood	honeysuckle
Christmas fern	mountain laurel	Christmas fern
black birch	blueberry	other ferns
cinquefoil	trailing arbutus	avens
avens	cinquefoil	hawkweed
other ferns	alumroot	cinquefoil
grape	mayapple	aster
(Vitis sp.)		staghorn sumac

Clearly, greenbrier, mountain laurel, and Christmas fern are the significant foods throughout the southern Appalachians. The other food plants are locally important—black birch in the Blue Ridge, dogwood and blueberry in the plateau, honeysuckle in the valley area—and their occurrence in the diet of grouse seems to depend on availability.

Greenbrier vines are well distributed on a variety of land types throughout the Appalachians but are especially prolific on cutovers and the edges of openings. Male and female flowers appear on separate plants, and the older, less productive thickets may contain mostly male plants. The leaves are deciduous but fall to the ground late in the season and are thus available to grouse even in winter. Fruits persist on the vine through the winter on some species; unlike such fruits as grapes and dogwood, they do not desiccate rapidly or attract ground-feeding mammals.

At least nine species of ferns have been identified in the grouse diet, but Christmas fern and grape fern occur most frequently. The tips of fern fronds are the most relished part. Other fern species include blunt-lobed wood fern, bladder fern, beech fern, rock cap, lady fern, climbing fern, and hay-scented fern. These evergreen ferns occur over a wide range of habitats and site conditions and are available to grouse during late winter, when many other low-growing plants have died back.

Mountain laurel leaves and buds are important to the fall diet but are more conspicuous in late winter. This broad-leaved evergreen prefers drier, south-facing mountain slopes. Laurel is an important cover for grouse at all times, and the tough leaves are consistently available as a food source.

Cinquefoil grows on a wide variety of sites but is especially abundant in grazed and ungrazed pastures, where it occurs as ground-cover among other grasses and forbs. It grows best on acid soils. The leaves at the base resist damage from freezing and are not affected by grazing cattle.

Black birch is one of the few tree species that constitute an important food source in the South. The leaf buds and male catkins are readily taken by grouse during the fall and winter, especially when snow cover and freezing temperatures persist. When snows cover the mountainous areas of eastern Tennessee and western North Carolina, for example, black birch is consumed more frequently than at other times. Birch grows in extensive stands at upper mountain elevations along ridges and in coves.

The seeds and leaves of avens are frequently eaten, but not in large volume. Seeds are available throughout the fall, and the leaves are winter-hardy. The plant is common on ungrazed pastures.

Honeysuckle leaves and fruits rank second

Nutritional values of fall and winter foods

This table presents the basic nutrient content, expressed as a percent of the oven-dried weight, of the most important fall and winter foods in the southern Appalachians. Nitrogen-free extract is a component that relates to the amount of carbohydrates; energy is expressed in Calories per gram weight of the plant. Some of the data come from Treichler et al., Spinner and Bishop, and Billingsley and Arner.

		Protein	Crude fat	Fiber	Nitrogen-free extract	Energy
greenbrier	leaves	10.8 %	10.4 %	15.6 %	59.4 %	4.7 C
greenbrier	fruits	9.1	7.6	14.9	65.4	4.5
Christmas fern	leaves	16.3	4.8	18.3	60.2	4.3
black birch	buds	9.3	2.5	33.0	39.1	3.7
black birch	catkins	14.41	8.44	22.97	50.87	–
mountain laurel	leaves	8.1	11.1	5.6	62.2	4.7
grape	seeds	6.6	7.40	–	59.74	–
avens	seeds	10.45	16.26	16.26	38.53	–
dogwood	fruits	6.49	18.75	–	38.44	–
sheep sorrel	leaves	20.6	4.0	7.9	62.7	4.4

Major fall and winter foods

In the southern Appalachians, greenbrier, mountain laurel, and Christmas ferns are most important in sustaining ruffed grouse over the winter. The information below was based on the diets of 311 ruffed grouse from across the region, in a study by Stafford and Dimmick.

Food item	% of diet
greenbrier	20.1
mountain laurel	14.8
Christmas fern	10.5
dogwood	4.3
cinquefoil	4.1
blackbirch	3.3
avens	3.2
honeysuckle	3.0
aster sp.	2.3
grape	2.3
alumroot	2.3
sheep sorrel (Rumex acetosella)	2.0
hawkweed	1.4
blueberry	1.3
other ferns	3.6
unidentified buds and leaves	2.5
all other foods	19.0
Total	100.0

among all foods in the valley region of North Carolina and Tennessee but are apparently not so significant in the Blue Ridge or plateau. Grouse eat the evergreen leaves more frequently than the fruits. In many areas of the valley, honeysuckle is the dominant groundcover plant, especially in moist, open ravines and pastures. Because of its climbing and entwining growth characteristic, it provides good cover for feeding grouse.

Grapes are a staple during autumn, when grouse eat great quantities of the fruits on the forest floor. The importance of grapes in the diet declines, however, by midwinter, and in some years grapevines do not produce enough fruit to last even that long.

The fruits of dogwood are locally important and, where available, consumed by grouse in large volumes. The seeds are eaten by many other wildlife species, however, and do not last long. In the plateau of Tennessee and North Carolina, dogwood ranks fourth by volume among all grouse foods.

The leaves of alumroot are used consistently by grouse throughout the winter, especially in mountainous areas. These plants are particularly abundant in moist covers and on shaded rock outcroppings, often growing among several of the ferns. The leaves are winter-hardy.

The bottom leaves of aster are eaten, along with the leaves of cinquefoil, hawkweed, and avens. Asters are common on open pastures, both grazed and ungrazed, throughout the southern Appalachians. Their green leaves persist throughout the winter.

Sheep sorrel is recognized as a common grouse food in most of the oak-hickory forests where grouse occur. This member of the buckwheat family grows in association with many other herbaceous plants on moderately to heavily grazed pastures. The leaves, not the seeds, are the food source.

Grouse eat the buds and fruits of the blueberry primarily during the early fall. Low-growing blueberry species are common on dry woodland sites, and the buds and fruits are easily picked by grouse feeding from the ground. Although the fruits of most species are available only for a short time after they reach maturity in the late summer or early fall, the leaf and flower buds are consumed throughout the winter.

—Steven K. Stafford

Cover

The importance of good habitat to the ruffed grouse goes without saying: where the habitat is good, grouse are abundant. Wildlife researchers, however, must turn that simple equation around and examine where grouse are abundant to find out what constitutes good habitat. In northern forests, Gullion and Marshall, Gullion, and Gullion and Alm have all reported higher survival rates of grouse in habitats dominated by aspen or mixtures of aspen and other hardwoods than in conifer habitats. The lowest survival rates have been observed where the understory was sparse and large pines dominated the overstory, and in young, regenerating stands less than eight years old. In addition, Boag and Sumanik, Rusch and Keith, Gullion and Alm, and Gullion have documented high levels of predation on grouse that occupy less suitable habitats. Higher survival in the better Wisconsin and Minnesota habitats is shown by higher breeding densities during both high and low years of the grouse cycle.

But what exactly is suitable habitat for the ruffed grouse? Must the bird always have aspen, for example? Given the grouse's wide range across the North American continent, with all the differences in terrain, elevation, climate, and vegetation that range encompasses, good cover in Georgia is not likely to look the same as good cover in Alberta. The species' ecological niche—taking advantage of the early stages of forest succession—

Since male ruffed grouse are easier to find than the well-camouflaged nesting hens and their elusive broods, research into habitat use has been concentrated on the spring drumming season. Recent studies, however, are bringing to light the different habitat needs of breeding females.

Picea mariana
black spruce

Geum canadense
white avens

Sambucus canadensis
elderberry

Ribes sp.
gooseberry

Salix nigra
black willow

remains the same, however, and an examination of cover needs through the year shows that wherever they live, ruffed grouse consistently seek habitats with common characteristics.

DRUMMING COVER

A drummer has three concerns: to attract females and breed, to defend his drumming sites, and to avoid being eaten. Habitat that provides good visibility at ground level and a low, dense cover overhead for protection will help him accomplish his aims.

The drumming stage itself is usually on a log. The species of log used varies considerably: aspen, oak, pine, spruce, fir, birch, chestnut, maple, whatever is available.

The drummer that occupies this log is taking advantage of excellent cover: the closely spaced fifteen-year-old aspens and the open forest floor protect him from sneak attacks.

Grouse appear to like one or more larger logs at least 20 centimeters in diameter and more than 2 meters in length. Other suitable drumming surfaces include log and rock piles, boulders, exposed tree roots, root hummocks of downed or tipped trees, dirt mounds, ant hills, and even snowbanks. Road culverts and remnants of old rock walls and foundations have also served as drumming sites where abandoned homesteads have reverted to forest, and stone walls are preferred sites in many such areas of the Northeast.

Just what drumming stage the grouse will choose depends on the quality of overhead and understory woody cover. Drummers prefer a vantage point to keep watch for approaching ground predators and other grouse, so the height of the drumming stage is a factor. In rolling or hilly terrain, drummers prefer sites on the gentler slopes, less than 45 degrees; the logs are often near the top but parallel to the contour. A guard object—a tree, snag, stump, root hummock, shrub thicket, or similar physical barrier—usually found within 1 to 3 meters of the drumming stage—provides security at the rear. Drummers also favor sites from which they can quietly slip away through good cover. If escape routes are inadequate, a drummer may occupy several logs and be very wary and difficult to approach. This behavior has been observed particularly in marginal or poor habitats, and during low grouse years.

Naturally enough, the quality and extent of drumming habitat largely determines the proportion of breeders that survive from year to year. It is not just in spring and fall that male grouse remain close to their drumming sites: most adult males occupy the surrounding habitats—within about 400 meters of the drumming site—for most of the rest of the year for the rest of their lives. Adult hens that have also learned what's good for them occupy similar habitats. It follows that expectations for grouse survival are greatest in habitats with dense understory and overhead cover dominated by tall shrubs and deciduous sapling trees—in other words, good drumming cover.

Although the tree species differ, good drumming habitats are structurally similar throughout the birds' range. Woody cover with suitably high stem densities occurs from Alberta through Idaho, Wisconsin, Missouri, and Ohio into Georgia. When stands of young, dense saplings are not available, drummers use older forest stands that have a dense understory of conifers or a shrub layer at least 1.5 meters tall.

The North. Many shrub species provide thick cover throughout the North. Alder dominates drumming sites in Michigan, for example, and white spruce is prevalent at sites in Alberta. Alder, hazel, dogwood, and winterberry commonly provide suitable drumming cover in Wisconsin. Other species that may provide cover in combination with these include serviceberry, viburnum, chokeberry, witch hazel, ninebark, thorn apple, and mountain maple. Prickly ash, grape, and gooseberry are locally important in oak-hickory forests and similar habitats in Wisconsin.

But most drumming grouse in the North can be found where aspens dominate. Stud-

Acer saccharum
sugar maple

Rhododendron maximum
great laurel

Senecio aureus
golden ragwort

Scirpus robustus
bulrush

Quercus velutina
black oak

Ilex opaca
American holly

Lespedeza virginica
bush clover (*left*);
Potentilla simplex
cinquefoil (*right*)

Nyssa sylvatica
black gum

Ranunculus acris
buttercup

Populus tremuloides
quaking aspen

ies between 1968 and 1982 on the Sandhill–Wood County areas in central Wisconsin indicate that mean density was 10.1 drummers per 100 hectares in aspen but only 2 in oak. Density has been highest in aspen habitats with alder understories, averaging 27.4 grouse per 100 hectares. Drummers seem to like both aspen saplings (six- to twenty-five-year-old trees) and pole-sized aspens (twenty-six years and older) that have alder understories. This understory of tall shrubs is critical, regardless of the age of the aspens: drummer density was only 5.4 grouse per 100 hectares in pole-sized aspen habitats that lacked alder.

Low densities in the North occur in stands under six years old, where the overstory trees have been cut. Then, as logging slash decays, woody stems thin out to less than 37,000 per hectare, and saplings grow taller than 5 meters, the number of drummers increases considerably. For the next twenty years drummer densities remain at high levels, provided the tall shrub understory is thick enough. In stands without tall shrubs, drummer densities have declined below the long-term mean, beginning at about sixteen years of age, as natural thinning creates an "open-grown" or parklike habitat that is unattractive to drummers. Similar declines in aspen habitats have been observed at the Mille Lacs Wildlife Area in Minnesota. And although the figures are somewhat lower, the same pattern was observed at the Stone Lake area in northeastern Wisconsin between 1976 and 1987: 10.4 drummers in five- to twenty-five-year-old aspens, and only 3 drummers in aspens twenty-six years and older. Clearly, drummers need a continuous supply of dense saplings, and there is but a short period when habitats devoid of good tall shrub understories are attractive to breeding grouse.

In central Wisconsin, a cutting program that maintains a good interspersion of young, dense, six- to twenty-five-year-old aspen stands has accounted for higher densities. Most cuts have been kept to 8 hectares or less, and at least 30 percent of the management area has consisted of six- to twenty-five-year-old aspen stands.

The low densities reported in central Wisconsin oak habitats have been attributed to a

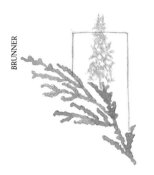

lack of different-aged trees, inadequate tall shrub and tree sapling cover, and a poor mixture of oak with aspen and other food resources important to grouse. More than 85 percent of these oak habitats are large stands of pole-sized trees with sparse shrub understories, and they support only about 2 drummers per 100 hectares. Grouse densities are higher in oak habitats elsewhere: 10.1 drumming grouse per 100 hectares in the oak-hickory forests of southwestern Wisconsin in 1976–1977 (two years of above-average grouse abundance), for example, and 7.4 drummers per 100 hectares in the oak-hickory forests of northeastern Iowa in 1967.

Densities were considerably lower in the habitats surveyed at Stone Lake, Wisconsin, except for swamp conifers with white cedar, which supported 4.2 drummers per 100 hectares, and balsam fir, 3.5 drummers. Lowest densities were 1.7 drummers per 100 hectares in northern hardwoods and 0.3 drummer in pine. By comparison, there were 2.2 drumming grouse per 100 hectares in red pine plantations in 1986–1988 in west-central Wisconsin. However, these plantations were either converted from oak or propagated naturally, and a good to excellent understory of tall shrubs or other woody cover (more than 20,000 stems per hectare) characterized portions of each stand. Understory woody cover in these stands was also considerably greater than in plantations established on old fields. Current statewide estimates of mean drummer densities (based primarily on Sandhill and Stone Lake data) are 8.6 drummers per 100 hectares in aspen, 3.7 in oak, 1.8 in northern hardwoods, and 1.2 in pine.

The marginal habitats for drummers are usually in large blocks of hardwoods or conifers that shade out tall shrubs and other desirable understory vegetation. The only suitable places for drumming grouse here may be along the edges or where breaks in the forest canopy allow understory plants to grow. Or the drummers may occupy habitats with dense conifer understories, usually along the edges of more suitable habitat. In any case, drumming grouse avoid habitats dominated by low-growing shrubs or woodlands with impenetrable horizontal cover, particularly where overhead cover is inade-

Thuja occidentalis
northern white cedar

Coptis groenlandica
goldthread

Populus trichocarpa
black cottonwood

Gaultheria procumbens
wintergreen

Prunus serotina
black cherry

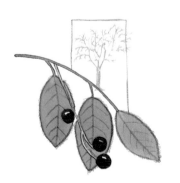

THE KINGDOM OF THE RUFFED GROUSE

Phegopteris connectilis
beech fern

Lonicera japonica
Japanese honeysuckle

Pinus rigida
pitch pine

Sassafras albidum
sassafras

Taxus brevifolia
western yew

quate—and for good reason: drummer survival in these habitats is risky.

Drummers often settle for the less suitable habitats during years of moderate to high grouse populations, which suggests that the best habitats are then occupied. Established older or dominant birds may also be nudging out inexperienced youngsters or less aggressive birds. This phenomenon has occurred during high grouse years on study areas in central Wisconsin, Kubisiak has reported. But during low grouse years, only the best habitats were occupied.

The Northeast. In New York, the drummer is less likely to find a log for his courtship and territorial displays than is a grouse in the historically forested habitats of the North. The New York habitats are often young, second-growth forests on abandoned farmland, where downed trees are few but stone walls and stone piles are common. Cerretani found that 61 percent of fifty-five Oswego County drumming stages were, in fact, on old man-made stone structures.

Male grouse here prefer drumming sites within young hardwood stands and tall shrub communities of alder and scrub oak, both characterized by high densities of small-diameter stems and sparse cover at the ground level. The density of stems 1 to 3 inches in diameter has been found to be greater at drumming sites than at randomly selected spots, even though the total number of stems of all sizes does not differ. This aerial shield of small stems permits the grouse here, as elsewhere, to detect raptor attacks, and the open nature of the ground cover, combined with the elevated position of the drumming site, enhances surveillance for approaching mammals and potential mates. Precisely which species provide all those stems appears to be inconsequential, except that stands of young aspen tend to be characterized by higher stem densities than other hardwoods.

In New York's older forest stands and other habitats without such ideal cover, male grouse appear to adopt one of two strategies to favor their survival. If young conifers are present, the grouse may drum directly under the hanging branches of a single conifer or within a clump of evergreens. Or the drummer may select a site on a ridge, knoll, or

In regions without aspens, drummers often seek hardwood stands, such as this oak forest with its dense understory of hazel and dogwood.

high wall to get an even better view of approaching predators. Nevertheless, many such drumming sites must be considered marginal or unfavorable, since they exhibit a high turnover in male occupancy or are sporadically or infrequently occupied.

Recent studies by Cullinan and Chambers show that the winter ranges of male grouse in central New York are almost exclusively different and much larger than the spring ranges.

Other things being equal, ruffed grouse in central and northern New York prefer forest stands that include or adjoin mature aspen trees. Of 106 drumming sites observed in central and northern New York over several years by Chambers, only 3 did not have at least several aspen within 80 yards. Given the fidelity of this association and the predominance of aspen catkins in the birds' spring diets, aspen should be considered a key component of spring courtship habitats in New York.

The West. In Alberta, northern Utah, and southeastern Idaho drumming ruffed grouse show a strong preference for aspen stands. Nevertheless, bigtooth maple stands can provide suitable cover for drumming in southeastern Idaho and northern Utah. In Washington, Brewer found that drumming males preferred deciduous stands in early successional stages. The common characteristic at all these drumming sites: the customary high density of small woody stems that create a prison effect and make the drum-

Oxydendrum arboreum
sourwood

Vitis sp.
grape

Rumex acetosa
garden sorrel

Pyrus melanocarpa
chokeberry

Aesculus glabra
Ohio buckeye

Zanthoxylum americanum
prickly ash

Rubus odoratus
raspberry

Betula pendula
white birch

Dryopteris goldiana
wood fern (*left*);
Dennstaedtia punctilobula
hay-scented fern (*right*)

Populus grandidentata
bigtooth aspen

Forests of oaks and hickories, common to the Midwest, offer male ruffed grouse dense, secure sites for their territorial and courtship displays.

ming stage essentially invulnerable to aerial predators.

Logs are not essential to western drummers, which have been observed on rocks and boulders and, when snow melt is late, on snowbanks.

The Midwest. Missouri drummers show a preference for three habitat types: seven- to twenty-five-year-old clear-cuts, old fields with a mixture of eastern red cedar and hardwoods, and mature oak-hickory stands with dense understories. These habitats all have high numbers of saplings, pole-sized trees, and shrubs.

Drumming grouse begin using clear-cuts in Missouri's oak-hickory forests when the new growth is about seven to ten years old. At this age the clear-cuts may have 12,000 to 35,000 saplings, stump sprouts, and shrub stems per hectare. Drumming sites in old fields and mature forests with dense understories contain an average of 6,500 stems per hectare. Stem densities in these habitats are lower than in clear-cuts, but in abandoned fields the combination of red cedar and hardwood shrubs, saplings, and poles provides cover nearly as thick. Eastern red cedar accounts for less than 25 percent of the stems in these habitats, but its low evergreen branches contribute more to the thickness of the cover than the same number of hardwood stems. Stem densities in oak-hickory forests average about 4,000 woody stems per hectare, so whether grouse are using clear-cuts or mixed eastern red cedar and hardwoods, they're selecting some of the densest cover available.

The Southeast. In the southern Appalachians, grouse have the same needs, and the same ideas about what constitutes a good drumming stage in a good habitat. But circumstances here are different than in other portions of the bird's range. Aspen stands being nonexistent, drumming sites here are typically found in mesophytic and northern hardwood forests. In the Blue Ridge, Cumberland Plateau, and Great Valley of the southern Appalachians, ridgetops are favored. In Georgia's mountainous areas, Hale and his colleagues reported that most drumming sites were situated on upper portions of ridges, at elevations of 620 to 1,230 meters, but not on the ridgetops themselves. Ridges and ridgetops in the southern Appalachians range from narrow, steep slopes to broad, gently sloping hillsides. The proximity of drumming sites is perhaps partially determined by the number, size, and relative flatness or broadness of moderately sloping ridges. These ridges often act as territorial boundaries. In the northern boreal and hardwood forests, by contrast, drumming sites are usually in lowland areas or at the foot of a slope.

Several researchers—Taylor in Tennessee, Hale in Georgia, and Stafford in North Carolina—have reported that although activity centers occur throughout a wide range of mountain elevations and slope aspects, steep slopes make unusual drumming sites: anything steeper than 25 degrees is generally avoided. In Tennessee and Georgia, drumming centers usually offer the grouse a north or northeastern view. It appears that these exposures permit the growth of suitable vegetative cover that is preferred by the drummers.

A common tree species used as a drumming stage in this region is the American chestnut, *Castanea dentata*. Some researchers have found that the species of log used by drummers does not reflect any preference for a particular species: it just so happens that since the late 1920s and early 1930s, when the chestnut blight swept through the South, the chestnut has provided the most downed trees over a large area of the Appalachians. Level logs that lie across ridge slopes rather than parallel to them are best.

What's overhead matters a great deal to a drummer, but only in the general physical structure of vegetation; the species of the overstory vegetation, like the species of drumming log, are less important than the

Quercus coccinea
scarlet oak

Rubus hispidus
dewberry

Rhododendron catawbiense
Catawba rhododendron

Rhus radicans
poison ivy

Quercus alba
white oak

Picea rubens
red spruce

Mitchella repens
partridgeberry

Morchella sp.
morel

Aster sp.
aster

Juglans nigra
black walnut

amount of protection they afford. Overstories around activity centers are characterized by a wide variety of tree species. In Tennessee and North Carolina, chestnut oak, pitch pine, sassafras, dogwood, mockernut hickory, and white oak are commonly associated with drumming sites. Yet similar overstory types are associated with nondrumming sites as well. The difference is the understory.

According to Hale, all vegetative layers contribute to suitable drumming sites, but the shrub stratum surrounding the drumming stage matters most. Shrubby thickets are ideal. Various studies have indicated that grouse prefer a moderately high understory density surrounding portions of their drumming stages. Stafford has reported that in North Carolina, density of shrubs and trees less than 3 inches in diameter was two and a half times greater around occupied logs. Taylor, Stafford, and Hale have all indicated that several heathlike shrubs, both evergreen and deciduous, are important. Such shrubs as mountain laurel, blueberry, and flame azalea are often associated with drumming logs. The growth characteristics and leaves of these shrubs provide overhead concealment yet good horizontal visibility from ground level to approximately 2 feet. In this stratum, grouse generally prefer sparse wood stems and leafy plants.

The heath-shrub thickets are used by grouse even when they are not drumming. Birds transplanted to western Tennessee, where no native birds remain, were found in them during the fall and winter, White and Dimmick have reported. Mountain laurel thickets offer evergreen cover in winter, and the leaves are used for winter food. But it is during the spring and fall drumming seasons, when the drummer is drawing the attention of mammalian and avian predators, as well as hens and rival cocks, that the vegetation surrounding his drumming stage is most important.

NESTING COVER

Grouse nests being difficult to find, the characteristics of good nesting cover have not been well documented. A great deal of attention has been paid to the types of vegetation near drumming logs; very little study has been made of the types of vegetation that provide conditions suitable for nesting. Nevertheless, two generalizations seem safe: that nesting hens use sites with similar features despite the different types of forests they inhabit, and that nesting sites contrast sharply with those chosen by drummers.

Because the drummer is conspicuous, he selects a habitat with dense cover that provides protection from predators. The hen, however, is completely camouflaged by her cryptic coloration and prefers a place with good visibility to allow her to detect approaching predators. Nature favors hens that sit tight on their nests and allow predators to pass by; if a hen remains motionless, she will be safe, so perfectly do her colors blend with

The orange tape marks the location of a ruffed grouse nest in Wisconsin. An opening in the overstory of oaks allows sunlight to reach the forest floor. Huckleberry, blueberry, and bracken fern thrive here. Relying on camouflage, nesting hens appear to prefer open sites that let them see intruders.

the dead leaves of the forest floor. If she flushes, however, she will expose her white eggs, and the nest may be depredated.

The best nesting sites are probably hardwood stands with tree stems 5 to 13 centimeters (2 to 5 inches) in diameter; Chambers reports trees with 8-inch diameters. Such stands have an unobstructed forest floor, which lets the hen see approaching mammalian predators and provides overhead protection from avian predators.

A ruffed grouse nest is a simple leaf-lined depression on the forest floor, usually at the base of some guard object, such as a tree, log, or stump. The nest must have an unobstructed escape route. Nests on slopes are therefore almost invariably set against the downhill side of the guard object: the hen has a clear field of view and can make a quick aerial getaway, whereas an uphill location would mean a climbing flight and thus a slow and chancy escape.

The daily range of a grouse hen is smallest during the nesting season. Although her an-

Acer grandidentatum
bigtooth maple

Rhus aromatica
fragrant sumac

Heuchera americana
alumroot

Ilex verticillata
winterberry

Robinia pseudoacacia
black locust

Acer spicatum
mountain maple

Smilax rotundifolia
greenbrier

Viburnum prunifolium
blackhaw viburnum

Trifolium pratense
red clover

Quercus rubra
red oak

nual range may take in 40 hectares or more, she may spend the entire incubation period within an area of only a single hectare. The nest must therefore be in or very near a source of food. It is no accident that by the time incubation is under way, the green leafy foods of spring are becoming available.

The North. Here, as elsewhere in their range, hens prefer upland sites that provide good visibility, and typically nest at the bases of trees or stumps but sometimes also at the edge of a bramble or shrub thicket. In central Wisconsin, the food source is usually aspen—as it is in Minnesota, according to Kupa and Schladweiler. Maxson, too, has found radio-marked nesting hens using aspen heavily in Minnesota, repeatedly going to selected feeding sites 28 to 185 meters from their nests. Habitats usually avoided by nesting hens in the North include recently cutover areas with logging slash and little or no tree cover overhead, and large areas of impenetrable horizontal cover, including dense grasses and sedge.

In central Wisconsin, sixteen grouse nests were found in pole-sized stands twenty-six years and older: ten in aspen, five in oak, and one in white pine. Another four hens had chosen dense six- to twenty-five-year-old sapling aspens. Nine nests were surrounded by an open ground layer, but the rest had moderate to dense low-growing or tall shrubs in the vicinity. Four hens were nesting in areas interspersed with moderate to dense ground layers of grasses and sedge.

The Northeast. Bump's years of study have shown that female grouse in New York's hardwood forests greatly favor the bases of large trees and stumps; brush piles are the third most frequent nest site. Of 1,270 nests found in New York, 56 percent were in hardwoods of pole size or larger, 11 percent were in overgrown, reverting farmland, and a similar percent in slashings left after forests were cut. Conifer stands accounted for only 4.4 percent of all nest sites. Considering the predominance of hardwood forests throughout the Northeast, it appears likely that habitat for nesting ruffed grouse is adequate.

The West. Nesting habits in the West are not well known, but the few hens that have been spotted know exactly what they like: aspen. In Alberta, for example, nineteen of

306

nineteen nests in a study by Rusch and Keith were located in aspen stands.

The Midwest. In the oak-hickory forests of Missouri, hens usually nest in upland stands of pole-sized or mature trees. These areas have more open understories, lower densities of woody stems, and less ground cover than those used by drummers and broods.

The Southeast. As in the West, nesting habitats in the Southeast are not well known. Until studies have been conducted and researchers have drawn their conclusions, the general characteristics of nesting habitat may be assumed to apply: the hen needs a clear field of view and a close source of food.

BROOD COVER

A ruffed grouse is never a nestling. The hen leaves the nest with her newly hatched brood as soon as the chicks are dry, and never returns. She leads her young birds to brood habitat, where they will spend the rest of spring and summer.

Grouse chicks from a successful first-attempt nesting are usually hatched in late May or early June. The young are incapable of flight for about the first ten days of life and able to fly only weakly the first three to four weeks—which makes them vulnerable to their predators. By midsummer they can better look after themselves, and the foliage of their habitat provides more secure cover. Nevertheless, of a newly hatched brood of ten chicks, only four are likely to be alive

Brood cover must conceal the chicks from their predators and provide an abundance of food. But the habitat cannot be so dense that it impedes the chicks as they take their first steps from the nest.

Tsuga mertensiana
mountain hemlock

Rumex acetosella
sheep sorrel

Tussilago farfara
coltsfoot

Rumex venosus
winged dock

Carpinus caroliniana
American hornbeam

Ostrya virginiana
ironwood

Physocarpus opulifolius
ninebark

Fagus grandifolia
beech

Maianthemum canadense
Canada mayflower

Larix laricina
tamarack

two or three months later, and another one or two will probably die before the fall dispersal is complete.

The brood-rearing season is thus the most critical season in the life of the ruffed grouse, and good brood habitat is essential to productive grouse range. Obviously, the better the brood habitat, the more juvenile birds that survive to autumn.

Young chicks prefer small forest openings or equivalent habitats supporting a diverse mixture of herbaceous plants that provide succulent leaves or fruits and host an abundance of insects. The growth at ground level should be relatively open and free of dense grasses that would impede the travel of chicks—and conceal a hungry fox. Patchy overhead cover of tree saplings, shrubs, brush, and brambles protects the birds from avian predators.

Such conditions exist where fire, timber harvest, abandoned farms, or other manmade or natural influences have created openings in the forest. The vegetation in new cutover or burned openings is usually too dense for grouse during the first two to four growing seasons, but it becomes suitable brood habitat when competition among woody plants results in a natural thinning. The age at which new openings become good brood habitat varies according to the site and the species of plants growing on it, but broods usually find conditions to their liking in four to five years.

After ten to fifteen years, the canopy closes over, blocking sunlight and killing many of the herbaceous plants. At this stage, the clearing loses its value as habitat for young broods but may provide seasonal cover for adult grouse.

Broods move about the brood range in search of insects, succulent herbs, and fruits. Ruffed grouse also adjust their movements according to changes in temperature, wind direction and velocity, precipitation, and relative humidity. During periods of extreme heat or high humidity, for example, the broods are likely to favor either shaded uplands or understories that are cooled by breezes. Such preferences are important to the birds: in search of the right food and cover, Bump found, hens may take their tiny chicks as far as a half mile.

The North. Here, grouse broods and hens favor aspen habitats. At Sandhill, 69 percent of 134 broods and 94 percent of 187 adults observed on flushing surveys from 1967 to 1975 were in aspen habitats, which accounted for half the area, and 94 percent of the broods and all the adults were either in aspen or within 100 meters. (The flushing transects were randomly distributed, and the habitats were sampled in close proportion to their occurrence in the area.) Of 30 brood flushes in Michigan, 23 were in aspen or aspen-hardwood mixtures, 5 in small openings, and only 2 in lowland hardwoods. In Alberta, Rusch and Keith also found that hens with broods and single grouse prefer aspen woods.

Grouse choose aspen habitats for security and food. The canopy of a stand of aspen is usually more open, allowing tall shrubs, tree saplings, and ferns and other ground-layer herbs to prosper. These habitats often provide good overhead and understory shade

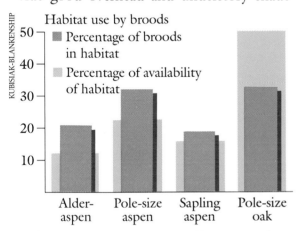

In the Sandhill Wildlife Area of central Wisconsin, extensive stands of oaks were available for brood habitat. The less numerous alders and aspens, however, were used more intensively by broods.

and protective cover as well as succulent foods.

Grouse broods and adults appear to prefer aspens at least five years old with alder understories, at least at Sandhill. Although six- to twenty-five-year-old aspens provide excellent vertical cover, the birds also liked pole-sized aspens twenty-six years and older with moderate to dense understories and ground layer cover. Principal tree species providing this understory cover were red maple, white birch, cherry, oak, and aspen; the main tall shrubs were alder, winterberry, hazel, chokeberry, and serviceberry. Most ground-layer cover was provided by bracken, cinnamon, and interrupted ferns. The principal forage species at ground level included dewberry,

Athyrium filix-femina
lady fern

Datura metel
thorn apple

Prunus pensylvanica
pin cherry

Cystopteris fragilis
bladder fern

Juniperus virginiana
eastern red cedar

Pinus contorta
lodgepole pine

Polygonum coccineum
swamp smartweed

Amelanchier laevis
Allegheny serviceberry

Elaeagnus umbellata
autumn olive

Pinus banksiana
jack pine

wintergreen, blackberry, blueberry, Canada mayflower, bunchberry, violet, and wild strawberry.

Broods in east-central Minnesota mostly use mixed hardwoods of white and yellow birch, trembling aspen, red maple, American elm, black ash, and tamarack, Maxson has reported. Alder, tamarack, white birch, and oak habitats are second choices. Aspen was not used, perhaps because it accounts for only 3 percent of the study area and was mixed with hardwoods, white birch, and oak. All habitats used by broods had sparse to dense understories with one or several species of tall shrubs (alder, hazel, dogwood, poison sumac, willow, bog birch) and ferns.

Another study in northeastern Minnesota, by Godfrey, found that broods prefer alder habitats with a mix of herbaceous food and cover plants at the ground layer. The broods are less partial to upland habitats of aspen, white birch, red pine, balsam fir, and mountain ash that had dense, hazel understories; such sites received considerably less use. Lowland conifers—balsam fir and tamarack— were used solely for roosting.

Grouse broods at Sandhill also occupy small natural openings, less than 10 meters wide. These areas attract insects and allow succulent herbs, ferns, forbs, shrubs, and other food and cover plants to prosper. Use of natural openings and early stages of woodland succession by grouse has also been observed in Iowa, New York, Pennsylvania, and Michigan.

The broods use pole-sized and larger oak forests less often. Such habitats offer only sparse understory and ground-layer cover. Exceptions occurred in portions of stands with hazel understories, which are used more heavily. Besides seeking relief from summer heat in cooling breezes, grouse may enter habitats with open understories if they are en route to a more desirable habitat or temporarily ranging along its periphery. Studying radio-marked birds, Godfrey found that broods travel through Minnesota's less desirable habitat to occupy alder thickets within their home range.

In Wisconsin, grouse broods appear to avoid large areas of dense grass, sedge, slash, or tangled brush, especially recent cutover or sheared areas less than five years old—a

310

choice also observed in Minnesota and Iowa. But broods do use edges of areas cut within the last five years, as well as stands with scattered slash piles, wind-thrown trees, and small brushy thickets. These spots offer temporary protective cover, particularly within or adjacent to more desirable habitat.

The Northeast. New York broods have likewise shown a marked affinity for the youngest stages of forest growth: woodland edges, abandoned and overgrown fields, forest clearings, alder stands, and berry patches. Common to all such habitats are overhead protection from avian predators and a relative abundance of insects and fruiting plants.

Bump and his colleagues reported that nearly 50 percent of the broods observed were seen in overgrown land; the other half were in cutover forested areas and second-growth hardwoods. The favorite habitats in Oswego County, New York, Lyons has reported, are sparsely stocked stands of white pine and hardwoods, Scotch pine and larch plantations, old fields, shrub swamps, and young hardwood stands. Data from her radio-marked broods indicate that the birds spend most of their time in and near berry patches, following the fruits as they ripen: strawberries, then raspberries, blackberries, and blueberries. Many kinds of flying insects are abundant in just such places.

Chambers has reported that broods prefer recently clear-cut openings to the surrounding forest; specifically, a six- to eight-fold increase in brood use of forested areas in central New York within six years after small areas (1 hectare) were clear-cut. Lyons, however, found virtually no broods in such openings where slash was piled around the edges; she found preferred use of old fields with an abundance of berries and insects. Bump noted that logged areas and alder stands were favored in extensive forests but that broods preferred old fields and woodland edges in regions containing a mix of forest and reverting farmland. Conifer habitats and conifers mixed with hardwoods are little used by broods.

The West. In southern Idaho, broods have been found most often in aspen or mixed aspen-conifer stands whose relatively open overstories encouraged dense understory and ground cover growth.

Carya glabra
pignut hickory

Rosa multiflora
multiflora rose

Betula alleghaniensis
yellow birch

Taraxacum officinale
dandelion

Carya tomentosa
mockernut hickory

Fragaria virginiana
strawberry

Hamamelis virginiana
witch hazel

Botrychium multifidum
grape fern

Lindera benzoin
spicebush

Pinus resinosa
red pine

In northern Utah and southeastern Idaho, lush growth of herbaceous plants seems to be an important aspect of good brood cover. Early in the summer, just after hatching, broods tend to be spread across slopes, often on upper slopes. As summer progresses and this vegetation dries up, broods gravitate to drainage bottoms and watercourses where they can enjoy moist microclimates. In central and northern Idaho, where substantial deciduous cover is lacking, broods tend to use Douglas fir and cedar-hemlock zones.

The Midwest. Missouri broods are usually found in young forest openings and clear-cuts more than five years old, and in lowland hardwoods with dense understories along creeks and streams. These habitats have greater than average densities of woody stems and good ground cover of herbaceous plants and low shrubs. The woody stems provide cover, of course, but the plants at ground level may also serve this function, especially in mature habitats without a great many woody stems. Areas with more ground cover may have more insects as well.

The Southeast. Brood habitat in the Southeast has been little studied, and brood habitat requirements are still poorly defined. From the research that has been done, however, several points can be made. Although hens in the Southeast enter a variety of habitats with their chicks, broods are found most often along forest edges, in recently disturbed sites, and in moist, forested areas with sparse understories but well-developed ground cover and plentiful insects. Steward found them to prefer two kinds of moist habitats: lowland areas containing hemlock, white pine, red oak, and poplar; and high knobs and ridges with red oak, sweet birch, and chestnut oak. Yet these moist forest types made up less than 15 percent of the study area, which suggests that a lack of attractive brood habitat may be limiting grouse populations. As summer wears on, broods seem to make more use of dry sites, where they feed on early-ripening blueberries.

A study by Hein found all broods on relatively level sites at elevations higher than 1,100 meters in near-climax communities of white oak and pignut hickory. In Georgia, hens with broods prefer upland hardwood

RUFFED GROUSE

At the edge of a woodlot, a drummer displays before another grouse. If the challenger cannot find suitable cover before the leaves fall, he will probably not survive the winter.

saplings, Harris found; next by preference are coves of hardwood saplings and upland hardwood pole timber. Habitats the broods avoid include regenerating hardwoods in uplands and coves, stands of pine sawtimber, and evergreen shrub thickets.

AUTUMN AND WINTER COVER

During the fall "shuffle" as young birds disperse, ruffed grouse enter just about any kind of habitat. Some juveniles may travel seven, eight, even ten or eleven miles from their summer brood areas; during this time, they are likely to occupy less suitable habitats, at least temporarily, as they seek what they judge to be good cover.

The juveniles' quest for fall cover is complicated by established adult males, who advertise their presence by drumming and even physically defend their territories. Encounters among birds are an integral part of fall dispersal and determine, in part, the distribution and density of birds in the area. Aggressive young males tend to find suitable cover, but the grouse that cannot find territories of their own may be relegated to poorer habitats. As long as most of the leaves stay on the trees, or suitable cover is available, these nonterritorial birds are relatively secure, but they will probably not survive the winter.

Until the shedding of deciduous foliage, in late October and early November, any habitat that offers adequate food probably has adequate cover as well. In fact, grouse show

Acer rubrum
red maple

Asimina triloba
pawpaw

Diospyros virginiana
persimmon

Rhus vernix
poison sumac

Quercus prinus
chestnut oak

Platanus occidentalis
sycamore

Staphylea trifolia
bladdernut

Kalmia latifolia
mountain laurel

Desmodium canadense
tick trefoil

Picea glauca
white spruce

more concern for food than for cover during the late summer and early fall, often concentrating in grape tangles and fruit-producing trees and shrubs, such as thorn apples, apples, viburnums, and dogwoods. These habitats attract and hold many grouse until the supply of soft fruit is exhausted; abandoned farmland is particularly favored at this time of year, given the abundance of fruiting plants found there. Similarly, forests containing beech and black cherry may become focal points for feeding grouse. Although many of these habitats appear to make excellent fall cover, they often lack the essential elements that qualify them as good year-round ruffed grouse habitat.

Ideal winter cover protects grouse from both the elements and their predators. It can be dense brushy or shrubby vegetation, hardwood saplings, or conifers that provide insulation and a profusion of cover at least 4.5 meters (15 feet) tall. Such conditions may exist in cutover woodlands where the tree saplings are about six to fifteen years old. Cover may remain adequate in these areas until the trees are twenty to thirty years old. Natural thinning of the trees then reduces the stem density below levels acceptable to grouse. There are many exceptions to this general rule, however. Shrubs and vines, such as mountain laurel, hazel, dogwood, hawthorn, grape, greenbrier, and honeysuckle, may continue to provide good cover well past the age of thirty, for example.

Older stands are another exception. Too sparse to make good cover, they can provide excellent sources of grouse foods, such as fruits, seeds, buds, and catkins. Some food-tree species don't become good producers until they are nearly 100 years old: the American beech, for example. Aspen stands, which provide suitable winter cover in the North at ten to twenty-five years, don't produce a good supply of buds for ruffed grouse until they are thirty.

These facts reveal two requirements for the best ruffed grouse habitats: an interspersion of plants of different ages, and an abundance of species that provide both food and cover. The food supply in a stand of mature trees, for example, will not hold grouse unless the birds can take cover in an adjacent stand of saplings. The aspens are particularly im-

314

As winter approaches, cold becomes another risk factor. Grouse in hardwood forests, like this Wisconsin stand of young oaks with an understory of hazels, will seek the protection and insulation of trees whose leaves will not fall until late winter.

portant dual-purpose trees in the northern forests, where winter snows may cover the foods at ground level. But one or more of the other fifteen native species of the genus *Populus,* the most widely distributed trees in North America, can be found in most parts of the ruffed grouse range.

The North. Ruffed grouse have adapted to survive winter in a variety of habitats throughout their range. In the North, highest survival rates occur in sapling aspen, alder, and upland brush habitats. Svoboda and Gullion have defined the best habitats for Minnesota most precisely: where five to seven mature, thirty- to fifty-year-old aspens per hectare grow within 30 meters of good fall-to-spring cover of dense shrubs and saplings. If the food source—the aspens—is more than 30 meters from the cover, the habitat becomes more risky.

In northern Wisconsin and similar parts of the grouse range, the days with snow deep enough for snow-roosting number about sixty; the longer a grouse can snow-roost, the better its chances for survival. In central and southern Wisconsin, however, there may be suitable roosting snow for fewer than thirty days, and frequently fewer than ten. In these areas—and wherever snow is inadequate—grouse seek the best insulation and protection they can find. Habitats with dense understories and thick overhead cover offer some protection from severe winter weather, but grouse may also use areas with thick grasses and sedges at the ground level—

Crataegus douglasii
black hawthorn

Cornus canadensis
bunchberry

Polystichum acrostichoides
Christmas fern

Phlox divaricata
blue phlox

Corylus americana
hazel

Pinus ponderosa
yellow pine

Vaccinium corymbosum
blueberry

Rhus typhina
staghorn sumac

Prunus virginiana
chokecherry

Populus balsamifera
balsam poplar

When the snow is not deep enough for snow-roosting, ruffed grouse often nestle into partial snow bowls. This bird has fluffed up its feathers for additional insulation from the cold.

habitats that may be flooded at other times of the year. Birds also roost in the protective cover of a blown-down or tipped tree, or where exposure to the radiant heat of the sun moderates the effects of cold weather.

Other habitats that provide protection from the cold include oaks and conifers. Young oaks that retain their leaves may be attractive, as are conifers whose living branches provide cover from ground level to at least 2 meters up. It seems that conifers are more suitable where they constitute a small proportion of the forest or occur in small patches. If the evergreens grow in large blocks, the edges are more likely than the interior to be occupied by ruffed grouse.

Northern birds need nutritious food as well as insulation. Where the buds of mature male aspens are the principal fall and winter foods, the supply of trees may limit the number of grouse that survive the winter. Grouse can, however, also feed on the buds, twigs, and catkins of several other species: hazel, birch, maple, willow, ironwood, cherry, serviceberry, dogwood, viburnum, sumac, hawthorn. Of these, hazel appears to be an important winter food for northern grouse. Hungry grouse may also be temporarily attracted to buds and other foods in recently cut areas, where slash and tree tops provide the principal cover. Depending on the site, various evergreen herbs and the mature fruits and seeds of wild and agricultural foods are eaten, too.

The Northeast. By early December, forest stands that include a mix of hardwoods and conifers and habitats where hardwoods adjoin conifers have become the primary haunts of New York ruffed grouse. Especially attractive are forest stands with many aspens, birches, black cherries, wild apples, and hop hornbeams—important food sources in those snowbelt areas where grouse forage on buds, twigs, and catkins. In the milder regions of southern New York, where ground-level foraging is possible through much of the winter, the nature of the hardwood overstory seems to be less important than the ground-layer herbs and shrubs that supply leafy greens and frost-hardy fruits.

Grouse in the Northeast usually shun the interiors of extensive evergreen stands, but they are also absent from large expanses of hardwoods that either are far from conifers or lack evergreens altogether. The reason is simple: when they cannot burrow into snow to keep warm, grouse prefer to roost in or under conifers. And because winters in New York and portions of many other northeastern states have warm spells and rains that ruin the snow cover for the purposes of the ruffed grouse, the birds choose conifers often. In fact, when snow-roosting is not an option, more than 90 percent of all winter roosts are in conifers.

Winter habitats for grouse south of the boreal zone may include small stands of conifers; here the birds seek shelter from the biting wind.

Young, ten- to twenty-year-old conifers of most types serve well as roosting cover. As they mature, pines tend to lose their value as nighttime roosts, but spruces, hemlocks, and firs continue to offer grouse a sheltered refuge from the cold under their low-hanging, pendant branches. During the day all conifer species, even mature pines and hemlocks, provide sites for just loafing.

Although Gullion has shown that mortality from raptors is higher in Minnesota habitats that include conifers, particularly older pines, Chambers believes that where the snow cover is inadequate in quantity or quality for snow-roosting, ruffed grouse select winter habitats that include or adjoin conifers. Whenever the snow is deep and

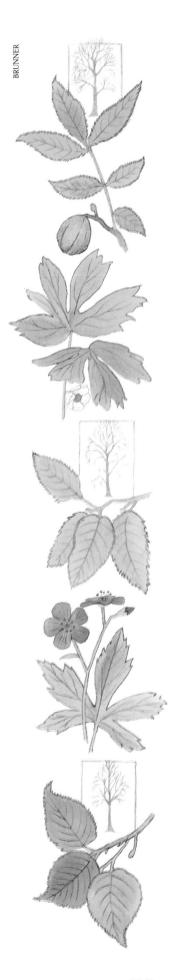

Carya ovata
shagbark hickory

Podophyllum peltatum
mayapple

Betula lenta
sweet birch

Geranium maculatum
wild geranium

Betula papyrifera
paper birch

THE KINGDOM OF THE RUFFED GROUSE

317

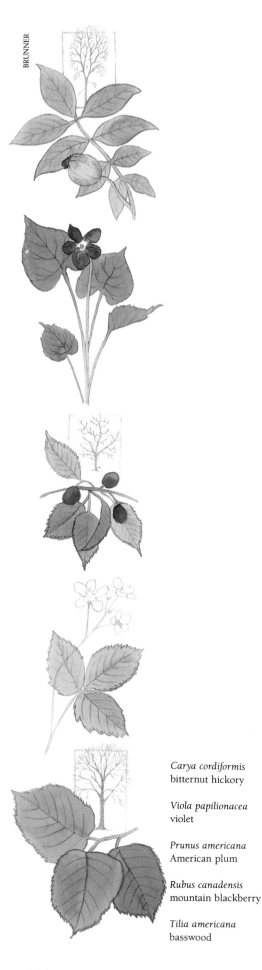

BRUNNER

Carya cordiformis
bitternut hickory

Viola papilionacea
violet

Prunus americana
American plum

Rubus canadensis
mountain blackberry

Tilia americana
basswood

soft enough to permit snow-roosting, New York grouse prefer hardwood stands and small forest openings, just like their Minnesota relatives.

The West. In the fall ruffed grouse lose their affinity for aspen and deciduous stands and begin to occupy more diverse habitats. In Alberta, Rusch and Keith found more grouse in spruce and bog habitats during the fall than in any other season. A similar pattern has emerged in southeastern Idaho, where Stauffer and Peterson found grouse using conifer and young, dense stands. This shift of habitat use in the fall is probably a result of the dispersion of young birds seeking new areas in which to live.

Western ruffed grouse feed heavily on aspen buds in winter and therefore tend to use aspen or mixed aspen-conifer habitats. The structure of favored stands is open enough to allow the accumulation of snow for snow-roosting. Where there is a fair amount of topographical relief, grouse tend to winter on the middle to upper slopes—apparently a response to the temperature inversions often encountered in mountainous terrain, where temperatures are usually warmer at higher elevations exposed to sunlight.

Conifers within the aspen habitats may be important as winter cover, since grouse roosting in evergreens receive good thermal protection when conditions are not right for snow-roosting. Conifers may also provide storm shelter. On numerous occasions in southeastern Idaho, Stauffer has observed five to fifteen sets of grouse tracks in the snow radiating from conifer patches after strong winter storms.

In late winter, as snow begins to melt, the grouse move toward south-facing slopes, where the first bare ground appears. These sites provide fresh herbaceous vegetation to supplement and eventually replace the winter diet of buds and twigs.

The Midwest. In Missouri the ruffed grouse's need for cover and food are met in old fields, which typically contain eastern red cedar. This tree (and possibly other types of low evergreen cover) seems to be important in the region because it provides relatively thick cover yet low stem densities. It offers the best available habitat in areas that

318

do not have stands of young hardwoods created by clear-cutting, but its real value may be as winter shelter. Grouse that roost in cedars, Thompson has found, conserve more heat and energy than those in deciduous cover. Only snow-roosting provides better insulation, but sufficient snow occurs rarely in Missouri.

Old fields also contain many foods important to midwestern grouse in winter. Clearcuts seven to twenty-five years old—the same habitats used by drumming males in spring—appear to make good winter cover in this region as well.

The Southeast. Although fall and winter habitats in the Southeast have been studied little—much of the published research on southeastern birds has come from studying grouse that have been transplanted to new areas—it is known that brushy areas resulting from clear-cuts and abandoned farmland are attractive to grouse. Both native and transplanted grouse prefer hardwood saplings to upland oaks. Yet grouse abundance varies considerably among stands of hardwood saplings, and the reasons are not fully understood. Moist sites in clear-cut areas seem to be attractive, probably because they offer more fruits and herbaceous leaves. Grouse also seem to have an affinity for thickets of young white pine in cutover areas. Working with transplanted grouse in Tennessee, White and Dimmick found that shrub thickets of laurel and viny thickets of greenbrier in upland forest areas were popular in early fall. Since laurel and greenbrier are two of the most common fall and winter foods of grouse in the Southeast, one might expect native birds to make similar use of such thickets.

In southern sawtimber and pole-timber forest stands, grouse also frequent rhododendron thickets. These habitats seem to provide adequate cover but lack sufficient forage. Nearby food sources—birch catkins, grapes on moist sites, acorns from the tree canopy—appear to allow a few grouse to survive in these food-scarce habitats.

> —*Harold L. Barber, Robert Chambers,*
> *Roy Kirkpatrick, John Kubisiak,*
> *Frederick A. Servello, Steven K.*
> *Stafford, Dean F. Stauffer,*
> *and Frank R. Thompson III*

Malus angustifolia
southern crab apple

Epigaea repens
trailing arbutus

Solanum dulcamara
bittersweet nightshade

Pseudotsuga menziesii
Douglas fir

Rhododendron calendulaceum
flame azalea

Cornus florida
flowering dogwood

The best year-round cover

Ruffed grouse numbers are greatest where young and old forest stands are distributed throughout an area—that is, where thick, woody cover occurs close to sources of food. But the extent of such areas and what surrounds them are important, too. Large contiguous blocks of upland aspen and oak forests of several hundred to a thousand acres or more have considerably greater potential for grouse than isolated or fragmented woodlands surrounded by cultivated fields or encroaching development.

To meet their needs year-round, grouse generally seek upland forests containing a high density of shrubs taller than 1.5 meters, and tree seedlings, saplings, and sprouts taller than 4.5 meters. Lowland forests with dense growths of tall shrubs or saplings may also be attractive during certain seasons. Stands of aspen, both young and old, that contain tall shrub understories are the best, but such habitats do not remain productive unless there is a continuous supply of dense stands of six- to twenty-five-year-old saplings. Aspen or oak plus conifers or other hardwoods may also provide suitable cover, if tall shrub thickets are mixed in.

These various combinations determine the structure of the habitat. Habitats with good vertical structure—more than 20,000 stems per hectare—with an overstory at least 4.5 meters tall provide shelter for grouse while frustrating their predators. Although grouse numbers may fluctuate regardless of habitat

Marginal habitat: the ruffed grouse can feed in these mature trees, but there is neither a sufficiently high density of understory trees nor any tall shrubby brush to provide adequate cover.

KUBISIAK

quality, grouse densities remain higher where good vertical cover is maintained.

Horizontal structure is another factor. Slash, tipped or blown-down trees, debris on the forest floor, and other impenetrable cover may restrict the movement of grouse on the ground and reduce their ability to spot predators. In the absence of good vertical cover, however, horizontal cover can provide grouse with shelter and concealment. Horizontal cover is probably more beneficial if it occurs only in small areas or clumps, rather than throughout a stand. Thus the birds can walk easily on the ground while finding some protection from the elements and their enemies.

Grouse may use unsuitable habitats temporarily to satisfy specific food or cover needs. They may also use small stands or patches of poor habitat surrounded by better habitat. Such areas may be too open, for example: pole- or sawtimber-sized woodlands twenty-six years or older with exten-sive parklike or sparse understories, or conifer plantations whose principal cover occurs too high in the tree canopy, or old fields and pastures with scattered trees and shrubs. These habitats may provide food or cover during summer or fall and allow easy movement of birds on the ground, but they are unsuitable as year-round cover.

Habitats may be too dense: areas with large amounts of logging slash following a clear-cut, or forested tracts damaged by windstorm, insects, or disease, or places where trees and brush have been bull-dozed or wind-rowed. Habitats may also be too dense for grouse if the understory and ground-layer cover are impenetrable: blocks of conifer where impenetrable cover occurs from ground level to 8 meters or more, or places where dense growths of vines, brambles, low-growing shrubs, grass-sedge, and forbs so dominate that desirable food and cover plants cannot take hold.

—*John Kubisiak*

Prime habitat: this site's interspersion of trees of different ages, from four years to fifty-six, offers the ruffed grouse both food and cover close together.

KUBISIAK

The essentials of habitat

*T*he first step in managing land for the ruffed grouse's—and the hunter's—benefit is finding out where the birds prefer to live and what foods they prefer to eat.

Ruffed grouse are generally found in the early successional stages of forests, including grasslands, shrubs, and early stages of tree reproduction—a wide variety of habitats. The birds do not occur uniformly throughout their geographical range, however. In 1973 Sharp suggested that ruffed grouse are tied to a particular niche by preferred food items, especially during the fall and winter months. The geographical variation in food habits reported in the literature may reflect the availability of food as well as the grouse's preferences. The art of wildlife management comes in applying this information.

Popular places

Comparisons of flushing rates—the number of birds flushed per hour—in different types of habitats should reveal the ruffed grouse's habitat preferences: the more birds flushed per hour, the more popular the habitat. But when Ferguson and, later, Brenner tested seven major forest types in Pennsylvania, the average number of birds flushed over a five-year period was relatively uniform. The data, however, do not tell us how many birds were flushed in each successional stage within a geographic region. It is possible that the majority of the birds lived in

In the North, grouse resort to willow buds only if aspen buds are unavailable. More than any other factor, the choice and abundance of winter foods may determine the extent of the species' range and its overwinter survival.

322

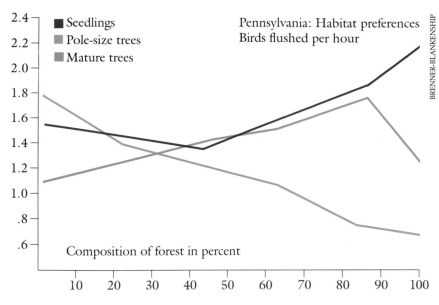

2.4
2.2
2.0
1.8
1.6
1.4
1.2
1.0
.8
.6

■ Seedlings
■ Pole-size trees
■ Mature trees

Pennsylvania: Habitat preferences
Birds flushed per hour

Composition of forest in percent

10 20 30 40 50 60 70 80 90 100

BRENNER-BLANKENSHIP

In Pennsylvania, forests with a high proportion of seedling trees support high numbers of grouse. Woodlands that consist entirely of seedlings are apparently most attractive.

early successional stages. Indeed, the number of birds flushed per hour increased in direct proportion to the amount of forestland in the sapling-seedling stage.

In Ohio's prime grouse range, the amount of oak-hickory forest cover varies from approximately 20 percent in the northeast to 53 percent in the southeast. Although the best grouse habitat is said to contain a high percentage of forest cover, according to Stoll, more grouse were bagged per hunter in the more open northeast. It remains to be substantiated, however, whether there are higher harvests in the northeast because the land is more open or because the hunters there are more persistent and more skilled.

In 1971, on a 2,560-acre area near Rochester in Alberta, Canada, Rusch and Keith confirmed that grouse like aspen. Of 135 drumming males, 96 percent occupied logs in the aspen woods. Within those groves of aspen, the grouse had selected drumming sites with a sparse canopy of low shrubs, a low density of saplings, and a high density of trees. But generally, the aspen woods had a high density of shrubs, which may have provided brood and escape cover. This protection is important: where grouse were killed by predators in aspens, the shrub cover was sparse, and a high percentage of birds were killed in the even sparser spruce woods.

Not surprisingly, after a nine-year study on the number of territorial males at two sites in Algonquin Park, Ontario, Theberge and Gauthier found that ruffed grouse densities were lower on sites where aspen were absent. One site contained mostly white spruce and balsam fir with some quaking aspen and white spruce; no aspens or other poplar species were present on the second site. Since they found no difference in the number of woody stems near drumming logs or in the number of perch trees (large pines, hemlocks, cedars) near drumming logs, Theberge and Gauthier concluded in 1982 that the differences in densities of drummers between the two sites could not be explained by differences in survival, the susceptibility of the habitat to predators, or spacing behavior. That left habitat selection.

What type of cover best ensures the survival of drumming males is controversial. Gullion and Marshall suggested that in Cloquet, Minnesota, grouse survival decreases as tall pines increase. Conifers, they concluded, are an unessential and even detrimental component of ruffed grouse habitat at Cloquet. The proportion of the total kills observed in spruce woods or spruce-aspen edges in Rochester, Alberta, appears to support this hypothesis. On the other hand, in 1986, Chambers suggested that conifer stands are an essential cover component of grouse habitat in the Adirondacks of New York. It is more likely, however, that all the vegetation within the home range of ruffed grouse influences, to some degree, their survival, Gullion and Marshall concluded in 1978. The lack of a relationship between vegetation and survival of drummers does not necessarily mean that vegetation has no effect on the survival of nondrumming males, hens, or broods.

Because ruffed grouse inhabit such a variety of habitats with such a range of vegetation, it is difficult to characterize the ideal or even the typical grouse habitat. Perhaps the best approach is to find the essential habitat components—the ones that are critical to the survival of the species in a given geographic area—and manage accordingly.

FAVORITE FOODS

Ruffed grouse have cosmopolitan tastes. Despite the variety of food species, however, certain items appear on the menu throughout their range. Unfortunately, because of the variation in the procedures used to analyze their feeding habits, it is difficult to compare the importance of one food species in one geographical area to that in another. Some authors report the number, weight, or volume of each item in the crop, in which case it is possible to rate each food item as a percentage of the total diet; others report only the percentage of crops that contained each item. Neither procedure, however, considers how much of the item the birds ate compared with its relative abundance in the area. If aspens are scarce but the grouse's crop nevertheless is full of aspen buds, for example, we would know that grouse want aspen buds badly enough to go looking for them. Nor do the procedures consider the nutrient quality of the food. To work these variables in, Stoll and his associates have calculated an importance index for each food item found in the crops of Ohio grouse:

$$\begin{aligned} \text{index} = {}&(\text{occurrence} \times 100) \\ &\times \% \text{ volume in crop} \\ &\times \text{specific gravity of food item} \\ &\times \text{nutritional value} \\ &\times (100 - \% \text{ availability}) \end{aligned}$$

In a similar effort, Woehr and Chambers have compared the feeding habits of grouse with the availability and the metabolizable available energy (MAE) of favorite foods in central New York. Such procedures can help determine the importance of various foods to ruffed grouse in different geographic areas or habitats within an area.

Despite the difficulties, grouse diets can be analyzed and compared, and a favorite topic of researchers has been the diet of ruffed grouse during the fall and winter. In Pennsylvania, analysis of eighty-eight crops collected statewide during December and January indicated that seeds and fruits, present in 44 percent of the crops, were the principal food items: grape, rose, cherry, greenbrier, and *Vibrium*. The remainder of the diet consisted of buds, twigs, and catkins (27 percent) and leafy material (29 percent). In northwestern Pennsylvania, seeds and fruits were also the principal food of ruffed grouse, accounting for 50 percent of the food items: dogwoods, followed by alder and black cherry. The rest of the matter was green leaves and buds, twigs, and catkins. In both studies, aspens occurred in fewer than 6 per-

cent of the crops and constituted less than 1 percent of the total weight.

Ruffed grouse diets vary seasonally, of course: fruits and seeds are of greater importance during the summer and fall, buds and catkins are a prime food in the early spring, and insects are important during the late spring and summer months, especially for young birds. But in Ohio the proportions varied by region. In northeastern Ohio, aspens were the principal food species during the fall and winter months, followed by hop hornbeam, poison ivy, greenbrier, and grape; in east-central Ohio, grapes were the most important food species, followed by aspens, poison ivy, dogwoods, and ferns. But in southeastern Ohio, aspens ranked seventh in importance and greenbrier was first. In the spring and summer, fruits and seeds constituted 38 percent of the diet in east-central Ohio but 49 percent in the southeast. Buds and twigs, the most important food in the northeast (45 percent), accounted for little more than half that in the other two regions. In all regions leafy material made up the difference.

In the southern Appalachians, ruffed grouse rely more on green leaves than on either fruits or buds. Leafy material amounted to 56 percent to 67 percent of their diet; fruits constituted 23 percent to more than 45 percent; buds and catkins did not exceed 10 percent, according to Stafford and Dimmick. In this region, greenbrier, mountain laurel, and Christmas fern were significant in the diet, and dogwood and honeysuckle were of local importance in the Cumberland Plateau and Great Valley regions, respectively. Throughout the region, herbaceous annuals and perennials of the forest floor (30 percent), leaves and fruits of vines (35 percent), and the foliage of woody shrubs (20 percent) were important foods; overstory trees contributed only 3 percent of the diet. Likewise, in southwestern Virginia, fruits and seeds constituted approximately 65 percent and leafy material, 34 percent, of the diet of grouse during the fall and winter months. During the spring and summer, not surprisingly, the proportions were reversed, Norman and Kirkpatrick concluded in 1984.

Leaves, fruits, and seeds are important in the New England states as well. McDowell

In some regions, oaks are the predominant tree species and the principal source of cover. Many other species besides aspen can support grouse.

reported in 1975 that the crops collected from 244 ruffed grouse from 1909 to 1968 contained more than fifty food species, of which the three most important were oaks, grapes, and birches. When McDowell listed the twenty-five most important food species for ruffed grouse in Connecticut, aspens ranked twenty-third.

Likewise, in 1970 Schemnitz reported that ruffed grouse in Maine fed extensively on leaves (46 percent), with seeds, fruits, and buds constituting 38 percent and catkins, 15 percent, of their diet. Schemnitz stressed the importance of ground cover, especially clovers, in the overall diet of the Maine ruffed grouse. With the onset of winter, however, buds became a major food. Although ruffed grouse were most frequently observed feeding on buds in aspen trees (38 percent), several other tree species, including white birch, apple, and cherry, were common sources of food. In Minnesota, however, Gullion found that aspens were *the* winter food for Minnesota ruffed grouse, and catkins were more important than buds. Gullion conjectured that buds, like twigs, were stuffing foods of poor nutritional value. But analysis of buds and catkins from a variety of species, including aspens, indicates that there is no significant difference in the nutritional value, or metabolizable available energy. The differences between these two studies are probably due to geographical variation in the availability of foods and the preferences of individual birds.

Woehr and Chambers found that in central New York, black cherry was the principal winter food of ruffed grouse. Apple and aspen were either second or third in importance, depending on the season and year. Aspen becomes an important food item during the spring, when other foods are less available to the birds.

Given the variety of foods that ruffed grouse eat, and the variation from one geographic area to another, management should center not on one or two species of plants but on at least ten to fifteen of the preferred foods in a region. Open grasslands should be interspersed with shrub, brush, and forest cover to provide an abundance of insects for young birds as well as vertical cover for nesting and escape from predators. Dense groves of conifers (particularly spruces), not single trees, spaced throughout the area may also be beneficial as winter cover for adult birds. The development of ruffed grouse habitat is probably more an art than a science, but any management plan should be based on the best scientific data available for the species in any given region.

—Fred J. Brenner

Summer cover for adult birds

*S*ummer is the time when grouse can find acceptable food and cover in a variety of habitats that may be unsuitable in other seasons. Although adult birds may use brood cover, their preferred habitats show certain special characteristics. Food must be plentiful, of course, but woody and herbaceous plants should provide concealment at the ground level, in the understory, and overhead. Brood use of certain dense habitats may be limited—the chicks, particularly those less than four weeks old, may be hampered by too much brush or impenetrable cover as they forage on the forest floor. But adult males and adult females without broods appear to spend considerable time in the densest, most secure cover available, particularly while molting.

In Michigan, Berner and Gysel have found that during summer, adult females without broods and adult males occupy coverts similar in structure—that is, in the distribution and density of vegetation from the ground up—to those used by drummers in the spring and fall. In east-central Minnesota, adult females without broods choose habitats with sparse to dense understories containing ferns and at least one kind of tall shrub: alder, hazel, dogwood, poison sumac, willow, or bog birch, but alder by preference. At Sandhill, in Wisconsin, small natural openings in the forests are attractive.

The need for cover is so strong that broods and adult birds sometimes seek cover or escape enemies in slash piles—cover that

would otherwise be unsuitable. In contrast, oak forests with open understories and sparse ground cover are generally avoided.

Come autumn, adult ruffed grouse spend most of their time in good year-round habitats where food and cover are available together. Birds may temporarily occupy habitats with less desirable protection if they find a good source of selected herbs, mature fruits, or other foods. Nevertheless, most of the banded adult grouse studied in Wisconsin appear to move a mere 400 meters or less during the fall—an indication that given good habitat interspersion, they can find their food and cover within about 25 hectares.

—John Kubisiak

Grouse feed primarily at ground level in the summer. The molting of flight feathers, and a consequent diminished ability to navigate in the air, may prompt adult birds to seek the densest possible cover.

Evergreen controversy

Puffed up against the cold, two ruffed grouse sit out a cold spell in an evergreen tree. Does this expose them to raptors or protect them from the elements? Competing theories argue the point.

*T*he most controversial aspect of the winter grouse habitat is the desirability of evergreen cover. Conifers have been described by some researchers as highly beneficial to grouse, by others as highly detrimental. To sort through the issue, it helps to look first at the role conifers play in the world of the ruffed grouse.

The ruffed grouse needs cover that lets it see predators before the predators see it. In winter, deciduous trees enable the grouse to see a raptor's overhead silhouette, but tall conifers with clean boles and dense canopies up high give the advantage to the predators. Moreover, those same tall conifers shade the ground so completely that the grouse's preferred cover plants cannot grow. Unable to

MAXSON

see its attackers and unable to take cover in any case, the ruffed grouse becomes, so to speak, a sitting duck. And indeed, several researchers have noted that stands of conifers expose grouse to severe losses from predation.

That is, in the North. In the southern grouse range, ruffed grouse use evergreen cover extensively in winter. With understory stands of mountain laurel, rhododendron, and young conifers providing cover near the ground, and with a mix of hardwoods, such evergreen woods support some of the highest grouse populations.

Whether evergreens are good or bad for grouse may be the wrong question; snow may be the real issue. The advantages provided by deep snow, thoroughly set forth by Gullion, bear repeating. The ruffed grouse lacks sufficient insulation to stay warm when the air temperature falls to −7°C. (20°F.). The bird's body responds by speeding up metabolism, which increases its energy requirements and can cause stress over an extended period. The temperature inside a snow drift, however, seldom falls below −7°C., even when the air temperature dips much lower. By burrowing into snow, the grouse can enjoy a snug winter roost wher-

ever deep snows persist through the winter.

But winter temperatures are often extreme where snowfalls do not permit burrowing, and it is the extremes, not the averages, that are the limiting factor. Temperatures as low as −34°C. (−30°F.) have been recorded in the southern grouse range. But even much more moderate temperatures stress the birds, and a grouse without shelter must increase its metabolic rate to stay warm. And at −17°C. (0°F.), a wind velocity of 32 kilometers per hour (20 miles per hour) creates a windchill factor of −40°C. (−40°F.), cold enough to tax any grouse's resources.

By providing shelter from the wind, rain, and cold, low-growing evergreens may supply an important winter need where snow is not deep enough for burrowing. No stand of conifers provides as much protection as a snow-roost, however. Perhaps it is the presence of snow, rather than any other difference in habitat or food, that accounts for the higher numbers of ruffed grouse in the North. If such a relationship exists, it is yet to be documented, and although this suggestion seems to contain more substance than some of the other explanations offered, it is intended here as food for thought.

—*Harold L. Barber*

About to enter the dark, sheltered space beneath a pine, this grouse will likely emerge again only to feed. If the snow is not deep enough for snow-roosting, the conifer tree may be the bird's sole option.

New York: Winter roosting preferences

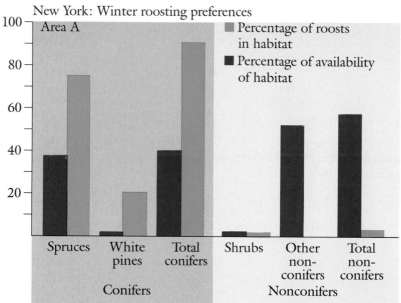

Area A

100
80
60
40
20

■ Percentage of roosts in habitat
■ Percentage of availability of habitat

Spruces | White pines | Total conifers
Conifers

Shrubs | Other non-conifers | Total non-conifers
Nonconifers

Ruffed grouse in New York clearly prefer evergreen cover for their winter roosting sites. Although three-fourths of study area B consisted of non-coniferous cover, few grouse chose to roost there – none at all, in fact, in deciduous cover that was not apple trees or shrubs. The findings were based on 101 birds studied in January through March.

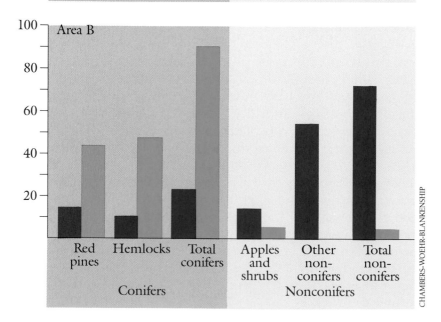

Area B

100
80
60
40
20

Red pines | Hemlocks | Total conifers
Conifers

Apples and shrubs | Other non-conifers | Total non-conifers
Nonconifers

RUFFED GROUSE

A home
on the range

In the West, coordination with logging operations holds great promise for improving grouse habitat. Wherever possible, cuts should be small—just large enough to encompass a home range or two—and riparian areas, which may provide critical brood-rearing habitat, should be protected with buffer zones. Abandoned logging roads and log decks can be seeded with preferred ruffed grouse foods, such as clover, grass, and cinquefoil.

A potential problem with habitat management for ruffed grouse occurs in the Rocky Mountains. Because of the intensive fire-prevention efforts made since the beginning of the twentieth century, few aspen stands have burned, and many are at least eighty years old. Stands of this age provide marginal ruffed grouse habitat now, and their utility declines every year. To encourage the young stages of forest succession that encourage ruffed grouse, fuelwood cutters and the developing markets for aspen lumber could be allocated cuts. Controlled burning would also help rejuvenate aspen.

Many areas of the West, especially public lands, are used for grazing livestock. Grazing should not be allowed in critical habitats, such as riparian areas, during the brood-rearing season. Once a brood is six to eight weeks old, however, the chicks are mobile, and grazing cattle and sheep are likely only to move the broods around, not to cause brood loss.

—Dean F. Stauffer

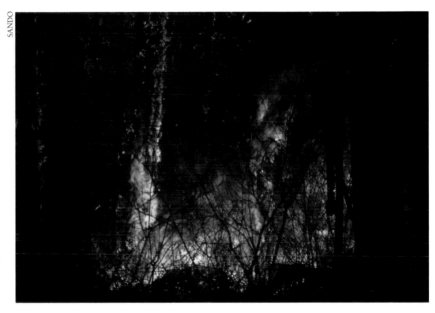

Forest fires—whether prescribed and controlled, or naturally ignited like the 1988 conflagrations that smoldered and raged across the West—can renew favorable habitat by clearing the old trees that hinder new growth below.

SANDO

Like a worshipper at dawn, this drummer faces east, catching the morning sun in his wings.

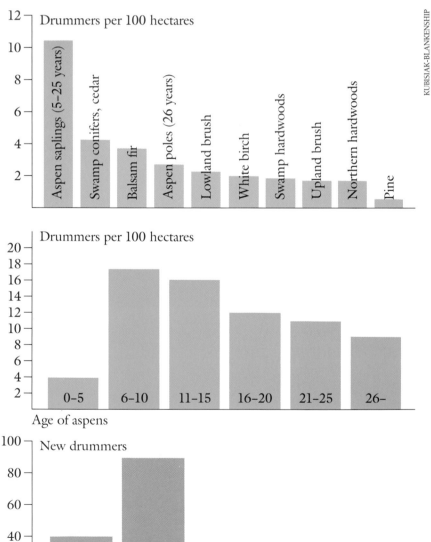

Drummers per 100 hectares

Aspen saplings (5–25 years)
Swamp conifers, cedar
Balsam fir
Aspen poles (26 years)
Lowland brush
White birch
Swamp hardwoods
Upland brush
Northern hardwoods
Pine

Drummers per 100 hectares

0–5 | 6–10 | 11–15 | 16–20 | 21–25 | 26–

Age of aspens

New drummers

0–5 | 6–10 | 11–15 | 16–20 | 21–25

Age of aspens

Aspens are the clear preference of grouse in the Stone Lake area of Wisconsin (top). But not all aspens will do. Studies in the Sandhill–Wood County areas show that most drumming sites are in aspens six to twenty-five years old (middle), and that new activity centers occur most frequently in the six- to ten-year-old stands (bottom).

Drummers per 100 hectares

■ Highest density in high grouse year   ■ Lowest density in low grouse year   – – Mean

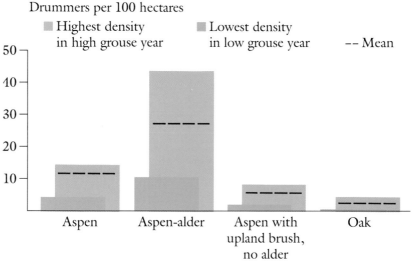

50
40
30
20
10

Aspen   Aspen-alder   Aspen with upland brush, no alder   Oak

KUBISIAK-BLANKENSHIP

Whether the grouse population has reached a high or hit the low point of its natural cycle, stands of aspen and alder support the greatest densities of drummers. Kubisiak studied population fluctuations in the Sandhill–Wood County areas of Wisconsin from 1968 through 1982.

Drummers per 100 hectares

■ Aspen with tall shrubs   ■ Aspen without tall shrubs

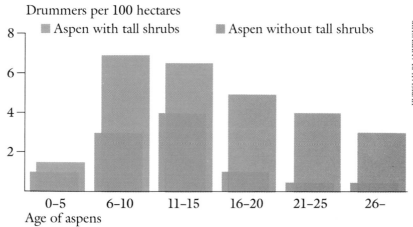

8
6
4
2

0–5   6–10   11–15   16–20   21–25   26–
Age of aspens

KUBISIAK-BLANKENSHIP

The importance of tall shrubs: whether overall populations are high or low (top), and whatever the age of the aspens (bottom), drummers seek activity centers with protective understories of alder and other shrubs, according to Wisconsin studies.

Managing the woods for the birds' sake

For maintaining a ruffed grouse population, it matters little how many birds occupy a certain covert in the fall and winter. With the exception of certain hens, who may travel 500 meters or farther in search of a mate or a nesting site, most ruffed grouse do not move far, if at all, from their winter coverts. If they fail to survive the winter, then, that covert is inadequate.

The best way to measure the overwintering capacity of a covert is to determine the number of drumming males in the spring. Although ruffed grouse are promiscuous, the usual spring sex ratio is nearly one to one; thus a drumming male may represent a breeding pair.

Density is determined, in part, by the individual's need for space, and for ruffed grouse males the minimum space requirement appears to be about 3 hectares (33 males per 100 hectares). That is, a male ruffed grouse will not tolerate another male within about 140 meters. This upper limit assumes a prime habitat, with abundant food and cover. Few extensive forest tracts are of prime quality, however, and a density of one drummer for every 4 to 5 hectares (20 to 25 males per 100 hectares) seems to be a more achievable goal. A spring population of this density should produce about one grouse per hectare in the fall.

Good habitats support densities better than one breeding male per 8 hectares (12.5

The number of drummers per given area in spring is the best measure of habitat quality: that a bird survived the winter testifies to the beneficial food and cover of the activity center he claimed the previous autumn.

Left: *A safe drumming log, or a trap that lures the unwary bird only to expose him to fatal risks? By late spring the answer will be known. Right: Small clumps of conifers have often been thought to enhance the quality of winter grouse habitat, but their value is closely related to the food and cover plants around them.*

per 100 hectares); densities that remain consistently lower reflect a deficiency in the habitat; anything less than a bird per 20 hectares (5 per 100 hectares) is poor or marginal for this species.

But generally the condition of ruffed grouse habitats is so poor across most of the birds' range that breeding populations seldom approach even the low density of 1 bird per 20 hectares. In most areas where population densities have been determined recently, grouse numbers tend to be one-fifth to one-tenth the density common in good habitats. But densities higher than 12.5 males per 100 hectares have been recorded in recent years on managed areas in Michigan, Minnesota, and Wisconsin.

Determining a valid density for ruffed grouse is not a simple matter. An extensive forest tract, for example, may have scattered pockets or narrow edges of grouse coverts in a primarily hostile environment. A determination of density should therefore be based only on the acceptable habitat and should exclude the inhospitable area.

In one Minnesota forest, for example, there are three pockets, each 3 to 4 hectares in size, widely dispersed in a 280-hectare, predominately pine forest. These small pockets are occupied by breeding grouse year after year (although one was vacant in eight years between 1958 and 1986), but the surrounding habitat is not a place for ruffed grouse to venture. If the whole forest is considered, the breeding density is 1.1 pairs per

100 hectares—clearly unacceptable—but if only the actual area of grouse habitat counts, the density approaches a respectable 20 pairs per 100 hectares.

Similarly, in western mountainous regions, ruffed grouse cover often consists of narrow stringers of suitable habitat along streams. These stringers may be no more than a few hundred meters wide but many kilometers long. It is inappropriate to include the intervening ridges when calculating grouse densities. The same is true in Appalachian forests, where ruffed grouse habitat is sometimes limited to small pockets of moist cove forests or areas along narrow valleys.

GOOD COVERTS, BAD COVERTS

Two questions help sort the adequate coverts from the inadequate: How often is a particular activity center occupied? And what is the longevity of the birds selecting that center? Some good centers in Minnesota, for example, have been used almost continually for at least a quarter of a century, and most of the occupants have survived at least two winters and breeding seasons.

But repeated or frequent occupancy is not always a good indication that a particular covert is a secure one. Some activity centers act as ecological traps, attracting birds with superior cover and abundant food, but having some flaw—scattered pine trees, say, or a stretch of clover at the forest edge—that dooms every occupant to a short life. One seemingly good activity center in Minnesota

MARTINSON

The brood is just about to leave the nest. Efforts in Pennsylvania to improve the cover for hens and chicks failed to increase the overall number of ruffed grouse: it is winter cover, not brood habitat, that ultimately determines population density.

attracted a succession of grouse from at least 1957 to 1972, but among the eleven birds using that center, only two survived to drum for a second season.

Nor does long survival of individual birds necessarily indicate that a site is a good place for ruffed grouse. There have been several activity centers in Minnesota that were used by single birds for four to six years, but once they died, they were not replaced. The longevity of those birds appeared to result from their being in such unlikely habitat that predators didn't bother to look for them.

How grouse respond

Although a considerable amount of habitat has been managed for ruffed grouse across the continent, only a few studies have attempted to document the birds' responses.

The New York study. One of the earliest efforts to improve grouse habitats and stabilize or increase their numbers was the New York study in the Adirondacks and Catskill Mountains from 1930 to 1942. This has long been the classic reference for ruffed grouse managers.

Gardiner Bump and his coworkers recognized the need for a diversity of habitats to meet the varying seasonal needs of these birds. In his twenty-year study of the 970-hectare Connecticut Hill area in New York, from 1927 to 1948, Bump observed abandoned farmland being invaded by woody vegetation. Even though most of the invading plants were aspen, alder, and other

hardwoods, the number of ruffed grouse decreased because habitat diversity disappeared. Working in maturing hardwood forests, Bump and his colleagues realized that blocks of early successional stages needed to be interspersed in the old forest. They therefore recommended devoting "25 to 30 percent of the covert to fully meeting grouse needs and the rest to producing other forest crops on a self-sustaining basis."

Because they had observed grouse making use of cover in hemlocks, spruces, firs, and pines in winter, they believed it imperative to have conifers scattered through the hardwoods. This has sometimes been a reason for widespread establishment of conifer plantations on wildlife areas and is still often included in prescriptions for grouse management.

Although some habitat management efforts were initiated as a part of this study, no evaluations have ever been published. However, the general concepts developed by the New York study remain valid, and current management largely represents a refinement of the ideas developed by Bump and his contemporaries during the 1930s.

Pennsylvania brood habitat work. Believing that a lack of suitable brood habitat was limiting ruffed grouse numbers in central Pennsylvania, Ward Sharp conducted an experimental cutting program. A total of 131 openings of 0.1 to 0.4 hectare were cut in a pole-timber hardwood forest, at a rate of 12 to 18 per year, from 1950 to 1957. The treated area was host to more grouse broods the year after the cutting began, and by 1955 there were twenty-one broods on the 297-hectare area—seven times the number in a similar but untreated forest nearby. But after seven to eight years the sapling canopy closed over, and the cuttings lost their value as brood habitat.

In conversations with Gullion in 1969, Sharp recognized the shortcoming of concentrating on brood cover. His brood management effort had provided for the needs of chicks and improved their survival rate, but it had not resulted in a higher ruffed grouse population because it had not changed the quality of winter habitat. The increased number of young birds had evidently dispersed into inadequate winter cover and been lost.

Seeding of trails and openings. Ruffed grouse feed heavily on clover, especially Dutch white clover, when it is available: grouse are commonly observed feeding on

Ruffed grouse are often observed feeding on clover along roads and trails, but encouraging them by seeding such places with their favorite foods may only expose them to predation, human and otherwise.

clover in the fall, and the crops of birds bagged by hunters are often packed with clover leaves. There has therefore been longstanding interest in seeding forest roads and openings to clover.

Although Wilder's and other studies have demonstrated increased grouse use of trails where clover was established, Gullion has not seen any studies that show a benefit to ruffed grouse. The demonstrated benefits have been to hunters and predators taking advantage of grouse feeding on this abundant supply of succulent greens. There are even some studies that have shown marked declines in grouse populations, declines that could, at least in part, be attributed to the practice of seeding clover.

RECENT MANAGEMENT STUDIES

Most studies of habitat use have dealt with how the birds fared in relatively stable forest situations, good or poor. These provided insight concerning what types of habitats ruffed grouse preferred among those available, but such studies seldom indicated what constitutes good habitat.

It has only been in the past twenty years that concerted, long-term studies have followed the response of ruffed grouse to habitat management that was either purposely or accidentally for their benefit. These studies began by monitoring the distribution and abundance of ruffed grouse in relatively stable, usually fairly mature forests. Then the response of grouse was followed as those forests were disturbed by logging or fire and as secondary forest succession developed.

To follow this sequence and document the changes, such an investigation must last at least fifteen to twenty years after forest disturbance. Add a three- or four-year predisturbance monitoring period, and a one- or two-year period during which the disturbance occurs, and the job of evaluating the impact of habitat change on a ruffed grouse population needs a quarter-century. Yet most efforts at habitat evaluation have lasted only two or three years.

The major difference between the earlier management prescriptions and those in vogue in the 1980s was the emphasis on aspen. Although aspen was identified as being especially attractive to ruffed grouse by the New York researchers, as well as by Fisher and by J. Bailey, it was not then singled out as the key species to be managed for their benefit. Identification of aspen's unique role in the life history of the species, across the greater portion of its range, has provided more direction to recent management programs.

Moreover, prolonged and intensive research has raised questions about the value of conifers as cover in ruffed grouse habitat. Young conifers and scattered clumps of older spruces, firs, or hemlocks do provide winter cover for these birds, but this cover may not be essential to their long-term welfare. Kubisiak in Wisconsin and current Minnesota research support the earlier New York findings of Bump and of J. Bailey, that if hardwood

Far left: *A commercial timber sale created this clear-cut.* Left: *By the end of the first growing season, aspens and various other woody and herbaceous plants are prospering. Within a decade, such land will support ruffed grouse at high densities.*

trees, especially aspen, are well distributed through young conifer stands, ruffed grouse can survive reasonably well at favorable densities.

But there is also considerable evidence that ruffed grouse live in higher densities in habitats subject to severe winter conditions despite the absence of coniferous cover. Conifer plantations that provide habitat for a decade or two eventually provide more security for grouse predators than for grouse. This results in increased ruffed grouse mortality and depressed populations for the next sixty to eighty years, until the trees are harvested and replanted, according to Gullion and Alm.

Several long-term projects jointly sponsored by the Ruffed Grouse Society and other agencies are currently under way in Vermont, New York, Pennsylvania, Michigan, Tennessee, Missouri, and Minnesota. In addition, Michigan, North Dakota, Pennsylvania, and Wisconsin wildlife management agencies have been monitoring habitat manipulation efforts since the late 1960s or mid-1970s. Several other states have initiated studies more recently.

There have been significant increases in ruffed grouse populations in response to forest disturbance on the older state-supported projects, one in the Gladwin Refuge in Michigan, and the Sandhill Wildlife Management Area in Wisconsin.

Michigan. The tree-cutting program on the Gladwin Refuge in Michigan began in 1962 and is scheduled to continue through 2050. Commercial harvesting proceeds at five-year intervals in 4-hectare strips (100 by 400 meters).

According to unpublished data provided by Prawdzik in 1986, there has been consistent, positive response by ruffed grouse to this treatment. Generally, grouse began using well-stocked aspen regeneration as breeding cover about five to six years after clear-cutting and reached peak densities of a drummer per 3 to 4 hectares (25 to 33 males per 100 hectares) three or four years later. The habitats were essentially devoid of conifers, which shows that these grouse did well wintering in areas lacking evergreen cover. At ten years, use of these habitats tapered off rapidly, and most were vacant when the aspens were seventeen to twenty years old.

Michigan has also evaluated the results of an experimental white-tailed deer management program on the Lower Peninsula. This involved clear-cutting 25 percent, 50 percent, and 75 percent of intolerant forest stands—mostly aspen and other plants that do not grow well in the shade of other vegetation—on six areas totaling 140 square kilometers between 1971 and 1975. By 1980 ruffed grouse had not shown much response to this program, but both deer and woodcock had responded. Woodcock responded best to the more extensive, 75 percent cutting, and deer to the 25 and 50 percent cutting, according to Bennett and his coworkers.

Wisconsin. The long-term study on the Sandhill Wildlife Area in central Wisconsin has also shown a significant, positive response to habitat management, especially where aspen regrowth has been encouraged. When Kubisiak began his study in 1968, breeding grouse numbers were nearly equal (7.2 males per 100 hectares) on both the area to be treated and an unmanaged control area nearby; both were 404 hectares. One area was then subjected to commercial clear-cut logging and shearing by chainsaws and by

A Wisconsin ruffed grouse is beautifully concealed in the hazel understory. Cover like this helps the birds survive to breeding age.

bulldozers equipped with cutting blades. Cuttings averaged 5.7 hectares and consisted of blocks or strips.

An increase in ruffed grouse numbers became evident about six years after this program commenced, and in stands of aspen that were six to ten years old, breeding populations reached densities approaching 18 drummers per 100 hectares. But population densities declined steadily thereafter, to only 8.9 males per 100 hectares in stands older than twenty-five years. There is very little coniferous cover in the Sandhill coverts, which indicates that as long as the aspens were suitable, these grouse survived very well in cold climates without high-risk evergreen cover.

In contrast to Sharp's experience in Pennsylvania, where the sapling canopy closed and broods abandoned the sites after seven or eight years, Kubisiak found that grouse broods were still making extensive use of the aspens fifteen years after the cutting. So where aspen management is involved, not only do densities of breeding ruffed grouse increase markedly for a decade or longer, but good brood habitat lasts at least that long.

Pennsylvania. An intensive study of the effect of a checkerboard pattern of small clear-cuts has been under way for about a decade on the Barrens area in central Pennsylvania. Based on a design developed in Minnesota by Gullion, this program involves clear-cutting 1-hectare blocks at four-year intervals in a four-stage rotation.

After eleven years, the number of breeding male grouse had increased more than 3.6-fold in treated areas, compared with only a 2.9-fold increase in a similarly sized untreated area. On the 550-hectare treated area, the numbers of breeding males increased from 9 (1.6 per 100 hectares) in 1976 to 33 (6 per 100 hectares) by 1986. There was also a marked shift in habitat use: the proportion of drumming males using cut-over sites rose from 5 percent in 1981 to more than 80 percent in 1986. There has also been a significant, positive response by nongame wildlife, according to Yahner.

North Dakota. The state began a management program in aspen forests in the Turtle Mountains in 1976, bulldozing 107 parcels totaling about 122 hectares by 1983. Schulz's design consisted of a series of 1-hectare clearings in a ten-year rotation. By 1982 the stands had not developed sufficiently to be considered prime habitat, but numbers of breeding grouse were increasing on the treated area. The major response is expected in the next few years.

Grafton, Vermont. A privately funded study of grouse response to habitat disturbance has begun to produce positive results in this southern Green Mountains setting. When the study at Grafton began in 1974–1975, only 15 breeding males were found on the 1,400-hectare area (1.07 per 100 hectares). Then, in 1976–1977, sixteen small sites were clear-cut. By 1987 the number of breeding males had nearly doubled, to 29 (2.07 per 100 hectares); 21 drummers were using sites not occupied in 1982 or earlier.

Cloquet, Minnesota. The longest tracking of ruffed grouse response to habitat change involves the Cloquet Forestry Center, a 1,362-hectare University of Minnesota forest research facility in northeastern Minnesota. This long-term study has recorded both marked decreases and increases in ruffed grouse numbers as changes occurred in available habitats.

Studies of ruffed grouse at Cloquet began with Ralph King's work from 1927 to 1936. After the early studies, grouse work consisted mostly of annual inventories using the strip-census method developed at Cloquet by King. In 1956, however, a more intensive study resumed.

In the 1930s the Cloquet Forest was still in the early stages of succession, recovering from the extensive logging under way when the area was acquired by the university in 1908–1909. Ruffed grouse were abundant. In 1933 King found at least 135 drumming males in the forest, at a density of 15 per 100 hectares. The spring population in 1933 was placed at about 535 birds (41.3 per 100 hectares), based on King's strip censuses (this is revised from a 61.8 per 100 hectares figure used earlier by Marshall and Gullion).

Two factors probably contributed to this high grouse population in the early 1930s. Most important was certainly the vast extent of young aspen forests on the surrounding 215,000 hectares scorched by the Cloquet fire of October 1918. What we now recognize as optimum, fourteen-year-old aspens dominated the wooded lands for many kilometers in all directions.

But also important was the extent of young growth on the Cloquet Forest. Because an active tree-planting program had been under way in the 1920s, there were not only extensive young aspen stands in the surrounding region but also many hectares of ten- to twelve-year-old conifer plantations in the forest. Together, these created a perfect habitat for ruffed grouse.

Wallace Grange was also at Cloquet for a short time in the early 1930s, trapping snowshoe hares to transplant to eastern states. Seeing the high snowshoe hare and grouse populations in young forests recover-

ing from the recent, widespread conflagration probably influenced his later writing, in which he recognized the importance of fire as an agent for creating and maintaining wildlife habitat.

In the next decade, however, the quality of habitat in the Cloquet Forest began to diminish. Normal successional development of the aspen stands reduced their value as grouse cover. At the same time the growth of the pine plantations changed what had been cover for grouse into cover for hawks and owls as the trees grew taller and lost their lower branches. As a consequence, ruffed grouse became increasingly scarce in the Cloquet Forest, even though it had been a game refuge since 1924. Peak spring populations were about nineteen birds per 100 hectares in 1942, and thirty per 100 hectares in 1950. But in 1946 ruffed grouse were so scarce that a density estimate was not even made.

Before intensive study resumed in 1956, logging had increased in the Cloquet Forest, with much of the cutting done in the maturing aspen and mixed aspen–jack pine stands. This logging continued through 1963, and much of the logged area regenerated to aspen.

In the late 1950s and early 1960s breeding ruffed grouse were widely scattered in the forest, mostly near lowland edges. In 1961, despite the considerable logging of the several preceding years, there was little evidence that ruffed grouse were benefiting from this disturbance. In fact, the initial response appeared to be negative, with forestwide grouse numbers declining by 1964 to a very low level (from 5.9 to 2.1 males per 100 hectares).

On one 266-hectare tract where 72 hectares had been logged from 1951 to 1963, the drumming male population declined from 22 in 1960 to only 5 in 1964. About 96 hectares of this area is uninhabitable muskeg and alder–black spruce–tamarack bog; the grouse density on the remaining land had thus declined from 12.9 males per 100 hectares—a fair density—to a marginal 2.9 per 100 hectares in those four seasons.

A marked turnaround in grouse population trends occurred in the late 1960s and early 1970s, and the 1972 numbers were sec-

The vast forest fire of October 1918 scorched many square miles of Minnesota's Cloquet Forest. By the early 1930s natural forest succession had created the perfect ruffed grouse habitat.

Freshly cut: a stand of aspens on the Sandhill Wildlife Area in central Wisconsin has been leveled by loggers.

Three years: looking like corn in a field, the aspen seedlings are uniformly dense, uniformly tall.

Four years: despite rapid growth, the aspens are still too young to provide year-round cover. Drummers and broods, however, may occupy the edges if suitable habitat is nearby.

Eight years: the saplings are closely spaced, providing excellent habitat for both drummers and hens. Because of natural thinning and tree mortality, the canopy admits sufficient light to encourage plants on the forest floor.

Eleven years: superb vertical cover forms a protective shield for grouse as they proceed through the pattern of their lives.

ond only to those of the early 1930s. In the stands of eight- to twelve-year-old aspens, ruffed grouse densities were as high as King recorded in 1933, but since only a relatively small portion of the Cloquet Forest had that quality of habitat, gross densities (at 9.6 males per 100 hectares) were still lower than in 1933. In 1970, 40 percent of the breeding grouse were concentrated in young aspen stands on 12 percent of the 1,362-hectare Cloquet Forest, at densities of 22 males per 100 hectares.

One interesting aspect of this response was an apparent change in the type of cover that ruffed grouse found acceptable. From 1969 to 1972 a number of young males could not find satisfactory sites for drumming in the regenerating forest and chose to wait for the opportunity to replace other drummers established in the new coverts. In 1972 Gullion estimated that one male was patiently "waiting in the wings" for every 2.3 birds established on drumming logs.

These young males evidently remained in or near these prime, new coverts, preferring to wait their turn rather than use any of a dozen or so older, vacant places that had been acceptable to their predecessors a decade earlier. In this young aspen cover the grouse were able to maintain high densities (29 males per 100 hectares) while numbers elsewhere in the Cloquet Forest and throughout the region dropped sharply (to 3.5 males per 100 hectares) in the cyclic decline of the mid-1970s.

In 1978 goshawks returned as nesting residents to the Cloquet Forest, after a ten-year absence, and quickly reduced the numbers of grouse in coniferous cover from 5.8 males per 100 hectares in 1978 to 1.9 per 100 hectares by 1980. But Gullion and Alm found that the goshawks had little impact on ruffed grouse living nearby in aspen cover.

By the mid-1980s, however, the successional development that had followed the 1933 high was being repeated. In addition, logging destroyed thirty-eight perennial activity centers. As a result, ruffed grouse numbers at Cloquet declined to the lowest densities recorded since the mid-1960s. Some birds were finding the old habitats to be the best coverts available and began using activity centers that had been vacant for two decades, even though these areas of the forest had changed since the 1960s.

Mille Lacs, Minnesota. A somewhat similar story has unfolded as the result of experimental habitat management for ruffed grouse in the Mille Lacs Wildlife Management Area. This is a state Department of Natural Resources' public hunting area in central Minnesota, about 115 kilometers southwest of Cloquet and 100 kilometers north of Minneapolis.

Intensive monitoring of the breeding ruffed grouse population began in 1966 on two areas, one 561 hectares and the other 582 hectares. Densities increased from 4.4 to 7 drumming males per 100 hectares from 1966 to 1968. This was a period of cyclic upswing throughout the region, and the increase in numbers was independent of management efforts. Most of the occupied activity centers were on south-facing aspects in this maturing forest. Only there could sunlight reach under the forest canopy and encourage a dense growth of shrub vegetation. These occupied habitats were often the alder-aspen cover found by Kubisiak to be so heavily used in Wisconsin. Elsewhere this hardwood forest was comparatively open and parklike, and a poor place for a grouse.

In 1968 the first clear-cuts were made as the initial part of a long-term program. These first cuts varied from 0.2 to 0.4 hectare in size. By 1972, 10 percent of the breeding males were in these five-year-old blocks. The grouse population had increased from a density of 4.4 males per 100 hectares to 11.6. This was a significantly better increase than was recorded on the similar, unaltered control area 8 kilometers distant.

In addition to the seventy-four small blocks cut from 1968 to 1973, five areas totaling 84.6 hectares were burned in 1968 and 1970. The low-intensity fire had little impact on the mature forest vegetation. Although aspen and various desirable shrubs sprang up, shade under the unbroken forest canopy discouraged sprout growth, and after four to five years this flush of vegetation had died, leaving most of the forest altered little.

On one 20-hectare sector of younger forest the fire did change the vegetation, and some very good grouse cover developed. From 1971 to 1982 this sector supported two or

Eleven years: aspens of this age also provide some food during the snow-free months.

Thirteen years: the density of trees is just beginning to thin, but ruffed grouse can still find adequate cover.

Eighteen years: the trees, now larger, are starting to crowd each other and compete for sunlight. Vertical cover is growing sparse, and suitability as year-round habitat is declining.

Twenty-seven years: these mature aspens are now excellent sources of food, but as cover they provide little protection from raptors and other predators.

Forty years: the parklike floor under the canopy is too open for the preferences of the ruffed grouse, but such habitats may be attractive for feeding, nesting, loafing, and other activities.

three drumming males annually. But by 1983 postfire succession had reached a stage that was no longer acceptable to ruffed grouse, and it has supported no breeding birds since.

The best response was to the 0.4-hectare dispersed, clear-cut blocks. By 1977, 65 percent of the breeding grouse in Mille Lacs were in these habitats, at a density of one male per hectare cut.

The early positive response by grouse to the small clear-cuts encouraged a more ambitious program. In 1974 there began a clear-cutting program to create forty-six interspersed 4-hectare strips, cut in four stages, at ten-year intervals. This expanded program also included treating 281 hectares in sixty-two blocks of 4 to 16 hectares on the control area. Later the cutting interval was shortened to six years.

By 1978 the first cutting rotation was complete, and the earliest cut blocks were already providing new coverts for ruffed grouse, and many other species of birds as well. On the area treated first, all the breeding grouse were in regenerated coverts by 1981, and on the treated portion of the former control area, this landmark was reached in 1985, eight years after clear-cutting had begun.

The lowland alder-aspen edges so heavily used before better habitat was created on drier, upland sites were completely abandoned by breeding grouse. Although those sites remained much the same as they were when used perennially before the clear-cutting of nearby areas, grouse ignored them.

A 162-hectare unaltered, old-forest control area that supported twelve to thirteen drumming males in 1971 and 1972, and eleven as recently as 1980, was without breeding grouse by 1985.

This consistent shift to the cutover habitats is interpreted as showing that the breeding males preferred the denser cover in the solid blocks of young aspen regeneration to the aspen-alder edges of the older forest. Hence the coverts that were most popular when this project began proved second-rate when higher-quality aspen sapling coverts developed a few years after clear-cut logging.

As at Cloquet, the transitory nature of good grouse habitat has been, or at least seems to have been, demonstrated at Mille Lacs as well—only faster. At Cloquet, developing aspen stands usually begin to be used as drumming activity centers when they are eight to twelve years old and continue to be heavily used for about fifteen years. Grouse prefer not to use the stands until the aspens, which may initially produce more than 100,000 suckers per hectare, have thinned to a density of about 17,000 stems per hectare. Use of the stand persists until continued natural thinning of the stand reduces stem density below about 7,400 stems per hectare. At Cloquet the first stage is reached eight to twelve years after an aspen stand has been clear-cut; the stand ceases to be attractive to grouse about fifteen years later.

In the warmer, better growing conditions at Mille Lacs, aspen coverts thin to acceptable levels in five or six years but continue to thin at a faster rate and lose their value as grouse cover about ten years later. As a consequence, all the 0.4-hectare blocks so popular with grouse from 1972 to 1979 were vacant by 1984.

But does it follow that good grouse habitats are transitory by nature? Perhaps not—since other factors may be at work. Exceptionally heavy hunting pressure on the Mille Lacs area has depressed breeding grouse numbers well below carrying capacity, and it is probable that if there had been fewer successful hunters, many of the coverts vacant for the past several years would have been occupied. The total absence of breeding grouse after 1984 from the control area, where there used to be seven to thirteen birds year after year, suggests the severity of this impact.

LONG-TERM TENANCY

Various factors can influence how long before grouse use the rejuvenating cover, and how long the early successional stage remains useful. Grouse respond most rapidly in stands where aspen grow most rapidly, putting forth a dense cover of sprouts and attaining height quickly. But these same stands are likely to be abandoned the soonest, as seen in the Gladwin Refuge in Michigan and some Cloquet and Mille Lacs sites in Minnesota. If the aspen growth is thinner and if other species, especially alder and hazel, are able to persist, grouse may take

Both the drumming log and the nesting site, flagged by a researcher's clipboard, are in this stand of aspen and alder. As grouse coverts, such mixed sites provide long-term, high-quality habitat.

longer to begin using those coverts, but use persists longer than in the purer aspen stands.

This appears to be the case on the Sandhill Area in Wisconsin, where Gullion found aspen sapling stands to be less dense than on the better Minnesota sites and on the Gladwin Refuge. Here, more grouse took up residence in the aspen-alder coverts (11.2 males per 100 hectares) than in pure aspen (4.4 per 100 hectares). Although they did not attract as many grouse as the essentially pure aspen sapling coverts in Michigan (25 to 33 per 100 hectares) and Minnesota (22 to 29 per 100 hectares), the mixed Wisconsin coverts played host to grouse several years longer.

As a covert for ruffed grouse, aspen mixed with other trees and shrubs seems to last longer than the usual ten to fifteen years, at least in Minnesota. This is especially true where hazel has been able to grow more thickly as the aspen thinned. Two Cloquet sites where this has happened were occupied well beyond the usual time-frame. One covert came into use in 1961, seven years after an aspen clear-cut, and in 1987 it was being used by its tenth consecutive drummer. Another center logged in 1961–1962 was vacant only one year before being reoccupied— probably because the hazel had not been severely disturbed by the logging—and in 1987 it had its twelfth consecutive occupant.

The hardwood forest on two areas totaling 40 hectares at Mille Lacs was knocked down by a bulldozer in the summer of 1970. Grouse were much slower finding satisfactory cover in these two areas, but sixteen years later these areas were receiving heavier use each season. Here the aspen regeneration was suppressed: it was bulldozed early in the summer, when a tree's food reserves in the root system are at a minimum. This allowed other hardwoods to be more successful in the recovering forest, increasing stem densities and prolonging the sites' attraction to ruffed grouse.

EXPRESSING THEMSELVES

Ruffed grouse that don't like the neighborhood will simply not live there. But even occupied habitats vary in how well they address a grouse's daily and seasonal needs, primarily secure cover and an easily accessible and ample supply of nutritious food.

Even before a newly created covert offers winter-long security, inquisitive grouse may "try it on for size." Grouse, presumably young birds, move into such coverts in the fall and may remain there well into the winter before dying or moving on. This scenario may be repeated several seasons before a bird finally survives the winter to breed there. Then a succession of grouse may use the site for a decade or longer before the cover thins below acceptable levels. At Cloquet one newly created site was used, in succession, by eleven grouse that survived only one or two winters; it was then abandoned. Another Cloquet site was host to six birds, each of which survived two or more winters.

In the best coverts, the drummer finds all his daily needs within a small home range. He usually uses one log, rock, or other stage that is clearly his preferred drumming site, although he may also make light use of two or three alternate sites. Remaining in the vicinity of his log and activity center throughout the year, he has an advantage: the less he wanders, the less chance he has of encountering a predator. In short, he is more likely to be a long-lived grouse.

But as the habitat begins to deteriorate and fails to provide adequately for the daily and seasonal needs, the resident bird begins to behave differently. He is forced to become more mobile and to increase the number of alternate sites, as well as his use of them. The amount of time he spends on his drumming log, as measured by the number of droppings, decreases. In secure Minnesota habitats the count often exceeds four hundred and sometimes a thousand droppings per season. But in insecure situations, the count may vary from less than a dozen to perhaps one hundred or so droppings. These counts do not necessarily correlate with the amount of drumming a bird does, but they do reflect the amount of time he spends on his drumming stage.

Besides becoming more mobile, the bird in poor habitat shows increasing uneasiness. Unlike his counterparts in secure sites, who are usually easily trapped for banding, he becomes increasingly difficult to capture. Re-

searchers have found that it often proves impossible to capture male grouse in poor habitats, whereas grouse in nearby premium habitats are taken the first or second time a trap is presented to them.

A bird in a deteriorating covert has two choices: either make the best of the situation and risk an early death, or move to a better site. The bird that makes the first choice seldom lives to breed a second season, but the one that moves usually adds at least another year to his life.

Nevertheless, grouse seldom abandon long-used perennial centers; a covert that has "gone by" becomes vacant only with the death of the occupant. The next bird to pass through the center, however, evidently does not recognize it as a place to stay. He moves on in search of something that better fits his perception of secure grouse habitat, and the old center remains vacant.

Where even the best grouse habitat available provides only marginal food and shelter, activity centers that would otherwise not be occupied will be used, perhaps persistently. In the late 1950s and early 1960s, before the extensive aspen regeneration became available at Cloquet, a number of activity centers in what is now considered marginal or submarginal habitat were used on a perennial basis. When better habitat became available, those same marginal centers were not used, even though the grouse population had nearly doubled, and several males, unable to occupy the better coverts, chose to wait a year or two rather than use the less desirable sites.

At Mille Lacs the long-used, perennial centers were completely abandoned in favor of the new coverts produced by clear-cutting, even though the habitat in the undisturbed forest had not changed.

THE ASPEN CONNECTION

Management of forests can affect ruffed grouse populations wherever aspens are an important part of the vegetation—and this includes 92 percent of the native range of ruffed grouse, and probably more than 95 percent of the ruffed grouse population.

Ruffed grouse probably evolved to fill the niche provided by aspen forests. That is, they take advantage of the ecological succes-

A small number of droppings betrays the insecurity of a drummer who moves from one log to another because his habitat is inadequate. The abundance of droppings on the log below, by contrast, indicates secure cover.

MAXSON

DIMENSIONS OF TIME AND SPACE

Effective habitat management for ruffed grouse can be accomplished as long as certain limitations are kept in mind. Because of their territorial behavior, there will be little impact on their numbers if management is limited to small areas. No matter how much work is done in a 3- or 4-hectare (10-acre) woodlot, only one pair of grouse will probably benefit, and the fall population will not exceed four or five birds. To support four pairs, or twenty-four to twenty-six grouse in the fall, there must be effective, dispersed disturbance on 16 hectares (40 acres). To support forty pairs and a larger huntable population, a portion of each 3- to 4-hectare area within 160 hectares has to be disturbed on a rotational basis.

To make significant changes in ruffed grouse abundance, then, fairly extensive tracts of woodland have to be altered. Recall that the 1918 Cloquet wildfire's significant boost to the numbers of ruffed grouse in the early 1930s involved the devastation of 215,000 hectares, and altogether more than 518,000 hectares burned in Minnesota that fall.

This brings us to another problem. The delay between the logging or fire that initiates forest succession and the increase in ruffed grouse is often disappointing to impatient landowners. The very regions where aspen predominates—and where grouse habitat management is most likely to be highly productive—have relatively short growing seasons and often less fertile soils. Under these constraints, it usually takes at least eight years, and more often ten to twelve years, before successional growth is inviting to ruffed grouse. For the eager landowner who wants more grouse to hunt, and has a fine new dog to help him, that is a long time to wait.

Commercial clear-cutting for pulpwood or other forest products may not create the most productive ruffed grouse coverts, but it is cost-effective. The increased demand for fuelwood, however, often justifies the more beneficial small clear-cuts, which would be uneconomical for a commercial logger.

Ruffed grouse make little use of regeneration in blocks less than 0.4 hectare, but benefits diminish as clear-cuts exceed 1 hec-

The burning and logging of forest tracts are beneficial to grouse only if large areas are treated, and even then, only after a decade of regeneration.

sion that follows the frequent catastrophic fires in northern forests. This is the disturbance that best maintains the aspen ecosystem, and it is the reason why the aspen is the most widespread tree on the North American continent.

Ruffed grouse are not a very adaptable species, but to some degree they have extended their range beyond the aspen forest to areas that offer a type of forest growth structurally like that in aspen sapling stands. There, in spots, ruffed grouse numbers may reach densities common in the northern aspen forests, but areawide densities are usually only a fraction of the numbers common in the periodically disturbed aspen forests of the North.

Ruffed grouse can be scarce in northern forests, too, especially where protection from fire or other disturbance has allowed conifers and long-lived, shade-tolerant hardwoods to crowd out the aspens. The Boundary Waters Wilderness Area in northern Minnesota is a prime example of an extensive conifer forest that provides minimal habitat for ruffed grouse. Many eastern hardwood forests, from Pennsylvania north through New England, likewise now provide little that ruffed grouse can use.

tare. In the larger clear-cuts, the distance from acceptable cover to essential food resources becomes excessive, and good cover goes unused.

Properly spaced, 1-hectare clear-cuts per 4-hectare area in forests containing aspen are the ideal. A 4-hectare clear-cut strip every 16 hectares should produce about 75 percent as many grouse, and a 4-hectare block every 16 hectares supports about 60 percent as many. When the clear-cut blocks reach 8 hectares, the number of grouse benefitting drops to 50 percent, and treatments 16 hectares in extent benefit only about 30 percent as many grouse.

The key to developing better habitats for ruffed grouse is providing the proper interspersion of forest age-classes. This means creating or maintaining situations where stands of young trees adjoin older forests: the high-quality young cover is used by breeding grouse and broods in spring and summer, and by juveniles and adults in fall and winter; the more open sites of the mature stands are preferred by nesting hens; and the flower buds of older trees are a prime food resource in winter. In the ideal world, top-quality cover is no more than 100 meters from nesting habitat and an adequate winter-long food supply.

If appreciable changes are to be made in area- or region-wide ruffed grouse numbers, extensive forest tracts need to be managed. This can be particularly difficult in eastern forests, where most of the land consists of small, privately owned parcels. The best opportunities for effective management of ruffed grouse are on county, state, and federal forest lands, or those of sympathetic industries, such as forestry.

Generally, however, the forest industry has not been particularly receptive to the management most productive for ruffed grouse. Aspen ranks low among the trees industrial foresters find profitable to grow: it is usually considered a "weed" tree, and more effort has gone into eradicating or controlling aspen than into encouraging it. Conversely, nearly all trees that have high commercial value are of little or no value to ruffed grouse. Fortunately, in some Lake States forests, aspen has become a favored species because of recent advances in wood technology

(for example, the development of the oriented-strand board).

Federal and state forests, and some county forests, have multiple-use mandates that justify less financially rewarding management. It is in these forests that management for ruffed grouse and other wildlife associated with the aspen ecosystem is most likely to occur.

PUTTING THEORY INTO PRACTICE

Although the general concepts of ruffed grouse management were spelled out by Gardiner Bump and his associates nearly forty years ago, there has been little concerted effort to apply them until recently. In 1965 a questionnaire was distributed to fifty-two wildlife research and management organizations, asking for evidence of beneficial response by ruffed grouse to management. None of the twenty-four respondents could cite such evidence, although several were convinced it had occurred. Given the lack of evidence, others questioned whether current management practices were beneficial.

In 1967 another questionnaire was sent to fifty individuals and agencies in the United States and Canada concerned with ruffed grouse management, asking about the status of habitat management projects. Only Minnesota, New York, Ontario, Pennsylvania, and Tennessee reported being engaged in programs they hoped would be beneficial to these birds. Most of their efforts involved general improvement of the forest habitat for wildlife by clearing openings, seeding trails and roadways, and planting fruit-producing shrubs.

A third questionnaire distributed in 1973 to twenty-seven agencies asked, "How many active projects involving habitat management for ruffed grouse do you have?" Six states (Connecticut, Michigan, Minnesota, Virginia, West Virginia, and Wisconsin) gave a positive response, listing projects ranging from a single 200-hectare project in Virginia to treatments on about 5,300 hectares in Wisconsin. Ten others said they were working with other agencies, such as state forestry departments or national forests, to improve habitat for ruffed grouse and other species associated with young forests.

Top: *The interspersion of aspens (the light-colored areas) and oaks (the dark) offers grouse the mixture necessary to carry out their life cycle, from secure activity centers to good nesting and brood habitat. Below: A three-acre site has been clear-cut and bull-dozed to encourage aspen regrowth.*

KUBISIAK

KUBISIAK

On the edge of an aspen clear-cut, a ruffed grouse takes advantage of the thick seedlings.

An increased level of activity was revealed by response to a questionnaire circulated in 1985 to forty-seven American and Canadian agencies. Nineteen agencies reported habitat management programs specifically designed to benefit ruffed grouse. These ranged from small, demonstration areas a few hectares in size in some of the New England states to operations involving thousands of hectares in the Lake States. Another fourteen states and provinces not directly managing habitat for ruffed grouse were engaged in other efforts felt to be beneficial to these birds, such as timber-harvesting programs that incorporated wildlife habitat enhancement, administered by state forestry departments. Other programs were sponsored by university extension services or the Ruffed Grouse Society.

Of great potential benefit to ruffed grouse and other wildlife is the recently revised forest management plan by the U.S. Forest Service for the 850,000-hectare Superior National Forest in northeastern Minnesota.

This plan, adopted in 1986, identifies more than 14,200 hectares of forestland to be managed for ruffed grouse. And timber management on an additional 515,300 hectares will include features beneficial to these birds.

The Superior National Forest is far from being alone in emphasizing ruffed grouse management in appropriate areas. This trend has been widespread in the national forest system for a number of years, with programs in the Mark Twain Forest in Missouri and the national forests in the Southeast, to name a few. National forests are usually large enough that favorable management programs within their boundaries can make significant contributions to regionwide grouse numbers.

Four decades after wildlife researchers recognized that quality of habitat limited ruffed grouse numbers more than predation and fall hunting, widespread efforts to apply this knowledge are now under way.

—Gordon W. Gullion

New strategies to encourage ruffed grouse

Extensive surface mining for coal continues throughout much of the eastern range of the ruffed grouse, from Ohio and Pennsylvania into the southern Appalachians. This disturbance of habitat would appear to be detrimental to ruffed grouse, but many of these sites have developed into excellent ruffed grouse habitat, primarily through natural succession of trees and shrubs that provide both food and cover. Many of the principal food species—aspen, black cherry, hawthorn, dogwood—pioneer on these sites within two or three years after mining operations cease.

Ruffed grouse have been seen feeding extensively on dogwoods, black cherry, hawthorn, and crabapples on two mine sites in Clarion County, Pennsylvania. Broods were observed only on the site where stems were abundant (averaging 160 per hectare); the number of insects per square meter was eighteen or greater; and the amount of ground cover was not so dense as to prevent the chicks from obtaining food.

Kimmel has suggested that a shrub canopy provides a more favorable microclimate for insects and herbaceous vegetation. In his 1982 study, a twenty-five-year-old mine planted with autumn olive provided the best cover for ruffed grouse broods. Brenner has only occasionally observed ruffed grouse feeding on autumn olive berries, but this food was found in the crop of one bird harvested in an area planted with autumn olive.

The forests are ever-changing. To ensure that ruffed grouse continue to find food and cover as their habitat proceeds through its natural succession, wildlife managers can take advantage of strip-mining operations and other commercial disruptions.

Cutting aspen trees encourages the growth of new shoots from the roots. These root suckers, called clones, grow rapidly from the established roots of the old tree. The treatment is a relatively easy way to achieve a mixture of aspens of different ages.

Because of the passage of the Federal Surface Mining Control and Reclamation Act (SMCRA) in 1977, current reclamation practices are often detrimental to the establishment and maintenance of ruffed grouse habitat. The regrading of mine sites to the approximate original contours and the planting of dense grass and legume cover, which provide the least favorable brood habitat for ruffed grouse, hinder the native trees and shrubs. Excessive regrading of the site compacts the soil, discouraging trees and shrubs and natural succession. And returning land to its original contours often produces long slopes that accelerate erosion.

Instead, installation of a series of short slopes and terraces would reduce erosion and enhance reclamation. If the terraces were planted with trees and shrubs, the overall area would be attractive to wildlife, including ruffed grouse. The species selected for the initial reclamation should include the ten to fifteen principal food and cover species native to the region. Brenner recommends a mixture of species, including dogwoods, blueberry, hawthorn, crabapple, honeysuckle, oaks, and possibly others, depending on local conditions. These should be planted in either strips or groups, interspersed with dense clumps of spruce. The strips should alternate with areas of grasses and legumes (clover) at least 3 feet in width; 10 to 12 feet would be better. In all cases, single-species monoculture should be discouraged.

If the site has previously been reclaimed with grass and legumes, it may be necessary to use chemicals to control the herbaceous vegetation prior to planting trees and shrubs. The herbicide Dalapan (Dowpon) gives good results where grass is a problem. Atrazine is an effective broad-spectrum herbicide, but it is toxic to woody seedlings. Roundup (glyphosate) is effective if applied during midsummer to early fall, and it has no residual effect. Since Roundup is absorbed through the foliage, the material must remain on the leaves for at least eight hours before a heavy rain.

In all cases, natural succession of preferred food and cover species, especially blackberries, strawberries, and other types of ground cover, should benefit ruffed grouse and other wildlife. Species that provide vertical cover should be selected.

On older mine sites with tree cover that has occurred through either planting or natural succession, management plans must encourage the establishment of the wildlife's preferred food and cover species. Many of these sites have been invaded by aspens; once established, the aspens develop clones by root suckering. The growth of these clones may be accelerated if the established trees are cut. The ideal time for cutting to promote aspen cloning is when the trees are between ten and fifteen years old, or 20 to 30 feet high. Root suckers will reach a height of 3 feet to perhaps 12 feet during the first twelve months. During the first growing season, the clones will be fairly evenly distributed within a radius of 15 to 20 feet from the base of the parent tree. Although a few suckers may grow the second year, the clones will not appear beyond the initial radius of 15 to 20 feet. In the fourth or fifth year after the initial cut, it may be advisable to cut a swath 33 feet wide along the edge of each new clone to encourage additional suckering and clone expansion. Discing aspen areas (using a conventional agricultural disc) following cutting by beavers will encourage aspen suckering. This procedure may also be advisable on mine sites.

Hicks and Samuel have provided an excellent framework for the management of aspen on mine lands, but single-species management may be a short-sighted approach to grouse habitat on mined and un-mined lands alike. Other food and cover species should be encouraged; controlled burning, for example, prompts the pioneering of woody as well as herbaceous species and open grassland areas, both beneficial to ruffed grouse. As in the initial reclamation of mined lands, emphasis should be placed on the ten to fifteen principal food and cover species used by ruffed grouse in that region. Managers should avoid, if at all possible, creating a single-species habitat.

The interspersion of young, middle-aged, and old aspens can be improved if commer-cial timber sales are well planned. Like other treatments, such sales should not exceed 8 hectares. Since the ideal is not always possible, cuts under 8 hectares should be spaced at least 90 meters apart, and larger cuts should be at least 180 meters and preferably more than 260 meters apart. In forests with a history of larger cuts, stands should be sub-divided wherever practical by distributing several smaller cuts or cutting portions of a stand before the trees mature. Contiguous stands should differ by at least five years to avoid creating large areas all of one age.

—Fred J. Brenner

Moving about

The ruffed grouse will go where it finds good food and good cover—that much, at least, seems clear. But there are also some less obvious factors that affect the movements of this bird.

Microclimate, for example. In 1951 Hungerford reported that ruffed grouse would rather be warm than cold, for the birds used the warmer places of Idaho ridges for drumming, nesting, and early brooding. During the latter part of the brooding period in August and September, the birds moved from their evening feeding sites to roost at higher elevations. In this case, Hungerford discovered, the grouse were responding to temperature inversions associated with the canyons and ridges of northern Idaho, and those roosting sites were 7° to 8°F. warmer.

Drumming is widely considered a mechanism for maintaining a safe space between competing males, as well as a way to attract females. Activity centers are usually spaced at least 450 feet apart, with little or no overlap. But some drummers may be found as close as 60 to 90 feet apart, with both birds pursuing apparently normal display activities. Perhaps in such an instance the two males are especially tolerant of other drummers, or maybe their behavior is a function of habi-tat. Archibald once observed two neighboring males who showed a marked preference for the border zone between lowland and upland habitats during the breeding season. The intensity with which each used the available space indicated that the size of the males' home ranges was restricted by the presence of a competing male.

Some wildlife biologists believe that the home ranges of ruffed grouse are smaller in the better habitats, and consequently these better habitats support higher densities. Whether this relationship always holds true is questionable, however: in some cases the best habitats may also attract other animals, including predators. Furthermore, if grouse are concentrated in the best habitats in relatively small, isolated areas, rates of predation may increase and thus complicate the data that would settle the question. But general conclusions may still be drawn: including the distance traveled during dispersal, the ruffed grouse needs areas at least 4 to 5 miles in diameter to carry out its life cycle—areas in the early stages of forest succession, with a variety of plant species and a minimum of debris that would hamper the movements of this ground-dwelling species.

—Gerald L. Storm and
John G. Scott

In captivity

The bobwhite quail, ring-necked pheasant, and wild turkey are easy to rear in captivity. Commercial production and large-scale programs for propagating and stocking have yielded a wealth of information on husbandry methods for these game birds. But comparatively little is known about propagation of ruffed grouse, except that the species is hard to handle. In the 1930s and 1940s, Gardiner Bump and his associates undertook an extensive research program on rearing ruffed grouse. These early researchers found that the ruffed grouse's naturally low egg production, low rate of chick survival, and complex breeding behavior were biological limitations that would be difficult to overcome. However, raising small numbers of grouse for special purposes is feasible. The few ruffed grouse now reared and kept in captivity are primarily research subjects.

HOLDING FACILITIES

Grouse can be maintained in seminatural conditions in large ground enclosures. Elevated cages with wire bottoms are sometimes used as well, the advantage being that sanitary conditions are easier to maintain. Ruffed grouse do well in outdoor enclosures and do not seem bothered by extreme cold, snow, or rain as long as they have adequate food and water and can remain dry.

At the captive wildlife research facilities at Virginia Tech, grouse are kept outdoors in multiple-cage units measuring 48 by 9 by 6½ feet high. Each unit contains eight cages measuring 6 by 9 by 6½ feet, each of which houses a single grouse year-round. Other sorts of pens have been used. Bump housed individual grouse in pens as small as 4 by 8 by 3 feet, but he also tried large overwintering pens measuring 25 by 110 feet that held 300 birds.

The pens at Virginia Tech are elevated at least 12 to 18 inches to provide easy access for removing droppings and spilled feed. The sides and top of the pens are covered with ½- or 1-inch mesh wire, but mesh at least ¾ inch is needed for the floor, so that droppings can fall through. A partial roof or other overhead cover protects birds from rain. Perch bars and limbs allow birds to roost under the protective cover of the roof. The pens at Virginia Tech have electric wire attached to and encircling the pens at floor level to repel predators. Because grouse frequently pace along the wire and attempt to peck each other, often resulting in feather loss around the head, the birds' view is blocked by strips of roofing felt.

Grouse can be caged together peaceably enough in summer, fall, and winter, but there is some risk of mortality from aggressive individuals. The floor area of large overwintering pens is therefore divided with low baseboards to discourage birds from chasing one another. For small captive flocks, housing birds singly is the simplest way to reduce the risk of mortality. In spring, when males begin to display, it is particularly important to separate aggressive males from each other and from less feisty individuals.

As grouse are easily excited and can injure themselves by flying into their wire enclosures, pens are secluded and out of sight of human activity. Wooded areas provide seclusion and protection from wind, but then the holding facility should be enclosed by a fence to keep out unwelcome visitors.

CAPTIVE BREEDING

Getting grouse to mate in captivity and produce large clutches of eggs can be difficult. Satisfactory results have been obtained by pairing males and females in pens with nest boxes before the breeding period commences. Bump used boxes 12 inches square and 6 inches high, lined with grass. Beckerton and Middleton have used artificial insemination to improve the odds that cap-

Pens for captive grouse are elevated for hygiene; electrified wire above prevents raptors from frightening the occupants.

tive hens lay fertile eggs. Once the eggs are in the nest, captive hens often become inattentive; researchers may elect to remove them.

Eggs collected from nests of wild grouse are packed in a warm container if the hen has begun incubation and are transported as quickly as possible to an incubator. Incubated at 99.5°F. at a relative humidity of 60 percent to 65 percent, using standard poultry incubating equipment, the eggs hatch in approximately twenty-three and a half days—about the same interval as in the wild. For artificially incubated eggs from nests of wild birds, hatching success rates of 76 percent and 91 percent have been reported by Fay and by Beckerton and Middleton, respectively. After the chicks have dried off, they are transferred to a heated brooder. Most mortality occurs in the first two weeks after hatching: this is the most critical period. Chick survival rates of about 75 percent for the first few weeks of life have been reported for artificially incubated wild eggs, compared with about 50 percent to 60 percent for chicks in the wild, where the young birds are subject to all the perils of nature. At six weeks of age, the chicks can be transferred to outdoor facilities, provided there is adequate protection from rain.

FEEDING

Because grouse nutrition has received little study, the nutritive requirements of captive birds have not been determined. Grouse can be maintained satisfactorily on commercial game bird feeds. However, these feeds, developed for seed-eating species like the bobwhite and the pheasant, have a lower crude fiber concentration and a higher metabolizable energy content than the natural diet of grouse, which consists of much more fibrous leaves, twigs, and tree buds. That captive ruffed grouse often become obese is probably the result of using these feeds with their unnaturally high energy levels. Because the size of the grouse's digestive system depends on diet quality, as Moss noted in 1972, any maintenance diet must be comparable to the natural diet, particularly if the birds will be used for nutrition-related research.

At Virginia Tech, the maintenance diet for winter contains 15 percent to 20 percent crude fiber and 2.5 kilocalories per gram metabolizable energy, the better to mimic the natural diet. In 1983 Beckerton and Middleton recommended protein levels of 11.5 percent and 20 percent for nonbreeding and breeding birds, respectively. Grouse will accept food in either mash or pellet form. Grit may not be necessary with commercial feeds, according to Robel and Bisset. Standard poultry feeding containers are used.

Chicks receive nourishment from their yolk sac and do not require feed for the first two to three days of life. However, scattered feed should be available immediately to initiate feeding behavior. The problem is that the natural diet for chicks consists of insects, not plant material. Since ensuring a steady procession of palatable bugs into the grouse chicks' pens is more than a little difficult, researchers use a starter feed containing 25 to 30 percent protein for the first eight weeks.

CAUSES OF MORTALITY

Accidental deaths are not uncommon among captive grouse. If disturbed, the birds may take suicidal flights into their cages. Hawks may harass grouse in outdoor pens, and mice or rats under the pens will agitate them. The captive birds' wings are therefore sometimes clipped, left just long enough to allow them to reach their perches. At the Virginia Tech facilities, where grouse are kept outdoors in a secluded area relatively well protected from disturbance, wing feathers are not clipped because of their value as insulation during cold weather.

Finally, captive grouse are highly susceptible to disease, the two most common being ulcerative enteritis and blackhead. Ulcerative enteritis is a disease caused by a common bacteria that may be present in the soil or in the droppings and digestive systems of birds. It causes ulcers in the intestines. Once a grouse contracts this disease, death can occur in several days. Blackhead disease, common in turkeys, is caused by a protozoan that invades the ceca and the liver. One possible solution to preventing these diseases was reported in 1963 by Fay, who found that adding the antibiotic oxytetracycline hydrochloride (terramycin) to the drinking water helped reduce mortality in young birds.

— Frederick A. Servello and Roy Kirkpatrick

Top: *Emerging from their artificially incubated eggs, these chicks will soon be transferred to a heated brooder.* Bottom: *Captive birds easily tolerate winter conditions as long as they can remain dry. Their preferred roosts are these elevated perches.*

MARTINSON

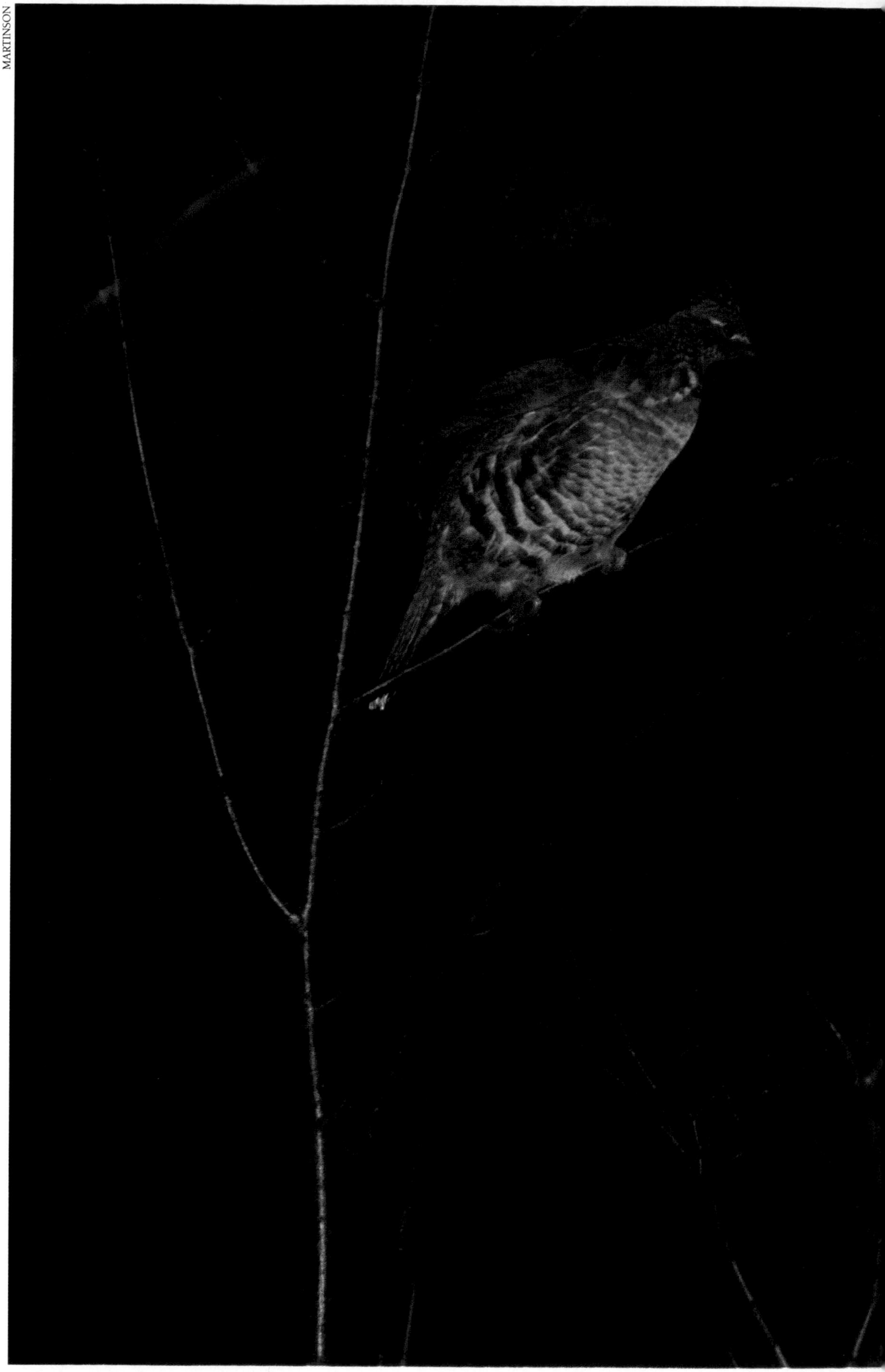

References

Aldrich, J.W. "Geographic Orientation of American Tetraonidae." *Journal of Wildlife Management* 27, no. 4 (1963): 529–545.

Aldrich, J.W., and W.J. Duvall. *Distribution of American Gallinaceous Game Birds*. U.S. Department of the Interior, Fish and Wildlife Service, Circular 34. Washington, D.C.: 1955.

Aldrich, J.W., and H. Friedmann. "A Revision of the Ruffed Grouse." *Condor* 45 (1943): 85–103.

Allen, A.A. "Sex Rhythm in the Ruffed Grouse *(Bonasa Umbellus* Linn.) and Other Birds." *Auk* 51 (April 1934): 180–199.

Amadon, D. "Avian Plumages and Molts." *Condor* 68 (1966): 263–278.

American Ornithologists' Union. *Check-list of North American Birds.* 5th ed. Baltimore: Port City Press, 1957.

Ammann, G.A. "Aging and Sexing Ruffed Grouse by Wing and Tail Feathers." Michigan Department of Conservation, 1948. Mimeo.

Ammann, G.A., and L.A. Ryel. "Extensive Methods for Inventorying Grouse in Michigan." *Journal of Wildlife Management* 27 (1963): 617–633.

Andrews, T.L., R.H. Harm, and H.R. Wilson. "Protein Requirement of the Bobwhite Chick." *Poultry Science* 52 (1973): 2199–2201.

Archibald, H.L. "Spring Drumming Activity and Space Use of Ruffed Grouse." Ph.D. dissertation, University of Minnesota, 1973.

———. "Directional Differences in the Sound Intensity of Ruffed Grouse Drumming." *Auk* 91, no. 3 (1974): 517–521.

———. "Temporal Patterns of Spring Space Use by Ruffed Grouse." *Journal of Wildlife Management* 39, no. 3 (July 1975): 472–481.

———. "Spatial Relationships of Neighboring Male Ruffed Grouse in Spring." *Journal of Wildlife Management* 40, no. 4 (October 1976): 750–760.

———. "Spring Drumming Patterns of Ruffed Grouse." *Auk* 93, no. 4 (October 1976): 808–829.

Aubin, A.E. "Aural Communication in Ruffed Grouse." *Canadian Journal of Zoology* 50 (1972): 1225–1229.

Back, G.N. "Impacts of Management for Ruffed Grouse and Pulpwood on Nongame Birds." Ph.D. dissertation, University of Minnesota, 1982.

Backs, S.E. *Sex and Age Criteria for Ruffed Grouse in Southeastern Vermont.* Grafton-Barrett Wildlife Project. University of Vermont, 1978.

Bailey, J. "Conifer Plantations as Habitat for Ruffed Grouse and Other Wildlife." *Transactions of the Northeastern Wildlife Conference* 1 (1958): 239–257.

Bailey, W.J., Jr., W.M. Sharp, R.B. Hazel, and G. Davis. *Food Habitat Trends of Ruffed Grouse in the Centre County 'Barrens.'* The Pennsylvania State University, College of Agriculture,

Agricultural Experiment Station, Bulletin 604. University Park, Penna.: 1955.

Bakke, E.L., and J.W. Schulz. "Movements and Habitat Use of Male Ruffed Grouse in the Turtle Mountains, North Dakota." *Prairie Naturalist* 17, no. 4 (1985): 177–184.

Barber, H.L. "The Ruffed Grouse." *Kentucky Happy Hunting Ground* 17, no. 6 (November 1961): 26–27.

———. *A Survey of Ruffed Grouse Populations in Kentucky.* Frankfort, Ky.: Department of Fish and Wildlife Resources, 1983.

Barker, I.K., A. Garbutt, and A.L. Middleton. "Endogenous Development and Pathogenicity of *Eimeria angusta* in the Ruffed Grouse, *Bonasa umbellus*." *Journal of Wildlife Diseases* 20 (1984): 100–107.

Barrett, R.W. "Behavior of Ruffed Grouse During the Breeding and Early Brood Rearing Periods." Ph.D. dissertation, University of Minnesota, 1970.

Beckerton, P.R., and A.L.A. Middleton. "Effects of Dietary Protein Levels on Ruffed Grouse Reproduction." *Journal of Wildlife Management* 46 (1982): 509–579.

———. "Effects of Dietary Protein Levels on Body Weight, Food Consumption, and Nitrogen Balance in Ruffed Grouse." *Condor* 85 (1983): 53–60.

Beer, J.R., and W. Tidyman. "The Substitution of Hard Seeds for Grit." *Journal of Wildlife Management* 6 (1942): 70–82.

Bendell, J.F. "Population Dynamics of the Tetraonidae: Introduction to the Symposium." *International Ornithological Congress* 15 (1970): 1–4.

Bendell, J.F. "Disease as a Control of a Population of Blue Grouse, *Dendragapus obscurus fulginosus* (Ridgeway)." *Canadian Journal of Zoology* 33 (1955): 195–223.

Bennett, C.L., Jr., D.L. Rabe, and H.H. Prince. "Response of Several Game Species, with Emphasis on Woodcock, to Extensive Habitat Manipulations." In *Woodcock Ecology and Management,* technical coordinators, T.J. Dwyer and G.L. Storm, 97–105. U.S. Department of the Interior, Fish and Wildlife Service, Wildlife Research Report 14. Washington, D.C.: 1982.

Bennett, G.F., and A.M. Fallis. "Blood Parasites of Birds from Algonquin Park, Canada, and a Discussion of Their Transmission." *Canada Journal of Zoology* 38 (1960): 262–273.

Benoit, J. "Les glandes endocrines." In *Traite de Zoologie Oiseaux,* edited by P.P. Grasse, vol. 15, 290–310. Paris: Masson et Cie, 1950.

Bent, A.C. *Life Histories of North American Gallinaceous Birds.* 1932. Reprint. New York: Dover Publications, 1963.

Berner, A., and L.W. Gysel. "Habitat Analysis and Management Considerations for Ruffed Grouse for a Multiple-Use Area in Michigan." *Journal of Wildlife Management* 33, no. 4 (1969): 769–778.

Billingsley, B.B., and D.H. Arner. "The Nutritive Value and

Digestibility of some Winter Foods of the Eastern Wild Turkey." *Journal of Wildlife Management* 34, no. 1 (1970): 176–182.

Bitely, R.A. "Drummer in the Forest." *Wildlife in North Carolina* 18 (1960): 1.

Blachly, L., and R. Jenks. *Birds at a Glance.* New York: Van Nostrand Reinhold, 1984.

Blevins, R.D. "Organochlorine Pesticides in Gamebirds of Eastern Tennessee." *Water, Air, and Soil Pollution* 11 (1979): 71–75.

Boag, D.A. "The Effect of Shrub Removal on Occupancy of Ruffed Grouse Drumming Sites." *Journal of Wildlife Management* 40 (1976): 105–110.

Boag, D.A., and K.M. Sumanik. "Characteristics of Drumming Sites Selected by Ruffed Grouse in Alberta." *Journal of Wildlife Management* 33, no. 3 (1969): 621–628.

Borror, D.J. *Dictionary of Word Roots and Combining Forms.* Palo Alto: Mayfield Publishing Company, 1960.

Boughton, D.C., and J.J. Volk. "Avian Hosts of Eimerian Coccidia." *Bird-Banding* 9 (1938): 139–153.

Bowman, T.J., and R.J. Robel. "Brood Break-up, Dispersal, Mobility, and Mortality of Juvenile Prairie Chickens." *Journal of Wildlife Management* 41 (1977): 27–34.

Bradford, A.S. "Some Notes on the Ruffed Grouse." *Passenger Pigeon* 9 (1947): 130–131.

Brander, R.B. "Movements of Female Ruffed Grouse During the Mating Season." *Wilson Bulletin* 79 (March 1967): 28–36.

———. "A Radio-package Harness for Game Birds." *Journal of Wildlife Management* 32 (July 1968): 630–632.

Braun, C.E., and W.B. Willers. "The Helminth and Protozoan Parasites of North American Grouse (Family: Tetraonidae): A checklist." *Avian Diseases* 11 (1967): 170–187.

Braun, E.L. *The Woody Plants of Ohio.* Columbus: Ohio State University Press, 1961.

———. *Deciduous Forests of Eastern North America.* 1950. Reprint. New York: Hafner Publishing Company, 1964.

Brenner, F.J. "Foods Consumed by Beavers in Crawford County, Pennsylvania." *Journal of Wildlife Management* 26 (1962): 104–107.

———. "Environmental Aspects of Coal Production in Pennsylvania: A Guide to Reclamation." In *Pennsylvania Coal: Resources, Technology, and Utilization,* edited by S.K. Majumdar and E.W. Miller, 415–422. Easton: Pennsylvania Academy of Science, 1983.

———. "Aquatic and Terrestrial Habitats in Pennsylvania." In *Species of Special Concern in Pennsylvania,* edited by H.H. Genoways and F.J. Brenner, 7–19. Pittsburgh: Carnegie Museum of Natural History, 1985.

———. "Land Reclamation after Strip Coal Mining in the United States." *Mining Magazine* (September 1985): 211–217.

Brenner, F.J., and S. Michalski III. "Evaluation of Surface Coal Mines as Ruffed Grouse Habitat." *Better Reclamation with Trees Conference* 4 (1984): 87–104.

Brenner, F.J., and R.P. Steiner. "Alternative Reclamation Strategies for Mined Lands." In *Environmental Consequences of Energy Production: An International Perspective,* edited by S.K. Majumdar, F.J. Brenner, and E.W. Miller, 115–130. Easton: Pennsylvania Academy of Science, 1984.

Brewer, L.W. *The Ruffed Grouse in Western Washington.* Washington State Department of Game, Biological Bulletin 16. 1980.

Brown, C.P. "Food of Maine Ruffed Grouse by Seasons and Cover Types." *Journal of Wildlife Management* 10, no. 1 (1946): 17–28.

Brown, L., and D. Amadon. *Eagles, Hawks, and Falcons of the World.* New York: McGraw-Hill, 1968.

Bryant, J.P., and P. Kuropat. "Selection of Winter Forage by

Subarctic Browsing Vertebrates: The Role of Plant Chemistry." *Annual Review of Ecological Systems* 11 (1980): 261–285.

Bump, G. "Food of Maine Ruffed Grouse by Seasons and Cover Types." *Journal of Wildlife Management* 10 (1946): 17–28.

———. *Wildlife Habitat Changes in the Connecticut Hill Game Management Area.* Cornell University Agricultural Experiment Station, Memoir 289. 1948.

Bump, G., R.W. Darrow, F.C. Edminster, and W.F. Crissey. *The Ruffed Grouse: Life History, Propagation, Management.* 1947. Reprint. Albany: New York State Conservation Department, 1978?.

Bussler, B.H., W.R. Byrnes, P.L. Pupe, and W.R. Chaney. "Properties of Mine Soil Reclaimed for Forest Land Use." *Soil Science of America Journal* 48 (1984): 178–184.

Cade, B.S., and P.J. Sousa. *Habitat Suitability Index Models: Ruffed Grouse.* U.S. Department of the Interior, Fish and Wildlife Service, Biological Report 82 (10.86). Washington, D.C.: 1985.

Campbell, B., and E. Lack, eds. *A Dictionary of Birds.* Great Britain: Pitman Press, 1985.

Cerretani, D.G. "Movements and Behavior of Ruffed Grouse During Late Winter and Early Spring in Central New York." Master's thesis, S.U.N.Y. College of Environmental Science and Forestry, 1976.

Chambers, R.E. "The Ruffed Grouse in the Barrens of Centre County, Pennsylvania." Master's thesis, The Pennsylvania State University, 1956.

———. "The Happy Valley Project." *Drummer* 12 (1986): 9.

Chambers, R.E., and W.M. Sharp. "Movement and Dispersal Within a Population of Ruffed Grouse." *Journal of Wildlife Management* 22 (July 1958): 231–239.

Chapman, F.B., H. Bezdek, and E.H. Dustman. *The Ruffed Grouse and its Management in Ohio.* Ohio Division of Wildlife Conservation, Department of Natural Resources, Wildlife Conservation Bulletin 6. 1952.

Clara, M. "Das pankreas der Vogel." *Anatomisher Ansager* 34 (1924): 257–266.

———. "Eine studie eur kenntnis der Langerhans schen Inseln." *Zeitschrift Fur Mikroskopie-Anatomische Forschung* 1 (1924): 513–562.

Collins, H.H., Jr. *Complete Field Guide to American Wildlife: East, Central, and North.* New York: Harper & Row, 1959.

Comsa, J. "Utilization of Anti-thyroid Action Test for Bioassay of Thymus Hormone." *American Journal of Physiology* 166 (1951): 550–554.

Cowan, I.McT., and C.D. Fowle. "Visceral Gout in a Wild Ruffed Grouse." *Journal of Wildlife Management* 8 (1944): 260–261.

Craighead, J.J., and F.C. Craighead, Jr. "The Ecology of Raptor Predation." *Transactions of the North American Wildlife Conference* 15 (1950): 209–222.

———. *Hawks, Owls and Wildlife.* Harrisburg: Stackpole Co., 1956.

Cringan, A.T. "Reproductive Biology of Ruffed Grouse in Southern Ontario, 1964–1969." *Journal of Wildlife Management* 34 (October 1970): 756–761.

Cullinan, T.P. "Winter and Spring Home Range and Habitat Use by Male Ruffed Grouse in Central New York." Master's thesis, S.U.N.Y. College of Environmental Science and Forestry, 1986.

Darrow, R.W. "Seasonal Food Preferences of Adult and of Young Grouse in New York State." *Transactions of the North American Wildlife Conference* 4 (1939): 585–590.

Dasmann, R.F. *Wildlife Biology.* New York: John Wiley & Sons, 1964.

Davidson, W.R., G.L. Doster, S.R. Pursglove, Jr., and A.K. Prestwood. "Helminth Parasites of Ruffed Grouse (*Bonasa umbellus*) from the Eastern United States." *Proceedings of the*

Helminthological Society of Washington 44 (1977): 156–161.

Davis, D.E. "The Anatomy of the Ruffed Grouse." In *The Ruffed Grouse: Life History, Propagation, Management,* by G. Bump, R.W. Darrow, F.C. Edminster, and W.F. Crissey, 721–740. 1947. Reprint. Albany: New York State Conservation Department, 1978?.

Davis, J.A. "The Postjuvenal Wing and Tail Molt of the Ruffed Grouse *(Bonasa umbellus monticola)* in Ohio." *Ohio Journal of Science* 68, no. 6 (1968): 305–312.

———. "Aging and Sexing Criteria for Ohio Ruffed Grouse." *Journal of Wildlife Management* 33 (1969): 628–636.

———. *Relative Abundance and Distribution of Ruffed Grouse in Ohio, Past, Present and Future.* Ohio Department of Natural Resources, Division of Wildlife, Inservice Document 62. Columbus: 1969.

Davis, J.A., and R.J. Stoll, Jr. "Ruffed Grouse Age and Sex Ratios in Ohio." *Journal of Wildlife Management* 37 (1973): 133–141.

DeStefano, S., R.L. Ruff, and S.R. Craven. *A Grouse in the Hand: Tips for Examining, Aging and Sexing Ruffed Grouse.* University of Wisconsin, Extension Publication G3227. Madison: 1983.

DeStefano, S., and D.H. Rusch. "Some Historical Aspects of Ruffed Grouse Harvests and Hunting Regulations in Wisconsin." *Transactions of the Wisconsin Academy of Sciences, Arts and Letters* 70 (1982): 27–35.

———. "Characteristics of Ruffed Grouse Drumming Sites in Northeastern Wisconsin." *Transactions of the Wisconsin Academy of Sciences, Arts and Letters* 72 (1984): 177–182.

———. "Harvest Rates of Ruffed Grouse in Northeastern Wisconsin." *Journal of Wildlife Management* 50, no. 3 (1986): 361–367.

Doerr, P.D., L.B. Keith, D.H. Rusch, and C.A. Fischer. "Characteristics of Winter Feeding Aggregations of Ruffed Grouse in Alberta." *Journal of Wildlife Management* 38, no. 4 (1974): 601–615.

Dorney, R.S. "1952 Ruffed Grouse Hunting Season Collection." *Wisconsin Wildlife Research* 12, No. 1 (1952): 109–117.

———. *The Relationship of Ruffed Grouse to Forest Cover Types in Wisconsin.* Wisconsin Conservation Department, Technical Bulletin 18. Madison: 1959.

———. "Sex and Age Structure of Wisconsin Ruffed Grouse Populations." *Journal of Wildlife Management* 27, no. 4 (1963): 599–603.

———. "A New Method for Sexing Ruffed Grouse in Late Summer." *Journal of Wildlife Management* 30, no. 3 (1966): 623–625.

Dorney, R.S., and F.V. Holzer. "Spring Aging Methods for Ruffed Grouse Cocks." *Journal of Wildlife Management* 21, no. 3 (July 1957): 268–274.

Dorney, R.S., and C. Kabat. *Relation of Weather, Parasitic Disease and Hunting to Wisconsin Ruffed Grouse Populations.* Wisconsin Conservation Department, Technical Bulletin 20. Madison: 1960.

Dorney, R.S., and A.C. Todd. "Spring Incidence of Ruffed Grouse Blood Parasites." *Journal of Parasitology* 46, no. 6 (1960): 687–694.

Drobney, R.D. "Effects of Diet on Visceral Morphology of Breeding Wood Ducks." *Auk* 101 (1984): 93–98.

Durbin, K. "The Forest Drummer." *Oregon Wildlife* (September 1979): 3–7.

Edminster, F.C. "The Effect of Predator Control on Ruffed Grouse Populations in New York." *Journal of Wildlife Management.* 3 (1939): 345–352.

———. *The Ruffed Grouse: Its Life Story, Ecology, and Management.* New York: Macmillan, 1947.

Edwards, M.G. "Ruffed Grouse Management in North Carolina." *Proceedings of the Annual Conference of the Southeastern Association of Game and Fish Commissioners* 11 (1957): 346–349.

Eng, R.L. "A Study of the Ecology of Male Ruffed Grouse *(Bonasa umbellus* L.) on the Cloquet Forest Research Center, Minnesota." Ph.D. dissertation, University of Minnesota–Minneapolis, 1959.

Eng, R.L., and G.W. Gullion. "The Predation of Goshawks upon Ruffed Grouse on the Cloquet Forest Research Center, Minnesota." *Wilson Bulletin* 74, no. 3 (September 1962): 227–242.

Erickson, A.B. "*Leucocytozoon bonasae* in Ruffed Grouse: Its Possible Relationship to Fluctuations in Numbers of Grouse." *Journal of Wildlife Management* 17 (1953): 536–538.

Erickson, D.L. "Movements and Seasonal Habitat of Ruffed Grouse on the University of Idaho Experimental Forest." Master's thesis, University of Idaho, 1961.

Eve, J.H., and W.R. Davidson. "Blood Parasites of Ruffed Grouse *(Bonasa umbellus)* from Kentucky, Maine, Michigan, and West Virginia." *Journal of Parasitology* 62 (1976): 142–144.

Fallis, A.M., and C.E. Hope. "Observations of Ruffed Grouse in Southern Ontario with a Discussion on Cycles." *Canadian Field Naturalist* 64 (January–March 1950): 82–85.

Fay, L.D. "Recent Success in Raising Ruffed Grouse in Captivity." *Journal of Wildlife Management* 27 (October 1963): 642–647.

Fenna, L., and D.A. Boag. "Adaptive Significance of the Caeca in Japanese Quail and Spruce Grouse (Galliformes)." *Canadian Journal of Zoology* 52 (1974): 1577–1584.

Ferguson, R.M. *The Timber Resources of Pennsylvania.* U.S. Forest Service, Bulletin NE-8. Upper Darby, Penna.: 1968.

Fischer, C.A., and L.B. Keith. "Population Responses of Central Alberta Ruffed Grouse to Hunting." *Journal of Wildlife Management* 38 (1974): 585–600.

Fish and Wildlife Comprehensive Plan. Madison: Wisconsin Department of Natural Resources, 1979.

Fisher, L.W. *Studies of the Eastern Ruffed Grouse in Michigan* (Bonasa umbellus umbellus). Michigan State Agricultural Experiment Station, Technical Bulletin 166. East Lansing: 1939.

Forbush, E.H., and J.B. May. *A Natural History of American Birds of Eastern and Central North America.* Boston: Houghton Mifflin, 1955.

Gabrielson, I.N., and F.C. Lincoln. *The Birds of Alaska.* Washington, D.C.: Wildlife Management Institute. Harrisburg, Penna.: Stackpole Books, 1959.

Garbutt, A., and A.L.A. Middleton. "Molt Sequence of Captive Ruffed Grouse." *Auk* 91(1974): 421–423.

Gasaway, W.C., D. Holleman, and R. White. "Digesta Flow in the Intestine and Cecum of the Rock Ptarmigan." *Condor* 77 (1975): 467–474.

———. "Digestion of Dry Matter and Absorption of Water in the Intestine and Cecum of Rock Ptarmigan." *Condor* 78 (1976): 77–84.

Giles, R.H., Jr., ed. *Wildlife Management Techniques.* 3d ed. Washington, D.C.: The Wildlife Society, 1971.

Gilfillan, M.C., and H. Bezdek. "Winter Foods of the Ruffed Grouse in Ohio." *Journal of Wildlife Management* 8, no. 3 (1944): 208–210.

Gill, J.D., and W.M. Healy, eds. *Shrubs and Vines for Northeastern Wildlife.* U.S. Department of Agriculture, Forest Service, Northeastern Forest Experiment Station, General Technical Report NE-9. Upper Darby, Penna.: 1974.

Gladfelter, H.L., and R.S. McBurney. "Mating Activity of Ruffed Grouse." *Auk* 88 (January 1971): 176–177.

Gleason, H.A., and A. Cronquist. *Manual of Vascular Plants of Northeastern United States and Adjacent Canada.* New York: Van Nostrand Reinhold, 1963.

Goble, F.C., and H.L. Kutz. "The Genus *Dispharynx* (Nematoda: Acuariidae) in Galliform and Passeriform Birds." *Journal of Parasitology* 31 (1945): 323–331.

Godfrey, G.A. "Home Range Characteristics of Ruffed Grouse Broods in Minnesota." *Journal of Wildlife Management* 39 (April 1975): 287–298.

Godfrey, G.A., and W.H. Marshall. "Brood Break-up and Dispersal of Ruffed Grouse." *Journal of Wildlife Management* 33 (July 1969): 609–620.

Godfrey, W.E. *The Birds of Canada*. Rev. ed. Ottawa: National Museums of Canada, 1986.

Goldston, E.F., and W. Gettys. "Soil Survey of Macon County, North Carolina." *U.S. Department of Agriculture Soil Survey Service No. 6* (1944): 112–114.

Graham, S.A., R.P. Harrison, Jr., and C.E. Westell, Jr. *Aspens: Phoenix Trees of the Great Lakes Region*. Ann Arbor: University of Michigan Press, 1963.

Grange, W.B. "Some Observations on the Ruffed Grouse in Wisconsin." *Wilson Bulletin* 48, no. 2 (1936): 104–110.

——. "Wisconsin Grouse Problems." *Wisconsin Conservation Department Publication No. 328* (1948): 153–157.

——. *The Way to Game Abundance*. New York: Scribner's, 1949.

Green, R.G. "Disease in Relation to Game Cycles." *Transactions of the American Game Conference* 18 (1931): 109–117.

Green, R.G., and J.E. Shillinger. "A Natural Infection of the Sharp-tailed Grouse and the Ruffed Grouse by *Pasteurella tularensis*." *Proceedings of the Society for Experimental Biology and Medicine* 30 (1932): 284–287.

——. "Progress Report of Wildlife Disease Studies for 1935." *Proceedings of the North American Wildlife Conference* 1 (1936): 469–471.

Gross, A.O. "Diseases of the Ruffed Grouse." *Auk* 42 (1925): 423–431.

Gudlin, M.J., and R.W. Dimmick. "Habitat Utilization by Ruffed Grouse Transplanted from Wisconsin to West Tennessee." In *Ruffed Grouse Management: State of the Art in the Early 1980's*, edited by W.L. Robinson, 75–88. The North Central Section of the Wildlife Society, and The Ruffed Grouse Society, 1984.

Gullion, G.W. "Food and Cover Occurrence and Availability as Influenced by Forest Practices." *Minnesota Department of Conservation, Game Research Project Quarterly Progress Report* 23, no. 4 (1964): 43–83.

——. "Evaluation of Food, Cover and Other Grouse Management Practices." *Minnesota Department of Conservation, Game Research Project Quarterly Progress Report* 24, no. 1 (1964): 26–137.

——. "Improvements in Methods for Trapping and Marking Ruffed Grouse." *Journal of Wildlife Management* 29, no. 1 (1965): 109–116.

——. "A Viewpoint Concerning the Significance of Studies of Game Bird Food Habits." *Condor* 68, no. 4 (1966): 372–376.

——. "The Use of Drumming Behavior in Ruffed Grouse Population Studies." *Journal of Wildlife Management* 30 (1966): 717–729.

——. "Ruffed Grouse Research and the Road Ahead." *Minnesota Conservation Volunteer* 30 (1967): 23–30.

——. "Factors Affecting Ruffed Grouse Populations in the Boreal Forests of Northern Minnesota." *Finnish Game Research* 30 (1970): 103–117.

——. "Factors Influencing Ruffed Grouse Populations." *Transactions of the North American Wildlife and Natural Resources Conference* 35 (1970): 93–105.

——. "Ruffed Grouse Investigations–Influence of Forest Management Practices on Grouse Populations." *Minnesota Department of Natural Resources, Game Research Quarterly Progress Report* 30, no. 2 (1970): 104–125.

——. "Selection and Use of Drumming Sites by Male Ruffed Grouse." *Auk* 84 (1970): 87–112.

——. "The Ruffed Grouse in Northern Minnesota." 1967. Rev. version. Cloquet: University of Minnesota, Forest Wildlife Relations Project, 1970. Mimeo.

——. *Improving Your Forested Lands for Ruffed Grouse*. Minnesota Agricultural Experiment Station, Miscellaneous Journal Series, Publication No. 1439. Coraopolis, Penna.: The Ruffed Grouse Society, 1972.

——. "Ruffed Grouse Habitat Manipulation–Mille Lacs Wildlife Management Area, Minnesota." *Minnesota Wildlife Research Quarterly* 36, no. 3 (1976): 96–121.

——. "Forest Manipulation for Ruffed Grouse." *Transactions of the North American Natural Resources Conference* 42 (1977): 449–458.

——. "Maintenance of the Aspen Ecosystem as a Primary Wildlife Habitat." *Proceedings of the International Congress of Game Biologists* 13 (1977): 256–265.

——. Personal communication. In "Criteria of Sex and Age," by J.S. Larson and R.D. Taber, 143–202. In *Wildlife Management Techniques Manual*, edited by S.D. Schemnitz, 4th ed., 183. Washington, D.C.: The Wildlife Society, 1980.

——. "Non-drumming Males in a Ruffed Grouse Population." *Wilson Bulletin* 93 (1981): 372–382.

——. "The Impact of Goshawk Predation upon Ruffed Grouse." *Loon* 53 (1981): 82–84.

——. "Rejuvenation and Maintenance of Forest Habitats for the American Ruffed Grouse." In *Proceedings of the Second International Symposium on Grouse*, edited by T.W.I. Lovel, 11–25. Edinburgh: World Pheasant Association, 1982.

——. *Managing Woodlots for Fuel and Wildlife*. Coraopolis, Penna.: The Ruffed Grouse Society, 1983.

——. "Ruffed Grouse Habitat Manipulation–Mille Lacs Wildlife Management Area, Minnesota." *Minnesota Wildlife Research Quarterly* 43, no. 4 (1983): 25–98.

——. *Grouse of the North Shore*. Oshkosh, Wis.: Willow Creek Press, 1984.

——. *Managing Northern Forests for Wildlife*. Coraopolis, Penna.: The Ruffed Grouse Society, 1984.

——. "Ruffed Grouse Management–Where do We Stand In The Eighties?" In *Ruffed Grouse Management: State of the Art in the Early 1980's*, edited by W.L. Robinson, 169–181. The North Central Section of the Wildlife Society, and The Ruffed Grouse Society, 1984.

——. *Sequence of Materials Handling for Sex and Age Determination of Ruffed Grouse and Comments Concerning Tail Patterns and Colors*. Rev. version. University of Minnesota, Forest Wildlife Project, SOP No. 5. Cloquet: 1984.

——. "Aspen Management–An Opportunity for Maximum Integration of Wood Fiber and Wildlife Benefits." *Transactions of the North American Wildlife and Natural Resources Conference* 50 (1985): 249–261.

——. "The Food Factor in Grouse Numbers." *Drummer* (June 1985): 14.

——. "Ruffed Grouse Research at the University of Minnesota Cloquet Forestry Center." *Minnesota Department of Natural Resources Wildlife Research Unit 1985 Report* (1986): 40–49.

Gullion, G.W., and A.A. Alm. "Forest Management and Ruffed Grouse Populations in a Minnesota Coniferous Forest." *Journal of Forestry* 81 (1983): 529–532, 536.

Gullion, G.W., and G.B. Evans. Interview by S. Smith. "Are We Overshooting Late Season Grouse?" *Wisconsin Sportsman* 11, no. 6 (1982): 18–23, 80.

Gullion, G.W., R.T. King, and W.H. Marshall. "Male Ruffed Grouse and Thirty Years of Forest Management on the Cloquet Forest Research Center, Minnesota." *Journal of Forestry* 60, no. 9 (1962): 617–622.

Gullion, G.W., and W.H. Marshall. "Ruffed Grouse Management." *Minnesota Conservation Volunteer* 23 (May–June 1960): 51–55.

———. "Survival of Ruffed Grouse in a Boreal Forest." *Living Bird* 7 (1968): 117–167.

Gullion, G.W., and F.J. Svoboda. "The Basic Habitat Resource for Ruffed Grouse." *Proceedings of Aspen Symposium, U.S.D.A. Forest Service General Technical Report NC-1* (1972): 113–119.

Hale, J.B., and R.S. Dorney. "Seasonal Movements of Ruffed Grouse in Wisconsin." *Journal of Wildlife Management* 27, no. 4 (October 1963): 648–656.

Hale, J.B., and R.F. Wendt. "Ruffed Grouse Hatching Dates in Wisconsin." *Journal of Wildlife Management* 15 (April 1951): 195–199.

Hale, J.B., R.F. Wendt, and G.C. Halazon. *Sex and Age Criteria for Wisconsin Ruffed Grouse.* Wisconsin Conservation Department, Technical Wildlife Bulletin 9. Madison: 1954.

Hale, P.E., A.S. Johnson, and J.L. Landers. "Characteristics of Ruffed Grouse Drumming Sites in Georgia." *Journal of Wildlife Management* 46, no. 1 (1982): 115–123.

Hamerstrom, F. *Birds of Prey of Wisconsin.* Madison: Wisconsin Department of Natural Resources, 1972.

Hardcastle, A.B. "A Checklist and Host-index of the Species of the Protozoan Genus *Eimeria.*" *Proceedings of the Helminthological Society of Washington* 10 (1943): 35–69.

Hardy, F.C. *Ruffed Grouse Studies in Eastern Kentucky.* Kentucky Division of Game, Federal Aid Project 18-R, Preliminary Report 26. 1950.

Harlow, W.M., and E.S. Harrar. *Textbook of Dendrology.* New York: McGraw-Hill, 1941.

Harris, M.J. "Spring and Summer Ecology of Ruffed Grouse in Northern Georgia." Master's thesis, University of Georgia, 1981.

Heacox, C.E. *The Gallant Grouse.* New York: David McKay, Inc., 1980.

Hein, D. "The Ruffed Grouse near the Southeast Edge of its Range." *Journal of the Elisha Mitchell Science Society* 86 (1970): 139–145.

Hess, E.H. "Imprinting in a Natural Laboratory." *Scientific American* 227 (1972): 24–31.

Hicks, R.R., Jr., and D.E. Samuel. *Surface Mine Reclamation: A Wildlife Habitat Opportunity.* Coraopolis, Penna.: The Ruffed Grouse Society, 1985.

Hill, W.C.O. "A Comparative Study of the Pancreas." *Proceedings of the Zoological Society (London)* (1926): 581–631.

Hjorth, I. "Reproductive Behavior in the Tetraonidae, with Special Reference to Males." *Viltrevy* 7 (1970): 183–596.

Hoffman, M.L., ed. "1986 May Count Summary." *The Maryland Yellowthroat* 6, no. 5 (1986): 5.

Hoffmann, R.S. "The Role of Predators in 'Cycle' Declines of Grouse Populations." *Journal of Wildlife Management* 22 (1958).

Howerth, E.W., L.F. Schorr, and V.F. Nettles. "Neoplasia in Free-flying Ruffed Grouse *(Bonasa umbellus)*." *Avian Diseases* 30 (1986): 238–240.

Huempfner, R.A. "Winter Arboreal Feeding Behavior of Ruffed Grouse in East-Central Minnesota." Master's thesis, University of Minnesota, 1981.

Huempfner, R.A., S.J. Maxson, G.J. Erickson, and R.J. Schuster. "Recapturing Radio-tagged Ruffed Grouse by Nightlighting and Snow-burrow Netting." *Journal of Wildlife Management* 39 (October 1975): 821–823.

Huff, Dan E. "A Study of Selected Nutrients in Browse Available to Ruffed Grouse." Master's thesis, University of Minnesota, 1970.

Hungerford, K.E. "Ruffed Grouse Populations and Cover Use in Northern Idaho." *Transactions of the North American Wildlife and Natural Resources Conference* 16 (1951): 216–224.

———. "Some Observations on the Life History of the Idaho Ruffed Grouse." *Murrelet* 34, no. 1 (1953): 35–40.

Hunyadi, B.W. "Ruffed Grouse Restoration in Missouri." In *Ruffed Grouse Management: State of the Art in the Early 1980's,* edited by W.L. Robinson, 21–35. The North Central Section of the Wildlife Society, and The Ruffed Grouse Society, 1984.

Inman, D.L. "Cellulose Digestion in Ruffed Grouse, Chukar Partridge, and Bobwhite Quail." *Journal of Wildlife Management* 37 (1973): 114–121.

Johnsgard, P.A. *Grouse and Quails of North America.* Lincoln: University of Nebraska Press, 1973.

———. *The Grouse of the World.* Lincoln: The University of Nebraska Press, 1983.

Johnson, R.A. "The Ruffed Grouse in Winter." *Auk* 44, no. 3 (1927): 319–321.

———. "The Fall Food Habits of the Ruffed Grouse in the Syracuse Area of New York." *Auk* 45, no. 3 (1928): 330–333.

Judd, S.D *The Grouse and Wild Turkeys of the United States and their Economic Value.* U.S. Department of Agriculture, Bureau Biological Survey Bulletin 24. Washington, D.C.: 1905.

Keith, L.B. *Wildlife's Ten-Year Cycle.* Madison: University of Wisconsin Press, 1963.

———. "The Ten-Year Cycle." In *The Encyclopedia of Mammals,* edited by D. MacDonald, 722–723. New York: Facts on File Publications, 1984.

Keith, L.B., and D.H. Rusch. "Predation's Role in the Cyclic Fluctuations of Ruffed Grouse." *Acta Congress of International Ornithology* 19 (1988): in press.

Keith, L.B., A.W. Todd, C.J. Brand, R.S. Adamcik, and D.H. Rusch. "An Analysis of Predation During a Cyclic Fluctuation of Snowshoe Hares." *Proceedings of the International Congress of Game Biology* 13 (1977): 151–175.

Kendall, R.J., G.W. Norman, and P.F. Scanlon. "Lead Concentrations in Ruffed Grouse Collected from Southwestern Virginia." *Northwest Science* 58 (1984): 14–17.

Kendeigh, S.C. *Ecology, with Special Reference to Animals and Man.* Englewood Cliffs: Prentice-Hall, 1974.

Keppie, D.M. "Dispersal, Overwinter Mortality, and Recruitment of Spruce Grouse." *Journal of Wildlife Management* 43 (1979): 717–727.

Kimmel, R.O. "Ruffed Grouse Brood Habitat on Reclaimed Surface Mines in West Virginia." Ph.D. dissertation, West Virginia University, 1982.

Kimmel, R.O., and W.M. Healy. "Imprinting: A Technique for Wildlife Research." In *Perdix IV: Gray Partridge Workshop,* edited by R.O. Kimmel, et. al. Madelia, Minn.: Minnesota Department of Natural Resources, 1987.

Kimmel, R.O., and D.E. Samuel. "Feeding Behavior of Young Ruffed Grouse in West Virginia." *Transactions of the Northeast Fish and Wildlife Conference* 35 (February–March 1978): 43–49.

———. "Implications of Ruffed Grouse Brood Habitat Studies in West Virginia." In *Ruffed Grouse Management: State of the Art in the Early 1980's,* edited by W.L. Robinson, 89–108. The North Central Section of the Wildlife Society, and The Ruffed Grouse Society, 1984.

King, P.B., and A. Stupka. "The Great Smoky Mountains—Their Geology and Natural History." *Science Monthly* 71, no. 1 (1950): 31–43.

King, R.D. "Spring and Summer Foods of Ruffed Grouse on Vancouver Island." *Journal of Wildlife Management* 33 (1969): 440–442.

King, R.T. "Ruffed Grouse Management." *Journal of Forestry* 35, no. 6 (1937): 523–532.

Kingsley, N.O., and C.E. Mayer. *The Timber of Ohio.* U.S.

Department of Agriculture, Forest Service Resources, Bulletin NE 19. Washington, D.C.: 1978.

Kingston, N. "On the Life Cycle of *Brachylecithum orfi* Kingston and Freeman, 1959 (Trematoda: Dicrocoeliidae), from the Liver of the Ruffed Grouse, *Bonasa umbellus* L. Infections in the Vertebrate and Molluscan Hosts." *Canadian Journal of Zoology* 43 (1965): 745–764.

Kittam, W.H. "October Foods of Ruffed Grouse in Maine." *Journal of Wildlife Management* 7 (1943): 231–233.

Korschgen, L.J. "Foods and Nutrition of Ruffed Grouse in Missouri." *Journal of Wildlife Management* 30, no. 1 (1966): 86–100.

Kress, S.W. *The Audubon Society Handbook for Birders.* New York: Charles Scribner's Sons, 1981.

Kubisiak, J.F. *Brood Characteristics and Summer Habitats of Ruffed Grouse in Central Wisconsin.* Wisconsin Department of Natural Resources, Technical Bulletin 108. Madison: 1978.

———. "The Impact of Hunting on Ruffed Grouse Populations in the Sandhill Wildlife Area." In *Ruffed Grouse Management: State of the Art in the Early 1980's,* edited by W.L. Robinson, 151–168. The North Central Section of the Wildlife Society, and The Ruffed Grouse Society, 1984.

———. *Ruffed Grouse Habitat Relationships in Aspen and Oak Forests of Central Wisconsin.* Wisconsin Department of Natural Resources, Technical Bulletin 151. Madison: 1985.

———. *Ruffed Grouse Harvest Levels and Population Characteristics in Central Wisconsin.* Wisconsin Department of Natural Resources, Research Report 136. Madison: 1985.

———. "Hunting Wisconsin Ruffed Grouse: Where Do We Stand Now?" *Wisconsin Sportsman* 15, no. 5 (1986): 50–52.

———. *Oak Forests: A Management Opportunity for Ruffed Grouse and Other Wildlife.* Coraopolis, Penna.: The Ruffed Grouse Society, 1987.

———. "Wildlife Habitat Guidelines for the Central Forest." Progress Report Study No. 231, in *Wildlife Resources Project Annual Report.* Madison: Wisconsin Department of Natural Resources, 1988.

Kubisiak, J.F., and K.R. McCaffery. "Species Management Guidelines, Wildlife: Chapter 42, Ruffed Grouse." Department of Natural Resources, Fish and Wildlife Comprehensive Plan, 1985. Mimeo.

Kubisiak, J.F., J.C. Moulton, and K.R. McCaffery. *Ruffed Grouse Density and Habitat Relationships in Wisconsin.* Wisconsin Department of Natural Resources, Technical Bulletin 118. Madison: 1980.

Kuhn, T. "Fall Foods of the Ruffed Grouse in Pennsylvania." *Pennsylvania Game News* 11, no. 10 (1940): 86–100.

Kupa, J.J. "Ecological Studies of the Female Ruffed Grouse (*Bonasa umbellus* L.) at the Cloquet Forest Research Center, Minnesota." Ph.D. dissertation, University of Minnesota, 1966.

Land and Resources Management Plan – Superior National Forest. Milwaukee: U.S. Department of Agriculture Forest Service, Eastern Region, 1986.

Landry, J.L. "Habitat Use by Ruffed Grouse in Northern Utah." Master's thesis, Utah State University, 1982.

Larsen, J.A., and J.F. Lahey. "Influence of Weather Upon a Ruffed Grouse Population." *Journal of Wildlife Management* 22, no. 1 (1958): 63–70.

Larson, J.S., and R.D. Taber. "Criteria of Sex and Age." In *Wildlife Management Techniques Manual,* edited by S.D. Schemnitz, 4th ed., 143–202. Washington, D.C.: The Wildlife Society, 1980.

Leopold, A.S. "Intestinal Morphology of Gallinaceous Birds in Relation to Food Habits." *Journal of Wildlife Management* 17 (1953): 197–203.

Levine, P.P. "A Report on an Epidemic Disease in Ruffed Grouse." *Transactions of the American Game Conference* 19 (1932): 437.

Lincoln, F.C. *Migration of Birds.* Rev. by S.R. Peterson. U.S. Department of the Interior, Fish and Wildlife Service, Circular 16. Washington, D.C.: 1979.

Little, T.W. "Ruffed Grouse Population Indices from Iowa." In *Ruffed Grouse Management: State of the Art in the Early 1980's,* edited by W.L. Robinson, 5–19. The North Central Section of the Wildlife Society, and The Ruffed Grouse Society, 1984.

Longwitz, R.J. "Some Aspects of the Ecology of Ruffed Grouse in Unmanaged Hardwood Forests of the Cumberland Plateau, Tennessee." Master's thesis, University of Tennessee, 1985.

Luttich, S., D.H. Rusch, E.C. Meslow, and L.B. Keith. "Ecology of Red-Tailed Hawk Predation in Alberta." *Ecology* 51, no. 2 (1970): 190–203.

Lyons, K.L. "Ruffed Grouse Brood Ranges and Habitat Preferences." Master's thesis, S.U.N.Y. College of Environmental Science and Forestry, 1981.

McBurney, R.S. "Drumming Behavior of Ruffed Grouse (*Bonasa umbellus* L.)" Master's thesis, Iowa State University, 1970.

McCaffery, K.R., and J.E. Ashbrenner. "Experimental Grouse Management on the Stone Lake Area." Progress Report Study No. 202, in *Wildlife Resources Project Annual Report.* Madison: Wisconsin Department of Natural Resources, 1987.

McDowell, R.D. "Fall Diets of Connecticut Ruffed Grouse, 1904–1965." *Transactions of the Northeast Fish and Wildlife Conference* 32 (1975): 80–94.

McGowan, J.D. "Fall and Winter Foods of Ruffed Grouse in Interior Alaska." *Auk* 90 (1973): 636–640.

Mackenzie, J.P.S. *The Complete Outdoorsman's Guide to Birds of Eastern North America.* Toronto: Paguarian Press, Ltd., 1976.

Madson, J. *Ruffed Grouse.* East Alton, Ill.: Winchester Press, 1969.

Major, P.D., and J.C. Olson. "Harvest Statistics from Indiana's Ruffed Grouse Hunting Seasons." *Wildlife Society Bulletin* 8 (1980): 18–23.

Mallette, R.D., and J.R. Slosson. *Upland Game of California.* 3d ed. Sacramento: State of California Department of Fish and Game, 1980.

Marjakangas, A., H. Rintamaki, and R. Hissa. "Thermal Responses in the Capercaillie *Tetrao urogallus* and the Black Grouse *Lyrurus tetrix* Roosting in the Snow." *Physiological Zoology* 57 (1984): 99–104.

Marquenski, S.V. "*Dispharynx nasuta* in Wisconsin Ruffed Grouse." Master's thesis, University of Wisconsin, Stevens Point, 1986.

Marshall, W.H. "Cover Preferences, Seasonal Movements, and Food Habits of Richardson's Grouse and Ruffed Grouse in Southern Idaho." *Wilson Bulletin* 58, no. 1 (1946): 42–52.

———. "Ruffed Grouse and Snowshoe Hare Populations in the Cloquet Experimental Forest, Minnesota." *Journal of Wildlife Management* 18, no. 1, (1954): 109–112.

Marshall, W.H., and G.W. Gullion. "A Discussion of Ruffed Grouse Populations – Cloquet Forest Research Center, Minnesota." *Transactions of the Congress of the International Union of Game Biologists, The Nature Conservancy, London* 6 (1963): 93–100.

Marshall, W.H., and J.J. Kupa. "Development of Radio-telemetry Techniques for Ruffed Grouse Studies." *Transactions of the North American Wildlife and Natural Resources Conference* 28 (March 1963): 443–456.

Maxson, S.J. "Activity, Home Range, and Habitat Usage of Female Ruffed Grouse During the Egg-laying, Incubation, and Early Brood Periods as Determined by Radiotelemetry."

Master's thesis, University of Minnesota, 1974.

————. "Activity Patterns of Female Ruffed Grouse During the Breeding Season." *Wilson Bulletin* 89 (September 1977): 439–455.

————. "Spring Home Range and Habitat Use by Female Ruffed Grouse." *Journal of Wildlife Management* 42 (January 1978): 61–71.

————. "A Nesting Study of Ruffed Grouse at the Cedar Creek Natural History Area, Minnesota." *Loon* 50 (Spring 1978): 25–30.

————. "Growth and Behavior of Ruffed Grouse Chicks." *Loon* 50 (1978): 106–112.

Meslow, E.C. "The Drumming Log and Drumming Log Activity of Male Ruffed Grouse." Master's thesis, University of Minnesota, 1966.

Miller, M.R. "Gut Morphology of Mallards in Relation to Diet Quality." *Journal of Wildlife Management* 39 (1975): 168–173.

Mohr, C.O. "Table of Equivalent Populations of North American Small Mammals." *American Midland Naturalist* 37 (1947): 223–249.

Monschein, T.D. "Effects of Hunting on Ruffed Grouse Populations in Small Woodlots in Ashe and Alleghany Counties, North Carolina." *Proceedings of the Annual Conference of the Southeastern Association of Game and Fish Commissioners* 27 (1973): 30–36.

Moser, M.A. "Habitat and Local Movement of Ruffed Grouse *(Bonasa umbellus)* in Southeast Ohio." Master's thesis, The Ohio State University, 1972.

Moss, R. "Effects of Captivity on Gut Lengths in Red Grouse." *Journal of Wildlife Management* 36 (1972): 99–104.

Moss, R., and I. Hanssen. "Grouse Nutrition." *Nutrition Abstracts and Review – Series B* 50 (1980): 555–567.

Murie, O.J. *A Field Guide to Animal Tracks.* Boston: Houghton Mifflin, 1954.

Narahara, A.M. "Dynamics of Drumming Site Selection by Ruffed Grouse in a Managed Forest." Master's thesis, University of Massachusetts, 1987.

Neave, D.J., and B.S. Wright. "The Effects of Weather and DDT Spraying on a Ruffed Grouse Population." *Journal of Wildlife Management* 33 (1969): 1015–1020.

Nelson, A.L., T.E. Clarke, and W.W. Bailey. *Early Winter Foods of the Ruffed Grouse on the George Washington National Forest.* U.S. Department of Agriculture, Circular 504. Washington, D.C.: 1938.

Nixon, C.M., M.W. McClain, and K.R. Russell. "Deer Food Habits and Range Characteristics in Ohio." *Journal of Wildlife Management* 34 (1970): 870–886.

Norman, G.W. "Nutritional Ecology of Ruffed Grouse in Southwest Virginia." Master's thesis, Virginia Polytechnic Institute and State University, 1980.

Norman, G.W., and R.L. Kirkpatrick. "Foods, Nutrition, and Condition of Ruffed Grouse in Southwestern Virginia." *Journal of Wildlife Management* 48 (1984): 183–187.

Oring, L.W. "Avian Mating Systems." In *Avian Biology,* edited by D.S. Farner, J.R. King, and K.C. Parkes, vol. 6, 1–92. New York: Academic Press, 1982.

O'Roke, E.C. "A Field Study of *Leucocytozoon bonasae* Clarke in Juvenile Ruffed Grouse, *Bonasa umbellus.*" *Journal of Parasitology* 26 (1940): 14, supplement.

Page, R.E., and A.T. Bergerud. "A Genetic Explanation for Ten-Year Cycles of Grouse." *Aecologica* 64 (1984): 54–60.

Palmer, Walter L. "Ruffed Grouse Population Studies on Hunted and Unhunted Areas." *Transactions of the North American Wildlife Conference* 21 (1957): 338–345.

————. "Sexing Live-trapped Juvenile Ruffed Grouse." *Journal of Wildlife Management* 23, no. 1 (1959): 111–112.

————. "Ruffed Grouse Drumming Sites in Northern Michigan." *Journal of Wildlife Management* 27, no. 4 (1963):

————. "Time Frequencies Between Successive Drumming Performances of Ruffed Grouse." *Wilson Bulletin* 81 (1969): 97–99.

Palmer, Walter L., and C.L. Bennett, Jr. "Relation of Season Length to Hunting Harvest of Ruffed Grouse." *Journal of Wildlife Management* 27 (1963): 634–639.

Palmer, William L. "The Barrens Grouse Habitat Management Study – State Game Lands #176 (Barrens)." *Pennsylvania Game Commission Project Annual Job Report,* Job No. 4, 1984.

Parker, G.H. "Copper, Nickel, and Iron in Plumage of Three Upland Gamebird Species from Noncontaminated Environments." *Bulletin of Environmental Contamination and Toxicology* 35 (1985): 776–780.

Parry, G., and R. Putman. *The Country Life Book of Birds of Prey.* Trewin Copplestone Publishing, Ltd., 1979.

Patrick, H., and P.J. Schaible. *Poultry: Feeds and Nutrition.* Westport, Conn.: Avi Publishing Co., 1980.

Peek, J.M. *A Preview of Wildlife Management.* Englewood Cliffs: Prentice-Hall, 1986.

Pendergast, B.A., and D.A. Boag. "Seasonal Changes in the Internal Anatomy of Spruce Grouse in Alberta." *Auk* 90 (1973): 307–317.

Peterson, R.T. *A Field Guide to the Birds of Eastern and Central North America.* 4th ed. Boston: Houghton Mifflin, 1980.

Petraborg, W.H., E.G. Wellein, and V.E. Gunvalson. "Roadside Drumming Counts – a Spring Census Method for Ruffed Grouse." *Journal of Wildlife Management* 17 (1953): 292–295.

Petrides, G.A. "Age Determination in American Gallinaceous Game Birds." *Transactions of the North American Wildlife Conference* 7 (1942): 308–328.

Pettingill, O.S., Jr. *Ornithology in Laboratory and Field.* 5th ed. New York: Academic Press, 1985.

Phillips, R. "Relationship of Ruffed Grouse to Habitat Types in the Wellsville Mountains, Utah." *Proceedings of the Annual Conference of the Western Association of Fish and Game Commissioners* 44 (1964): 216–221.

————. "Fall and Winter Foods Habits of Ruffed Grouse in Northern Utah." *Journal of Wildlife Management* 31, no. 4 (1967): 827–828.

Polderboer, E.B. "Cover Requirements of the Eastern Ruffed Grouse in Northeast Iowa." *Iowa Bird Life* 12, no. 4 (1942): 50–55.

Porath, W.R. "Population Ecology of Ruffed Grouse in Northeast Iowa." Master's thesis, Iowa State University, 1968.

Porath, W.R., and P.A. Vohs, Jr. "Population Ecology of Ruffed Grouse in Northeastern Iowa." *Journal of Wildlife Management* 36 (July 1972): 793–802.

Portmann, A. "Le developpement postembryon – naire." In *Traite de Zoologie Oiseaux,* edited by P.P. Grasse, vol. 15, 270–289. Paris: Masson et Cie, 1950.

Pough, R.H. *Audubon Water Bird Guide.* Garden City, New York: Doubleday, 1951.

Powell, D.S., and T.J. Considine, Jr. *An Analysis of Pennsylvania's Forest Resources.* U.S. Department of Agriculture, Northeast Forest Experiment Station, Forest Service Resources, Bulletin NE-69. Broomall, Penna.: 1982.

Prawdzik, T., J. Hammill, and A. Boyce. *Gladwin Field Trial Area Management Plan – 1977-2050.* Michigan Department of Natural Resources, 1977.

Prosser, C.L. and F.A. Brown, Jr. *Comparative Animal Physiology.* Philadelphia: W.B. Saunders, 1961.

Pumphrey, R.J. "Sensory Organs." In *Biology and Comparative Physiology of Birds,* edited by A.J. Marshall, vol. 2, 69–86. New York: Academic Press, 1969.

Radford, A.E., H.E. Ahles, and C.R. Bell. *Manual of the*

Vascular Flora of the Carolinas. Chapel Hill: University of North Carolina Press, 1964.

Rasmussen, G., and R. Brander. "Standard Metabolic Rate and Lower Critical Temperature for the Ruffed Grouse." *Wilson Bulletin* 85 (1973): 223–229.

Ridgway, R., and H. Friedmann. *The Birds of North and Middle America.* U.S. National Museum Bulletin 50, Part X. Washington, D.C.: 1946.

Rinell, K.T. *Productivity of Ruffed Grouse Populations.* West Virginia Division of Game and Fish, Federal Aid Project W-39-R, Preliminary Report. Charleston.

Robbins, C.S., B. Bruun, and H.S. Zim. *A Guide to Field Identification: Birds of North America.* New York: Golden Press, 1983.

Robel, R.J., and A.R. Bisset. "Effects of Supplemental Grit on Metabolic Efficiency of Bobwhites." *Wildlife Society Bulletin* 7 (1979): 178–181.

Roberts, T.S. *A Manual for the Identification of the Birds of Minnesota and Neighboring States.* Minneapolis: The University of Minnesota Press, 1955.

Robinson, W.L., ed. *Ruffed Grouse Management: State of the Art in the Early 1980's.* The North Central Section of the Wildlife Society, and The Ruffed Grouse Society, 1984.

Rodgers, R.D. "Ratios of Primary Calamus Diameters for Determining Age of Ruffed Grouse." *Wildlife Society Bulletin* 7, no. 2 (1979): 125–127.

———. "Ecological Relationships of Ruffed Grouse in Southwestern Wisconsin." *Transactions of the Wisconsin Academy of Sciences, Arts and Letters* 68 (1980): 97–105.

———. "Factors Affecting Ruffed Grouse Drumming Counts in Southwestern Wisconsin." *Journal of Wildlife Management* 45 (1981): 409–418.

Rose, G.A., and G.H. Parker. "Effects of Smelter Emissions on Metal Levels in the Plumage of Ruffed Grouse Near Sudbury, Ontario, Canada." *Canadian Journal of Zoology* 60 (1982): 2659–2667.

———. "Metal Content of Body Tissues, Diet Items, and Dung of Ruffed Grouse Near the Copper-nickel Smelters at Sudbury, Ont." *Canadian Journal of Zoology* 61 (1983): 505–511.

Roussel, Y., and R. Ouellet. "A New Criterion for Sexing Quebec Ruffed Grouse." *Journal of Wildlife Management* 39 (1975): 443–445.

Rue, L.L., III. *The World of the Ruffed Grouse.* Philadelphia: J.B. Lippincott, 1973.

Ruff, M.D. "Nematodes and Acanthocephalans." In *Diseases of Poultry,* edited by M.S. Hofstad, H.J. Barnes, B.W. Calneck, W.M. Reid, and H.W. Yoder, Jr., 614–648. Ames: Iowa State University Press, 1984.

Rusch, D.H. "Ecology of Predation and Ruffed Grouse Populations in Central Alberta." Ph.D. dissertation, University of Minnesota, 1971.

———. "Upland Game." In *Manitoba's Wildlife Heritage – A Guide for Landowners,* edited by R.B. Oetting, R.W. Nero, and H.D. Goulden, 35–43. Winnipeg: Manitoba Department of Mines, Resources and Environmental Management, 1973.

———. *The Wildlife Cycle in Manitoba.* Manitoba Department of Mines, Resources and Environmental Management, Information Series No. 11. Winnipeg: 1975.

Rusch, D.H., S. DeStefano, and R.J. Small. "Seasonal Harvest and Mortality of Ruffed Grouse in Wisconsin." In *Ruffed Grouse Management: State of the Art in the Early 1980's,* edited by W.L. Robinson, 137–150. The North Central Section of the Wildlife Society, and The Ruffed Grouse Society, 1984.

Rusch, D.H., and P.D. Doerr. "Broad-Winged Hawk Nesting and Food Habits." *Auk* 89, no. 2 (1972): 139–145.

Rusch, D.H., M.M. Gillespie, and D.I. McKay. "Decline of a Ruffed Grouse Population in Manitoba." *Canadian Field Naturalist* 92 (1978): 123–127.

Rusch, D.H., and L.B. Keith. "Ruffed Grouse–Vegetation Relationships in Central Alberta." *Journal of Wildlife Management* 35, no. 3 (1971): 417–429.

———. "Seasonal and Annual Trends in Numbers of Alberta Ruffed Grouse." *Journal of Wildlife Management* 35, no. 4 (October 1971): 803–822.

Rusch, D.H., L.B. Keith, and E.C. Meslow. *Natural Vegetative Communities Near Rochester, Alberta.* Alberta Department of Lands and Forests, Fish and Wildlife Technical Bulletin 4. Edmonton: 1971.

Rusch, D.H., E.C. Meslow, P.D. Doerr, and L.B. Keith. "Response of Great Horned Owl Populations to Changing Prey Densities." *Journal of Wildlife Management* 36 (1972): 282–296.

Samuel, D.E., D.R. Beightol, and C.W. Brain. "Analysis of the Drums of Ruffed Grouse." *Auk* 91 (1974): 507–516.

Sanders, D.A. "Manson's Eyeworm of Poultry." *Florida Agricultural Experiment Station Bulletin* 206 (1929): 565–585.

Sando, R.W. "Prescribed Burning of Aspen-Hardwood Stands for Wildlife Habitat Improvement." Paper presented at the Midwest Fish and Wildlife Conference 34, Des Moines, 1972.

Scanlon, P.F., R.C. Oderwald, T.J. Dietrich, and J.L. Coggin. "Heavy Metal Concentrations in Feathers of Ruffed Grouse Shot by Virginia Hunters." *Bulletin of Environmental Contamination and Toxicology* 25 (1980): 947–949.

Schalk, A.F., L.M. Roderick, H.L. Foust, and G.S. Harshfield. *Avian Tuberculosis: Collected Studies.* North Dakota Agricultural Experiment Station, Technical Bulletin 279. 1935.

Schemnitz, S.D. "Fall and Winter Feeding Activities and Behavior of Ruffed Grouse in Maine." *Transactions of the Northeast Fish and Wildlife Conference* 27 (1970): 127–140.

Schladweiler, P. "Movements and Activities of Ruffed Grouse *(Bonasa umbellus* L.) During the Summer Period." Master's thesis, University of Minnesota, 1965.

———. "Feeding Behavior of Incubating Ruffed Grouse Females." *Journal of Wildlife Management* 32 (April 1968): 426–428.

Schneiders, H.O. "The Pugnacious Partridge." *Passenger Pigeon* 9 (1947): 63.

Schorger, A.W. "The Ruffed Grouse in Early Wisconsin." *Transactions of the Wisconsin Academy of Sciences, Arts and Letters* 37 (1945): 35–90.

Schultz, J. *Ruffed Grouse Population Data.* North Dakota State Game and Fish Department, unpublished P-R Report, Project W-67-6-23, Study BXI. 1983.

Schulz, J.W. "Manipulation of Habitat for Ruffed Grouse on the Wakopa Wildlife Management Area, North Dakota." In *Ruffed Grouse Management: State of the Art in the Early 1980's,* edited by W.L. Robinson, 109–121. The North Central Section of the Wildlife Society, and The Ruffed Grouse Society, 1984.

Schulz, J.W., A.A. Aufforth, and J. Woods. "Fall Foods of Ruffed Grouse." *North Dakota Outdoors* (October 1983): 12–15.

Seehorn, M.E., R.F. Harlow, and M.T. Mengak. "Foods of Ruffed Grouse from Three Locations in the Southern Appalachian Mountains." *Proceedings of the Annual Conference of the Southeastern Association of Fish and Wildlife Agencies* 35 (1981): 216–224.

Servello, F.A. "Regional Variation in the Nutritional Ecology of Ruffed Grouse." Ph.D. dissertation, Virginia Polytechnic Institute and State University, 1985.

Servello, F.A., and R.L. Kirkpatrick. "Sexing Ruffed Grouse in the Southeast Using Feather Criteria." *Wildlife Society Bulletin* 14 (1986): 280–282.

———. "Fat Indices for Ruffed Grouse." *Journal of Wildlife Management* 51 (1987): 12–15.

———. "Regional Variation in the Nutritional Ecology of Ruffed Grouse." *Journal of Wildlife Management* 51 (1987): 749–770.

Servello, F.A., R.L. Kirkpatrick, and K.E. Webb, Jr. "Predicting the Metabolizable Energy in Ruffed Grouse Diets from Van Soest and Total Phenol Analyses." *Journal of Wildlife Management* 51 (1987): 173–177.

Sharp, W.M. *Management of a Poletimber Forest for Wildlife Food and Cover.* State College, Penna.: The Pennsylvania State University, 1957.

———. "The Effects of Habitat Manipulation and Forest Succession on Ruffed Grouse." *Journal of Wildlife Management* 27, no. 4 (1963): 664–671.

———. "The Role of Fire in Ruffed Grouse Habitat Management." *Proceedings of the Tall Timbers Fire Ecology Conference* 10 (1970): 47–61.

Shillinger, J.E., and L.C. Morley. *Diseases of Upland Game Birds.* U.S. Department of Agriculture, Farmer's Bulletin 1781. 1937.

Sibley, G.G., and J.E. Ahlquist. "The Relationship of Some Groups of African Birds, Based on Comparisons of the Genetic Material, DNA." In *Proceedings of the International Symposium on African Vertebrates,* edited by K.L. Schuchmann, 115–161. Bonn: Zoologisches Forschungsinstitut und Museum Alexander Koenig, 1985.

Siegfried, L.M. "Neoplasms Identified in Free-flying Birds." *Avian Diseases* 27 (1983): 86–99.

Small, R.J. "Mortality and Dispersal of Ruffed Grouse in Central Wisconsin." Master's thesis, University of Wisconsin–Madison, 1985.

———. "Predation and Hunting Mortality of Ruffed Grouse in Central Wisconsin." Master's thesis, University of Wisconsin, 1985.

Small, R.S., and D.H. Rusch. "Poncho versus Backpack Attachments for Radios on Ruffed Grouse." *Wildlife Society Bulletin* 13 (1985): 163–165.

Snoeyenbos, G.H. "Tuberculosis in a Ruffed Grouse." *Wildlife Disease Association Bulletin* 2 (1966): 9.

Snyder, R.A. "Drumming Sites and Early Winter Foods of the Ruffed Grouse." Master's thesis, West Virginia University, 1973.

Sousa, P.J. "Characteristics of Drumming Habitat of Ruffed Grouse *(Bonasa umbellus)* in Grafton, Vermont." Master's thesis, University of Vermont, 1978.

Spinner, G.P., and J.S. Bishop. "Chemical Analysis of some Wildlife Foods in Connecticut." *Journal of Wildlife Management* 14, no. 2 (1950): 175–186.

Stafford, S.K. "Data on Ruffed Grouse Drumming Sites and Activities in Haywood County, North Carolina." Unpublished report, 1972.

———. "Fall and Winter Foods of Ruffed Grouse in Eastern Tennessee and Western North Carolina." Master's thesis, University of Tennessee, 1975.

Stafford, S.K., and R.W. Dimmick. "Autumn and Winter Foods of Ruffed Grouse in the Southern Appalachians." *Journal of Wildlife Management* 43, no. 1 (1979): 121–127.

Stafseth, H.J., and S. Kotlan. "Report of Investigations on an Alleged Epizootic of Ruffed Grouse in Michigan." *Journal of the American Veterinary Medical Association* 20 (1925): 260–267.

Stauffer, D.F. "Seasonal Habitat Relationships of Ruffed and Blue Grouse in Southeastern Idaho." Ph.D. dissertation, University of Idaho, 1983.

Stauffer, D.F., and S.R. Peterson. "Ruffed and Blue Grouse Habitat Use in Southeastern Idaho." *Journal of Wildlife Management* 49, no. 2 (1985): 459–466.

———. "Seasonal Micro-habitat Relationships of Ruffed Grouse in Southeastern Idaho." *Journal of Wildlife Management* 49, no. 3 (1985): 605–610.

Stewart, R.E. "Ecological Study of Ruffed Grouse Broods in Virginia." *Auk* 73 (1956): 33–41.

Stiven, A.E. "Food Energy Available For and Required By the Blue Grouse Chick." *Ecology* 42 (1961): 547–553.

Stokes, D.W. *A Guide to Nature in Winter: Northeast and North Central North America.* Boston: Little, Brown and Company, 1976.

Stoll, R.J. *Indices to Ruffed Grouse Abundance and Distribution in Ohio.* Ohio Department of Natural Resources, Division of Wildlife, Federal Aid in Wildlife Restoration Final Report. Columbus: 1979.

———. "Indices to Ruffed Grouse Hunting Success in Ohio." *Wildlife Society Bulletin* 8 (1980): 24–28.

Stoll, R.J., and G. Honchul. *Ruffed Grouse Habitat Management Guidelines.* Columbus: Ohio Department of Natural Resources, 1983.

Stoll, R.J., and M.W. McClain. *Weights of Ohio Ruffed Grouse.* Columbus: Ohio Department of Natural Resources, 1983.

Stoll, R.J., Jr., and M.W. McClain. "Distribution and Relative Abundance of Ruffed Grouse in Ohio." *Ohio Journal of Science* 86 (1986): 182–185.

Stoll, R.J., M.W. McClain, R.L. Boston, and G. Honchul. *Characteristics of Ruffed Grouse Drumming Sites in Ohio.* Columbus: Ohio Department of Natural Resources, 1975.

Stoll, R.J., Jr., M.W. McClain, R.L. Boston, and G.P. Honchul. "Ruffed Grouse Drumming Site Characteristics in Ohio." *Journal of Wildlife Management* 43, no. 2 (1979): 324–333.

Stoll, R.J., M.W. McClain, and G.C. Helt. *Ruffed Grouse Fall and Winter Cover Preferences.* Ohio Department of Natural Resources, Division of Wildlife, Inservice Note 370. Columbus: 1977.

Stoll, R.J., M.W. McClain, C.M. Nixon, and D.M. Worley. *Foods of Ruffed Grouse in Ohio.* Ohio Department of Natural Resources, Division of Wildlife, Fish and Wildlife Report 7. Columbus: 1980.

Stoll, R.J., C.M. Nixon, M.W. McClain, and P.W. Worley. *Fall and Winter Foods of Ohio Ruffed Grouse.* Ohio Department of Natural Resources, Division of Wildlife, Inservice Note 22. Columbus: 1973.

Stollberg, B.P., and R.L. Hine. *Food Habit Studies of Ruffed Grouse, Pheasant, Quail, and Mink in Wisconsin.* Wisconsin Conservation Department, Technical Bulletin No. 4. Madison: 1952.

Stresemann, E. "Sauropsida: Aves." In *Hundbuch de Zoologie,* edited by W. Kukenthal and T. Krumbach, vol. 7, pt. 2. Berlin: Berlin-Leipzig, 1934.

———. *Ornithology from Aristotle to the Present.* Cambridge: Harvard University Press, 1975.

Sumanik, K.M. "The Drumming Sites and Drumming Activity of Territorial Ruffed Grouse in Southwestern Alberta." Master's thesis, University of Alberta, 1966.

Svoboda, F.J., and G.W. Gullion. "Preferential Use of Aspen by Ruffed Grouse in Northern Minnesota." *Journal of Wildlife Management* 36, no. 4 (1972): 1166–1180.

Tanner, W.D., and G.L. Bowers. "A Method for Trapping Male Ruffed Grouse." *Journal of Wildlife Management* 12 (1948): 330–331.

Taylor, D.A. *An Analysis of Some Physical Characteristics of Ruffed Grouse (Bonasa umbellus) Drumming Sites and Logs in Middle and Eastern Tennessee.* Tennessee Wildlife Resources Agency, Technical Report No. 75-25. 1976.

Terres, J.K. *The Audubon Society Encyclopedia of North American Birds.* New York: Alfred A. Knopf, 1980.

Terrill, L.McI. "Notes of Food of the Ruffed and Spruce Grouse." *Canadian Field Naturalist* 38, no. 4 (1924): 77.

Tester, J.R. "Changes in Daily Activity Rhythms of Free-ranging Animals." *Canadian Field Naturalist* 101 (1987): 13–21.

Theberge, J.B., and D.A. Gauthier. "Factors Influencing Densities of Territorial Male Ruffed Grouse, Algonquin Park, Ontario." *Journal of Wildlife Management* 46, no. 1 (1982): 263–268.

Thompson, D.R., and J.C. Moulton. *An Evaluation of Wisconsin Ruffed Grouse Surveys.* Wisconsin Department of Natural Resources, Technical Bulletin 123. 1981.

Thompson, F.R., III. "Ruffed Grouse Seasonal Habitat Use, Survivorship, and Winter Energetics in Missouri." Ph.D. dissertation, University of Missouri, 1987.

Thompson, F.R., III, D.A. Freiling, and E.K. Fritzell. "Drumming, Nesting, and Brood Habitats of Ruffed Grouse in an Oak-Hickory Forest." *Journal of Wildlife Management* 51, no. 3 (1987): 568–575.

Thompson, F.R., III, and E.K. Fritzell. "Fall Foods and Nutrition of Ruffed Grouse in Missouri." *Transactions of the Missouri Academy of Science* 20 (1986): 45–48.

——. "Ruffed Grouse Winter Roost Site Preference and Influence on Energy Demands." *Journal of Wildlife Management* 52, no. 3 (1988): 454–460.

Todd, K.S., Jr., and D.M. Hammond. "Coccidia of Anseriformes, Galliformes, and Passeriformes." In *Infectious and Parasitic Diseases of Wild Birds,* edited by J.W. Davis, R.C. Anderson, L. Karstad, and D.O. Trainer, 234–281. Ames: Iowa State University Press, 1971.

Treichler, R.R., R.W. Stow, and A.L. Nelson. "Nutrient Content of some Winter Foods of Ruffed Grouse." *Journal of Wildlife Management* 10, no. 1 (1947): 12–17.

Trippensee, R.E. *Wildlife Management.* New York: McGraw-Hill, 1948.

Uhlig, H.G. "Weights of Ruffed Grouse in West Virginia." *Journal of Wildlife Management* 17, no. 3 (1953): 391–392.

U.S. Department of Agriculture. *Wildlife Management Handbook: Southern Region.* Atlanta, 1971.

Vanderschaegen, P.F. "Food Habits of Ruffed Grouse at the Cloquet Forest Research Center, Minnesota." Master's thesis, University of Minnesota, 1970.

Vanderschaegen, P.F., and J.C. Moulton. "Winter Food Habits of Ruffed Grouse in Young Aspen Stands." *Passenger Pigeon* 37, no. 1 (1975): 47–48.

Van Tyne, J., and A.J. Berger. *Fundamentals of Ornithology.* New York: John Wiley and Sons, Inc., 1966.

Weber, A.J., and F.B. Barick. "Eleven Years of Ruffed Grouse Censusing in Western North Carolina." *Proceedings of the Annual Conference of the Southeast Association of Game and Fish Commissioners* 17 (1963): 13–15.

Wenstrom, W.P., P.F. Vanderschaegen, and G.W. Gullion. "Ruffed Grouse Primary Molt Chronology." *Auk* 89 (1972): 671–673.

West, G.B. "The Nature of Avian and Amphibian Sympathin." *Journal of Pharmacy and Pharmacology* 3 (1951): 400–408.

White, D.W., and R.W. Dimmick. "Survival and Habitat Use of Northern Ruffed Grouse Introduced into West Tennessee." *Proceedings of the Annual Conference of the Southeastern Association of Fish and Wildlife Agencies* 32 (1978): 1–7.

——. "The Distribution of Ruffed Grouse in Tennessee." *Journal of the Tennessee Academy of Science* 54, no. 3 (1979): 114–115.

——. *The Distribution of the Ruffed Grouse in Tennessee.* Tennessee Wildlife Resources Agency, Wildlife Research Report No. 79-6. 1979.

Wilder, E.H. "Walking-Trail Developments for Hunters on the Nicolet National Forest." *Journal of Wildlife Management* 33 (1969): 762–768.

Wilson, A., and H. Wilson. "The Tymus in Myasthenia Gravis." *American Journal of Medicine* 19 (1955): 697–702.

Wingfield, G. "Winged Hunters." *Birds of Nebraska, NE-BRASKAland Magazine* 63, no. 1 (January–February 1985.)

Woehr, J.R. "Winter and Spring Shelter and Food Selection by Ruffed Grouse in Central New York." Master's thesis, S.U.N.Y. College of Environmental Science and Forestry, 1974.

Woehr, J.R., and R.E. Chambers. "Winter and Spring Food Preferences of Ruffed Grouse in Central New York." *Transactions of the Northeast Fish and Wildlife Conference* 32 (1975): 95–110.

Woolf, A., R. Norris, and J. Kube. "Evaluation of Ruffed Grouse Reintroductions in Southern Illinois." In *Ruffed Grouse Management: State of the Art in the Early 1980's,* edited by W.L. Robinson, 59–74. The North Central Section of the Wildlife Society, and The Ruffed Grouse Society, 1984.

Yahner, R.H. "Effects of Forest Fragmentation on Winter Bird Abundance in Central Pennsylvania." *Proceedings Pennsylvania Academy of Science* 59 (1985): 114–116.

——. "Structure, Seasonal Dynamics, and Habitat Relationships of Avian Communities in Small Even-aged Forest Stands." *Wilson Bulletin* 98 (1986): 61–82.

Glossary-index